Dancing Through History

Joan Cass

Prentice Hall
Englewood Cliffs, New Jersey 07632

Library of Congress Cataloging-in-Publication Data

Cass, Joan.
   Dancing through history / Joan Cass
      p. cm.
   Includes bibliographical references and index.
   ISBN 0-13-204389-0
   1. Dancing—History. 2. Folk dancing—History. 3. Ballet—History.
4. Modern dance—History. 5. Dancing—Europe—History. 6. Dancing—
United States—History. I. Title.
GV1601.C28   1993
792.8'09—dc20

                       93-106
                        CIP

Production Editors: **Maureen Richardson/Kerry Reardon**
Interior design: **Maureen Richardson**
Acquisitions Editor: **Ted Bolen**
Cover Designers: **Jayne Conte/Karen Salzbach**
Prepress Buyer: **Herb Klein**
Manufacturing Buyer: **Robert Anderson**

Photos courtesy of Martha Swope

 ©1993 by Prentice-Hall, Inc.
A Simon & Schuster Company
Englewood Cliffs, New Jersey 07632

Printed in the United States of America

10 9 8 7

ISBN   0-13-204389-0

Prentice-Hall International (UK) Limited, *London*
Prentice-Hall of Australia Pty. Limited, *Sydney*
Prentice-Hall Canada Inc., *Toronto*
Prentice-Hall Hispanoamericana, S.A., *Mexico*
Prentice-Hall of India Private Limited, *New Delhi*
Prentice-Hall of Japan, *Tokyo*
Simon & Schuster Asia Pte. Ltd., *Singapore*
Editora Prentice-Hall do Brasil, Ltda., *Rio de Janeiro*

CONTENTS

Part II   European Ballet Tours

PREFACE

Part I of *Dancing Through History*, is designed to acquaint you with the wide-ranging activity of dance as it has existed throughout the world. We begin with general concepts, and go on to a sweeping overview of tribal, ethnic, and folk-dance forms. In Part II, we look at ballet, from its origins in Renaissance Europe to the present. In Part III, we discuss twentieth-century modern dance and jazz, including the contemporary scene which is international and eclectic. All three sections offer you a context for understanding the Western dance art as we find it the 1990s.

The book discusses significant dance artists, historical background of styles, and major works of choreography. It includes theoretical ideas such as the relationship between music and dance, and the psychology of performing. The purpose of these discussions is to clarify trends and to stimulate thinking on the dance art and human society. To move further in this direction, one or more questions are posed at the end of each chapter.

In writing this work, I have drawn heavily on the literature in the field. You will find a listing of the books I have consulted in the Bibliography. Noted dance photographer Martha Swope has provided all the illustrations from her extensive collection. In particular, I would like to express grateful acknowledgement to Wesleyan University for permission to quote liberally from three excellent books: Ivor Guest's *The Romantic Ballet in Paris* and *Fanny Elssler*, and Selma Jeanne Cohen's *Doris Humphrey*.

In addition to relying on other historians, I have had the good fortune of personal involvement in the dance scene since the 1940s. I began as a student of Martha Graham, Doris Humphrey, Louis Horst, and others, and went on to be a critic and lecturer. Interviews with hundreds of choreographers and dancers, and innumerable concerts which I reviewed for newspapers and magazines proved to be excellent primary sources of material for this work. Dance always cries out to be performed and seen, rather than talked about. It is my hope that these pages will add insight and pleasure to your experiences in the field.

J.C.

PROLOGUE

A HISTORICAL SENSE OF DIRECTION

The study of dance history confronts us from the start with two problematic subjects: dance and dance history. What is dance? For our purposes, I give it the broadest possible definition: Dance is the making of rhythmical steps and movements for their own sake (as against steps and movements done in order to go somewhere, to do work, or to dress oneself). Dance has been present in just about every known human society (and even some animal groups!). We see dance in art, in religious observance, in communal activities, in courtship, in healing, in education, in war, in physical training—and that's not all. Given such a widespread existence and such a wandering character, it is no wonder that we run into trouble when we try to pin it down.

As for dance history, its study is obviously more than a compilation of facts. It involves organization and interpretation. It is carried on by people who use their personal philosophies to guide them through a minefield of explosive questions. From what point of view do you deal with the tons of available information? Which facts do you emphasize? Which do you omit? At what event or period do you start? In short, what is the direction of your thinking? (If you are interested in knowing about dance history as a discipline, the place to start is CORD, the Committee On Research in Dance, which is based at New York University.)

In this book I will try to acquaint you with dance as it has appeared over time, around the world. I have chosen to focus on Western theater dance as an art form, both because of my own interests and experience, and because I believe it is the most relevant way to introduce the subject of dance history to an American reader. My aim in this book is to give you as full a background as possible for what you see in today's concert halls and studios. The material is organized with two themes in mind: *tradition* and *creativity.*

Tradition is a familiar flower in the field of dance. There are traditions in the repertory, in the technical training of dance performers, in creative theory, in the social life of dancers, and in the ways they earn a living. Over and over again we hear of great dance artists who were themselves inspired by traditions in the dance world. If these traditions are familiar to you—if you know something about the people who shaped them and can trace the development of a style and the origins of a particular dance composition—then your enjoyment of each concert increases greatly. In short, dance history is your key to being at home in the American dance world.

To illustrate the theme of creativity, I would like to contrast Western European (and hence American) culture with Asiatic, tribal, and ancient cultures. I realize that these categories are immense, and any characterizations about them are open to criticism as superficial generalizations. Nevertheless, I offer them to you in the belief that a broad, even if inexact, outline is a better way to represent a subject to beginners, than an accurate picture whose meaning is obscured by fussy details. Considered in contrast to non-European cultures, the central theme of Western theater dance is the search for fresh ideas. The situation is different in Asia or in Africa, where dance is closely related to a religious service, a royal ceremony, or a tribal ritual; and where the form and content of these activities are handed down from generation to generation. Not only are they familiar by their repetition to the people of a given culture, this familiarity is preferred to change and variation.

In contrast, Western theater dance is not part of religion, it is not ceremonial, and it is not practiced by the whole community together. Western theater dance features individual skillful performers, choreographers, directors, and companies. It is professional, theatrical spectacle that stands or falls on its ability to attract and please paying audiences. Western audiences quickly tire of repetition. They are constantly on the lookout for novelty and originality. Of course it is the artists themselves who are at the forefront of restless creativity. Reforming dance into a more *dramatic, expressive* art form were Jean Georges Noverre in the 1700s and Michel Fokine in the early 1900s in ballet; and Isadora Duncan in the 1890s and Martha Graham in the late 1920s in modern dance. On the other end of the emotional scale, the Renaissance dancing masters—Petipa, Merce Cunningham, and Twyla Tharp—sought novel entertainment in the *manipulation of materials* of the art form.

In practice, each of these artists meant something very different by the pursuit of reform and novelty. However, all of them had the same theoretical objectives: infuse the art of dance with new life; make it possible for dance to express new ideas; and arouse the interest of easily bored Western audiences. Although reform and novelry have been sought throughout the years of Western dance history, you will note how periodically, a new fashion is all the rage. It immediately becomes subject to endless imitation. Inevitably, this casts the dance art into the pit of triteness, and results in second-rate pieces, which soon enough are perceived as repetitions of the same old thing. In time, an inspired genius arises to let in the fresh air of creative inspiration and a new fashion takes hold.

It is this search for novelty that paradoxically connects Western theater dance with traditional dance forms of the non-Western world. To infuse their work with new life, you will frequently see choreographers draw on time-honored alien forms of dance, which are ancient in their own cultures but unfamiliar in the West. Consider the ancient spring ritual that appears in numerous cultures throughout the world.

In 1913, Nijinsky, perhaps the best-known figure in ballet, shocked Paris audiences into a violent physical battle at the premiere of his composition *The Rite of Spring* by using a score by Stravinsky. The scandalous dance was seen only six times before it was withdrawn from view. In 1984, Martha Graham, the most famous modern dancer, prepared her own interpretation of the work. In the years between, at least eleven choreographic versions of *The Rite of Spring* were staged by well-known modern dancers like Mary Wigman, and famous ballet choreographers like Leonid Massine (who starred Martha Graham in his 1930 production!). Even Walt Disney did one for his 1940 musical cartoon film *Fantasia*.

All of these works dealing with the rite of spring are about tribal sacrifice that celebrates the cycle of the year and of life. They honor the promise of spring—the season of fertile growth, mating, and rebirth after the frozen death of winter.

At first glance, this seems to be strange content for twentieth-century urban theater. Why would the most sophisticated dance artists—Nijinsky, Graham—hark back to the most primitive (and animalistic) instincts and experiences? The answer lies first of all, as with so many dance works, in the music. Stravinsky created a harsh score, twanging with dissonances and agitated phrases, for Diaghilev's *Ballets Russes*. Nijinsky followed Stravinsky's rhythms and score by twisting his dancers into grotesque shapes. The others used the music in their own ways.

Of course, music always sets people dancing. How much more does it propel and inspire professional dancers to reflect rhythmic sounds in movement! Many a choreographer frankly points to music as the conductor of his dance imagination; and Stravinsky's *The Rite of Spring* is a particularly potent composition. However, music is not the only force. Later, we

The history of Martha Graham's "Rite of Spring" (1984) goes back many centuries.

will explore Nijinsky's artistic environment as well as Graham's. We can go on to guess what the artists didn't tell us about the images and feelings that inspired them but we can never know these things with certainty. Dancers are stimulating and important to us precisely because they give physical expression to feelings and ideas that the rest of us sense only dimly. Artists are interested in basic impulses of primitive human nature. They are not bound by convention to deny the existence of instincts, as other people prefer to do. Most of us like to think of ourselves as rational and sophisticated in our behavior. The truth of the matter is that we all take part in rituals.

What spring rituals do you attend: an Easter parade or Sunday Mass? A Passover seder? An annual dance recital? A Mardi Gras? Spring cleaning? A spring prom? We can safely say that your spring rituals, as well as Nijinsky's and Graham's, have their roots in distant cultures. Incidentally, if you do go to a prom—or any party—the chances are that you may do some dancing, but not in the style of modern dance or ballet. As you know, jazz is the dominant form of social dancing in the Western world, and further, its presence is strongly felt in contemporary theater dance.

Jazz was both long ago and far away. It began as an offshoot of tribal African culture, and developed among black Americans. Jazz dances and music spread from New Orleans and the South through vaudeville, movies, dance halls, and discothèques, where they were taken up by entire communities. After that, serious musicians and choreographers, whose bodies responded to the magnetic beat, began to use jazz. Similarly, most national folk dances have been adapted at one time or another for a theatrical work. Hindu dance and Spanish dance in particular have always been a source of inspiration to ballet and modern choreographers; and in their original ethnic forms, (most often arranged to suit the requirements of the stage) they have enjoyed great popularity among Western audiences.

To sum up, the most characteristic stance of Western dance is the untiring quest for novelty, and the creativity it brings forth. At the same time, there is always present an awareness of what has gone before—an appreciation of tradition and a sense of continuity, such as that provided by an opera house where operas and ballets have been staged for centuries. Academies of music and dance lend stability to the scene (even though the conservatism of the academy is often bitterly resented by the artist). So alongside creativity, look for tradition, because it acts as a rudder for you to grasp while navigating hundreds of specific, complicated events that express great diversity.

Now we are ready to begin our a broad overview of dance in world culture through the ages. This will not only help you to appreciate the tribal, folk, and ethnic companies that appear on our stages, it will also call attention to traditions that have inspired many artists in Western theater dance.

1   TRIBAL RITES

THE LIFE OF STONE AGE MAN

We start our explorations of dance as far back as we can go, with the life of early man in preliterate, Stone Age tribal societies. Wasn't the Stone Age tens of thousands of years ago? How then can we know about the customs of people who left no written records and particularly about dance, which is the most transitory of activities? The answer is that Stone Age culture is not strictly a chronological classification. Rather, it is one based on methods, skills, and social arrangements. Therefore, when nineteenth-century anthropologists found the same tools and methods of hunting and cultivation that led them to classify Stone Age man in the first place, they figured that Stone Age tribes were still around. They assumed that in the distant past, tribal life had the same characteristics that they saw among Native American tribal groups, Aborigines in Australia, tribal groups of the Amazonian rain forests, and certain African peoples.

The argument makes sense up to a point. However, there are problems. First of all, with increasing speed, tribal cultures have been disappearing. Tribal peoples adapted to the customs of technologically more advanced peoples, and also, conquerors forced them to change. Second, the nineteenth-century anthropologists who provided the bulk of our accounts of tribal ritual repeatedly noted the presence of dance, but gave only the most casual references to the actual forms and movements. You have probably noticed that even experienced dance critics find it difficult to describe dance in words. These anthropologists had no training in our art form. Additionally, they were often prejudiced against the dancing they saw.

As Roderyk Lange wrote in *The Nature of Dance, An Anthropological Perspective*, these early scholars mentioned dances from all over the world:

> only in conjunction with customs and music. Dances appeared to many of them as very "exotic," "wild" and "indecent." Sometimes they explained them as manifestations of lower developed peoples. The "civilised" [sic] observers themselves would never have dreamt of performing such uninhibited movements.

However, if we keep certain reservations in mind, we can accept the eyewitness accounts of anthropologists, missionaries, and travellers as our sources for tribal life from the distant past. Fortunately, we also have as witnesses contemporary men and women who are trained observers of dance. Their reports do seem to confirm in essence what the others have said.

Ritual

From the beginning, we are struck by the fact that our subject looms large. Dance is a feature of every significant occasion and event crucial to tribal existence as part of ritual. The first thing to emphasize is that early dance exists as a ritual element. It does *not* stand alone as a separate activity or profession. For an understanding of tribal dance, therefore it is necessary to begin with the phenomenon of ritual.

Rituals are traditional clusters of actions. Their function is to cast powerful magic spells to placate and influence gods and spirits. Complicated rituals, passed along from one generation to the next, are practiced in every tribe to influence the future. They are performed in connection with fertility, initiation, hunting, healing, death, and war. They may last for hours, even days.

There is no clear separation in tribal societies between religion and government and art; between tilling the soil and magic; between illness, health, and superstition. All these areas cross over and touch one another. In any survey of tribal customs, you will find traces of the arts of dance and music, as well as drama, poetry, and painting (on bodies and on the walls of caves), rubbing shoulders with elements of worship, social mores, laws, medicine—and indeed most aspects of more advanced civilizations. All of these cultural patterns are observed in tribal rituals. In other words, tribal ritual is equivalent to what we call *social organization*. It is the form in which tribal groups respond to the business of living.

Rituals may be specific or cyclical. A specific ritual has a particular, one-time purpose. A cyclical, or general, ritual is repeated at the same time each year or season. A specific ritual may be devised to cure a person of ulcers, to expel an evil spirit from a person or a hut, or to mourn a death and prepare a proper burial. For example, a madman may be buried in the forest, away from the village, and told not to return and afflict others with his madness.

For descriptions of rituals, we turn now to written accounts. The literature shows that because so many communities developed their belief systems and histories in fearful isolation from their neighbors, the details of ritual are infinitely varied. In addition, because rituals are concerned with every aspect of life, they do not fit easily into categories. Nevertheless, there are common elements that appear frequently enough to be considered characteristic. In order to get a general idea of the nature of tribal ritual, we will focus on their content, considering examples of rituals grouped according to their purpose.

Fertility Rituals. The most basic concern of early man was (and remains!) fertility. Without food, or without new offspring, the tribe would perish. This gives utmost importance to the cycle of the seasons, the fertility of the soil and of the human and animal populations, and the abundance or absence of rain. Thus the community's most important efforts go into rituals to promote fertility. Their aim is to influence various supernatural powers by casting spells on the gods and spirits in charge of the animal population, agriculture, and childbearing.

These rituals follow a cyclical pattern, parallel to the repetitive rhythms that are such a direct part of experience: the recurrence of the seasons with their wet and dry or cold and hot weather; the cycles of the sun; the lengthening and shortening of days; the alternation of day and night; the waxing and waning of the moon; the sowing and harvesting of food; and the patterns of plant and animal life that are echoed in man's. As seeds slumbering in the winter soil sprout again in the spring, so individuals are born and grow. Before they decline and die, they assure the continuity of life by reproducing the next generation. Thus there is a close connection between rituals of human fertility and those of funerals, agriculture, and the hunt.

In agricultural communities, the greatest anxieties are connected with the times of sowing and planting. What will happen between now and the harvest? Will malicious spirits blacken the sun, withhold the rain, cause the crops to fail? How can the tribal leaders get the spirits to look kindly on them? So they do their best, each tribe devising rituals to appease the gods: ceremonies to demonstrate the desired outcome of fertility and abundant growth; magic spells to force the spirits to perform properly; sacrificial gifts to buy their favor. Rain dances are a prime example of ritual as magic power to promote fertility. The gardeners among you know how important rain is for crops. Charms to bring rain are found everywhere among tribal peoples.

In general, the times of most intense, prayerful activity are bound up with fertility and the regeneration of life. Because fertility is so fraught with meaning, and there are so many aspects of existence associated with it, we find endless variations on our old friend, the spring ritual. As Lois Ellfeldt wrote in *Dance From Magic to Art*;

> The solar seasons are important in the calendar of celebrations of all planting cultures. . . . Winter is the season of the dead, with its sleep and rebirth with the sun. . . . Rather than take a chance on the return of spring, with its renewed life, there are rites to insure this. There are literally thousands of forms, but the essence is in sacrifice.

The people of Bengal perform these rituals at the time of planting the rice crop. Boys and girls of a Munda village go to the forest and cut a young Karma tree. Singing, dancing, and beating drums, they carry the tree and plant it in the middle of a special dancing ground. They decorate its branches with colored cloth and plaited straw jewelry, offer it a sacrifice, and with linked arms dance in a great circle around the tree. As preparation for this festival, the daughters of the village headmen have already cultivated fast-sprouting barley blades, which they bring to this same spot, and place them with reverence at the foot of the small tree. The ritual is then concluded with the tree being uprooted and thrown into a stream.

When you hear that the Mundas believe the gods of the forest are responsible for crops, the idea behind these actions becomes clear. The tree spirits have been reminded by the example of the fast-growing barley blades to do the right thing, that is, to quicken the growth of the rice crop. Submerging the tree in water acts as a rain charm.

The *circle form*, present in tribal ritual, Asiatic religious ceremonies, and folk dancing, is also common in our art dance. As Curt Sachs points out, the circle takes on a spiritual significance:

> This is not the result of a development of understanding but rather of the connection between an idea and its motor reflex—to encircle an object is to take it into possession, to incorporate it.

Therefore, magic powers are most often tapped through rhythmic motion within a circle. And this circle often turns around something—a fire, a pit, a post, or a person. Mysticism aside, we can see how in a more obvious psychological way the circle creates a community. It enables you to face everybody at once, and to define a space. This also allows you to tell secrets and be part of an in-group, and to keep out the enemy. We see the circle form in initiation ceremonies in East Africa where the Wayao circle a fire during the circumcision of youths, and among the California Indians who dance around a newly matured girl.

Initiation Rituals. Close to rites of fertility are rites of *initiation* for boys and girls, as they reach the age of puberty. Among the Sotho in northwestern Transvaal, boys undergo circumcision as part of their initiation to adulthood. Before the cutting, novices sit facing the west—afterward, towards the east. The idea is that the immature boy dies and reawakens as a man. During the initiation, the adult men of the East African Wayao circle around the fire. A California Indian maiden, at her first menstruation, must dance forward and backward, at all times keeping her face turned toward the east. The east, the direction of the rising sun, is the direction of life, while the west is the direction of the dead. As she dances, she swings a rattle made of an animal's hoof (this relates to a hunting charm).

Rituals of the Hunt and of Animals. Just as the rituals of spring and fertility of the soil appear in planting cultures, similar impulses give rise to different forms where hunting and fishing provide food. There is a natural affinity between man and the animal populations in his environment. Even when he uses animals for food, he respects their life form, and may call on their spirits to protect him. An animal dance may serve as a hunting charm. The dancer wins power over the animal he imitates, and will be able to entice him within killing range. Or, specific ritual may be devised to make a new fishing net, thereby creating proper conditions that ensure a good catch. African Pygmies celebrate an elephant kill by building a huge wooden framework to represent the elephant, and pinning the tail of the slain animal on the structure. Then to a beating drum, the hunters reenact their search, closing in on the elephant, and finally plunging attacks with their spears.

Healing and Funeral Rituals. The health and strength of tribal members are obviously of utmost importance. When illness strikes, witch doctors, priests, and the entire community practice *magical healing rites*. Healing rites are found everywhere. When someone is sick, the shaman, (we also call him the witch doctor or the medicine man, although it is interesting to note that the shaman is often an elderly woman) places the sick person in the center of the magic circle and leads a chorus in dancing around until they overpower and chase away the evil spirit of sickness.

You may have picked up a connection between tribal healing rituals and modern-day practices. Since the 1940s in this country, various people have felt the healing power of dance (and other arts) on some forms of illness, to the point where there is now a large American Dance Therapy Association, and in our society, dance therapy is a recognized profession, although its recognition is not wholehearted in all circles. In tribes of course, there was never any question.

When a Senegalese is dangerously ill, a devil dancer is called in. He makes offerings to the devils, and dancing in the masks appropriate to them, conjures the demons of disease, one after the other, out of the sick man's body and into his own. The idea is that because it is possible to shift a load of wood or stones from our own back to the back of another, it is equally possible to shift the burden of pains and sorrows onto another. This is what the Senegalese devil dancer did when he took the demons of illness into himself. Curt Sachs comments:

> Having thus successfully extracted the cause of the malady, the artful dancer lies down on a bier, shamming death. He is carried to an open place outside the village. Here, being left to himself, he soon comes to life again, and hastens back to claim his reward.

Malvina Hoffman, a sculptor who travelled the world to find models for the Hall of Man exhibit at the Chicago Field Museum, describes this healing ritual among the Ainu of Japan in *Heads and Tales*:

> They feel that illness is the possession of the body by demons. These demons hate certain smells, so the Ainu medicine—man seeks out what will be most odious to their sense of smell. Certain wildflowers (one of them is the convulvus root) are chewed and then spat out over the unfortunate invalid. The "doctors" rush about howling and spitting this evil-smelling root, waving swords, and generally doing their best to terrorize the demons of disease, and I should think scare the patient into a state of collapse. The result must often be successful, for the custom persists, and this form of exorcism is resorted to repeatedly all over the globe.

When healing rituals fail, and death results, there is a funeral. For obvious reasons, *Funeral rituals* may include activities to stimulate fertility. At funerals, dancers of the Pangwe of Cameroon must whirl their loin cloths in the air to expose their genitals; from the same impulse, at the death of a girl on the Island of Yap, women throw their grass skirts in the air to show their private parts. When a chieftain of Yap dies, the dancers who follow his body engage in passionate sexual motions.

War and Weapons Rituals. Although there are many ritual themes that we haven't considered, we will look at only one more major kind: Curt Sachs says, "The weapon dance is extremely widespread: handling a weapon is still man's favorite sport." (These words were written in the thirties. If anything, they are truer today than they were then.) In New Ireland, the dancers, each holding a battle spear, form a double row. Their bodies are in continuous motion, legs and feet make quick tripping motions from side to side, forward and backward. Meanwhile, spears are swung and thrust against invisible opponents. These movements, having been rehearsed with great care, are executed simultaneously by all.

Other Ritual Elements Found in Dance

Up to now we have taken note of rituals that include movement. Now let us consider other ritual elements that are also found in the dance art. One such element is *sounds*. These may include drum beating, chanting, and singing. The drummer is the main music maker in a tribe; and since it is felt that the gods speak through drums, both the man and the instrument are associated with the sacred. The most common ritual arrangement has the drummers in a clearing; the dancers face the drummers while they dance, sing, clap, and stamp; and the tribe forms a circle around the performers. The first drums were animal skins stretched over cooking pots, or across the ends of a hollow tree trunk. Drumsticks were cooking spoons. To honor their sacred character, many rituals are observed in connection with manufacturing the drums. For example, among the Lotuko, when new skins are provided for drums, the men do a dance wearing women's clothing. At various times and places, rattling instruments, bone whistles, and reed flutes were added to drums, and you had the beginnings of accompaniment—as well as that of the jazz band!

Body decorations may include the adornment of the body with masks, feathered or grass costumes, colored stones and shells, and painted make-up for faces or bodies. A common element used in summoning magic power is the *mask*. The dancer assumes a special supernatural identity with a mask or headdress. You know from watching horror films the effect of a mask on a spectator. Think for a moment of the effect on the wearer. Perhaps you've been at a Mardi Gras, or a masquerade, or worn a mask on Halloween. As in any striking costume, you feel different, removed from your familiar self. It hides you. The mask enables you to do things you might not otherwise do. Would ordinary southern businessmen have been able to take part in the lynching of black men if they had to face one another in their everyday faces?

And how much more does donning a mask affect you if you believed, with tribal man, that the mask changes your actual identity and merges you with the spirit that the mask represents? Among the Dogon tribe, the mask by itself is a fearsome object, attracting great magical force. It is dangerous to the very men who make it, and for protection before and during their wood carving, they perform sacrifices and obey strict rules. Thus the masked dancer, becoming one with tribal ancestors, or with good or evil spirits, is powerful indeed.

The *setting* involves going to a particular place, like another village or a clearing in the woods, or a cave, or a sick person's hut. Preparation for the ritual may include decorating the place. A bower may be erected in the clearing or on a cave wall. Finally, an element common to both ritual and dance is *fire*. It is a given that before the invention of electricity, fire was present at all nighttime ceremonies to provide light. However, fire also serves other purposes. It may be used for sacrifice, or as a focal point to dance around, or to carry in the form of torches. Fire is very much a part of modern ritual. You may or may not have attended a candlelight procession, whether at an initiation into a club, or a memorial service. But you have certainly sat at a campfire and felt the awesome attraction of its dancing flames.

Crossover Rituals. In this chapter, I have offered you a number of types and examples of rituals and ceremonies. Under each type, you will find activities that could just as well have been put into a different classification, since all the traditional motifs of tribal dance are creatively combined in ever-new relationships. You have already been warned that a subject as broad as world dance is not easy to pin down. However, since our methods of study—and certainly our books—are constructed in a linear fashion, we are stuck with the necessity for drawing lines, often in a rather arbitrary manner. Anthropologists sometimes use the term *crossover rituals* to deal with this problem. Actually, it is a rare ritual that does not cross over.

For example, we see crossover rituals in the many vegetation rituals that begin with the idea of human fertility. In other dances, moments of sexual intercourse are brought into the dance and combined artistically with it. The weapon dance crosses over to fertility rites. There is a very ancient relationship between battle dance and love dance, which we see in the deep significance of the weapon dance when it is performed at sowing and reaping, girls' rites, weddings, and funerals. The same actions may have a number of purposes. Flagellation and stamp dances (beating on the earth) occur in initiation rituals, at funeral dances, as rain charms, and in fertility rituals, and so on. Now that you have a clear concept of ritual in the life of tribal man, we will look more closely at the dance itself, as it was and is found in ritual.

Questions for Review

1. Think of a private ritual you attended with friends or family. What similarities can you find with tribal rituals?

2. Can you think of a public political ritual which took place recently? Discuss the elements that were present.

2 DANCE IN TRIBAL SOCIETIES

FORMS OF RITUAL DANCE

The reason we find the presence of dance over and over again in rituals lies in the nature of dance as a form of motion. However you define it, dance is a special kind of activity. Its motions are rhythmical, planned, and focussed. They are bigger than life, that is, above and beyond everyday movement. Dance has power. We know from our own experience that when people who are worn out from a day's labor start to dance, they become refreshed, energized, and enjoy dancing for hours. "Every dance is and gives ecstasy," is the way Curt Sachs put it in his *World History of The Dance*. Havelock Ellis went further in *The Art of Dancing*: "Dancing is the loftiest, the most moving, the most beautiful of the arts, because it is no mere translation or abstraction from life: it is life itself.".In short, dance lifts us into a special state. It is therefore not strange that when people in preliterate tribes seek to perform magic or to formalize their basic attitudes towards the world they turn to the dance as a central feature in their behavior. Be advised, however, that ritual dance does not always conform to what is ordinarily thought of as dance. It may be merely exaggerated movement, such as jumping and howling, running about, or flinging or whirling articles of clothing. Now we will explore the characteristics of ritual dance..We begin with the classifications that Curt Sachs makes in *The World History of The Dance*, because he was perhaps the first scholar to analyze the elements of tribal dance in ways that are useful to students of dance theory.

First, Sachs offers a major division of dance types into *harmonious* and *ecstatic.* In harmonious dances, the motions and rhythms are repetitive, hypnotic, and the patterns simple. Movements include shuffling, stamping, hopping, lunging, and stamping or stepping with a bent knee and a slide backward from one foot to the other—all performed with a relaxed spine. The arms, hands, head, shoulders, trunk, and pelvis may swing from side to side. .In contrast, ecstatic dances build to ever-greater heights—literally, with high leaps and jumps, and emotionally, with the performers becoming increasingly more excited. The movements may involve whirling or twirling; every part of the body may shake or tremble; the head rolls and spins; legs and arms are thrust into the air with great speed, making the thigh muscles quiver or throwing any part of the body into high-speed vibrations or convulsive trembling, all of which demand great facility and strength.

Sachs mentions the presence of whirling dancers in Mediterranean and Asian countries as far back as 1300 B.C. He himself repeatedly saw the following ritual in Cairo, in 1932:

> Ten monks soar forth, spread their arms out horizontally like the wings of an airplane, and begin to whirl in such a manner that the many cowls worn one over another form a large bell around them.
>   Four of the dervishes make up a small circle, six a larger one, and as they whirl about constantly, the eldest moves slowly and continuously between the two circles, again counter-clockwise.
>   These old men with outspread arms spin like tops for a full half hour—an astonishing, inconceivable performance.

Deben Bhattacharya wrote in *Dance Magazine* (February 1965):

> At one time the cult of the whirling dervishes spread from Turkey to the Balkan countries and throughout the Middle East into India. But following the Westernization of Turkey and the ban on dervishes by Turkish authorities in 1925, most of the Arab countries outlawed the movement.

Time and again we will hear how political and religious authorities ban or encourage dance practices for reasons that lie outside the field of aesthetics.

The climax of an ecstatic dance is often a *trance state* for one or more of the participants, led by the priest or shaman. Ecstatic dances may end with the dancer in a hypnotic state, or a trance. The tribal members consider that he (or very often she) is possessed by a spirit. Trance dances have been observed in many parts of the world. Convulsive dances leave the participants almost unconscious. They are unaware of their surroundings and show little reaction to outside stimuli. There are frequent stories about dancers in a trance who do not feel the touch of burning coals nor painful needles, and in fact their flesh emerges unscarred. Sometimes the spectators are affected as deeply as the performers.

Anthropologist Erika Bourguignon, in *"Trance Dance"*, (*Dance Perspectives*, Number 35), presents an insightful discussion of the whole subject. Dance is often used to bring about mystic states, sometimes with the aid of drugs and potent liquors. This is ecstatic dancing in the most literal sense. It reappears time and again in religious movements as diverse as eighteenth-century Hasidism; the dancing sects and manias of Christianity during the Middle Ages; the whirling dervishes of North Africa, Turkey, Malaya, and Indonesia; and the Shakers in the United States.

Sachs gives us a report of ecstatic dancing from the Solomon Islands. Imagine an open village square surrounded by the low huts of the natives, the darkness intensified by the palms and other dense foliage. In a wide circle, the naked figures squat and lie, lighted up by the flickering glow of a fire. Four or five older men walk noiselessly into the center with spears, bows, and arrows. The younger men soon join them and arrange themselves in rows, like the spokes of a wheel, with the old men in the center. The half-grown boys take places in a circle on the outside. Now the old men in the center begin howling. Gradually, the young men and boys join in and at the same time the entire throng begins to move slowly around a central point. Soon the pace is quickened and the dancers on the outer edge must make long jumps to keep up with the rest. As they turn, the dancers whistle shrilly; they rattle their weapons and toss themselves into the air. The excitement gradually reaches such a point that individual dancers break away from the rest and roll on the ground in wild ecstasy.

Possession trance cults are known today all over the world, particularly among West Africans and their descendants in Cuba, Jamaica, Haiti, Trinidad, and Brazil. A central practice in possession trance cults involves dancing for two purposes: first, to invite spirits to take part; and second, as a way of the dancer impersonating (in a sense becoming) a spirit. Adult women are the most frequent performers in these cults. After they awaken from a trance, they don't remember what happened or what they did when the spirits took over their bodies.

Bourguignon describes the rituals of possession trance cults in Haiti, where she did field work. The person in a trance performs dance motions which imitate familiar Haitian spirits, such as the coquettish wiggling of the female spirit Erzulie Freda; and the aggressive, machete swinging of male spirits like Ogun.

Another useful distinction that Curt Sachs makes about dance applies to gesture. Just as we speak of choreography today as either dramatic or plotless, so does Curt Sachs classify tribal dances as *mimetic* or *imageless*. Even if the dance ritual has a purpose, its movements can be rhythmic and generalized, that is, imageless, with the power coming not from the gestures themselves, but from their rhythmic repetition and other ritual aspects. However, if the action portrays an entire event, in order that nature may be moved to imitate the action, we call the ritual mimetic, that is, the movements portray an image. The rituals in the previous chapter in which high jumps and skyward leaps were done to inspire the gods of agriculture to make the crops grow tall were mimetic. Also mimetic are tribal dancers who mimic animals with great skill. Among the Berg Damara of South Africa, for example, there are at least twenty-two different animal dances. There is a natural affinity between man and the animal populations in his environment. Even when he uses animals for food, he respects their life forms and may call on their spirits to protect him.

Performers. Who performs rituals dances? Is it the general population, or are there specially trained dancers? This aspect varies tremendously. At times, all tribal villagers may take part, if only for the pleasurable purpose of strengthening communal feelings in the tribe. At other times, it is limited to priests or dance specialists, or by sex.

Pygmies of Central Africa love to dance and do so spontaneously in the contented hour after supper. Someone will get things started by tapping out a rhythm on the drums or piping on a whistle. A man may dance a jig by himself while laughing and clapping his hands. Soon a dozen men, women, and children will have risen to follow one another in a circle, waving their arms, singing, stamping, and laughing. They can dance all night if the moon is full. In other cases, the performers are specially trained and skilled. The best-known dancers of Africa were in the Watusi tribe, an aristocratic race of very tall, long-limbed, graceful blacks, who astounded travellers in the late 1800s and early 1900s with their dance prowess, calling forth comparisons with Nijinsky and other ballet stars for their breath-taking leaps and jumps.

Odette Blum, trained in ballet and modern dance spent two years in Africa. While she was in Ghana, Blum not only observed tribal dance, she studied it on site with native teachers. These circumstances make her writings especially valuable to us. In her article *"Dance in Ghana"* (*Dance Perspectives* Number 56), Blum describes the basic styles of African dance movement. In general, Blum tells us:

> There is a going with gravity; the spine is more at ease, less held (than in European-rooted dance). The feeling is down rather than up. The body posture reflects modesty . . . To have a "lifted" position is considered haughty, and is used to depict overweening pride, or a comic effect . . .
>
> African movement consists basically of "free flow" . . . a movement in one part of the body will *cause* a movement in the neighboring parts and beyond .
>
> The precise placement of a limb in space is not significant; the stress is placed on the continuous, free-flowing motion.

Ghanian dance movement involves manipulation of costumes. The dancers, men and women, wear long lengths of material (eight to ten yards!) wrapped as skirts or as togas. These tend to slip. The cloth may be flung with a wide, sweeping gesture, which begins a turn, while the whole body rises and lowers. This projects a feeling of "power, pomposity, a desire to display."

Sexual Roles in Dance

Male and female differences in styles and roles is something we will come across time and again as we follow the history of dance. In ritual dance it is a dominant factor. According to Curt Sachs, it is chiefly *men* who do the all-important dances of war and of the hunt. In contrast, women's dances most often deal with the moon, planting, or caring for the bodies of the dead. Their dance style tends to be toned down. They do not do the spreading leaps or make the highly labored exertions of the men. Sachs writes:

> Almost everywhere the dance of women shows evidence of suppression and diminutions. The bold leap, the separation from the ground, is reduced to a stretching on the toes, and the large stride degenerates into a timid tripping. A dance of women will return almost certainly to a close form.

He notes a few exceptions, such as the predominantly sexual "frivolous" jumps of the women of Palau in the Caroline Islands in honor of a feminine divinity. And the Massai young girls entreatingly approach their lovers with short jumps. If the men respond by leaping into the air, it is taken as a sign of agreement that they will meet in the evening.

According to Sir James Frazer (in *The Golden Bough*) male and female have equal dance status when sexual rituals are ordained. That is, when they perform a direct imitation of mating, or actually have sexual inter-course. This could be at coming of age (initiation) ceremonies, as a magic influence on crop growth, or sometimes to propitiate the spirits in times of general stress and trouble. On the other hand, Sachs maintains that rituals that feature couples dancing in direct contact are very rare in tribes. They show up at later stages of civilization.

Odette Blum confirms these sexual characteristics when she tells us how movements of men and women are differentiated in style in a traditional fashion:

> In a dance called *Adowa*, the women sway gently from side to side as they travel forward; the torso bends low on the way, with small wave-like motions flowing through it, the head gliding serenely on top. The men move with more drive: the whole torso tends towards a more frontal, direct appearance; the wave-like torso motion is broader.
>
> In the *Kobine*, the men travel with easy runs in a spacious circle. The women form their own circle within the men's. Unlike the men however, the women will travel throughout in the same direction.

> In the *Husago*, the women performed an even, unaccented, continuous flow of motion. . . The men's movements were clearly separated.

In modern Ghana, however, she notes that the women's roles are increasing. Now they alternate with men in doing variations and, in fact, frequently join the men's circle.

TRIBAL CULTURE AND THE MODERN WORLD

Only in the last fifty years or so, have Western scholars begun to appreciate the richness of tribal cultures. Up until that time, the usual Western attitude ranged from amusement and contempt to outright hostility. At best, they ignored native arts; at worst they deliberately destroyed them. W.E.F. Ward wrote in his *History of Ghana* (1958):

> Ghana was an African state with a civilization which owed little or nothing to Europe, and may indeed have been in some respects superior to the civilization of Europe in the age of Charlemagne. . .
> Ignoring magnificent medieval developments in West Africa, European historians have repeatedly stated that Africa produced no civilization of its own.

Malvina Hoffman, a sculptor whose book *Heads and Tales* was referred to previously, observes that only in the 1930s did our western "intellectuals" begin to awaken to the fact that art is a record of a people's culture as well as intrinsically valuable. In Hawaii, she bewailed it as a tragedy that the missionaries had destroyed all the idols, gods, and other carvings of the natives.

Similar awful things occurred in Africa. Odette Blum tells how in the late nineteenth century, when the British ruled the African Gold Coast, they allowed the African chiefs to continue as political administrators. However, they left education largely to the missionaries, who held the native culture in contempt. These pious preachers considered traditional music to be barbaric, and traditional dance to be lascivious and sinful. Blum writes: "As a result there grew up a class of educated Africans who were ignorant and often ashamed of their own heritage and considered the European superior." It is no surprise that tribal dance began to die out at an accelerating rate. At times, intertribal warfare contributed to this downfall. Such was the case among the Watusi.

Lewis Cotlow reports the complicated history of this tribe in his book *In Search of the Primitive (1966)*. When Cotlow first saw them, the Watusi were a haughty, aristocratic race:

. . . giants six and a half to almost eight feet tall, slender and graceful. And their clothing was just right—long flowing robes like a Roman senator's toga, snowy white and with sunbursts of gold or broad red stripes.

They may have migrated from Egypt to central Africa, where they became the rulers of the native Bahutu, a small, docile people whom the Watusi enslaved and often treated with great cruelty. After the Belgians conquered the area, they allowed the Watusi to continue as the dominant tribe. When the African peoples revolted during the 1950s and 1960s against their white colonial masters, the Bahutu rose both against the Belgian administrators and the Watusi overlords. Ten years of slaughter followed, at the end of which the Bahutu triumphed. In his book, Cotlow concludes, "the fantastic Watusi are done for."

Fortunately, the picture elsewhere was more cheerful. With the spread of nationalism and independence movements throughout the tremendous continent of Africa, and with the changing climate in cultural attitudes worldwide, there was a deliberate, conscious reversal of cultural trends. Sometimes tribal leaders led the effort to revive traditional arts; sometimes sympathetic and talented Westerners took part in these efforts.

In 1957, the Gold Coast became the first African country to regain its independence and its name: Ghana. The new-old state under Kwame Nkrumah fostered a return of pride in African culture and tradition. The

These African dancers staged a tribal war ritual.

University of Ghana invited Odette Blum to teach modern dance and Labanotation at the University of Ghana from 1966 to 1968. (Shortly, we will discuss *Labanotation*, a system of recording movement on paper. Ghanians were eager to learn it so they could spread the old dance forms throughout the country.)

All over the world, similarly ravaged natives have begun to reverse the process by preserving and restoring age-old artifacts and traditions. In 1966, King Sobhuza II, Lion of Swaziland, joined his people in a six-day *Incwala*, or ritual ceremony. Dressed in animal skins and elaborate plumage, they performed dances that would ensure the renewal of the land, the king, and the people.

Now we come to the skilled and caring people from the outside who have assisted tribes with this renewal. One such black woman, an outstanding American modern-dance artist, is Pearl Primus. Primus has been a very successful concert performer. At the same time, she along with her husband Percival Borde, a West Indian dancer, has been a tireless researcher and advocate of authentic native African dance. Born in Trinidad, Pearl Primus achieved a Ph.D. in anthropology. In 1948, on a Julius Rosenwald Fellowship, Primus made a survey of dances in Africa. Ric Estrada, in *Dance Magazine* (November 1968) tells us about this New York trained modern dancer in Africa:

> She covered the Gold Coast, Angola, Cameroons, Liberia, Senegal and the Belgian Congo. Her trek from village to village was telegraphed by the talking drums booming across the bush "Little Fast Feet is on her way."
>
> At every village she explained that she came from a country across the sea and that she wished to see their dance so that she could tell her people about them. But despite her simplicity, her hosts considered her an ancestral spirit, returned to them in human form. Her own dynamic dancing confirmed their suspicions.
>
> She was adopted by the dancers of His Royal Highness, King of the giant Watusi. She was renamed *Omowale* (Child Returned Home) by the spiritual head of the Yoruba people of Nigeria, and designated *Jaibundu*, (First Among Dancers).

In 1951, Pearl Primus presented performances based on these dances and rituals back in the United States. In 1959, she spent six months in Liberia, sponsored by their government, where she instituted a program designed to preserve native dance and related arts. Since that time, she has been moving back and forth between both continents, studying, dancing, and teaching.

Labanotation and Choreometrics. At the same time that there was a growing consciousness of the fragility of ethnic cultures, two important tools to aid in their preservation appeared. The first was *Labanotation*, the second *choreometrics*. Labanotation is a thorough system of analyzing and notating physical movement. It was developed by Rudolf Laban whom we will meet later in connection with German modern dance. Laban's basic concept, known as *effort-shape*, is described in his book *The Mastery of Movement*.

In order to make a written record of something as complicated as movement, it is necessary to analyze and describe many things. These include: the shape of the body and all its parts in each position; the dynamic force used in transit (percussive, gliding, swinging); the position of each body in the stage space; and the total design of the group. This must all be done in combination with rhythmic phrasing, and in relation to the musical accompaniment. It sounds complicated, doesn't it? It is. Actually, the principles are not hard to grasp, but mastering the details of the system is a matter of long, concentrated study.

Laban worked out much of his movement analysis during World War II for English industry, where he conducted time and motion studies to increase worker efficiency. Dancers have become very interested in Labanotation to preserve and analyze choreography. Psychologists and therapists use it to understand body language that may express emotional problems. In this country, their work is centered at the Dance Notation Bureau in New York City. Labanotation has been applied by scholars, like Odette Blum in Ghana, to record dance rituals and to investigate patterns of similarities and differences among groups of people.

The second tool, choreometrics, grew out of a project directed by Alan Lomax at Columbia University that was concerned with recording and measuring the qualities of tribal music. Irmgard Bartenieff and Forrestine Paulay, leading experts in Laban's dance analysis, worked with Lomax to apply his approach to Dance.

In the *Filmmakers Newsletter* (Volume 4, Number 4, February 1971), Alan Lomax defines Choreometrics as both the measure of dance, and the measure of man. How did Lomax, Bartenieff, and Paulay measure dance? They produced a rating system that assigned numbers to the qualities of movement behavior as classified by Laban. Then, by using films from all over the world of people both at work and dancing, they created profiles that could be computerized and compared. Here are their conclusions:

> We find within any one culture area, one or two distinctive movement profiles . . . In simple cultures, one such description characterizes most activity. . .
>
> Naturally there are differences between individuals, between persons of different ages and sex, but these differences are likely to grade away from a baseline movement signature . . . notable in the stance adopted by a people and in the tempo of their activity. . .
>
> In broad terms, Choreometrics affirms the existence of a very few large

and very old style traditions: 1) the primitive Pacific, 2) black Africa with Melanesia and Polynesia, 3) high culture Eurasia, and 4) Europe. There also seems to be an Arctic style tradition that links northern Europe across Siberia to aboriginal North America.

Contrast these observations of Eskimo and Polynesian cultures, reported by Irmgard Bartenieff in *CORD Preliminary Conference on Research in Dance*, 1967:

> ESKIMO: One absolutely consistent body attitude. High intensity through an active use of strength, speed, and force. Sharp angularity in work movement. The endless going on of the drum dance, perhaps exemplifying the Eskimo's boundless endurance and patience in waiting for the seal to surface from the ice hole. The stress on speed and strength in all games. The directional use of space. The stress on simultaneous use of all parts of the limbs used, producing maximal impact.

> POLYNESIAN: The use of two body attitudes. The predominance of indirectedness, moderate speed, and fleeting use of force. The use of several transitions, including both round and angular. The indefinite use of space in shape. The successive use of body limbs, never with forceful impact. The undulating style of the dance.

The purpose of ethnographic filming is not only for pure analysis and research. Lomax believes it will lead to feedback and cultural renewal. He says:

> The voices and the images of the nonliterate underprivileged are, unlike ours, seldom amplified by the big communication systems...But broadcasting sound and film, especially song, dance, drama, narrative, ritual and the like, can put the human race on terms of parity, for all aesthetic systems carry their own messages of perfection.

Tribal Dancing on Western Stages. In this century, next to the efforts of native leaders and western dance scholars, there have been commercially motivated attempts to revive native cultures. This happened more and more as theater managers became aware of the possibilities of mining age-old rituals for their artistic and commercial possibilities. When for commercial reasons, non-Western groups appear on our stages, the effect is not always positive. We will discuss this further in the chapters to come.

Before we leave tribal dance, I want to tell you about a rare experience that was both completely authentic and marvelous theater: the Yaqui Indian Josè Daniel Avilez, appearing in the Mexican Ballet Folklorico's *Deer Dance* as the hunted deer.

Mine was the critic's job of reviewing Avilez and the Folklorico Ballet. Each time I saw him—in 1968 in Mexico; again that year in Boston; and once more in 1973 in Israel—I was overwhelmed by his gripping, brilliant performance in a dramatic animal dance.

Avilez, his torso bare except for a necklace, wearing a fringed loincloth, a stuffed deer's head with antlers, and dried gourds filled with gravel around his legs, held a large gourd rattle in each hand. He was chased, cornered, and finally killed by two hunters. His silent springing steps, his crouching, breath-held leaps, his awful fear, and finally his shuddering death throes were a tour de force of mime and exquisite technical control.

Before attending the concerts, I was lucky to find an excellent background piece by Olga Maynard in The January 1964 issue of *Dance Magazine*. From Maynard I learned that the *Deer Dance* is an authentic sacred dance, a ritual of sacrifice whose purpose is to ensure a new cycle of life for the Sonora Indians. This tribe is unique. In all Mexico, only this tribe maintained its independence, refusing to lay down its arms until it was granted the right of self-government. Thus following their traditions from prehistory, venerated elderly men of the Sonora tribe taught the deer dance to Avilez, among others, when he was a very little boy. Strong and talented, he went on to perform it from the age of five, beginning in 1950.

When Olga Maynard first visited the dance company for her article, she found Avilez "a little savage." When the sixteen-year-old wasn't rehearsing or performing, he was like an acquisitive child, wearing two watches at once, and ill-matched jackets, trousers, and a dreadful, oversized hat. Or he sat around with a sullen face. Three years later, when she saw him again, he was able to laugh at himself. He was learning English and his ambition was to know all kinds of dancing and to "dance everything" like the wonderful Russian he saw on tour. (This was in 1961, in Paris, when Rudolph Nureyev defected to the West, and when the Ballet Folklorico won the Paris competition for best folk dance company.) He also enjoyed social dancing (the twist was a favorite) and spectator sports.

I have tried, without success, to discover what happened to that innocent tribal boy, with his two wristwatches and his sad-looking offstage clothes. Did he achieve his ambitions? Or did adulation go to his head, making him spoiled and lazy? Is he still alive? I would like to think that he returned to his tribe, and that now he is a tribal elder, teaching the deer dance to the next generation of boys.

Question for Review

1.   What dance performance have you attended in which you can identify ritual connections?

3 ASIAN CEREMONIES

ORIENTAL DANCE, PAST AND PRESENT

Leaving tribal culture, we come to a fork in the road. We can follow dance and ritual into Asia, or we can move first to the Mediterranean region, from where we trace most of our Western culture. I choose to turn to the East, because that is where the traditions we are following continued in an unbroken development. I keep using the phrase "our Western culture." This may strike you, who think of the whole world as your home, as provincial. However, when in the late 1800s Kipling said, "East is East and West is West and never the twain shall meet," he expressed an opinion that was widely held among intellectuals as well as ordinary people. Ironically, just around the time that Kipling wrote those lines, we in the United States and Europe began to have real contact with Asia. And over the last hundred years, Asian dancing and other arts have gradually made a strong impression on the Western mind.

Actually, this happened during earlier periods too, on and off since Marco Polo's voyages in the 1200s. Later in our history we will meet Jean Georges Noverre who in 1754 choreographed *Les fetes Chinois*, (The Chinese Festivals), which went over very well with Parisians who found the Chinese "exotic"; and later still, Ruth St. Denis, an early modern dancer who was inspired by themes of Eastern dance. More recently, in the 1960s, young people from the West (including the Beatles) went to India by the thousands to "get off" on drugs and meditation. In our field, this is when John Cage and Merce Cunningham adopted Buddhist *chance practices* in making artistic decisions. In the late 1900s, such contacts as these have led you to be familiar with Oriental foods and practices like Yoga, and with pupils from far-off countries. Perhaps you even consider yourself a child of the Far East. Nevertheless, for the purpose of understanding the history of dance and its traditions, it is useful to treat Eastern culture as separate from Western. Even today, in this age of television satellites and worldwide cultural blendings, one can still find sharp differences between hemispheres and nations. And in the past, these differences were much sharper and more pervasive.

When we look at civilizations that have evolved beyond tribal forms, we find that in contrast to Western dance, which developed as art, entertainment, and recreation, Asian dance remained closely linked with religious content. Even when it was attached to royal courts, Oriental dance kept its content of national myth and legend, with god and demon characters. Up to the present, Easterners still look on dance as a form of spiritual communication. In line with this, they have adhered to age-old forms and legends in choreography, costume, and accompaniment. In contrast, Westerners have been partial to novelty. When compared with Western styles, there are general characteristics commonly found in Oriental dance movement. Obviously you will come across exceptions, but these observations apply if you take a broad overview of cultures, as do the practitioners of choreometrics described previously.

Eastern body stance is fluid. The spine undulates; the hips, rib cage, and head shift from side to side; the shoulders ripple and shake. Knees are most commonly bent. With the feet and legs held in fixed positions, the dancer lunges, springs, stamps, and turns. The Eastern dancer's movements glide low over the ground and often sink down altogether, until the dance is performed in a seated position. Arms, hands, fingers, and head perform the most subtle and expressive motions. Stylized facial gestures of the eyes, brows, nose, cheeks, mouth, and chin are part of the choreography.

In contrast, European dance presents a stable spine, with hips, shoulders, and arms held quietly. Face and hands are generally left to the individual performer. The dancer reaches upward, favoring high jumps and leaps into the air, which are rare in Oriental dance. The European dancer bends his legs and feet in order to stretch them still straighter. Western dance often features women in spectacular exhibitionism. In Eastern dance, there is a sharp distinction between the broad and vigorous movements of the males, who spread their legs in wide lunges, and the females, whose gestures are more subtle and who keep their bent knees modestly close.

Hindu Dance. Asian styles share a common origin in Hindu dance, perhaps the oldest of the world's developed dance forms. Mrinalini

Sarabhai, performer and scholar of Hindu dance, tells us in *"The Eight Nanikas"* (*Dance Perspectives*, Number 24) that the earliest known reference to Indian dance occurs in the Rig-Veda, which is believed to have been written before 5000 B.C. Hindu dance embodies a philosophy that is not easy for the Western mind to grasp. The problem is that in the West, religion is regarded as a spiritual matter related to the soul, while the body is separate, and the seat of wicked impulses. Western religious teachings set very specific limits on sexual pleasure. On the other hand, Hindu dance is an expression of both sexual love, and of religious devotion. Sarabhai says:

> The perfect form of worship is surrender to love....The passion of the love poems of India is the passion of the seeker. Lovemaking is taken to the divine height of ardent desire for the perfect union of man and God.
>   Love through poetry, through dance, through painting, was extolled as a means of achieving salvation. Spiritual release was indicated by the utter surrender of the worshipper to God, through all the known phases of love.

Now you will learn some Sanskrit terms. *Mudras* refer to the specific, literal sign language of gestures. For example, the sixty-seven gestures of the hands, in various combinations with thirteen gestures of the head, or the thirty-six different glances, can project several thousand different meanings!

Bharata Natya is a female solo dance practiced in the temples. Its content is totally sexual. The present form of *Bharata Natya* was set in the early eighteenth century by four well-known teachers. Although the dance is now performed on the stage, instead of in the temple, it still opens with an invocation to the gods who represent the triumph of good over evil. The dance then proceeds through a rigid structure of lyrical, rhythmic, and dramatic passages. The lyrics and the movements tell of the bliss of sexual love through the predicament of a heroine. By now there are three hundred and eighty-four varieties of heroines, but they are based on eight basic classical types.

Sarabhai describes how each heroine dances to express her love for the god Krishna, according to different circumstances. For example, one heroine is happily waiting for her beloved, repeatedly looking to see if he is coming. Another is lonely, suffering the separation from her lover. Or, a heroine is full of remorse because she has quarreled with her lord. Perhaps a heroine is grieved, because her lover has not come as he had promised. In accordance with her mood, which may be expressed as eagerness, anger, gentle mockery, impatience, and so on, each heroine has her own language of gesture, her own rhythm, her own musical mode. Through the consecration of this sacred dance, the body is rid of human weakness, and purified into a medium of spiritual beauty. Neither the musicians, who sing and strike cymbals, nor the dancer in a richly decorated sari, pause until the performance concludes with a coda of pure dance after about three hours.

The dances of the Nautch-Wali, dating from the 1500s, are in a completely different class. La Meri tells us (in Chujoy's Dance Encyclopedia) that these dancers were originally imported from Persia for the entertainment of rulers. Their dance style was popular, but not in favor with India's upper castes, because the Nautch girls were known for their loose morals.

Kathakali is a vigorous, difficult dance-drama, performed mostly by boys and young men. Kathakali presents the entire gamut of great epics of Hindu literature: the creation of the universe: the gods and their rivalries, spiritual tests, battles, and sexual exploits. The style is bigger than life, with movements that tend to be forceful, full of stamping rhythms reinforced by an orchestra of ear-splitting percussionists.

Kathak, performed by men and women, is mainly concerned with music and rhythm, rather than story. Adorned with ankle bells, the feet act as percussive instruments and work closely together, often one crossed in front of the other, stamping out very complex rhythms. The signature movement of Kathak is the chukra, a brilliant whipping turn executed on one spot.

Manipuri has a soft, restful quality. Its light, graceful movement dramas are performed by many dancers, supported by dialogue and song.

In the early years of this century, two Indian men made it their mission to revive the great Indian classical dance and restore its lost prestige: the poet Rabindranath Tagore and the charismatic dancer Uday Shankar. Shankar not only aroused a great surge of interest in Hindu dance with his many tours, (he came repeatedly to the United States, beginning in 1931, and was always well received), but he was responsible for reviving and preserving the ancient arts in his own country by establishing a research institute and school.

Through conquest and trade, the influence of Hinduism spread widely in Asia. Here again, we are faced with our twin principles of tradition and creativity. While there are many similarities in dance among all Oriental peoples, at the same time, each nation has expressed its unique personality in individual variations.

National Variations of Asian Dance

Java. Today Javanese traditional dances are preserved at court, along with other art forms. There is not one, but a number of aristocratic courts in Java which are centers of dance. Although dance performances are presented in theaters, the theatrical dance of Java is virtually a religious ceremony, known for its slow, swaying rhythms. In Heads and Tales, sculptor Malvina Hoffman describes a performance of wayang wong, a highly polished court dance that lasted throughout the night and the following day. Wayang wong is built on spiritual principles of balance and moderation.

Court dancers of Java show time-honored ceremonies.

Hoffman found the technique of mudras to be highly developed, and was impressed that at court, "The art of dancing is considered the chief delight and occupation of the young men and women from childhood until they come to marrigeable age."

Miriam Morrison presents an excellently detailed discussion of Javanese dance in *Dance Chronicle* (Volume 2, Number 3, 1978). She describes in very specific terms the dance style known as *Bedaya-Serimpi*. Stemming from the original women's style of dancing, it evolved into men's and women's dance and is basic to the aesthetic of Java.

> Delicate arm and hand movements, subtle tilts and turns of the head, slow, measured steps forward and gliding movements to the side made with imperceptible movements of the feet . . . .
>
> Fingers are held in positions and much wrist movement is used, creating delicate circling movements. A dance scarf, tied around the dancer's waist, falls to her ankles . . . It is gently picked up, flipped over the hand and wrist, dropped, placed over the elbow, held by the tips of two fingers, and so on . . .
>
> In the *Bedaya*, lasting forty to ninety minutes, the dancers never change their facial expression and there is no change in dynamics.
>
> It is *not* literal dance-drama. Although the action alludes to a story, all movement remains highly stylized, abstract and symbolic.

Bali. The dances of Bali are not centered at court, as are the Javanese. The style of their movement and music is more impetuous and vigorous. Mastery of the quick and difficult movements of Balinese dance requires rigorous training. Walter Sorell in *The Dance Through the Ages* describes the most famous of their dances, the *Legong*:

> The whole body seems to be in movement, from eyebrows and neck to wrists and fingers, from shoulders and elbows to knees and feet. . .
>
> The *Legong* is a pantomime dance performed by two young girls dressed in rich and flowery garments set off by beautiful headdresses and fans.

Only in a recent modernized version called the *Djoged*, has this dance become more of a communal affair. A girl dances in the traditional *Legong* style and is joined by boys from the audience.

Ceylon. The Ceylonese dancers are the Oriental exceptions who excel in spectacular leaping turns. They specialize in fire dancers, who cover themselves in flames without getting burned, and in the devil dance, which mimics the demonic spirits to the point where the performers spin into transports of ecstasy.

Cambodia. The articulated gestures of arms, hands, and feet— extreme even in the Orient—are outstanding in Cambodian dance movement styles. These intricate postures are the focus of delicate, hypnotic motions. The major part of the dancers' training for the first five years consists of exercises that bend and wrench their joints until they can perform these exquisitely stretched contortions. Unfortunately, this age-old style is of less importance in world dance today than it was two decades ago. What happened in Cambodia in the 1970s is a terrible lesson in the way political events impinge on seemingly unrelated matters like art. The Khmer Rouge not only killed 90 percent of the country's dancers, they destroyed all the relevant literature. In a painstaking attempt to re-create the art form, the Cambodian nation has had to rely on one lame woman, Chea Samy, for the memory of steps, gestures, and stories to rebuild the tradition-stamped repertory.

China. When Malvina Hoffman travelled to China in the early 1930s and brought back seventy-eight photographs of *mudras* used in Tibetan religious ritual, she rightly regarded it as a remarkable find. Although ceremonial dance in China goes back many centuries, little was known in the West about Chinese dance. In recent years, however, information about Chinese dance forms has been increasingly available to Westerners. La Meri tells us in Chujoy's *Dance Encyclopedia* that the remnants of Chinese classical dance survive only in Chinese drama, where each character type has a specific hand gesture. For example, only the *shen* (male) uses strong, spread fingers, while the *tan* (female) has "helpless" hands.

An outstanding feature of Chinese dance is related to costume. We have seen the use of the scarf in Javanese dance movement. In China, an elaborate art of the sleeve has been practiced since at least 400 B.C. Gloria Strauss discusses this complex form in *"The Art of the Sleeve in Chinese Dance"* (*Dance Perspectives,* Number 63). *Shui hsiu* (water sleeves) made of thin white silk, at least one and a half feet in length, are separate items, attached to the dancer's costume. In Chinese opera, the *hsiu* (sleeve gesture) is used for communication in the same way that Hindu performers use the *mudra* (hand gesture). Although some sleeve gestures are purely decorative, most have a specific dramatic meaning. Strauss gives examples:

> *chang hsiu*: the left sleeve is placed on the stomach and the right sleeve is placed at the back of the head, indicating that a person is being beaten. Does a young girl wish to indicate that she is pleased with her appearance? She places her left hand over her right one, with the left palm upward and the right palm downward. The sleeves, which have been hanging down, are now swayed from side to side. This is *cheng hsiu*. Does a character wish to signify happiness? It can be done by lifting the hands with the palms downwards until they are in front of the chest. Then turn both hands outwards with a flicking motion. This is *shuang yang hsiu*.

The tradition of sleeve dancing has been preserved in the Peking Opera, where set character motions are as much a part of the presentation as the words. A Chinese opera performer is required to be as skilled a dance-mime as he is a singer. In a review of the Peking Opera (*Dance Magazine,* November 1980) Tobi Tobias wrote that *The Monkey King Fights the Eighteen Lo Hans* presents:

> a dazzling display that mingles tumbling, juggling and martial arts, is the center of the piece and it is physically thrilling. Nearly all of the fabled acrobatic feats are here: cartwheels and somersaults catapulted into the air; resilient descents onto the hands, a shoulder or a rubbery spine; stagewide diagonals of non-stop flipflops; vaulting springs from motionless preparations.
>
> While the mere achievement of these stunts is remarkable, the appeal to the dance fan lies in the dynamic variety they display—the contrast of supple and tough, trajectory and suspension....

In contrast, *The Jade Bracelet* presents:

> gentle, rhythmic patterns of movement: symbolic configurations of supple fingers, play of the hands in and out of the long, white silk kimono cuffs, little postural inclinations and undulations, eloquent manipulations of a fan.

Japan. The dance arts of Japan show influences of both the Chinese ceremonial dance and the Hindu. *Gagaku*, the name of the all-male Japanese Imperial Household Musicians and Dancers, means noble and elegant music, and was introduced from China into Japan in the eighth century. Membership in the group is hereditary. Its dance is known as *Bugaku*. It is a pure, stately dance style, emphasizing symmetrical movements and the use of paired dancers. However, its offshoots include acrobatics and mimicry. From these, in the fifteenth century, the *Noh* drama evolved. *Noh* is a highly symbolic theater that offers a dramatic situation with singing and dialogue, and then comes to a climax in mime and dance that are precisely timed. It is always performed with the musicians on the stage of a covered platform with a painting of a pine tree representing the area of a shrine. Sorell tells us:

> The five basic positions used in the *Noh* drama are: an erect stance and movement to the left, right, forward and backward. The erect stance is the primary position and from it the actor unfolds his own variations. The symbolism is further accentuated by the wearing of wooden masks which, like the elaborate costumes, have a specific meaning.

Japanese artists have made a tremendous impression on Western stages with *Kabuki* theater. Many elements of *Kabuki* can be traced to primitive ritual, especially its most characteristic movement, which is stamping. In Japan, farmers practiced the age-old custom of stamping the ground to rouse the good spirits and drive out the evil ones to ensure a good rice crop. *Kabuki* itself is not, however, an ancient art form. It originated in 1603. O-Kuni, a female dancer at a Shinto shrine, is credited with creating this form of dance play. The fact that O-Kuni was a woman is especially noteworthy because *Kabuki* turned into a men's theater art, with men performing women's roles as well as men's.

The story goes that when O-Kuni went on tour to raise money for her shrine, she got carried away and began performing with more sensuous pleasure than pious reverence. Gradually, she brought other girls into her troupe, and arranged litle dance plays to popular songs along with mundane jokes and puns. But just because they were an all-female troupe, they had problems in gaining respectable recognition. O-Kuni handled this by having all her female dancers disguised as men. *Kabuki* became popular, and immediately other women founded such groups. The trouble here was that many of the women were professional prostitutes rather than dancers. This caused the authorities to step in and put a stop to the whole business, which was corrupting public morals.

However, entrepreneurs saw good commercial possibilities in the new theater form. Finally, they hit on the idea of using all men, training some of them to become convincing "females." But now there was a moral danger from the homosexual element, who found an erotic appeal in the transvestites. Again, an outcry against corruption. Another solution was found, and this seemed to work. At least it has lasted to this day. The female impersonators were stylized in the manner of a widespread puppet tradition: their faces were covered with bizarre make-up; over a thick, liquid white-rice powder, straight eyebrows and rosebud lips were painted. Then the performers were trained not to smile. Only the eyes could be expressive. Knowing this tradition is helpful not only in appreciating *Kabuki*, but also in approaching contemporary Asian dance such as *Butoh*, a startling Japanese avant-garde dance form that has risen in recent years to present performers with their heads shaved and their bodies covered in a uniform white paint—among other weird get-ups.

Asian Dance Today. In connection with tribal dance, we noted how Westerners like Pearl Primus, and Odette Blum are working hard to preserve and revive ancient rituals. The same thing is occurring today in Asian dance with people like Michael Alum, a New York City based modern dancer who recruited (*and trained*) a group of Malaysians in their own dances. Commissioned by The Asia Society, Alum travelled to Malaysia where he tracked down dance-dramas far from cities like Kuala Lampur where, he observed in a *Dance Magazine* (June 1991) interview that "the performers see too much Madonna and bureaucrats encourage them to smile for tourists." In New York City, the group performed Alum's versions of *makyong* and *manora* (dance-dramas), *penca silat*, which is a martial art, and *wayang kulit* (shadow puppet plays). Alum found the martial art form the closest to his own modern dance techniques.

I must mention the fact that a Western art form has also taken firm hold in the East. In recent years, native ballet companies have arisen in China, Japan, and throughout the area to present impressive productions of European ballet.

Folk Dance

Alongside legendary dance theaters, folk dances are a vigorous feature of the Asian scene, for example, in India. In her review of *Traditions of Indian Folk Dance* by Kapila Vatsyayan (in *Dance Chronicle* 1978–1979), Renée Renouf makes the point that "dance in India is a slice of life, particularly its intricate interconnection with life and social processes at the folk level... folk and classical traditions must and do coexist, and folk forms continue to vitalize and feed the classical stream."

Lois Ibsen Al Faruqui, in *Dance Scope* (Winter 1976–1977), observes that in Islamic folk dancing there is no conscious effort to plan performances rigidly, or to do the dances the same way each time. Muslin folk dance spans a tremendous geographical area from Morocco all the way to the Philippines, where four categories of dance appear:

1. **Combat dances.** There is at least one variation of the sword dance in almost every Muslim country. They are danced by paired male "combatants" carrying weapons and include advancing and retreating movements as well as skillful weapons maneuvers.

2. **Solo improvisation** (*raqs al sharqi*). As professional dance, this is most often done by a woman, although at informal communal gatherings, a male amateur performs. It has been labelled the "belly dance" in the West, a term that Arabs consider offensive. The movements that require strict control over individual muscles include: the head shifting laterally from shoulder to shoulder; undulations of hands and arms; shaking the shoulders; trembling or horizontal motions by breasts, hips, and abdomen; swirling turns; backbends; manipulation of scarfs; and tapping of tiny metal castanets.

3. **The Chain dance** (*dabkah*). Both men and women perform chain dances, but not together. Linked together by clasping hands or linking arms at the elbows, the chain dance involves foot stepping or stamping with the torso held still.

4. **Dances in mystical** (*Sufi*) orders. Only a small percentage of Islam's adherents find dancing compatible with religious practice. It is done as part of a chanting session.

In the Philippines, ritual dancing has never stopped in isolated areas, but Philippine folk dances were dying out until their conscious revival in the 1920s. The Bayanihan Company has kept the movement techniques straightforward and simple, but raised folk dancing to a spectacular theatricality with the joyous use of bamboo poles clapped together, glasses and lighted oil lamps balanced on the head, and the like.

Questions for Review

1. Why is it said that Hindu dance combines the most sensual aspects of human nature with the most sublime?

2. What ritual elements can you find in Kabuki dance theater?

4 EARLY MEDITERRANEAN CIVILIZATIONS

OUR DANCING ANCESTORS

Moving westward, we seek our roots in ancient civilizations of the Mediterranean, during the period beginning approximately in the fourth millennium (4000 to 3000 B.C.) Here, although the dances of that period do not continue to be performed as they are in Asia, we still find much information about them, because these people have left written records. Thus we can trace rituals with which we became familiar in primitive tribes that continued to be performed in the religious observances of more developed societies. Please keep in mind that despite elaborate written descriptions of rituals and ceremonies, we can *not* re-create the actual dance motions performed, except in conjecture. Movement is transitory. Once it ceases to be part of a living, ongoing culture, it disappears, unless of course it has been filmed, or set down in some form of movement notation. We now consider the specifics of ritual and dance in Babylonia, Egypt, Greece, Rome, as well as in early Judeo-Christian societies.

Babylonia

The geography of Babylonia is no doubt familiar to you under its present name: Iraq. Before the 1991 military campaign known as Desert Storm, you probably would have had trouble finding this country on a map, unless you are interested in archaeology. This is a fascinating center of archaeological discoveries, including a large library of clay tablets which are the source of much information about ancient religions and festivals.

Akitu was an important Babylonian festival. They celebrated spring by reenacting their creation myth: the fight of the god Marduk against the dragon of chaos. This dramatic rendition was staged at an elaborate, pyramid-shaped temple, which also served as the site for gazing at the heavens and observing the moon, stars, and planets, whose motions were imitated in their rituals.

The figure of the King symbolized the high god Marduk. It shouldn't surprise us to learn that the early Babylonian kings claimed to be gods. Royalty traditionally has retained a connection to divinity. From primitive tribes, where the chieftain was often one and the same as the priest, down to Louis XIV and other kings who have ruled by divine right, (Great Britain's monarch is crowned in a cathedral), there has been a very close identity between secular and religious authority.

Back in Babylonia, as the great battle began, chaos won the first round, destroying law and order, and stripping the king of his power. Then the tide turned, order was restored, and the king regained his throne. Along the way there was a water theme of rain making, and also one of sun worship. The victory of the king-god meant the victory of all good things. The triumph of right was then celebrated by the divine nuptials. That is, the king, who had the power to approach the high god in charge of crop regeneration, had sexual intercourse with a chosen priestess in a room decorated with leaves and flowers, symbols of fertility. During this ritual, offerings were made to the dead, the idea being that in the season of rebirth, the dead would be resurrected. The main purpose of the Babylonian rite of spring was to ensure the fertility of the land for another annual cycle.

Egypt

The pyramids and other ancient monuments in Egypt have long held a great fascination for many people. You know them well if only as mysteriously romantic settings for movies. Who can regard these ruins without wondering about the past? Among my favorite lines of poetry are Shelley's inscription on a wrecked tomb half-buried in desert sand: "My name is Ozymandias, King of Kings: Look on my works, ye Mighty, and despair!"

Of concern to kings and commoners alike was the lush growth along the banks of the Egyptian Nile. Their fertility rituals centered around the river, which annually floods its banks. Without the Nile, Egypt would be entirely desert. Therefore the Egyptian religion understandably was built around a king-god (Osiris) identified with the Nile and the sun, elements essential for the growth of crops. Osiris introduced the cultivation of wheat and barley to the Egyptians as well as the technique of brewing beer from barley. He taught his people how to set up vineyards and ferment the juice of grapes for wine. By giving his people law and religion, he transformed them out of a state of savage cannibalism.

At first it seems strange to learn that Osiris was god of the underworld, until we look more closely at the myth. It is a complicated story of a god whose jealous brother had him buried alive in a coffin and thrown into the river. After many adventures, the dead body of Osiris was discovered, and this time dismembered by the same brother. Isis, the sister and wife of the dead king-god who was murdered in his prime, mourned and lamented his death so sadly that the sun god took pity. Osiris was resurrected and made king of the dead in the underworld.

Thus Egyptian fertility rituals celebrated the flooding of the Nile, which irrigates more than a thousand miles of land on either side of the river, with the reenactment of complicated legends of the death and resurrection of Osiris. At the same time, this expressed the Egyptian belief in immortality. The goddess Isis, the wife-sister of Osiris, had a big part in these legends, and she was also the center of her own cult. Isis introduced dancing and singing to the Egyptians. Dance and music played a great part in two major Egyptian agricultural ritual pageants: the festival for Isis, when the Nile started to rise each year, and the festival for Osiris, when the harvest was in. Egyptian priests, who were also astronomers, did a dance of the stars, in which they imitated the turning of the sun by moving from east to west around a sun altar while making signs of the zodiac.

Featured in these and other rituals were specially trained dancers maintained by the courts and the temples. Their function was ceremonial, like that of a church choir. Many movements were not what we would consider spiritual, however, but gymnastic. For example, there are pictorial representations of a woman being hurled through space between two men, or doing somersaults or deep backbends into a bridge position, or jumping high into the air while crossing the feet.

Greece

Isadora Duncan tells us in her autobiography that when she and her brother Raymond first landed in Greece, they knelt down and kissed the soil:

> Indeed, we were half mad with joy. We wanted to embrace all the inhabitants of the village and cry, "At last we have arrived in the Sacred Land of Hellas! Salute, O Olympian Zeus! And Apollo! And Aphrodite! Prepare, O ye Muses to dance again! Our singing may awaken Dionysus and his sleeping Bacchantes!"

When we come to our modern dance story, we will see how this passionate artist used her ideas of Greece in her own work. For our purposes we must note that neither she, nor Lillian Lawler in her exhaustive study *The Dance in Ancient Greece*, nor any other modern scholar can re-create a phrase of Greek dancing as it was actually performed at the time. However, legends and information about it have come down to us which lead us to believe that Greek dance was capable of awakening such feelings as Isadora expressed.

The art of dance, along with music, poetry, and drama, had a rich flowering among the ancient Greeks during their great classical period (before and after 500 B.C.). Believing that dance was originally an activity of the gods, they used it liberally in religious ritual. A pyrrhic dance was done at funerals to infuse life into the dead, or at least to affirm the life force in the living. After a ferocious battle, it was by no means considered strange for Sophocles, one of the most famous Greek dramatists, to be so well trained in dance and music that he was chosen to lead a victory dance after a battle. Similarly distinguished generals and statesmen performed through their adult years. You see, dance was an important part of education and was taught to youths as part of their military training. Aristocrats danced at their dinner parties and banquets. Thus the dance freely crossed the line between religious and secular life. It is noteworthy that professional dancers, often slaves, were *not* well respected even though they provided entertainment. Contests were held among singer-dancer groups that were trained and supported by patrons. But these competing groups were made up of members from the upper classes, and not the professionals.

The rites best known to us from ancient Greece, and extremely popular at the time to the point of being a craze, were the *Dionysian*. The very word, referring to Dionysus, the god of wine, has come to mean wild, abandoned, licentious behavior. Although done in the dead of winter, when frenzied women ran through the frozen woods while waving burning torches, this was really a rite of spring. Like Nijinsky's dance, it was a wild incantation in the frozen wastes to bring regeneration and the promise of fertility. Kings opposed the Dionysian rites, because they easily got out of hand and disrupted law and order. However, while rulers did succeed in toning them down some, they never managed to eliminate them completely.

In direct contrast to the Dionysian rites, and regarded as most important in religious worship, were the dignified fertility rites dedicated to Demeter, the goddess of grain and agriculture, and to her daughter Persephone, goddess of vegetation and also of the underworld. (You remember the primitive crossover rituals that ensured good crops at the same time as they appeased spirits at a funeral.) Like the Dionysian, these rites were performed by women. However, in this case the women were high-born matrons and the mood was solemn and chaste. Further, they

were mysteries, not only done in secret, but never discussed with noniniti-
ates. These two contrasting rites are an excellent illustration of the distinction made by Curt Sachs between ecstatic and harmonious dances.

To sum up, dance, poetry, and music fused in the dramatic art of
the Greek stage, where tragedy and comedy reached a high point that has
seldom, if ever, been equalled in human history. After the Greeks lost their
supremacy to the Romans, their arts deteriorated sadly. However, through
the centuries, the memories of their greatness never died out completely.
By the middle of the eighteenth century, artists and archaeologists were
rediscovering the glories of Greece and Rome. One of these was Byron,
who fell in love with Greece, ancient and modern, to the point where he
joined an attempt to liberate Greece from Turkish rule. It was his lines—
"The isles of Greece, the isles of Greece Where burning Sappho loved and
sung"—that Isadora Duncan quoted as she neared the famous shore.

The Roman Empire

The talents of the Romans lay primarily in engineering and government.
Rather than appreciating the comparatively tame pleasures of dance, their
favorite spectator sport involved watching gladiators killing one another in
the arena. However, they did develop enormous skill in one area of movement: pantomime. For information on Roman pantomime, we turn to A.M.
Nagler's *A Source Book in Theatrical History*. Here we find a passage from
Livy, in Book VII, Chapter 2 of his *History of Rome*, (written at the opening
of the Christian Era) that speaks of the origin of mimetic dances, which
were to become a characteristic feature of the Roman theater. During a time
of plague, (364 B.C.), with the object of appeasing the gods and turning
away their wrath, they staged entertainments that featured gesticulation to
music. In Nagler's anthology we also learn that pantomime made its
Roman debut as an art form in 22 B.C. with the tragic dancer Pylades and
the comic dancer Bathyllus. Here we find these observations by Lucian of
Samosata, who lived during the years A.D.125 to 180:

> A first-rate artist of Pantomime must have memory, sensibility, shrewdness,
> rapidity of conception, tact, and judgment; further he must be a critic of poet-
> ry and song, capable of discerning good music and rejecting bad . . .
>
> He must be perfectly proportioned: neither immoderately tall nor
> dwarfishly short; not too fleshy nor cadaverously thin...His frame must be at
> once supple and well-knit, to meet the opposite requirements of agility and
> firmness. . .
>
> In Pantomime there can be too much of a good thing. An actor of repute
> was acting the madness of Ajax, and so lost control of himself that one might
> have been excused for thinking his madness was more than feigned.

With that, Lucian goes on to describe the actor's tearing the clothes from one of the drummers, and then snatching a flute from a musician and using it to beat the head of the actor who played Ulysses. This emotional outburst set off the audience, who began to leap, yell, and tear at their own clothes. The audience was split between admiration and amusement. However, the actor seems to have repented, because when he was asked to repeat the performance, he recommended another actor for the role of Ajax.

In time, the art of pantomime deteriorated into a corrupt, smutty form. But in spite of (or maybe because of!) this, the public remained devoted. Walter Sorell in *The Dance Through the Ages* notes that pantomimists became wandering entertainers who kept alive the idea of theatrical dance "through the Middle Ages into the days of the Renaissance." We will mention them again later, when we trace the origin of ballet.

The Judeo-Christian Era

Now we meet the Jews and the Christians, both of whom suffered badly under the Romans. Early Jewish and Christian rituals contained dance elements, as was true among the pagans. Their holidays had a dual origin: they commemorated events in history and legend, and they also marked the time to till the soil, to plant, to harvest and to mourn the darkness and celebrate the light. Only gradually did these ritual practices give way to an attitude of total separation between body and spirit, with the body holding all that was evil in humanity, and the spirit all that was good. This attitude was to influence and stunt the growth of dance in our Western culture down to the present.

Dance in Judaism. We know that among the biblical Hebrews various dances were performed, because they are mentioned in the Old Testament. Some of these were not regular rituals, but rather spontaneous occasions, such as Miriam the prophetess leading the women in a dance with tambourines to celebrate crossing the Red Sea; or dancing around the golden calf in the desert (which aroused the wrath of Moses).

The most joyful rite of spring observed among the early Jewish people (right up until today) was Purim. Purim is based on the legend of how Queen Esther and Mordechai saved the Jewish people in Persia from annihilation by the villainous Haman, around 400 B.C. The holiday, however, also pays tribute to nature's rebirth and renewal. It's time to drive out old man winter and bring back warmth and light, to feel the joy of the blossoming earth. Furthermore, there is also an exhortation to drink. The sages have actually written that on Purim a man must get so drunk he no longer knows the difference between "Haman be cursed" and "Mordechai be blessed." That's why they call this holiday "ad delo yada," which is Hebrew for "until he will not know."

At the end of the New Year holiday in the autumn, there is the festival *Simchat Torah* ("Joy of the Law"), when the leaders of a congregation remove the sacred scrolls from their cabinet and, together with all the men of the congregation, march in a circle around the synagogue, singing joyfully. To note how customs change through the centuries, you may be interested to hear that *Yom Kipur* ("Day of Atonement,") today the most solemn day of the entire Jewish year, was not always such a serious time. In the Talmudic period (around the fifth century B.C.), the knowledge of God's grace made people happy. During the afternoon, whole communities gathered in the vineyards outside Jerusalem to sing and dance; and maidens, dressed alike in white garments, called upon young men to choose their partners.

Dance in Christianity. The Christians started out using ritual movement in their services. Havelock Ellis tells us in *The Art of Dancing*: "The very idea of dancing had a sacred and mystic meaning to the early Christians, who had meditated profoundly on the text: 'We have piped unto you and ye have not danced.'" In the second century, there was a hymn that described the Last Supper. The Apostle John tells us that Jesus gathered his disciples and instructed them to dance around him in a circle, and said, "Whoso danceth not, knoweth not the way of life." This was no less than a description of sacred dance.

In time, however, the church fathers developed a strong opposition to ritual dance, indeed, to any dance. This represented the triumph of the theological attitude, that is, since the body is the source of all impurities, its use could only harm the worshipper by coming between him and God and diverting his spiritual thoughts to lower matters. This puritanism arose in part from the desire to protect Christians from the seductive, dissolute practices of pagans among whom they lived.

When Christianity changed from a persecuted minority religion to the dominant religion in the west, it gained enormous secular authority. Its leaders did not confine their antidance edicts to religious worship, but were able to limit the use of dance even in public festivals. This did not happen all at once. Christianity spread slowly in the Middle Ages, through what is now Spain, France, England, Germany, and beyond. It did not win out in the Scandinavian countries until around the year 1000. In any case, it was a long time before ecclesiastical banishment of ritual dance prevailed. According to Havelock Ellis: "In English cathedrals, dancing went on until the fourteenth century. In France the priests danced in the choir at Easter up to the seventeenth century. In Toledo, Spain it survives to the present in a few special festivals." But the banishment did prevail. In this respect, Western religious authorities caused the art of dance to move in a direction opposite to the arts of the East. Even in our time, the idea of ritual dance in church strikes many people as sacrilege.

Nonetheless, we note that there are artists and religious ministers today who want to restore dance to Christian worship. Both Ruth St. Denis and Ted Shawn were active in this mission. There is now a Sacred Dance Guild that conducts classes and meetings to advise would-be dance choirs at religious institutions of any denomination. And what about outside the church? How did secular dance fare during these centuries of philosophical piety? For answers, we will look at Europe as it moved through the Middle Ages.

Questions for Review

1.   What were the ritual characteristics in the culture of Ancient Egypt?

2.   Why did Isadora Duncan and others regard ancient Greek society as a model for the art of dance?

5 FOLK DANCE DEVELOPMENT IN MEDIEVAL EUROPE AND TODAY

THE CHURCH VERSUS SECULAR DANCE

Perhaps you saw the movie *The Red Shoes*. Then you remember Moira Shearer, the lovely English ballerina, who was so happy to put on a pair of crimson satin toe shoes until she found they made her dance—and dance and dance and dance—until she dropped. Oh, how you ached for her. How you understood the magic spell the dance can cast. But, come now, you say, *The Red Shoes* was just a children's story, an innocent fable by Hans Christian Andersen. Innocent? Are fairy tales, their landscape cluttered with jealous sisters, power-mad kings, and blood-thirsty giants, really so innocent? Let's face it, the raw material of fairy tales is, and always has been, the dark side of human history.

The *Red Shoes* takes us back to the Middle Ages when, beginning with the eleventh century, numerous reports have come down to us of a dance curse—a compulsion to dance that possessed people who couldn't stop until they fell of total exhaustion. As we noted many pages back, much of dance is ecstatic. Here, however, we are concerned with ecstatic dance that is uncontrolled and compulsive, with the quality of a seizure or nervous disorder, and affecting not only one person, but seizing entire groups—an epidemic of insanity. We are told that crowds of peasants would circle hand in hand, or singly, in hideously distorted movements for hours at a time until they collapsed, foaming at the mouth. Curt Sachs reports that the sight of this madness caused spectators to enter the circle, quivering and grimacing, to take up the frenzied dance. The evil would last for months, immune to the treatment of doctors or priests.

The place of choice for these scenes was a churchyard, where dement-
ed souls sought communion with the dead. This is the origin of the term
danse macabre, or "dance of death." Church councils opposed the practice as
obscene, and did their best to root it out. No matter what countermeasures
they took, however, dance manias continued to break out at least through
the seventeenth century. It has been suggested that dance mania was set off
by horrible happenings, like the fourteenth-century Bubonic Plague which
wiped out half the population; or the cruelty of the crusading armies which
left Europe to fight the infidel in the Holy Land at intervals from 1095 to
1272, and ravaged the countryside along the way.

Of course we know that horrible happenings were not invented during the Middle Ages. And we know too, that dance manias appeared
among tribal peoples even in their rituals, what we have referred to as
trance dance. Curt Sachs had an interesting theory about dance mania:

> What is revealed in these dances is not a "relic" of "paganism," but a piece of
> ecstatic inner life, which since the Stone Age has been disguised and con-
> cealed, but never extinguished, and which must break out through all
> restraints at the favorable moment.

Is this a warning that we must be on the lookout for a recurrence? Never
mind, let's look on the brighter face of folk dance.

Folk Dancing

To this day, folk dancing is a recreational activity in most countries, despite
the fact that it has to compete with America's jazz and pop styles for the
favor of the youth of Europe and Asia. What characterizes these folk
dances? Scholars agree that their origin is in the ritual of early man.
Benjamin Hunningher in *The Origin of the Theater* explains:

> Just as in the rest of the world, primitive man in Europe depended upon the
> succession of the seasons; deviations in nature's periodicity immediately put
> him in peril of death. He too longed for the return of summer and fertility; he
> too did his best to compel the ruling forces, by charms and by dances, to con-
> form to his desires.

From the vast number of examples, he cites the *Perhtenlauf* and the Morris
dance. The *Perhtenlauf* prevails in parts of the Alps. During the period from
Christmas until Twelfth Night:

> young men wearing masks of terrifying aspect, clad in sheep- and badger-
> skins,with bell-girdles around their waists, dance and run with great uproar
> through town and field. . . They may break into houses and annoy the

inmates, or they may only pass, yelling and dancing, till suddenly the wild Perht appears among them: the Unknown One.

Then they break into an ecstatic, breath-taking dance, and in growing frenzy they jump higher and higher...

Easter brought the Morris dance to England as well as to the Continent, a procession of disguised dancers with blackened faces (blackened for the "Moors" from whom the custom derived its name)....Wild behaviour suited such participants, who carried staves and wooden swords and often caused turbulent situations.

It is no coincidence that these "rites" occurred during Christian holidays. Throughout the Middle Ages, the church, well aware of both the appeal and the danger of folk customs, waged war against them. Their appeal stemmed from two human qualities which do not respond easily to reason: fear and the love of pleasure. The fear was a superstitious one. If the people didn't follow the old rituals, they might antagonize the gods who control the all-important growth of crops, rain, and the like. Love of pleasure made people long for the merry festivities that interrupted the bone-crushing monotony of hard work in a grim environment. Even members of the clergy took part in the fun.

From the church's viewpoint, these rituals were dangerous not only because they were pagan, but also because of their open references to fertility, which meant obscene expressions and forms that went against church morality. To stamp out these offenses, the church first of all passed decree after decree of condemnation. The fact that this didn't do the trick is shown by the fact that the edicts, which began about 500, continued at least until 1600. Pope Gregory the Great tried a different approach. He came up with a policy of "adoption," that is, whenever possible the church incorporated these folk customs into Christian ritual after carefully sanitizing them. In 1223, for example, Saint Francis is said to have introduced the Christmas carol dance around the crèche. We learn from Suzanne Aker (in *Dance Magazine*, December 1964):

> Unexpected as it seems to us now, during the Middle Ages the verb "to carol" meant to dance, not to sing....Carols of that time were not pious acts of singing, but joyous dance...
>
> As the illiterate peasants circled round the crèche singing and dancing, they felt themselves participating in the nativity, much as the primitive peoples identified with sacred images in their circular sacramental dances.

We can see how the church's attitude towards folk customs affected ordinary people by turning to studies like *Medieval People* by Eileen Power. This is a charming but thoroughly researched work on the life of six characters from the Middle Ages. Bode was a real peasant who lived and worked with his wife Ermentrude and their three children on an estate near Paris during the reign of Charlemagne (about 800). Although he was a superstitious man, Bode went to church where they taught him to substitute the names Jesus Christ and Mary for Father Heaven and Mother Earth when he placed a cake in a furrow and chanted a prayer for a good grain crop or recited a charm for bees. Church authorities, however, were not happy on saints' days. Power tells us that Bode and his friends:

> were not content to go quietly to church and quietly home again. They used to spend their holidays in dancing and singing and buffoonery. . .They were very merry and not at all refined, and the place they chose for their dances was the churchyard...
>
> Over and over again we find the Church councils complaining that the peasants (and sometimes the priests too) were singing "wicked songs with a chorus of dancing women." Over and over again the bishops forbad these songs and dances, but in vain.

Characteristics of Folk Dance. Just as dancing differed from tribe to tribe, folk dances developed differently from place to place. Every local group has its own peculiarities of movement stemming from physical build, occupation, and *national quality* as this term is used by choreometrics scholars. Happily, most folk dancing does not spin off into the shuddering fits of dance mania. Whatever its primitive, ritualistic beginnings, folk dancing has usually been performed to give pleasure, first of all to the dancers, and then to the spectators. In every Western country there is a repertory of dances, some of which are done on specific occasions and others that are done at any festival or simple social gathering. So again, we can trace both universal traditions and local creativity, although we usually mean creativity of the group and not of the individual when we speak of folk dance.

The Movements of Folk Dance. When folk dance is done for recreation by ordinary Westerners, its motions are simple. Basic steps are running, walking, hopping, skipping, and moving sideways by crossing the feet in front or in back of each other. These are endlessly combined into dance steps like the polka, the grapevine, the waltz, the do-si-do, the schottische, and others. Further variation is supplied by clapping the hands or clasping them high to form an arch. The rhythms are generally 2/4, 3/4, or 6/8.

The Maypole. By now you won't be surprised to hear that the maypole dance is really a primitive fertility ritual, even if we don't first stick a live tree or a pole into the ground and sanctify it as a fertility center as did our tribal ancestors. This pole motif is found everywhere. Northern Europeans dance around the maypole on bright summer nights as do

Basque sword dancers. The motif of holding long, gaily colored ribbons that are tied to the pole, and twisting them one over another, is found in the *Himmeltanz* of Alsace; the *Bandltanz* of southern Bavaria; the *ballo della cordella* of Sicily; the dance of the women weavers of Provence; and the Spanish *danzas del cordon*.

Another spring ritual is performed on May Day in Sweden, when two characters act out a little pageant. One actor plays Winter, clad in furs; the other plays Summer, decorated with fresh leaves and flowers. They make a procession through the village. At each house they get presents of food. In return, they sing, dance, and enact a drama: first there is a battle; Winter throws ice and snowballs; the contest goes back and forth until Summer finally wins out.

In Russia, a pagan festival is reenacted at Eastertide. A girl lies "dead" on the ground. Her name is Kostrubonko, which means spring. Maidens circle her in a funeral procession, mournfully singing. Suddenly Kostrubonko jumps up. Spring is reborn! Everybody sings and dances joyfully. It is believed that long ago, there really was a dead girl—a sacrifice. Here you have the origin of Nijinsky's idea for his *Rite of Spring*.

Courtship Dances. Havelock Ellis wrote: "Dancing is not only intimately associated with religion, it has an equally intimate association with love." When Ellis expounded on this thesis, it became clear that when he said *love* he meant *courtship*, and when he said *courtship*, he meant *sex*. Dance is the art of the body. As we have seen, the body was held in very low esteem by Western authorities, and dancing was frowned upon, as was sex. However, the common people of the West did not buy into this. Like all people everywhere, they found a way to express themselves in dance and in sex, often both at the same time.

The popular couple dances of European countries prove their age-old courtship origin by their alternation of generalized rhythmic passages with mimed drama (remember the primitive mimetic dances?). The generalized sections have steps that trace patterns like the wheel, the arch, the two opposing lines, and, of course, the circle, which are easily traced to tribal dancing. The drama consists of the courtship (fertility) theme that is acted out. For example, we find this structure in the Balkan *kolo,* the Bohemian *husicka,* and the Italian *bergamasco*. In between dance sections, pantomimes are performed: the male woos the female; she coyly withdraws; he makes threatening gestures; she finally yields, perhaps even with a kiss and a hug.

High Style and Professionalism. During the late Middle Ages, in the 1300s and after, folk dancing was enjoyed not only by the common people, but was also taken up in high society, at courts first in Italy, and then elsewhere. Professional dancing masters codified the peasant forms and taught aristocrats to dance them in a stately manner that had elements of chivalry and noble pride. These were the preclassic dances that we shall soon follow into the ballet. It is ironic that this most elegant of courtly forms evolved in part from the wildest, most bawdy behavior of the lower classes.

Alongside of folk dancing, there was a continuation of the remnants of dance spectacle, such as the Roman pantomimes that were discussed previously. Music historians tell us about minstrel entertainers: *jongleurs* in France and *Gaukler* in Germany, who kept alive some of these forms. However, these performances were limited, again because the church banned them whenever possible. For the most part, this kept them out of the larger population centers, although they turned up repeatedly at town fairs and in castles, entertaining the aristocrats. Dance spectacle too may have had an influence on the court dancing that became ballet. We can't be more specific because of the lack of evidence. You see, for our knowledge of the history of those years, we are dependent on clerical writers, since there were very few people outside of the church who could read or write. (That's the reason for the term *Dark Ages*, which used to be the name given to medieval Europe.) Because of official disapproval, dancing was an area that church scholars did not care to investigate. Therefore we too are left in the dark.

Development of National Folk Dances

Spain. Now we turn to the country where the common people's dance has grown into a complex art of spectacle and tradition. Spanish dance, which may be the most consistently popular style the world has ever known, combines elements of folk dancing with those of spectacular entertainment. Spanish dance is the oldest extant European dance art and is also a point of contact between Eastern and Western dance. The Moorish invasion of Spain in the 700s made a strong mark on the dance of Andalucia, and from there, on all of Spain.

La Meri, in her book *Spanish Dancing*, informs us that folk dances have been seen on the Iberian Peninsula since 1600 B.C. It is no wonder then, that one cannot speak of a unified Spanish style. There are, in fact, three broad types: regional dances which comprise the communal, provincial forms like the *fandango* and the *jota*; school dancing, also known as *bolero* plus classical dance, which is mostly a nineteenth-century academization of the varied regional dances with a slight admixture of ballet; and *flamenco*. Within the regional dances alone, there are three major stylistic divisions: of the northern, of the central, and of the southern provinces, from which there come over one hundred accepted, unchangeable traditional dances. From all the possibilities, here are a few examples that will remind you of age-old customs.

In honor of spring, young people throughout Galicia dance with swords, or around beribboned poles. The Basques have a popular recreational dance, the *Aurresku*, which is both spectacular and erotic. It concludes with a "challenge" section, in which each man tries to leap the highest. This leaping is thought to have originated as a primitive ritual to make the crops grow well. The Navarros do a *Multidanzak* on feast days and weddings. Men alone take part. The circular form, the stiffness and gravity of the style, and the step directions from side to side point to a connection with archaic ceremonies. In Cataluñya many dances began in ancient times. Both the *Sardana* and the *Contrapas* are danced to lyrics which relate the Passion of Jesus. The *Ball de la Teya* is a street dance in which a live tree is burned, recalling pagan sacrificial fires.

From Curt Sachs's *World History of the Dance* I offer you quotes that resound with the enthusiastic tone heard over and over again about Spanish dances. Sachs himself says, "The courtship dance of Spain reaches a perfection which never fails to enchant the spectator anew. In the provocative rhythms of the castanets in which 3/8 and 3/4 time are mixed with such charm, the courtship dance of the *fandango* rushes on deliriously." Casanova, history's most famous lover, saw the *fandango* in 1767 and wrote, "Each couple, man and woman, never move more than three steps, as they click their castanets with the music of the orchestra. They take a thousand attitudes, make a thousand gestures so lascivious that nothing can compare with them. This dance is the expression of love from beginning to end, from the sigh of desire to the ecstasy of enjoyment. It seemed to me impossible that after such a dance the girl could refuse anything to her partner." A German scholar wrote in 1799, "The *fandango* is always danced by only two persons, who never touch each other even with the hand. But when one sees how they challenge each other, now moving away, now approaching again; how the woman at the moment when she seems about to surrender, slips suddenly away from the victor with renewed vivacity; how he pursues her, then she, him; how in all their glances, gestures and positions they express the various emotions which enflame them both; when one sees all this, one cannot help confessing with a blush that this dance describes Cythera's battles as truly as the final cannonade of a fireworks display describes the actual thunder of cannons before a besieged fortress." (Cythera refers to the erotic Greek cult of Aphrodite, although I'm sure you got the point even without that bit of information.)

As you see, the above quotes all refer to the *fandango*. The strands that make up this form and its origin are lost in history. There is no doubt, however, that the *fandango* became a craze in the eighteenth century to the point where Havelock Ellis could claim "The Church tacitly encouraged it. An Aragonese Council saw it as a useful safety-valve for the emotions, despite its occasional indecorum."

The same thing happened two centuries later to *flamenco* dancing. The *flamenco*, originated by the Gypsies, consists of moody improvisations within traditional rhythm forms such as the *farucca*—to the accompaniment of guitarists and onlookers who clap, stamp, and shout. It features *tacaneo* (heel work) which is exclusively Gypsy and may have originated in the emphatic floor-contact motions of the Middle East, castanets, (clacking, hand-rhythm instruments of wood), and what is typical in all Spanish dance: the proud carriage of head, torso, and arms. *Flamenco* is an improvised expression, within a strict form, of the Gypsy's pride in being, his sexual passions, and his forebodings of death. At its height it sweeps the performer, and the small intimate circle of simpatico viewers who catch and reinforce the mood, into heights of ecstasy.

This form was not presented on stage until this century. Once it was shown, it became a craze. Mistakenly, most of the foreign public considers *flamenco* to be synonymous with the whole of Spanish dance. Antonio, a famous virtuoso of the 1960s, complained to me: "The entire second half of our program is *flamenco*. Managers insist on a lot of it. I believe audiences would like a more varied program, but I have no choice. You can never really do the program you want!" It is obvious that for the more restrained Westerner, part of the heart-stopping appeal of the *fandango* two hundred years ago and of the *flamenco* today is the permission given the spectator to enter into an unusually sensuous experience in the name of art.

We must note one big difference between these two dances. While the steps and motions of the *fandango* are carefully set (differently, of course, in each local version), the *flamenco* is like a jazz jam session. That is, the performers get into the mood with familiar sequences, and then improvise their own variations that express their private passions as the spirit moves them . It is this spontaneity and presence of real feeling that bring the genuine excitement to both performers and spectators, who spur each other on to ever-greater heights of emotion and invention. Needless to say, it is very difficult to let oneself go in this fashion before an audience, to improvise on demand. Antonio explained, "Some nights we can be more emotional than on other nights—that depends on the response out front. The audiences differ so that we are never the same twice!"

Both inside and outside of Spain, during the long history of Spanish dance, it is not surprising that the popularity of these forms has risen and fallen with the place, the time, and the individual artist. When we get to the romantic era, we will see how in 1836 Fanny Elssler won the hearts of Parisians, and later of New Yorkers, with her performance of the *Cachucha*. When Massine created *The Three Cornered Hat* for Diaghilev (1919) he followed the scenario of a nineteenth-century Spanish play and included three Spanish dances: a *farucca*, a *fandango* and a *jota*. Massine is neither the first nor the last choreographer to have incorporated chunks of Spanish dance into a composition. Modern dance as well as ballet choreographers have been attracted by this form. Petipa gave *Swan Lake* a Spanish dance for two couples. *Viva Vivaldi* (Joffrey Ballet) quotes Spanish mannerisms throughout. In modern dance, noteworthy examples are Doris Humphrey's bull fighter, in *Lament for Ignacio Sanchez Mejias*, who moves in a Spanish stance; and José Limón's entire technique, where the body carriage reflects his Mexican (and therefore part Spanish) origin.

After Spanish dancing suffered a decline at the end of the nineteenth century, in the 1930s there was a great revival of the art by La Argentina, who was especially magnificent in the use of castanets. She was followed by dozens of artists and companies, among them Argentinita, Pilar Lopez, José Greco, Antonio, and Rosario, all of whom won glowing reviews when they toured the West. By the early 1970s, as these dancers passed their peaks and no one comparable took their places, there was a sharp drop-off in bookings and popularity. Then, in the middle of the 1980s there was another revival led by the great movie hit *Carmen*, in which Antonio Gades presented sexy scenes in the lives of Gypsies who dance the *flamenco*. So styles move up and down in fashion, like an elevator. But sooner or later the public always comes back to Spanish dance.

Israeli Folk Dance. Folk dance was one of the many ways in which the development of Israel was different from that of other countries. Everywhere else, folk dances grew naturally, and were passed along from one generation to the next, their origins lost in the haze of the past. On the other hand, the folk dances performed by Jewish immigrants who had come to the state of Israel sprang up in a short period of time. In the immigrants' baggage were skills and traditions that included dances and songs from their old countries. These were immediately embraced by the settlers. At the same time, however, traditional European and Yemenite folk dances took on special qualities, marked by the character of the pioneers.

For example the *hora*. The *hora* came from Rumania, but the original Rumanian *hora* is no longer recognizable in Israel. The shoulder chain was abandoned in favor of simple hand holding, giving more freedom of movement. The energetic stamps and leg swinging disappeared and made room for small, light, elastic steps, with accentuated body turns. All the movements became narrower and more restrained, in short, more Oriental. Similar changes occurred in the Polish *krakowiak*, the Russian *tcherkessia*, the Jewish *sherele*.

Now we come to a well-known personality in the realm of folk dance: Sara Levi-Tanai. Sara Levi-Tanai's parents came to Israel from Yemen in the early 1900s. They had twelve children, but only Sara (born in 1911) survived. Then, when Sara was six years old, her mother died and Sara was raised in a Safed orphanage. The orphanage was run by European

The Moiseyev Company performs Russian dances with theatrical verve.

immigrants, and Sara's education was based on European culture, certainly not Yemenite. Finally, in 1946, the shy young woman felt ready to go off and work with her own community. She went to Tel Aviv, where she gathered a group of Yemenites and held informal classes. The best dancers became her company. Sara wanted to make something "deep and delicate, something like filigree." We are told in *Dance Perspectives* Number 59 how she learned Yemenite steps and songs from the company, particularly from Margolit Ovid, whom Sara recalled as "more than a dancer—an inspiration."

In 1949, Sara Levi-Tanai officially formed a company that became the Inbal Yemenite Dance Theater. Her early programs presented folk dances. In 1953, her ambitious *Yemenite Wedding* pointed to her real goals: "What has always impressed me is the holiness of an act in life, how Judaism makes sacred even the most mundane, heightening its meaning. My concern in the *Wedding* was to show this by theatrical means." The Inbal Company attracted the interest of American choreographers Jerome Robbins and Anna Sokolow, who advised and taught them frequently. Inbal has toured at home and abroad since the mid 1950s using a repertory including *Story of Ruth* and *Ode to Shabazzi*. Theirs is an expanding repertory, created at first exclusively by Sara Levi-Tanai, and then later with contributions from other choreographers. Well-known artists such as David

Sharir, Anatole Gurevitch, Naftali Besem, and Dani Caravin have designed sets and costumes.

In the 1950s, in the deep freeze of the cold war, Russia's Moiseyev Dance Company won many friends in the West. Their success inspired many nations to sponsor the formation of folk dance companies. And earlier in the century, we have seen how Uday Shankar of India, and Argentina of Spain revived the arts of their own countries. These groups are greeted with special warmth by spectators who feel a personal tie with the culture being portrayed, either because they have a family connection or because they wish to express political solidarity with the nation.

Presenting Ethnic Dance On Stage

For general audiences, the first viewing of any new foreign style has an obvious appeal. One is always interested in meeting other people, and the dance offers an attractive way to get acquainted. Part of the appeal of folk and ethnic dance forms is their very unsophisticated clarity and open sincerity. Many a viewer who has become fed up with the expressionless impersonality of too many contemporary dance forms finds it a relief and a pleasure to identify with the ethnic performer as an energetic human being. However, as the novelty wears off, audiences become sated quickly. The problem is that these dances were not created with foreign audiences in mind. Therefore, unless the company directors are talented in arranging varied programs—no matter how skilled their dancers are in performance—their simple, repetitive patterns may strike the viewer as monotonous.

You may be surprised to learn that as often as not, folk and ethnic dance programs you see do *not* consist of age-old works, lovingly treasured and passed along from generation to generation. Instead, they may include works that were created recently, maybe even specifically for the festival you attend. Does this mean they are not "genuine?" Not at all. If they are built on folk materials: the basic themes, the steps, the body carriage, the rhythms, and the native gestures and byplay, then they are surely a genuine expression of a people's culture.

Doris Humphrey wrote (in a letter quoted in *Dance Chronicle*, Volume 1, Number 1, 1977) about Japanese dancing which she saw in 1925 when she was with Denishawn touring the Far East:."The Geisha dancers are all they have been cracked up to be, very pretty and young and exquisitely dressed, and the dances are always graceful if a bit too long and monotonous." If a brilliant and sensitive choreographer feels that way, how much more will the lay audience! This leads impresarios to be seduced by vulgar commercialism, as were the managers about whom Antonio complained in his remarks about too much *flamenco*. We have all seen more than enough cheap performances of pseudo jazz dance. Of course, next to these, you have to place high-class, commercially successful creations in a jazz style by Jerome Robbins, Bob Fosse, Gwen Verdon, Marge and Gower Champion, not to mention Gregory Hines. Whatever the quality, there are always plenty of events with the ethnic or folk label on our stages. Africa, Malaysia, Korea, the Philippines, Mexico, Hawaii, Japan, Native America, Russia, Cambodia, Poland, Yugoslavia, Israel, Cuba, and of course Spain are only some of the places that have been represented in ethnic festivals, or alone, since the late 1980s. And they keep coming.

In Part I, we have circled the globe and reached far into the past to look at dance, both to get some understanding of (to us) exotic forms and also better to appreciate Western theater dance. In the next section, we will visit the Italian Renaissance. As we trace the development of classic ballet from European court spectacles and popular folk dances, we move closer to our own dance world.

Questions for Review

1.   Describe an ethnic dance performance that you saw. Did you find it gratifying? Give your reasons.

2.   Why do you think Spanish dancing is so consistently popular?

6 NOBLE BEGINNINGS

ARISTOCRATIC ENTERTAINMENT 1300 TO 1600

Ballet is a kind of special behavior. If you take lessons, the teacher demands control of your limbs and shapes your body into a geometric design while you hold yourself proudly, formally, and gracefully. At a ballet performance you enter a dream world in the company of noble kings and queens at spectacular court ceremonies, or with beautiful romantic creatures floating through the night, or perhaps where magnificently shaped gymnasts turn and leap with superhuman skill. Where did these manners come from?

Renaissance Manners and Luxury

Ballet was born in Europe during the period we call the Renaissance, approximately 1300 to 1600, at the courts of the Italian and French ruling nobility. The story of Romeo and Juliet reflects the manners and values of the beautiful people of that epoch. To get an idea of the atmosphere reflected in the art of ballet, picture yourself in the setting of Romeo and Juliet, a couple that lived and died in an Italian Renaissance town. Shakespeare's play mirrors quite accurately the formal splendor as well as the violence of life in that setting.

The Renaissance saw an influx of wealth into European society. Some of this came from the rise of capitalistic business enterprises, and some from the great quantities of gold and silver that poured into the treasuries of Europe from the recently discovered mines of the New World (North and South America). Together with this affluence there was an emphasis on the experiences and objects that money can buy. Political power, scientific knowledge, family love, physical beauty, and the arts all claimed respectable attention. An outstanding feature of the Renaissance was the search for a lifestyle that was pleasant, joyful, and luxurious.

The leaders of Renaissance society were the wealthy, noble families of Italy like the Medicis and the Sforzas (the Capulets and the Montagues of Shakespeare's *Romeo and Juliet*). Each family was prominent in a particular city. There was no nation of Italy at that time. These aristocrats lived in magnificent palaces and fostered whatever they thought would add to the beauty of their environment and daily pleasure. In their luxurious activities and interests, we can find the seeds of the art of ballet. For example, they lent tremendous support to architecture, painting, and sculpture. Magnificent cathedrals, statues, and paintings by brilliant artists like Leonardo da Vinci, Botticelli, and Michelangelo testify to their active encouragement of the arts. Further, they treated their fellow townsmen to generous rounds of public festivals which included carnivals, spectacles, sports contests, and processions.

Public Spectacles. Renaissance townspeople took part in a procession to show off their dignity and sumptuous clothing, or just to have fun. To get an idea in today's world of a Renaissance spectacle, we would have to attend an English coronation, like that of Elizabeth II. Flanked by the toy-soldier-like palace guards, Her Majesty and officials of government and church, resplendent in historical costumes, assemble, and then strut in measured, stately formation to Westminster Abbey. Or we would have to attend a Mardi Gras celebration in Latin America, where each city works for months to prepare floats to dazzle the population. As these floats roll by one by one, depicting scenes from religious or folk legend, the rest of the population turns out en masse in sparkling costumes and masks. They throw confetti, eat, drink, dance, and watch fireworks. Such celebrations occurred frequently in Renaissance towns. The fanfare of trumpets and announcements by town criers would proclaim the visit of a foreign prince, an important wedding, or a day dedicated to a saint. Crowds would form in the streets, and others would gawk from their windows at the appropriate ceremonies and processions that would take place.

Life at Court.　The noble Italian families like Romeo's and Juliet's organized an elaborate court life for themselves, their upper-class associates, and their attendants. A daily routine of civilized, refined existence made artistic rituals of the most ordinary activities like dressing and conversation. Endless time and effort were devoted to personal fashion by both men and women in assembling and putting on the various garments of one complete outfit: gowns and underdresses, hose, doublets, cloaks, fancy shoes, hats for indoors as well as out, all in stiff magnificent fabrics, and all excessively ornamented with quantities of jewelry. Women not only coiled or braided their hair into intricate shapes, they also dyed it or piled on masses of false silk hair. They used paints and perfumes and plasters to adorn and color every feature, including their teeth. Perfumed rolls of money were not unheard of, for both men and women .

Politeness, tact, and delicacy at all times were the order of the day. Specific etiquette for all kinds of situations was set in writing, taught, and what is more—actually followed! Proper behavior dictated how to address a nobleman, whom to proceed and whom to follow into a room, and when to rise and sit when in the company of others. A social evening might be regulated in detail. For example, a distinguished lady would be elected president, to rule for an evening. She would decide who would entertain, whether with music, stories, poetry, or dance, and her word was law for that occasion. In other words, proper behavior was not only considered an art, it was also a requirement if one were to be invited out and accepted in high society.

There was an emphasis on merit. People were welcome in high society in proportion to their accomplishments and skills. Degree of noble birth counted less, although if one were to gain the admired skills, obviously money or position was necessary. Everyone who had the leisure and the means took lessons of many kinds, striving to become expert in important areas such as swimming, wrestling, gymnastics, track running, horseback riding, and dancing, one of the most prized activities of all. Here, of course, women were included. The cultivated aristocracy constantly partook of banquets, dances, and private entertainments, where their devotion to clothing and appearance, to manners and to accomplishments paid off in both enjoyment and achievement of social position. And conversely, you can picture the misery of the unattractive, clumsy bore, who was not invited out much and spent his time brooding about his bad luck, cut off from fun and social advancement.

Romeo and Juliet

The high-society etiquette of the period plays a part in the familiar story of Romeo and Juliet. The lovers first met at a ball given by Juliet's prominent family, the Capulets. Her father knew that Romeo came from the hated Montague clan, and had sneaked into the ball wearing a mask. But Capulet was more concerned with having a pleasant party and exercising the proper etiquette for a host than in letting nephew Tybalt throw Romeo out. "Let him alone," he told Tybalt, who was furious when he discovered Romeo's presence. "He is known to be a virtuous, well-mannered youth. Not for all the wealth in town would I allow him to be harmed in my house. And as for you Tybalt, stop frowning. A face like that doesn't belong at a party."

Featured dancer Diana Weber presents Juliet in a hopeful moment in the San Francisco Ballet Company's "Romeo and Juliet."

In fact, old Capulet was daydreaming about his own youth, when his days were spent like Romeo's, mooning after one girl or another. Don't forget, Romeo's friends dragged him to this party to take his mind off his wild adoration of Rosalind, a girl too poor to accept his love; and Romeo protested, warning them that he wouldn't dance because he felt so heavy from despair, sick from unrequited love. He soon changed his mood and his mind after Capulet called a welcome to all the gentlemen present and announced to the ladies, "If one of you will refuse to dance, I'll swear it's because she has ugly corns on her feet. Come musicians, play! Everybody clear a space—now, dance!" At this moment, Romeo saw Juliet and was overcome. The fifteen-year-old Juliet certainly knew how to dance. So did Romeo. They did not miss a step when he, struck by love at first sight, maneuvered to a place at her side and took her hand as a partner. They were both so familiar with the steps of the dance that they could go through them automatically while exchanging flowery speeches about pilgrims, saints, and holy shrines—all poetic ways of working up to a kiss. If Rosalind had entered the room at that moment, Romeo would have had trouble remembering her name.

Dancing Masters

The mastery of dance depicted here was not unusual. Dancing was one of the prime accomplishments of any lady or gentleman. It was considered essential for a place at court. To provide the required lessons in dancing, many noble houses had in residence a dancing master who taught the steps and proper bearing. The most famous dancing master of the Renaissance was Guglielmo Ebero (William the Hebrew), born before 1440. He was attached to the Medici court of Florence and other great houses, teaching social dances and arranging the entertainments for court festivities, like the magnificent wedding of Costanzo Sforza and Camilla d'Aragon in 1475. As this wedding linked the two great houses of Sforza and Aragon, so Guglielmo might well have been Romeo and Juliet's teacher, and had they married, he might have presided over their wedding dances for the Capulets and Montagues.

However, we know that these lovers were not fated to marry because of hostility between their two families. The psychologists can offer us many explanations for the coexistence of refinement and barbaric cruelty that characterized the Renaissance. There were many victims of the bloody customs of the day—like Romeo and Juliet. The deaths of these young lovers were caused by the fashionable regard for honor, as defined in a rather petty way, which lead to feuds among families that were as common at the time as devotion to pleasure. These vendettas left a trail of stabbings and murders. (We still see examples of this bloody feuding amongst the mafiosi, today in Italy and Sicily.)

Thus the families of Romeo and Juliet, the Capulets and the Montagues, had been waging a feud, with Capulet and Montague youths and their friends duelling merrily and killing in the streets. This caused the young lovers to meet and marry in secret, and die in a fog of hasty errors. Only after the double shock of their deaths did the heads of the families shake hands in peace. And turning again to the decorative side of Renaissance life, first Montague and then Capulet promised to have a statue built from pure gold of the other man's lost child. Like the bereaved parents, we also will turn away from the grim sight of lifeless youth and beauty, to remember brighter hours. Let's go back and take a closer look at the dances that Romeo and Juliet were automatically performing while staring into each other's eyes, burning with their freshly kindled love.

Preclassic Dance

These were the preclassic court dances. We say *preclassic* because theirs were the steps that led up to the *classic* ballet that you may be studying; and we say *court* because they were the forms executed by the nobility in their palace settings—their courts. Where did these forms come from? They had evolved from a combination of merry peasant folk dancing and dignified court processions like those at Elizabeth's coronation. When they were taught as dancing steps for court ballrooms, it was always with an emphasis on formal, pompous manners. The dances fell into two types: the *Basse Danse* (meaning "low to the ground"), a combination of mostly slow steps; and the *Haute Danse* (meaning "high off the ground"), a series of lively jumps and hops. This division of slow and fast dances corresponds to our ballet exercises today that are divided into *adagio* and *allegro*.

As for style, the dance techniques consisted of very limited body movement and simple footwork. This was because the people who performed them were not professional dancers and did not spend all their time at lessons, and because both men and women wore the most voluminous clothing. That is to say, all the dances were made up from a few basic steps that were fairly easy to do. But there were many variations and combinations, and sometimes a particular dance could be quite complicated in its final form.

Really, you can see a similar setup in a first-year ballet class today All class work is built on basics like the plié, the relevé, the five positions, the battements, the rond de jambe, the arabesque, the pirouette, and the jeté. Yet at the end-of-the-year recital, the student has to practice hard to get a part in a prearranged choreographic number just right. Thus you can imagine these courtiers as first-year ballet students—although encumbered by fancy, heavy clothing—learning to do a number of set dances.If we read the instructions supplied by their dancing masters and set down in books by Guglielmo and others, we also see that the nobility were not taught technique the way you are. There is no emphasis on straightening the leg to a pointed toe, or on controlling the muscles of the hips (after all, these were well hidden by clothing). However, attention was given to the style of doing the steps and to overall behavior.

Thoinot Arbeau (1519 to 1596). Consider dancing master Thoinot Arbeau's lessons in *Orchesography,* a manual on dance (also fencing, piping, and drumming) edited by Julia Sutton. On one figure in a *Basse-Danse,* Arbeau instructed his male students (like Romeo) on the proper way to perform the *branle*:

> By keeping the heels together, and turning the body gently to the left for the first bar; then to the right, glancing modestly the while at the spectators for the second bar; then again to the left for the third. And for the fourth bar, to the right, again with a discreetly tender sidelong glance at the damsel.
> You must be careful not to take strides that suggest you wish to measure the length of the hall, as the damsel who is your partner cannot with decency take such long steps!

He dictates that in the slow *pavane* it is all right for the cavalier to wear his cloak and sword. The steps proceed with decorum and measured gravity. As for the damsels, they keep their eyes lowered, although it is permissible to cast an occasional glance of virginal modesty at the onlookers. The *pavane* was frankly used by kings, princes, and great lords to display their fine mantles and robes of ceremony on days of solemn festival. Similarly, the queens, princesses, and great ladies accompanied the men, with the long trains of their dresses let down and trailing behind them. At a ball, before beginning this dance, the performers walked gravely around the room and saluted the great dignitaries who gave the ball.

The steps of the *pavane* were the simplest possible. The gentlemen walked behind their ladies, leading them by the hand; a few gliding steps and a great many curtseys followed, and everyone regained his place. Next, one of the gentlemen advanced alone and, describing a slight curve in the middle of the ballroom, went *en se pavanant* (strutting like a peacock) to salute the lady opposite him. Finally, taking some backward steps, he regained his place, bowing to his own lady.

In contrast, the fast *galliard* had a vigorous gaiety, containing a great number of leaps and leg thrusts (kicking motions). The musical phrase of the galliard had six beats, but the dancer took only five steps, because on the fourth beat he jumped, which meant he was in the air for the fifth beat and landed on the sixth. The galliard usually followed the pavane. An alternation of slow and fast dances made for variety and also allowed the dancers to catch their breath after the dances involving the jumping. Incidentally, this arrangement of slow and fast dances was the origin of the musical suite, which developed into the sonata, and then finally into the symphonic forms. The slow dances gave the elderly (or fat!) courtiers a chance to participate, while the faster ones allowed the young energetic ones to show off.

The *Allemande* had a slow, flowing grace, especially of the arms, and it is the only court dance in which partners held both of each other's hands. It was tender and sentimental, and musically was in 4/4 time with a flowing quality that resulted from melodic lines with many sixteenth notes. Again, in contrast, a running, playful form was the *courante*, a great favorite in a fast-paced double or triple rhythm. Another slow dance was the *sarabande*, which resembled the pavane in most respects except that it was in 3/4 time, while the *pavane* was in a 2/4 or 4/4. The most exciting, speedy dance was the *gigue*, which could be in 3/8, 6/8, 9/8, or 12/8 time. Passionate and furious are two moods associated with the lively *gigue*. The *minuet* was characterized by artificial, mincing behavior with its short, dainty steps. It became for many years the most popular of all the court dances.

All these, with a few lesser-known forms, were the dances practiced at all the courts of Europe in the 1500s and 1600s. These are what the dancing masters taught the nobility and their attendants; and what Romeo and Juliet and all the others danced at their parties and balls. As has been pointed out, dancing was taken very seriously. Therefore, although it was recreational, as Thoinot Arbeau pointed out, the performer's dance served as a kind of silent speech. In dance "the speaker," without saying a word, persuaded the spectators through his movements that he was gallant and worthy to be acclaimed, admired, and loved.

Thus a clarity of communication was called for, and it was indeed present partly from the dependent relationship between the dancer and the music. Thoinot Arbeau asserted that without the rhythmic quality of music, dancing would be dull and confused. Guglielmo backed this up. He left us a list of six qualifications for a good dancer. He put first *rhythm*, the ability to keep time with the music. Second was *memory*, keeping in mind the right steps and correct sequence of movements. Third was the use of *space*, an awareness of the size and layout of the space to which he must regulate the size and proportion of movements. Fourth was airy *lightness* (ballon). Fifth was *coordination* between steps of the feet and use of the body. Sixth was *inclination* for body movement, the gift for *expression*. We can see that to a large extent the style and body attitude of these preclassic court dances still characterize the classic school of ballet technique. If we think of technique as a learned system for moving the body properly in dance, then the advice of Guglielmo and Arbeau referred to above are not that different from the instructions that a contemporary teacher might give to pupils in a ballet class.

However, ballet is more than a series of technical movements, steps, and exercises done in a certain style. It is also a theatrical art form that includes elements in addition to dance: namely music, costumes, setting, and a plot, theme, or idea. Sometimes it also contains poetry, or dialogue, spoken or sung.

Court Entertainments

During the period we have been discussing—the Renaissance—there were court entertainments in addition to the balls. They combined all the theatrical elements mentioned above. In fact, dancing was probably the least interesting of all the aspects of a court entertainment. If Juliet had gone ahead and married the suitor that her parents had chosen for her, instead of eloping with the forbidden Romeo, the Capulets would undoubtedly have arranged a smashing celebration. This would have been climaxed by a showy pageant—a court entertainment—that would have contained the sketchy outlines of ballet spectacles with which we are familiar, except that the dancing itself would be severely limited.

Performers. The pageant performers would have been members of Juliet's family and other courtiers. These worthies would have looked forward to the event quite eagerly. They would have spent hours preparing for their parts and planning their costumes. Each day they delighted in dressing up, so how much more fun it was to don a costume. They spent much time in front of the mirror trying to achieve a special effect, not to mention the money laid out for special materials and props, often in a frank attempt to look more splendid than their best friends.

Masks were a complete source of fun in themselves, and many courtiers had a supply of them, which they used to disguise themselves during a festival when they might mingle in the streets with the ruder peasants, boisterously making merry. Or they might appear at a court party to flirt outrageously with dance partners married to someone else or otherwise forbidden, as Romeo did at the Capulet ball. Needless to say, this was a pretense easily seen through. Tybalt recognized Romeo's voice immediately, even though he and his friends had crashed the Capulet party wearing masks. Most of the time, however, everyone willingly went along with the game. Juliet's father boasted wistfully to his guests about his youth when he would wear a mask "and could whisper naughty pleasantries into a lady's ear—but that was long ago, and is now just a memory."

Thus all the most energetic, talented, and fun-loving courtiers would want to be in the show, which would consist of a musical introduction and then a series of tableaux, pantomimes, and special effects. While the performers were amateurs, there would also have been professional musicians, poets, and scenic artists who would have contributed their skillful talents or organized the whole affair.

Musicians. The musicians surely would have been professionals. Music was a great favorite with all classes of people. Every court had its resident composers and instrumentalists. Music had changed from the meandering chants for religious prayer that had been in service during the Middle Ages to new rhythmic melodies that were sung and played on instruments whenever people gathered together. Of special significance for our story is the fact that this was a time when almost all the great music being composed was specifically dance music, called pavanes, sarabandes, gavottes, and so on, after the dances that were so well-known at court.

Themes and Ideas. Either a professional or an important favorite courtier might come up with the themes and ideas on which pageants were based. Literary content—stories and legends—particularly those harking back to the pre-Christian era, had great appeal in the fifteenth and sixteenth centuries after the saturation of the Middle Ages with Jesus legends. The directors of Renaissance spectacles took their ideas largely from Greek and Roman mythology and history. Julius Caesar, Cleopatra, and Achilles were frequently portrayed, as were Venus, Cupid, and Hercules. The guests at these affairs were well acquainted with ancient tales. They enjoyed seeing and identifying these characters and the events connected with them, along with the pleasure of figuring out which well-known courtiers, personal friends, and other subjects for gossip hid behind each elaborate mask and costume. Poetry would have been recited about ancient Roman heroes and Greek gods, mixed in with flattery to the assembled company. Capulet might have been compared to Jupiter in his wisdom and power, for example, or Juliet to Venus. Perhaps Cupid would have been praised for uniting such a loving couple.

Scenic effects contributed much to the visual spectacle and perhaps made the biggest impression on the viewers. Scenes featured floating clouds, rumbling chariots, and larger-than-life animals, all involving complicated machinery like platforms on wheels and rollers, "flying" harnesses, hooks and pulleys, as well as trap doors, and the like. Creating effective props that functioned in a convincing manner occupied the attention of the finest Renaissance artists. Leonardo da Vinci himself was responsible for designing the contraptions at some shows. And, of course, trained engineers were called upon to build them.

Dancing. Finally, even if the prime element wasn't dancing, it was present. Performers were expected to remember to be graceful and to carry out all instructions in regard to steps and gestures, keeping time with the music, and leaving room for the other performers. The dancing masters often spent hours with their noble pupils, patiently teaching them simple pantomimic motions and steps that would be suitable to their roles. Then, after the show, the whole company of guests would participate in ballroom dancing which would go on through the night hours. They would all have practiced regularly and taken lessons with the same dancing master to get the steps and patterns just right.

To sum up, in the preclassic court dances, taken together with the pageants and the processions of the Renaissance, we can see the barest outline of ballet as we know it. As we continue our pursuit of dance history, we shall see how the steps and movements developed in complexity and in brilliance beyond recognition, and were given over completely to professionals. Still, as a technique of physical movement and as a kind of behavior, ballet continued—and still continues—to be characterized as a courtly, dignified, technical system with an emphasis on clear designs made by the dancer's limbs and torso in a refined and elegant style. We shall also see how choreographic productions maintained a showy spectacular character, even while varying considerably in style of themes, music, stage design, and costumes as well as movement.

Romeo and Juliet in Ballet

Shakespeare's *Romeo and Juliet* is important to the dance fan not only because its setting is an Italian Renaissance town, and therefore shows us a lot about the birthplace of court ballet. It also has served as the source and inspiration for a large number of dance works. At least a dozen totally different versions have been produced during the last twenty-five years alone. Before that, it made up the scenario for no fewer than eighteen operas, almost all of which had some dance in them, as well as song.

Let's pause and consider the charactes of Romeo and Juliet. First of all, why are they the most famous lovers in Western civilization? Certainly, the image of two beautiful young people bursting with passion to the extent that they are willing to defy their families and turn their backs on money and social position in order to be together is in itself very striking and appealing. But I think the real secret lies in their tragic fate. How striking this passion becomes when it is set against the ugliness of blood feuds and the muddy complications of capricious chance that finally cause the emotionally charged youngsters to take their own lives in confusion. Thus the beauty and appeal of the starry-eyed lovers is considerably heightened by its contrast with the darker tones of tragedy.

But what kind of dance can one make of such a play? Shakespeare provided a lot of material to choose from: a frustrated Romeo being kidded by his friends and urged to crash a party; a glittering ball; several lovers' meetings; a couple of murderous duels; Juliet seeking help at a friar's chapel; a funeral procession—these are only some. Each choreographer decides on an overall plan and then chooses the scenes he wants to use, and treats them according to his idea. In 1938, the Russian Mikhail Lavrosky followed Shakespeare's plot and action closely, making his ballet almost a work of pantomime. In 1943, the Englishman Antony Tudor, in the U.S., concentrated on the subtleties of a danced love affair between the two main characters, bringing in some of the rest of the action as a stylized portrait of the Renaissance in Italy. His Romeo and Juliet were mature—no teenagers here! In 1962, John Cranko (a South African who came to Stuttgart by way of England) combined lyrical dancing and lively pantomime, as did Kenneth MacMillan (1965) in England, to give their own interpretations of universal love in an historical setting. There is a movie of MacMillan's version (in which Juliet is once again a young girl). In addition, there are a number of versions of the *pas de deux* of the lovers, performed by dozens of artists, like Rudolf Nureyev and Lynn Seymour.

In fact, the musical drama *West Side Story* created (1957) by Jerome Robbins and Leonard Bernstein was based on this same wonderful drama. Here the timeless elements of teenage passion and feuding tribes were transposed from rival families in sixteenth-century Verona to street gangs in twentieth-century New York. Instead of the Italian Montagues and Capulets, there were the Puerto Rican Jets and Sharks, each ruling their own street and guarding it with knives against forays by the opposition. The tragedy occurred when a sister of a Shark fell in love with a Jet leader. After the show was a success, a movie version followed. Another up-to-date interpretation was Béjart's *Romeo and Juliet* (1966) which presented the Renaissance noblemen as contemporary teenage boys, counting out loud, doing gymnastics, and tumbling, along with the more conventionally staged lovers' duets. In the 1970s, the American John Nueumeier's Hamburg Ballet danced his own version of the story, based in part on the earlier Cranko work, with many personal departures.

Anyway, you can see from this quick international tour that there is more than one way to express the same thought. Thus art is a form of communication, and its statements and styles must reflect the feelings dominant in a particular culture, or a particular artist. Yet at the same time, ballet has remained an art of visual spectacle and technical skill, its personality a product of its birth in the courts of Renaissance Italy. Our story moves now with Catherine de Medici, from Italy to France.

Questions for Review

1. Why do we say that the style of ballet comes from Italian Renaissance manners?

2.   What is the relationship between preclassic dances and musical forms?

3.   How would you treat the story of Romeo and Juliet in a ballet?

7 COURT SPECTACLES

Catherine de Medici (1519 to 1589)

Catherine de Medici (1519 to 1589) was married at fourteen years of age to Henry, heir to the French throne. Like Juliet, Catherine too had fallen in love on her own with handsome, curteous, highly cultivated cousin Ippolito. Unlike Juliet, she was content to ignore these stirrings of romantic desire in order to go along with the political schemes of Pope Clement VII. This cooperative attitude sprang from her central interest in life, which from a very early age was the achievement of political power.

While Juliet was affectionate, spontaneous, playful, and had grown up secure, surrounded by a loving family and protected by a motherly nurse, Catherine's nature was serious, introspective, and shaped by a very different childhood environment. Not only was she orphaned at birth, her life was constantly threatened by civil war in her native Florence; and as one of the few last representatives of the great Medici family, her future was the subject of political negotiations for many years. Catherine grew up in dangerous political waters, and she learned to swim in them so well that she became a champion.

Marriage has always been considered a way of uniting not just a man and a woman, but also their families. Among high-born rulers, it has also been a method of forming political alliances among states. Catherine and Henry were thus brought together as part of a very complicated plot, involving several major powers. Catherine's prize was to reside at the French court from 1535 to 1589, first as a duchess, then as a queen; and after the death of her husband King Henry in 1559, as the queen mother. As the power behind the throne, queen mother Catherine virtually ruled France, acting through her children who in fact occupied it.

Catherine's Luxurious Court. History remembers Catherine de Medici primarily as a cold, hard schemer, responsible for bloody massacres in the religious wars between Catholics and the new Protestants. There was another side to her reign that interests us more in the story of ballet. When Catherine moved to France, she brought with her a great pile of wealth and the memory of splendid entertainments and pageants, as described in the previous chapter. Talented artists followed her from her native land and created a luxurious, Italian-style court in France. In fact, Catherine kept herself busy with the arts through the first ten years of marriage, before her first child was born; and after that, partly to console herself for what turned out to be a sad marriage. Her husband King Henry occupied himself openly with his beautiful mistress Diane, who was constantly at his side, and who received more admiration and attention from the court than did Queen Catherine. So the queen surrounded herself with Italian artists and their work flourished as a consequence.

Catherine's contributions to this early stage of ballet development were not through her own dancing. Rather, like Sergei Diaghilev (whom we will meet later on), Catherine encouraged musicians, dance teachers, scenic designers, and poets to exercise their talents for the instruction and entertainment of the French nobility. Needless to say, her encouragement also took the form of financial support, and she allocated thousands of francs to mount lavish shows. This continued even after her children began to arrive, sometimes with events designed especially in their honor. An outstanding celebration even for this showy period was arranged for her son Francis, the first one of her children to marry. Francis was coupled with Mary Stuart of Scotland.

Again, we are talking about a political marriage of teenagers: the bride and the groom were both fifteen years old. Their wedding in 1559 was a splendid Renaissance affair, clearly showing the luxurious Italian influence that Catherine had brought with her. A detailed description of the wedding is found in Antonia Fraser's fascinating biography *Mary Queen of Scots*. The ceremony took place at the cathedral of Notre Dame, which was embellished with a special outside structure that made a kind of open-air theater, which included a twelve-foot-high arch. Swiss guards, resplendent in their dress uniforms, entered the theater to the sound of tambourines and fifes. Then came a duke and a bishop, followed by a procession at the head of which was a corps of musicians, all dressed in yellow and red, playing trumpets, violins, and other musical instruments. Next came a hundred gentlemen-in-waiting of the king, and gorgeously attired royal princes.Magnificently dressed high churchmen: abbés, bishops, and cardinals bearing jewelled crosses appeared. Then Francis and Mary entered, each one led by a king and a duke.

Mary Stuart wore a robe as white as lillies, so sumptuous that the observer who left us this account could not find words to describe it. Her immensely long train was carried by two young girls. Tall and elegant, Mary glittered like the goddess of a pageant, with diamonds around her neck, and on her head a golden crown garnished with pearls, sapphires, rubies, and one huge red gem worth over 500,000 crowns. Catherine de Medici, led by a prince, and several grand noblewomen followed Mary, all in fabulous robes and jewelry. When this noble crowd entered the church, the Mass was performed under a resplendent gold canopy with gold carpets. After Mass, the guests enjoyed a long, elaborate banquet, with hours of dancing. The whole group then proceeded to the palace. The gentlemen rode horses adorned with crimson trappings. The ladies were carried in chairs and the bride sat with Catherine de Medici on one made of gold.

Now came supper, and a second ball, more splendid than the first, this time punctuated by an endless series of pantomimes and tableaux, in

Margo Fonteyn does the proud steps of a Renaissance court dance in La Scala's "Romeo and Juliet."

which members of the royal family took part. Twelve artificial horses made of gold and silver cloth were brought into the ballrooms. Young royal princes mounted the horses and drew along a series of coaches, each containing a number of bejewelled occupants, singing. (The singers were supposed to represent poor pilgrims, despite the glittering jewels!) Next, six ships were drawn into the ballroom, their silver sails made ingeniously so that they seemed to be billowing in the wind while the ships themselves gave the impression of floating on the floor. Each magic ship had room for two sailors, and the noblemen who were steering each one chose a noble lady for his partner—the choices dictated of course by the rank and position of the ladies at court. As the observer noted, no one could decide what lit the room more brightly, the torches along the sides, or the flash of royal jewels. Nor was this the end. More festivities followed over several days.

Ballet Comique de la Reine

Balthasar de Beaujoyeux (birthdate unknown, died 1587), a key figure in the entourage of Catherine de Medici, had himself arranged other, similar spectacles. An Italian violinist who had attached himself to her court in Paris around 1555, Beaujoyeux was given the responsibility for royal entertainments by Catherine. Beaujoyeux capped his career in 1581 with the production of *Ballet Comique de la Reine*, which is referred to by most dance historians as the first real ballet. Of course, this ballet, arranged to honor another marriage with political overtones, did not spring to life without antecedents. We have already seen Mary Stuart's wedding and other banquet entertainments that had been the custom at courts for over one hundred years. But the production of the *Ballet Comique de la Reine* was on a grand scale not yet seen: it lasted for five hours; it contained a large number of dance sequences; and its sets included fountains, water machines, a palace, gardens, and a chariot float. There was a specially written poetic script. Commissioned music was performed by not one, but a number of ensembles. The finale alone was danced by sixteen courtiers. We can get an idea of the style of this early ballet from this description, set down by the choreographer Beaujoyeux himself, and reproduced in *Dance as a Theater Art*, edited by Selma Jeanne Cohen.

The hall was set with a wooded grove, an immense overhanging cloud, and Circe's garden and her castle. Everyone present knew that Circe was a sorceress who could hold men frozen in enchantment. A noble messenger ran out, dressed in silver cloth adorned with jewels, and explained that Circe had captured him. He said that he had managed to escape for the moment, but he sought the king's help in order to keep his freedom. (The real king was, of course, seated among the spectators.) Next, Circe appeared, holding her magic wand of gold, and in verse, complained angrily about the escaped prisoner.

Circe exited and out came three mermaids and a sea god, with tails of gold and silver scales, their bodies entwined with gold thread. They all carried golden mirrors and circled the hall singing in praise of King Henry, who was more noble than Jupiter. The mermaids ended up at a fountain which contained three basins adorned with gold and silver sculpture, with scented water flowing through them. In twelve golden niches around the large basin sat the queen and eleven other royal ladies, who were supposed to be nymphs, in dresses of silver cloth and many precious stones. Ten violinists in white satin, adorned with egret feathers, entered to play the first dance diversion. The nymphs formed a line with a triangle in front, the queen its forward point. They revolved in accord with the music, winding backward around each other in different steps. Having arrived close to the king, they proceeded to go through twelve geometric figures, all different from one another. Evil Circe appeared again and touched each nymph with her wand, freezing them into statues. When she returned to her garden she had a bold, happy face to show that she had won a great victory.

Suddenly there was a clap of thunder. The overhanging cloud began to descend, bringing Mercury down. He sprinkled a potion, intended to subdue Circe, but instead she conquered him, and sat above him in her garden, where there was a procession of man-sized animals: dogs, lions, elephants, and others—all enchanted forms of men she had bewitched. Another thunderbolt signalled the arrival of Jupiter, who represented King Henry, and he managed to overcome the wicked Circe, whom he led as a captive over to the real king. The grand finale now took place, with fifteen passages in it, each one ending with the performers facing the king. Then they danced the grand ballet of forty passages, or geometric figures, which were exact in their shapes: square, round, or triangular, with smaller figures inside. The choreographer commented that it could have been a battle array, so well was the order and also the rhythm kept. The art of choreography consisted mainly of designing floor plans, like line drawings. The spectators sat above the dancers, and could clearly make out the patterns. TV directors make use of this effect sometimes when they use an overhead camera to focus on a circle of dancers inside another circle.

At least nine hundred important dignitaries saw the patterns in *Ballet Comique de la Reine*. Further, Beaujoyeux published a libretto and description (from which the above scenes were taken). Along with the libretto and notes on the choreography, copies of the music were sent to every court in Europe. In short order, it became a model and was imitated by many other court artists. In 1581, travel was not as fast nor as comfortable as it is today. Nevertheless, the aristocracy of Europe visited one another and were quick to bring back to their own courts whatever pleasant diversions they found elsewhere. Throughout the period that followed the 1581 production of this spectacle, we hear about entertainments that resembled the *Ballet Comique de la Reine* as far afield as Portugal, Sweden, and England. Therefore, if one must point to a single event as the "first" ballet, then *Ballet Comique de la Reine* deserves the distinction.

Ballet In England

When artistic ideas spread from one country to the next, they take on different colorings in each place. For example, when John Lennon moved from England to America, his music was influenced by the political protests that he found in his new home. Similarly, as the ballet moved into one European court after another, its shapes varied with the cultural behavior already in residence. In England, for instance, French court dances became very popular. Henry VIII was very proud of his ability to dance and of the occasional musical accompaniment he composed for it. The great passion of his daughter Queen Elizabeth I was dancing. She exercised every morning by doing six galliards, a tiring dance, full of leaps and kicking steps. This may be a good time to pause and consider British court life in other aspects.

A few pages back, a description of the brilliant French wedding of Mary Stuart was given. Her sickly husband died in less than two years and the pretty widow returned to Scotland where she had a claim not only to the throne of that country, but also of England's through a distant grandparent. Queen Elizabeth didn't like this threat to her position and she found reasons to have Mary imprisoned in England for nineteen years, and finally executed in 1587. Meanwhile, Mary's son James (by a second marriage) held the Scottish throne. James not only didn't answer his mother's appeals for help against Elizabeth, he appeared satisfied at her death, since it left him undisputed ruler of Scotland, and in due course, of England.

Martha Graham choreographed *Episodes* in 1959. This dance presents Mary's hopeless struggle with Elizabeth, treating it as a flashback in Mary's memory as the unfortunate queen mounts the executioner's scaffold. In London, under the same Elizabeth who coldly isolated Mary from society; and then under that same James who cruelly turned his back on his mother's desperation, there were continuous merry celebrations—a contrast similar to that of Renaissance Italy. In dance spectacles, there were new heights achieved in the *masque* form, through the collaboration of Ben Jonson and Inigo Jones.

Ben Jonson (1572 to 1637). Jonson was a comic dramatist who breathed the same intoxicating air that stimulated Shakespeare's creativity. For a while, he turned his genius to writing poetic scenarios for court entertainments, and spiced them up considerably with comic, even grotesque, scenes. Before his time, most court productions had maintained a stilted, noble tone, designed to dish up flattering tributes to kings and dukes. Certainly, that was the style of the *Ballet Comique de la Reine*. Jonson worked on the introduction of antic humor, like the scene in his *The Hue and Cry After Cupid*, where the spirit of Love was attended by twelve boys, who represented the lighter, playful moments of romance. They wore silly clothes, instead of the customary jewelled silver cloth; they carried torches; and to suitable music they went through odd, unexpected movements and steps, making funny faces and ridiculous gestures all the while. Jonson also brought on ugly characters, like old, hobbling witches, who made deliberately clumsy, distorted movements. With such scenes, Jonson took advantage of that most basic idea of contrast: variety makes for better entertainment than monotony. A scene is always more effective when it is set next to one of opposite mood. Graceful nymphs and valiant heroes are much more attractive when they follow heavy, ugly figures.

Inigo Jones (1573 to 1652). In these masques, Jonson worked together with Inigo Jones, and because ballet was an art of visual splendor, Jones really stole the spotlight. Jones's contributions were in designing marvelous scenic changes with complicated machinery and new stage arrangements that he found on the Continent. He also offered handsome, witty costumes, better adapted for body movement than those in use elsewhere, topped by richly expressive masks. Jones was also adept at positioning people in theatrically impressive groupings. These included the geometrical patterns that we found in the *Ballet Comique de la Reine*, as well as floor plans that traced the names of royalty to be honored and other popular symbols. For many years, these English productions excelled in interest and showy display.

Eventually, however, religious bigotry got into the act and dimmed the glowing English stage. This occurred under the Puritans, who rose as a sect to purify not only the corrupt English church, but the soul of all Elizabethans. Numerous sermons against dancing like this one were heard: "This dancing is madness—men and women together, turning and jumping in public places, with such beastly slobberings, kissing and other misdemeanors! Every leap or skip in dance is a leap toward hell." Finally, in the next century, these Puritans got into the government with Cromwell, and put a decisive halt to the development of theatrical dance in England.

Ballet On the Continent

Fortunately, no such prohibitions occurred in Catholic France or Italy. In Italy, artists continued to make significant contributions to European theater art, both through the design and construction of theater buildings and with the introduction of opera, which is drama that unfolds through music and song. In Italy, opera developed separately from ballet, while in France, they were combined to some extent.

Meanwhile, dancing moved forward in France, with the continued patronage of the nobility, including the kings. Louis XIII was the son of another domineering de Medici woman. Marie repeated Catherine's story. Sixty-seven years later, she came from Florence, Italy to marry a French King—Henry IV. This was in 1600. Like the first de Medici, Marie ruled through her son Louis, who hesitantly mounted the throne—at the age of nine—after his father died in 1610. Here is a drama of political intrigue that you may well see some day as an episode on one of those historical TV miniseries that have recently become so popular. Louis did not prove to be such a compliant son. Teenage King Louis started out by developing interests in ballet and in hunting to occupy his time when his overbearing mother Marie made it clear that she would keep him out of state affairs. Queen mother Marie ran the show, partly with her favorites, Concini and his wife. The Concinis were a Florentine couple who had followed Marie to France. She conferred very high positions on Concini, who soon won the hatred of the French nobility because he was so greedy, and because he kept his position secure with the help of an elaborate spy system that he set up among the nobles. They tried to organize a rebellion against him, but Concini prevailed.

Then, in January 1617, young King Louis (sixteen years old) chose the plot and danced the lead in a court ballet: *The Liberation of Renaldo*. He used a well-known story about the Crusades to make the political point to his court that he considered himself to have come of age, and he was prepared to take over the reins of government. Louis didn't say so in so many words, but he didn't have to. Courtiers were quite accustomed to figuring out the parallels between a ballet story and a struggle at court. Sure enough, a couple of months later, King Louis XIII had Concini assassinated and his wife burned as a witch; and he followed this up by exiling his mother from court.

The Liberation of Renaldo concerned a sorceress, Armida, who set fire to the armed camp of the Crusaders and took prisoners of all the Christian knights. Only Renaldo resisted. He escaped, delivered Jerusalem from the Moslems, and saved Christianity. There was an obvious parallel between Armida, the evil witch, and Marie de Medici; while King Louis himself portrayed the Demon of Fire, transformed into the knight who saved Jerusalem. The message was clear: Louis intended to rule as an absolute king for the good of France, freed from the evil power of queen mother Marie. If we look at this ballet as an example of court entertainment, rather than political maneuvering, we find that the spectacle form continued to reflect its residence at court well into the 1600s.

Performers. Dancers were still primarily aristocrats, who were chiefly concerned with flattering others and with publicly displaying their close relationships with prominent people. Professionals helped the amateurs with skillful guidance, and distributed the parts according to the performers' abilities rather than their noble ranks. The less talented courtiers appeared as drunken peasants, students, and tramps. Professional dancers kept the difficult parts for themselves and shared with the best amateurs the complex figures of the grand ballets. Noblemen enjoyed playing servants and other people of the low classes just for fun. The only trouble was that they couldn't always bring themselves to dress in an appropriately poor fashion. Women's parts were generally taken by men wearing masks, although a noblewoman would appear sometimes in a mask. On those occasions, the choreography had to respect the delicacy and shyness of their sex and avoid frolicsome capers, preferring noble grace to virtuosity and expressiveness. Children often took part, appearing as birds, monkeys, dogs, or cats, and also as midgets or cupids. New ballets were constantly created for important state occasions, or in honor of distinguished people.

Dramatic versus Ballet à Entrées

In one respect there was a resemblance to contemporary ballet in the theoretical distinction between *dramatic* (mimetic) productions and *entrées*, which we would call *divertissements*, or just dancing, loosely organized by an indefinite theme. Three hundred years ago, these two types went in and out of fashion alternately, as they do today Then, as now, there were works that combined elements of both types. But usually, the dramatic ballet would feature action around an actual plot or story line, borrowed either from the classical literature of ancient Greece and Rome, or from medieval legends about knights and the Crusades.

Dramatic Productions. The subject matter of dramatic court ballets often concerned Jerusalem. As Jerusalem is often featured in today's headlines, so it has been the object of world attention through the centuries. The plot of *The Liberation of Renaldo* was based on a popular poem of the 1500s, Tasso's *Jerusalem Revisited*. This city figured prominently in European culture as a subject for literature and ballet scenarios, which were often based on memories and fantasies about the Crusades, including the siege of Jerusalem and the conquest of Palestine. Heroes were European Christian Crusaders, and villains were Turks and Moslems. Jerusalem served as both a spiritual symbol as well as a focus for bitter battles.

This fascination has lasted down to the present. In 1950, William Dollar, an American, choreographed *The Duel*, after *Jerusalem Revisited*. It is very different in style from the court ballet *The Liberation of Renaldo*, suiting twentieth-century tastes with its limitation of characters and its condensation of plot. In *The Duel*, four Crusaders in armor and high-plumed helmets stand lined up in battle formation. A strange, lone Moslem warrior enters, and unafraid, challenges one of them. They duel and the Moslem triumphs, killing the Crusader. During the fight, the challenger's helmet suddenly falls off, and with her long black hair streaming down, the victor is revealed to be the beautiful Turkish woman warrior, Clorinda. Tancred, the leader of the Crusaders, is struck by her bravery and beauty and falls in love with her. Later, on another battlefield, the Christian Tancred enters, chasing a Moslem warrior. The enemy is once again Clorinda, but neither recognizes the other, since their faces and heads are completely covered. They duel. She wounds him. He replies with a mortal thrust. As she is dying, he discovers the identity of his beloved, and cradles her in his arms. Clorinda leans against him, showing her love too late. Tancred sadly carries the dying woman off the field. At the end, he realizes that he must prepare himself to seek out the enemy again, since the fight is by no means over.

We find that the plots of the sevententh-century ballets, whether from a love poem by Ovid or a tale of Jerusalem, were carried forward through miming and appropriate costumes and scenery, mixed in with artificially dragged-in dance scenes. In addition, poetry and singing were usually present. While we sometimes use all these combinations today, we would probably call the result musical comedy or mixed media, rather than ballet. In the 1600s, all ballets included poetry. Some verses were spoken or sung, to introduce each section of the action. Others might give a summary of the action, and were distributed to the audience as program notes, before the performance, to let them in on the plot. And as we have seen, many poems were simply dedicated to important people who were present, in order for the poet to attract attention and receive promotions and favors. Then, as now, there was always music, specially composed by resident musicians of the court. Finally, there were sections of dance that represented grotesque monsters, water sprites, or military conquerors.

Ballet à Entrées: Dance *Divertissements*. This nondramatic court entertainment was also called figured dancing, or ballet mascarades. In such a program, the general scheme usually followed was: entrance of musicians, a set of dances by masked performers, the grand ballet, and then general social dancing for all the guests. Beyond that there was no exact formula.

Choreography differed with the type of entrée. In an *entrée figuree*, the choreography was of geometrical inspiration and consisted of figures traced on the floor along rigorous paths, representing a name or a sign that symbolized courage, all-powerful love, or immortal fame. This approach predominated in the grand ballet. In an *expressive entrée*, featuring characters or action, there was a motley crew of characters. There were sliders who fell all over themselves; or a man in debt fighting two policemen for his coat; or sprites in feathered costumes, showing off their jumping ability. Contrasting effects and surprises were always sought by the choreographer. Midgets grew tall; cripples threw away their crutches and started jumping around; and shy nymphs turned into impudent hussies. Acrobatics were commonly used: human pyramids, somersaults, even tightrope dancing. Any skill could be put onstage. Painters made portraits while dancing; glass blowers turned out beautiful pieces; and grooms swept the village square in the stage set.

Novelty and entertainment were the only objectives. To a viewer of today, many of these productions would seem enormously involved and cluttered up. The *Ballet du Chateau de Bicetre* included interludes with the following types: tramps, drunken peasants, gypsies, youths, ladies, deities, ghosts, counterfeiters, judges, and sergeants. The birth of Louis XIV was celebrated with the *Ballet de la Felicité* (1639), with his arrival represented by a prince onstage who enters with Felicité, causes fighting to stop, and is then greeted by Fame. This kind of obvious approach was quite popular.

Although the birth of a king could produce acclaimed productions, when ministers of state tried to stage them for the purpose of building patriotic enthusiasm, they weren't too well received. *The Ballet of Four Christian Kings* (1635) and *The Ballet of the Success of the French Army* (1641) were full of impressive scenes of military strength and grand marching. However, these seemed to have elicited the same reaction as ballet about military victories might from a modern audience. In the seventeenth century, as in the present, the viewer preferred airy flights of fancy and acrobatic tricks to scenes of national boasting and propaganda. It isn't that the audience objected to military conquest as a dance subject in these unsuccessful productions. Rather, it was the serious, preaching tone that they didn't like.

The courtiers particularly appreciated a telling point when made in a light vein, another similarity to today's dance, whose public also favors humor and satire. The story is told that Louis XIII once showed his disapproval and "punished" two of his musicians by cutting their salaries in half. Thereupon the pair danced before the king, one in only a jacket, although a gigantic jacket, and one dressed only in breeches, also oversized, to imply that they could afford to be only half dressed, since that was all their salaries allowed. The performance amused the king and the musicians were once again in his favor, and presumably restored to their former financial status. Anyway, the entertaining idea was put to use in another ballet, where it was enjoyed for its own sake.

So many ballet mascarades were performed during this period—there were eight hundred between 1589 and 1610—that standards for choreography received the attention of serious theorists. We noted previously that the qualifications of a good dancer were listed a century earlier by Guglielmo, and can still be applied as criteria today. So can the principles set down for the choreographer by Saint-Hubert, who participated in court ballets during the reign of Louis XIII. His small pamphlet from 1641 tells *How To Make a Successful Ballet*. It can be found in Selma Jeanne Cohen's anthology *Dance as a Theater Art*. Even today, many pleasing dance productions are created according to Saint-Hubert's advice.

Questions for Review

1.   How would you describe the features of the court ballet in sixteenth-century France?

2.   Discuss the masque as developed by Ben Jonson and Inigo Jones.

3.   What happened to court ballet in England in the seventh century?

8 THE SUN KING DANCES

FRENCH ROYAL BALLET FROM 1650 TO THE 1700s

Louis XIV

The most famous dancing king, Louis XIV (1638 to 1715), leapt onstage with two men who resided at his court: Lully and Beauchamps, both important to our story. Because of the nature of the Sun King's court, and its interactions with all of French culture, we now begin to see the beginnings of a professional ballet tradition, such as the kind we associate with today's scene. A casual first glance seems to reveal the opposite of professionalism. Dance, more than ever, was an aristocratic plaything, as the court of Louis XIV reached a new height in exaggerated, elegant, artificial, ceremonious lifestyle.

Louis himself demanded to be treated like a god. He rose from bed in the morning, ate his meals, and sank to sleep at night as the star—or the sun—of a public spectacle in which the greatest noblemen of France competed for the privilege of helping him dress, undress, or reach his wine cup. It was considered an honor to be allowed to hold the sleeve of his royal nightshirt while his royal arm entered it. Courtiers who served as his valets or washing-bowl attendants were themselves of noble birth.

This also had been true in Renaissance courts, but Louis magnified the scale, increasing his royal household from six hundred to ten thousand people! No one was considered worthy of eating with him, but those favored were allowed to watch him put food into his royal mouth. While this insistence on being the focus of all eyes arose from a belief in the importance and total power of all kings, especially himself, at the same time, Louis XIV staged these daily events with conscious courtesy and pompous ceremony. The style of classic ballet owes a great deal to the personal mannerisms of Louis. These in turn were rooted in the elegance of Renaissance court life, together with Louis's own cultivation of physical grace through a daily routine that included dancing lessons, exercises with weapons, and fencing. It is no wonder that a king with an over-blown ego who delighted in breakfast rituals in which noblemen devoted themselves to his adoration also enjoyed being the center of attention on an actual stage. For this most total, absolute, despotic monarch loved dancing. He amused himself not only with lessons and frequent formal dancing parties, but with active participation—in leading roles—in the ballets that his courtiers produced. Louis XIV danced in court ballets for at least twenty years, beginning as a teenager when he, like his father before him, was under the domination of a queen mother.

La Ballet de la Nuit, 1653. At the age of fourteen, Louis presented himself in *La Ballet de la Nuit*, this time not as a declaration of independence from his mother, but partly in support of her, in answer to the Fronde, a collection of rebels from all classes who had unsuccessfully tried to overturn the monarchy, as represented by his mother Anne. The monarchy won, and this ballet was Louis's statement that the royal ruler was the sun around whom the kingdom revolved, and on whom it depended for its life. Therefore, when he finally occupied the throne as the real power in France, Louis XIV set about engraving an indelible image of a Sun King whose rays could warm his people and make the country grow strong; but whose same rays could be lethal, if directed against enemies of France or of Louis—which amounted to the same thing. "I am the State," he maintained. His appearances in ballets and his starring role at his daily wash-up were all part of this patriotic self-glorification.

In *La Ballet de la Nuit*, Louis took no less than six roles, among them the rising sun. He liked this picture of himself so well that he eventually took the sun as his personal symbol. The production embodied all the characteristics of seventeenth-century ballet that we saw under his father, Louis XIII. *La Ballet de la Nuit* had forty-three *divertissements* in four acts, following the progress of the hours through a night:

ACT 1. Sunset. Assorted "dark" characters romped about, including hunters, bandits, shepherds, gypsies, lamp lighters, beggars, and cripples.

ACT 2. The night as the hour of court entertainment. This allowed an introduction of the "old-fashioned" courantes and sarabandes in masquerades and pantomimes—a ballet within a ballet.

ACT 3. Fantasies of the night. The moon as a lover. A moon eclipse, observed by astrologers Ptolemy of Egypt and Zoroaster of Persia. A witches' dance and a burning house complete with fleeing children and thieves.

ACT 4. Sleep and silence, and then the rising sun (Louis), accompanied by happy spirits, symbolizing honor, grace, love, riches, victory, fame, and peace. Their function was to praise the Sun King.

All these little scenes took hours to present, in combination with poems, songs, and intricately designed and engineered sets—like illusions for the fire, moon, sun, and so on—that were surely more spectacular and advanced than the dancing. From there on, there were many such ballets for Louis to star in. He even designed some of his own variations. We can't fault the king for holding the center stage in court ballet. His financial support to the art form and his many personal appearances certainly promoted its popularity.

All this sounds like more of the same court entertaining that we found in the Renaissance Italian palaces and later under Catherine de Medici and Louis XIII in France. And, of course, there were great similarities. But now we come to another aspect of Louis XIV's monarchy.

Louis's New Order. The reign of Louis XIV was not just pleasure oriented, ceremonious, and tyrannical. It was also total, absolute, despotic, and in today's language, a systematically organized, tightly controlled dictatorship. The new addition was an orderly system. The French monarchy was a complex organization, ruled from the top, and characterized by a worship of geometric order for its own sake. René Descartes, philosopher and mathematician, expressed the spirit of the age with his declaration that everything in the universe works according to logical principles that can be understood with the use of systematic, intellectual reasoning. It doesn't serve our purpose to set forth the workings of this orderly dictatorship in foreign and economic policy, taxation, and religion. Rules and systems were in evidence in all these departments, suffice it to say. Of more interest to us is the application of detailed rules to every aspect of cultural life.

Etiquette for every situation was strictly prescribed. The French language was codified. Words and expressions considered *proper* were listed in a dictionary that took fifty-six years to prepare. The board of an academy of painting and sculpture decided how these arts should be taught and applied; which artists were worthy of receiving commissions and prizes; and even whose work would be exhibited. A court poet wrote a book that dictated acceptable approaches to drama and poetry. Incidentally, while artists usually hate to be told what to do, and work badly when they are, at this time the authoritarian supervision was quite successful. Beautiful, expressive, interesting works were produced in all fields.

Dance and Music Academies

Dance and music were by no means neglected, which is not surprising, considering how much the king enjoyed them. Academies were founded to fix objective standards for the perfection of technique and artistry, sometimes treating music and dance separately, and sometimes coupling them under one organization, or perhaps linking them variously with drama and poetry.

Jean Baptiste Lully (1632 to 1687). Again, an Italian was the key figure here. A brief side trip to peek into his personal story offers insight on this historical period, since some very instructive facts are involved. First, it shows how the aristocracy looked at lower-class people as things—even as property. An important nobleman brought Giambattista Lulli, a peasant boy of seven, from Florence, Italy to France as a "present" for his high-born niece, who put the child to work as a kitchen assistant. Secondly, it demonstrates that low birth was not a permanent obstacle to advancement. The boy annoyed the other servants by practicing the violin. This came to the attention of the lady of the house—probably as a complaint from the staff—who recognized his talent and got a teacher for him. Thirdly, it tells us that immigrants, then as now, changed their names to harmonize with their new surroundings. As Jean Baptiste Lully, this precocious youngster was soon playing in, and then conducting, a string orchestra. From there, he became the king's music master, and then the director of the Royal Academy of Music, dominating the music and dance scene in France and beyond, until his death in 1687.

A final lesson contained in Lully's story is the capricious games that fate sometimes plays on individuals, and through them on the culture of a period. At the age of forty-eight, Lully accidentally pierced his foot with his oversize conducting baton. Gangrene set in and the wound caused his death. Most significant to the dance historian is the close connection between developments in the art of movement and those in the art of music that occurred in Lully's career—a connection that is to be made time and again in our story. Lully is best known as a composer. But he was also a director, a producer—and a dancer! He therefore understood and was interested in the problems of writing music for ballets, and further, he helped create a form of opera that featured a lot of dance. He also worked closely with Beauchamps, who was dancing teacher to Louis XIV as well as a choreographer and a top performer.

Pierre Beauchamps (1636 to 1705). Beauchamps directed the Royal Academy of Dance. In keeping with the spirit of the time, with the rules and analytic systems set forth for language and the other arts, Beauchamps listed and described the technique of Ballet as far as it had advanced in his day. He noted the five basic foot positions, the arm positions, the known patterns of movement and steps, and the rules for executing them, with emphasis on the crucial turnout of the legs.

Beauchamps stressed technical excellence rather than expression of ideas and emotions. As we continue this dance history, we repeatedly find some ballet masters who primarily seek to display technical skill, while others are interested in dance principally as a means of communication—a way of talking through the body to convey thoughts or feelings. Beauchamps was in the first group. In his theory, his teaching, and his own fine dancing, he detailed the conquest of skills. He emphasized vigorous pirouettes and leaps that covered space. According to the precise, orderly style that was so fashionable, he arranged these in balanced, well-proportioned designs that leaned towards the geometrical. Beauchamps was also responsible for establishing the practice that dancers should always face the front of the stage, with the line towards the audience being the most harmonic one possible. The turnout of the legs helped this positioning.

Theater Design

The emphasis on a frontward-facing dancer resulted partly from the location and design of the theatrical stages that came into use during this period. Theaters had been common in ancient Greece and Rome, but during the Middle Ages they disappeared. Churches became the theaters for morality plays that presented scenes from the Bible, and especially the New Testament, with the birth, death, and resurrection of Jesus celebrated at Christmas and Easter. There were similar performances in outdoor market squares, but here lighter entertainment might be included among the religious episodes. Then, as we have seen, during the Italian Renaissance, spectacles and entertainments primarily for pleasure were staged in large halls of palaces and other great dwellings, sometimes preceded by outdoor processions.

First in Italy and then in England, platforms were erected, both outdoors and in ballrooms. Then, scenic backgrounds were introduced along with movable flats, props, and scenic machinery. Finally, by the close of the 1500s, theater buildings were specially constructed with permanent stages that allowed the use of elaborate settings. By the end of the 1600s, Italian stage engineers brought these designs to other European cities.

Separate theater buildings were constructed everywhere, or palaces were at least furnished with their own theaters, including tremendous, well-equipped stages (such as those at the Louvre and Versailles). Thus dancers and actors began to perform as they do today, on a raised stage, making a series of pictures framed by a proscenium arch, while the audience sat opposite—not watching from haphazard angles as they would have out in the street, or seated all around the hall as they did in the ballrooms during court entertainments. Stage sets were designed so that the action might appear as a series of moving pictures taking place behind the proscenium arch, while the entire audience watched from one viewpoint. On the stage would be a house or a street, painted "in perspective" on a backdrop and side wings, which gave a three-dimensional illusion of depth and distance.

Most of our theater buildings today are modelled after the sixteenth-century Italian design that had a raised proscenium stage at one end of the hall, with the audience spread out in front of it. This arrangement affected more than the stage design and the placement of performers, who would always be seen at the best advantage from a front view.

On the performing side, the way was open to theater and dance becoming totally professional activities. Dancers and actors were separated from the audience, first by the physical existence of the proscenium arch, and more importantly, by the removal of the productions from the court. This meant that the amateur courtiers were no longer the principle source of performing talent. The class of paid, professional entertainers had never really died out since ancient Roman times, but it had shrunk considerably during the Middle Ages. Now it was to increase continuously, both in numbers and in respectability.

Also affected was the makeup of the audience. Separate theater buildings brought with them the practice of charging admission, and this meant that performances were no longer private spectacles to be enjoyed by invitation only. Now almost anyone with the price of a ticket could attend. The audience began to come from the population at large, and not just from the nobility. It was generally true that the theater tended to attract those who had some understanding and background in the arts. First of all, this meant the nobility, and secondly, the professional and business middle class, rather than workmen. But in the London of Elizabeth I, all classes were present, much as they might be at a movie house today.

Of course there were always seats for different prices. The most expensive ones were in exclusive boxes, to which the wealthy and high-born came, as much to be seen and admired as to see the production. Or they may have wanted to watch a favorite dancer or singer. Then they would retire to a private little room adjoining their box, to play cards, to eat, to flirt, or to gossip. They returned to their box seats only when an attendant called them to tell them that something was about to happen onstage that they wouldn't want to miss. Elements of this kind of pampered, selfish behavior are still very much with us at all theatrical events, especially ballet and opera performances.

The court may have been the whole world to the aristocrats and their attendants who lived among them. But there were many more people outside the nobility. They were of the middle class, in businesses and professions; and of the lower class as farmers, laborers, and tradesmen. Many from these two classes were also spectators at all kinds of performances. The commercial theater manager searched for new kinds of theatrical shows, different in subject and tone from the court spectacle, to attract and keep the patronage of this mixed audience, now so much wider than the selected "invited guests" at a court entertainment. No longer could the sole content of a production be the flattering of a duke on his birthday, delivered in a courtly, pompous manner. More substance, humour, and action that concerned a broader segment of humanity were now called for. Finally, the combination of a dance and music academy with a commercial theater meant that the performers were separated once and for all from their audiences: socially, physically, and in their schooling for the arts. No longer did dance represent an activity with which courtiers amused themselves. It now became a profession. *La Triomphe de L'Amour*, a French ballet in 1681, saw the appearance of the first professional premier danseuse on record: Mademoiselle de Lafontaine (1655 to 1738). This was a double innovation, because up to then most women's roles had been danced not only by the courtiers, but by men. Occasionally, ladies did agree to appear in a production, but they would be in scenes with all women, or at least they would pretend to conceal their identity behind a mask.

Because this is a dance history, every dance detail is magnified, while other things are mentioned only in passing or skipped over altogether. Don't let this give you a distorted picture of history. Please keep in mind that every past age was at least as complicated as our own. And as for entertainment, audiences were more likely to go to these new theater buildings to watch plays and operas, rather than just ballets. In fact, the dancing they saw was usually a part of a total dramatic production, whether spoken or sung.

Moliére (1622 to 1673). If you mention Moliére to the average cultured person, his name will call to mind a group of excellent satirical plays that hold up to ridicule many silly habits and customs of seventeenth-century Frenchmen. For example, one of these plays, produced during any recent season, is *The Imaginary Invalid*. It is a rollicking comedy about a hypochondriac who tries to marry off his daughter to a doctor, so that he can get free medical treatment. The viewers of this play may not know that Molière also worked with Lully and Beauchamps at the court of Louis XIV for several years, turning out a series of *comédie-ballets* which were to be the ancestors of today's musical comedies. This ignorance is understandable, because the comédie-ballets tend to be the lesser-known works produced by Molière. However, in their day, the combination of his witty plots and characters, Lully's fine operatic airs, and Beauchamps's lively dance patterns made outstanding theatrical evenings.

Béjart's Molière. These entertainments, together with Molière's life and times, inspired a contemporary choreographer to create *La Molière Imaginaire*. Maurice Béjart, responsible for the modernistic *Romeo and Juliet* mentioned earlier, applied his inventive imagination in 1976 to seventeenth-century France. His work, *La Molière Imaginaire*, combines dancing, singing, and acting to make what Béjart described on the program as a "Ballet Comedy." This deliberate reversal of the seventeenth-century term *comédie-ballet* was to show that Béjart wanted to emphasize the dance aspect, while paying respects to an older form that he was reviving with up-to-date modifications.

The décor and costumes, the music and the action are all in a combination of seventeenth-century court style and bold modern surrealism. The leading figure sometimes represents a modern-day actor, or one of the characters found in Molière's plays, or perhaps Molière himself. Two nearly-naked lovers dance their embraces to represent Molière's constant searching and respect for human truth. They are set in contrast to figures in wigs and hoop skirts, who mince around, representing the phony manners, dress, and personalities of the society that the playwright satirized. Molière's words are used throughout. Movements and patterns feature an elegant minuet and modern dance. Once again, we have a work that demonstrates how artists and audiences alike share in and draw on the richness of our cultural traditions.

Certainly, the image of the dancing King Louis XIV is indelibly engraved on our view of the past, and it helps enlighten us about ballets in the present. King Louis's reign saw court ballet at its most courtly. Yet by the time he died in 1715, the dance scene was marked by professionalism in every aspect The academic technique, the schooling, and the commercial theater that were to influence the future of ballet, all developed under this most noble, dignified monarch. He left the stamp of his royal mannerisms on the style of our art form. However, we can't yet call ballet fully professional. After all, side by side with the professional Mademoiselle de Lafontaine, Louis himself took part in entertainments like *La Triumph de L'Amour*, or if he didn't, his courtiers did. For the totally professional scene, we must wait a little longer, until the eighteenth century. That is the subject of the next chapter.

Questions for Review

1. Discuss *La Ballet de la Nuit* as an artistic work and as a political work.

2. What were the contributions of Jean Baptiste Lully to our story?

3. Was the ballet professional during the reign of Louis XIV?

4. How did the Royal Academy of Dance reflect the spirit of the age?

9 ENTRECHATS AND REVOLUTIONS

PROFESSIONAL BALLET 1714 TO 1789

The Royal Academy of Dance

Our next scene takes place in Paris, in 1725. Picture a special ballet class for a small group of advanced and professional pupils. The teacher is Françoise Prévost (ca.1680 to 1741) the outstanding female dancer of her day. Jean Balon (1676 to 1739) was her partner. His name is easy to remember because his dancing was outstanding for its quality of ease, and the word we use for lightness in elevation is *ballon*.

Among Prévost's pupils were two talented young females whom Prévost addressed by their family names, Mademoiselle Camargo and Mademoiselle Sallé, in order not to cause confusion, since both were named Marie. The rest of the advanced students didn't like the two Maries because they were obviously the teacher's pets. When the time came to practice jumping exercises, Camargo used to show off, continuing to jump easily, long after everybody else had to stop, completely out of breath. As for Sallé, she would often interrupt an exercise with questions that the other students found very silly, like: "What if we tried to bend this way when we do the pirouette?" "Wouldn't that look like a leaf spinning in the wind?"

In the previous chapter, we noted the appearance of Mademoiselle de Lafontaine, the first female dancer of status. Next in line came Françoise

Prévost, who made her debut at the opera in 1699. For thirty years. Prévoste was the foremost prima ballerina of her day, widely admired for lightness and expressive elegance. With the appearance of Camargo and Sallé, the place of the female dancer was secure. In fact, with them began the rivalry between ballerinas, which we will hear of time and again in dance history. Camargo and Sallé eventually divided the Paris dance public into two opposing camps, and you can be sure that each was very conscious of her standing as reflected by salary, the type of roles assigned, bouquets received, and all the other trappings of fame. Although ballerinas were popular, we still have to wait more than a hundred years for women to dominate men in professional ballet. In fact, the outstanding dancer of the early eighteenth century was a man, Louis Dupré.

Louis Dupré (ca. 1697 to 1774). Dupré was referred to as *le grand*, both because of his height (almost six feet) and because of his artistic greatness. Lillian Moore tells us (in *Dance Magazine*, June 1960) that Dupré made his debut in 1714, and was soon acclaimed for his graceful elegance. He became the favorite partner of Marie Sallé. Dupré was the *premier danseur noble* of his day. He was by inclination and temperament a classical, rather than a dramatic dancer. In fact, Jean-Georges Noverre, one of his pupils, criticized Dupré for always dancing abstract *chaconnes* in which he excelled, instead of varying his style to suit the theme of a particular ballet. At the same time, Moore quotes this admiring description that Noverre wrote of his teacher:

> The elegance of his figure and the length of his limbs were wonderfully suited to the execution of *developpés éffacés* and the intricate steps of the dance...
>
> This rare harmony in every movement earned for the celebrated Dupré the glorious title of *Dieu de la Danse* (God of the Dance.)

Dancing as a Career. The mark of professionalism from the time of Camargo, Sallé, and Dupré was that dancers from then on would be totally dedicated to their careers. They were not noble dilettantes, amusing themselves on occasion, but people from middle and lower classes who put a tremendous amount of effort and time into their art—their work. Dancing lessons, rehearsals, and tours became the focus of their daily existence. They competed with one another for the public's approval, and sought roles in productions not just to show off among their friends, but to earn money and establish positions for themselves in a society which was rapidly changing.

During the eighteenth century, European culture made a somersault from a court-centered pyramid to a more stimulating, fluid, middle-class leadership that allowed a mixture of money and talent to prevail. Widespread changes were in evidence. In government, the French and American revolutions were about to burst upon the world. In economics, mass production and industrialization were on the way. In education, literacy was increasing and freer intellectual attitudes prevailed. The dancer moved gracefully into this open environment; taking the role of producer and salesman of entertainment; trying to please a broad public and get as many people as possible to buy his merchandise. No wonder, then, that he strove for *popularity*, a word which took on new meaning with the appearance of cheap, daily newspapers. Through newspapers, theatrical gossip and critics' opinions were distributed to anyone who cared to read them. Journalists had no small part in promoting both the careers and the theatrical rivalries of Camargo and Sallé.

The two Maries had a lot in common, in addition to their first names. They were both ambitious and artistically daring. They both made performing debuts at very early ages: Camargo at nine; Sallé at ten. Yet they were to present their public with a choice of ballet idols that differed sharply in style. In the eighteenth century, as in the present, a ballerina's charm included an image of her private life superimposed on her stage personality. Of course then, as now, the public sometimes had a distorted picture of a dancer's biography.

Marie Anne de Cupis de Camargo (1710 to 1770). Camargo had an exotic "foreign" background. She was born in Brussels to a Spanish mother and an Italian music-master father. Before making her debut at the Paris Opera when she was sixteen, she appeared successfully in Rouen and Brussels , beginning at the age of nine. Later, Camargo followed the fashion of Parisian society by being linked with a succession of high-born wealthy lovers. Noverre, whom we shall soon meet as a prominent ballet master, wrote of her: "Mademoiselle Camargo, so gay on the stage, was by nature melancholy and serious." Many performers presented this kind of mystery. There was no mystery, however, about her appeal to audiences. She was outstanding in speed and drive: in short, a brilliant technician.

If the general level of skill was considerably lower than it is today, you must remember that an audience can judge only in the framework of the times. Camargo was probably the first dancer to execute the *entrechat quatre*, which was fantastic for the 1700s. She was particularly famous for shortening the voluminous eighteenth-century skirt. This extended the range and virtuosity of women's movements beyond anything yet seen. To exhibit women's ankles so shamelessly was a bold move. In addition to shocking current standards of female modesty, her action also flew in the face of Rule XIII of the opera: "Artists are obliged to sing and dance in the clothing assigned to them." However, the academy administrators must have quickly appreciated the advantages of freeing the legs in this manner (even though we would consider it a very limited freedom indeed!). Anyway, Camargo was careful to wear special underwear under these shorter skirts to protect her modesty.

Not only did Camargo thrill her public with technical virtuosity and daring costume, she also had a fine musical sense. As Noverre wrote of her: "Mademoiselle Camargo enjoyed that precious gift of appreciating naturally and easily the movements of the most difficult melodies. This gift, plus an exact precision, accorded to her dancing a spirit of vivacity and gaiety which is never found in those dancers who have less sensitivity to music." Please note carefully Noverre's comment on the importance of music. Musicality is the prime quality that raises the dance technician out of the class of the athlete and places him squarely among the artists. Musical sensitivity makes the dancer beautiful, as well as skillful.

Marie Sallé (1707 to 1756). Sallé brought a different side of dance to the public. This second Marie was born into show business. Her father was an acrobat in her uncle's successful touring company of actors, comedians, tumblers, and clowns. The troupe came to Paris every spring and summer to entertain at numerous fairs, and while they were in the neighborhood, Marie's family arranged for her to study with Prévost and Balon. Obviously, she had a special aptitude for dancing, and her performing family, always on the lookout for new talent, must have spotted it when she was very young. In fact, Marie Sallé made a big hit on a London stage when she was only nine years old. Together with her brother, she appeared for two months as a harlequin in a dancing act that followed a melodrama (*The Unhappy Favorite*). Their engagement was so successful that it was extended to over one hundred performances in all.

One evening when Prévost, her teacher, was ill, she allowed Sallé, a girl of fourteen, to dance in her place at the prestigious opera house. The reason for Sallé's substitution lasting for only one night, however, was that the audience had responded to the young ballerina very enthusiastically, and Prévost, who was over forty, did not care for this at all. Middle-aged people in every profession are resentful when faced with the threat of fresh young talent. This is an ever-recurring problem, particularly in our field. Since the instrument of the dance art is the body, a dancer, like an athlete, achieves his greatest technical skill quite early in life, usually somewhere in his twenties. Reaching the heights of interpretation, musically and dramatically, can take longer. But it is a rare dancer who can maintain his superiority well into his forties, or even continue to please the public. And the forties are the very years in which the dancer achieves an important position in a ballet or a theater company. This makes constant struggles inevitable between the mature performer and the newcomer who is pushing for his turn in the spotlight. This is an unpleasant, but inescapable fact of dance life. After her short one-night stand at the opera, Sallé continued to tour with her uncle's troupe and to appear in London with her brother. When she finally landed an appointment at the Paris Opera, she was twenty. Then she had leading roles in all important opera productions. As well, she had her share of roles in ballets at court. There Sallé was much admired and she made friends with important people like Voltaire. In her personal life, she was not particularly happy. Along with her constantly growing dance fame came increasingly more discomfiting gossip and backstage intrigue. The regular Parisian opera goers enjoyed scandals as much as ballets. They were disappointed that Sallé didn't openly take lovers the way Camargo did. In her teenage years, she was neurotically preoccupied with her brother, and after his marriage and shockingly early death, she showed a preference for women over men. If the scandal-loving public enjoyed discussing details of ballerinas' love affairs, you can imagine what they made of an unconventional private life. The more private Sallé tried to be, the more she whet the appetites of the gossips. Journalists catered to this appetite, inserting many nasty innuendos in their newspaper columns. They did this for the same reason that they enjoyed inflating the rivalry between Sallé and Camargo. Scandals stimulated newspaper circulation and boosted the journalists' egos.

Artistically, Sallé also had her problems with the opera administration. Many of the rigid, artificial aspects of court ballet had made their way into the opera, and remained there even after it became professional. Star dancers appeared in an opera, doing dance entrées tailored to fit their own abilities. As a result, these entrées often had little to do with the action of the work in which they were performing. These stars also used their favorite piece of music, not caring whether or not it harmonized with the style of the opera, or was written by the same composer. Such spirited prima donnas also refused to consider the logical or dramatic requirements of a role when they chose their costumes. They might be representing Greeks, or Indians, or peasants. Yet they dressed solely for prestige, in elaborate costumes, insisting on the tallest hairstyles, the fullest skirts, and the most glittering jewelry possible.

These costumes caused quarrels between Sallé and the opera's director, because her approach to dance was indeed a revolutionary one. Like Camargo, she also was interested in changing and simplifying dance costumes, but for a completely different reason. Camargo shortened her skirt so that she could execute more difficult, splashy jumps. Sallé, on the other hand, was interested in dance not as a form for exhibiting technical skill, but as one for expressing feelings and portraying situations. Because of the attitude of the Paris Opera management, Sallé had to return to London to put her theories into practice.

Pygmalion

In London, Sallé triumphed in *Pygmalion*, her best-known work, in 1734. Through this ballet, she realized several ambitions: creating choreography; performing as a dramatic dancer, capable of every nuance of expression; and designing dance costumes that suited the dance idea and at the same time allowed freedom of movement—the very opposite of the tinsel and clutter of French operatic ballet dress. Sallé dared to wear a simple muslin dress, draped in the style of classic Greek sculpture; slippers without heels; and her hair, without any ornament, falling loosely around her shoulders. Starting as a statue, she came to life before the eyes of the audience. An observer from the newspaper *Mercure de France* described it this way:

> The statue, little by little, becomes conscious, showing wonder at her changed existence. Amazed and entranced, Pygmalion takes her hand, leading her down from the pedestal. Step by step she feels her way, gradually assuming the most graceful poses a sculptor could possibly desire, with steps ranging from the simplest to the most complex.

George Bernard Shaw took this ancient myth and changed it around quite a bit to bring it up to date—that is, to 1912, when he wrote the play *Pygmalion*. The original tale is of the sculptor, Pygmalion, who creates a statue of such an appealing woman that he falls in love with it, or her, Galatea by name. Galatea then comes to life. Shaw moved the ancient tale into modern England. He made the sculptor Pygmalion into Henry Higgins, a language expert; and the statue into a lovely English lady whom Higgins creates from the "raw clay" of Eliza, a rough lower-class girl who sells flowers. In turn, this play was made into *My Fair Lady* in the 1950s, with dialogue, songs, and dancing. Then, from the musical comedy, they made the popular movie. Thus *My Fair Lady* traces its lineage to comic opera and ballet, which relate to court entertainments and the comédie-ballet form perfected by Lully and Molière. This family of artworks and art forms is like a large tree, with many intertwined branches.

Meanwhile, back in the eighteenth century, the London audience responded with enthusiastic excitement to *Pygmalion*. This was the high point of Marie Sallé's career, when she was twenty-seven. After that, she performed intermittently with varying success both in London and Paris, until 1752. She died in 1756, but her appearance in ballets like *Pygmalion* left an unforgettable image with the public of the dancer as an instrument for creating emotional images. Noverre wrote of Sallé:

> We have not forgotten Mademoiselle Sallé's artless expression. Her graces are always in our thoughts. Even though many other dancers have since copied her style, they have not succeeded in overshadowing the nobility, the

harmonious simplicity, the tenderness, the fullness—yet the always modest movements—of that pleasant ballerina.

For while there were many other dancers during that period who took their share of the spotlight, no one compared with the two Maries. Camargo brought technical virtuosity to a high point, and Sallé did the same for expressive emotion. These remain the two great facets of the dance art: formalized movements performed with skill and musical sensitivity on the one hand; and gestures that are made expressively to communicate feeling, on the other. This second facet was the overriding interest of Jean-George Noverre, a name that has been mentioned in passing several times. Now we owe our full and respectful attention to the most famous person of eighteenth-century dance.

Jean-Georges Noverre

Noverre (1727 to 1810) was born the year of Sallé's debut at the Paris Opera. Because of him, 1760 stands out as a memorable date in dance history. By then, ballet had progressed to the point where it boasted a long list of able, professional performers. It had spread through Europe with companies in residence in many cities. This came about with the increasing spread of theater buildings and opera companies beyond Italy, England, and France to Sweden, Austria, Portugal, and so on. Along with an impressive number of fine performers, ballet had also developed a host of problems and shortcomings. After all, if we date the first ballet as 1581—the *Ballet Comique de La Reine*—then by 1760 we are talking about something almost two hundred years old, even if its professional life was much younger. No wonder there were problems!

Anyway, 1760 saw the publication of Noverre's *Letters on Dancing and Ballets*, a series of essays whose main purpose was to attack the same ridiculous approach to choreography and costuming that had caused bad feelings between Sallé and the directors of the opera. We have the book available to us today in a translation by Cyril Beaumont (issued by Dance Horizons). In this excellent work of criticism, Noverre laid down at length and in clear detail his own—and to some extent Sallé's—philosophy of dance. It was one that emphasized this art form as a means of communication: of speech without words. In fact, Noverre held that in expressing emotion, dance was often superior to words. He wrote:

> There are undoubtedly, a great many things which pantomime can only indicate. But in regard to the passions, there is a degree of expression to which words cannot attain—or rather there are passions for which no words exist. Then, dancing allied with action, triumphs.

> A step, a gesture, a movement, and an attitude express what no words can say. The more violent the sentiments it is required to depict, the less able is one to find words to express them. Exclamations, which are the apex to which the language of passions can reach, become insufficient and have to be replaced by gesture.

In order that dance may best reflect nature, Noverre advised the ballet master to observe constantly how the people around him, every day, in every walk of life, move both in their occupations and in their dealings with one another. These and many other thoughts were well appreciated, both during Noverre's lifetime and since then. Fame came to his writings in part because he was such a fine performer himself. Also, several of his pupils rose to high places in and out of dance: Marie Antoinette, the ill-fated queen of France during the revolution, the great dancer Vestris, and the choreographer Dauberval. But most important of all to building his fine reputation was the fact that he himself proved his theories over and over again with renowned, successful entertainments which he created in his position as ballet master at the court of Stuttgart.

Jason and Medea, 1763. This was the best-known work that Noverre produced. Again from Greek mythology, the terrible story went like this. Jason, in order to get back his throne from a wicked uncle who grabbed it unlawfully, needs to find the golden fleece (gold was contained in the magic wool that covered a ram). This treasure is guarded by a dragon, and Jason seeks the help of Medea the sorceress to slay it. In gratitude, Jason stays with Medea for ten years, and she bears him two children. But finally, Jason falls in love with a more appealing young nymph and he runs off with her. Medea goes mad with jealousy. First, she sends a gift of a poisoned mantle to Jason's young beloved, and when the nymph puts it on, it burns her to death. Still not satisfied, Medea kills the two children of Jason's that she bore, and in some versions she serves their hearts to him at a banquet.

With his treatment of this legend, Noverre had a tremendous success. In fact, the work was revived repeatedly with or without his permission, especially by Vestris, who starred in the premiere and broke precedent by appearing without a mask, according to Noverre's direction. In this way he could use facial expression as well as gesture to carry out his heroic role. Incidentally, copying choreography without authorization is a practice that continues. There is no real protection against it because the ballet master can change things around so that his version isn't identical with the original. Better copyright laws have helped, but probably won't entirely eliminate the problem.

Jason and Medea was not universally loved. There were some who objected to a horror story as the scenario for a ballet. As one critic later complained: "I do not wish to see Jason's children strangled, while dancing—perishing on the beat 'neath rhythmic blows by their mother dancer. . ." In fact, in Saint-Hubert's advice on *How to Compose a Successful Ballet*, mentioned in our discussion of the seventeenth-century ballet art, he had warned against doing Homer's *Illiad* in ballet form because the "burning of Troy would scare the ladies." How much worse would they be affected by seeing a mother murder her children? And indeed, it was reported from Stuttgart that at one point during *Jason and Medea* some in the audience fainted, while others fled the hall.

A basic argument over what should be suitably dealt with in dancing still goes on. Martha Graham choreographed *Cave of the Heart* in 1946, telling this same story. Scorn and ridicule, as well as the most ecstatic praise, have been heaped on Graham for such grim creations. In recent years, there have been performances of *The Miraculous Mandarin*, with its complicated plot about multiple murders. It can be gruesome when the same character is killed and rises only to be killed again, which happens here several times. This work has been through many choreographic versions. In the eighteenth century, few ballets were about such gory events as the ones in *Jason and Medea*. Much more usual themes were adventure stories, many with exotic glimpses of far-off places like Turkey, China, and ancient Greece. Then in 1789, a few months before the French Revolution smashed the Old Regime, *La Fille Mal Gardée* appeared in a French provincial theater. This ballet was a story of peasant life, and marked a departure from the heroic themes that had dominated up to that time.

Jean Dauberval

Dauberval (1742 to 1806) choreographed *La Fille Mal Gardée* (1789) to apply Noverre's theories to comedy. Up to then, the master himself had emphasized tragic and lyric emotions, as had those who followed in his footsteps. While it may seem that here was a democratic interest in "the people," particularly considering the nearness of the revolution, today we can see that works like this were almost as exotic and artificial as an eighteenth-century balletic portrait of the Crusades. *La Fille Mal Gardée* was a rose-colored image of "happy peasant" villagers. After all, villages were not far away in actual distance from the theater and the courts; but they were far enough from the life experiences of the middle and upper classes to be wrapped in a romantic glamor. Marie Antoinette, before she lost her head to the revolutionary guillotine, used to enjoy playing peasant maid with some of her ladies-in-waiting at a picturesque, miniature dairy farm, set up specially for her amusement. Whatever one thinks of the nature of these "games," the very fact that stage room was even given to a complete work set in a peasant village did indicate some change in the consciousness

Carla Fracci and Ivan Nagy are the light-hearted lovers in the American Ballet Theater's production of La Fille Mal Gardée.

of the eighteenth-century ballet world about the way people in general spend their lives.

La Fille Mal Gardée has another distinction for a dance history. It is considered the oldest ballet—not the first, still the Ballet Comique de la Reine, which had been produced over two hundred years earlier—but the oldest that is still current in the repertory of several companies in England, the United States, Denmark, and elsewhere. Please keep in mind that these versions are not authentic revivals. Dauberval's choreography and the first musical accompanying score have long since disappeared from both memory and other records. What remains is the village setting, the rough outlines of a comic plot, the idea of combining naturalistic pantomime with dance interludes, the mixture of folk dance and academic ballet steps which today we call caractère, and the use of music based on French folk tunes.

The plot of La Fille Mal Gardée, now as then, concerns a wealthy widow who owns a farm and seeks a suitable marriage for her daughter Lisette. Arranged marriages were as accepted in eighteenth-century village life as they were earlier in the Italy of Romeo and Juliet, and at the French court of Catherine de Medici. Money, not noble birth, is the prize sought here. The widow Simone does find a rich man who owns a vineyard and is eager to find a bride for his son Alain, a good-natured dope. These practical adults agree on a marriage between Lisette and Alain. Of course, Lisette, being a high-spirited beautiful girl, already has a sweetheart of her own choosing: the honest, handsome, but poor Colin.

The attractive couple shares the friendship of all the merry young villagers, and they cooperate to help Lisette and Colin give the old matchmakers the runaround. Since this is a lighthearted comedy, the couple manages to tease old Simone into blessing their union, and the foolish boy and his father take themselves grudgingly off the scene.

Along the way, the action includes byplay with a butter churn and an umbrella, which silly Alain swings around while everybody gets wet in a sudden rainstorm. Dance interludes include a harvest festival in which the young people weave in and out of streamers, and wave kerchiefs, sheaves, and strike tambourines while doing polka and other folk steps in balletic precision. A love duet in straight classical adagio technique, is provided for Lisette and Colin. As much comedy pantomime as possible is milked from the foolish, clumsy Alain, his pushy father, the bossy buxom widow, and the fun-loving villagers. As the curtain lowers on *La Fille Mal Gardée*, we bring to a close the first stage of our ballet history.

Questions for Review

1.   Which balletic style do you prefer, that of Marie Camargo or that of Marie Sallé? Why?

2.   Discuss Noverre's philosophy of dance.

3.   Do you believe that murder is a fit subject for dance?

4.   Describe the choreographic elements of *La Fille Mal Gardée*.

10 HISTORICAL PARADOXES

ART AND SOCIETY IN FRANCE FROM 1789 TO 1820

Ballet in 1789

To refresh your memory, here's a brief review of what the dance world was like on the eve of the French Revolution. Ballet had come of age. Choreography included virtuoso dance sections combined with rhythmic miming. Plots tended to have some unity in either the heroic, the lyrical, or the comic manner. A wide public attended performances in commercial theaters, and were served both by gossipy pieces and by more serious articles about dance in daily newspapers. These factors and the establishment of total professionalism of dance all reflected changing social conditions.

Each generation from 1700 onward was to see an enlargement of academic ballet vocabulary and a soaring of virtuoso dancers. At the same time, new themes and styles of choreography would accord with the spirit of each age, and can be traced to other art forms as well. For example, there are clear generational resemblances between *La Fille Mal Gardée*, Mozart's opera *The Marriage of Figaro*, and Fielding's novel *Tom Jones*—all comedies about boisterous, lower-class figures.

Our art form had travelled far from the *Ballet Comique de la Reine*. Academic technique had developed a long way from amateur courtiers' slow processionals with a few faster, but crude jumps, leaps, and kicks. Now onstage were professionally trained dancers with strong bodies. Their legs turned out at the hips. They made long leaps, high-speed pirouettes, and all kinds of high jumps, including the entrechat, a jump with beating calves.

Carlo Blasis (1795 to 1878). A pupil of Jean Dauberval, who had choreographed *La Fille Mal Gardée*, was to become one of the most important theorists of academic ballet technique. Carlo Blasis made his debut at the age of twelve, and was a premier danseur in Italy, England, and Russia. He recorded his formidable knowledge of dancing in several books. The best-known of these are *The Elementary Treatise* (1820) and *The Code of Terpsichore* (1828).

Carlo Blasis organized the technique of ballet which had been developing for over two hundred years. He is credited with setting the standards and vocabulary of classical ballet technique, which to this day are the basis of traditional schooling. Blasis taught most of the great nineteenth-century dancers.

By 1800, folk steps were also part of the professional vocabulary, stylized and neatened to accord with ballet. Pantomime was studied as well. While there continued to be many changes, after 1789 the general direction of ballet had been determined, and most developments would echo in one way or another what had taken place so far. In addition, we have seen how the major issues that confront the dance world today had for the most part already been raised. For example, is dance an art form suitable for expressing the deepest emotions and human situations, from the most comic to the most tragic, as choreographers from Noverre to Martha Graham have asserted? Or is it best treated as a form of light entertainment, designed to present pleasing designs and impressive displays of skill as justified by Saint-Hubert and Lincoln Kirstein (an important patron of American ballet)? Is the function of the dancer to be primarily a technical virtuoso, like Marie Camargo, or an interpretive actress like Marie Sallé? How should we regard the egotistic rivalries of performers, and the backstage intrigues that are set in motion? Can the journalist-critic serve a useful function for the art form as a whole, or does he merely cater to a malicious, gossip-loving, snobbish public? There are respected, mature artists all over the world today who differ sharply on these issues.

Dance and Politics

Indeed, what is the nature of history itself? Remember that *La Fille Mal Gardée* was produced in July 1789, in the same year and country that saw the start of the bloody events known as the French Revolution. Yet you can examine the ballet in vain for any signs of violence or even of an unsettled population; and you certainly will not find in the choreography any positions regarding the founding of a republic. The ballet ignored government upheaval, just as there was no mention of this—or any ballet—in the declarations issued by the many political assemblies that gathered that year. How can two such completely different human expressions as the French Revolution and a playful ballet exist in one historical time and place? The answer is that history isn't a single stream of feelings and events that sweeps everything along together in one direction. Rather, it is made up of an unending quantity of separate activities large and small, distributed among a tremendous number of fields.

Today's newspaper headlines may scream about a presidential election, yet other things will also be happening in art, science, religion—and dance, with some people paying more attention to these than to the change in government. Our concern here, like that of the choreographer Jean Dauberval and the dancers in his company, is ballet. Professional dancers, whether in 1789 or 1989, have always taken their daily barre practice through political upsets and even wars. Your teacher will explain the importance of pointing the toes properly no matter who is chosen to serve in the government. And choreographers still arrange movement patterns for dancers to perform, with the intention of creating beautiful artworksrather than taking part in political action. However, no matter how apolitical dancers may be, the ballet world could not continue pirouetting in its own orbit, totally undisturbed by King Louis XVI losing his head, or the plots of the Paris terrorists, or the feats of Napoleon. All people are inevitably affected by the large, ongoing events of their time. During the frightening period known as the Reign of Terror (1793 to 1794), when about twenty-five hundred people were executed at the guillotine, many French aristocrats fled across the Channel to England. With them went a number of dancers, who transferred their activities to London theaters.

A government that orders an endless round of killings, on thin political excuses, will press its heavy hand everywhere—including the arts. During these years, a Committee of Public Instruction decided that artists had to be inspired by patriotic ideals, and that their works should promote good citizenship. Good citizenship, of course, was to be defined by those in political control. For example, a painting contest was arranged so that the subject, The Death of Brutus, could be presented as the fate of a noble character who died for liberty and his country. We are not surprised to find, at this same time, a theatrical tragedy with several ballet sections, entitled *Brutus*, by order of executive power in 1793. Interestingly enough, after several rehearsals and the construction of some of the scenery, this was never performed because of political troubles.

However, a lyric *divertissement* with ballets by Gardel, called *The Triumph of the Republic*, whose stated purpose was to deepen the "love of liberty," was performed ten times, beginning on January 27, 1793. And from April 24, 1794, there were twenty-four performances of *The Assembly of August tenth*, or *The Inauguration of the French Republic*, produced by the Committee of Public Instruction. This was a five-act patriotic pageant which included recitals, songs, dances, and artillery salutes, with flowers placed around stage sets of the Bastille and the Arch of Triumph. A procession of actors portraying blind youths represented the newborn citizens of the nation.

The dance art simply doesn't thrive when it is called upon to offer moral-political teaching. Therefore, there were relatively few of these pageants during the French Revolution. For the most part, when unsafe streets didn't close the opera house, the ballet was left to follow its old patterns of entertainment, with Greek and Roman generals, gods and goddesses figuring in pantomimic phrases and fancy stage machinery; and with the action constantly varied by passages of group dancing designed to be pleasing to the eye. One such ballet was choreographer Gardel's *The Judgment of Paris* (1793), which enjoyed a successful run of many years.

Salvatore Viganò (1769 to 1821). Viganò was the outstanding name in dance history from 1789 to 1810. Although born in Italy, he followed the French innovators of our story in a direct line. Viganò studied with Jean Dauberval, who not only choreographed La Fille Mal Gardée, but was also one of the finest pupils of the great Noverre. Viganò first became known as a performer. He and his wife Maria toured European cities in the 1790s, where they made a great hit, having cigars and hairstyles named after them. Viganò not only arranged the choreography for their shows, but much of the music.

Particularly memorable was Maria's appearance in Vienna (1793 to 1795), where she struck a series of poses on stage that were inspired by Greek statues. The sensational two-year run of this number can be attributed less to inventive choreography than to the startling revelation of Maria's naked body, covered only by transparent veils.

Since the 1790s, nudity has been "rediscovered" repeatedly, always causing shock waves of excitement to ripple through the dance atmosphere—notably by Ruth St. Denis who upset prudish Boston in 1906 by arriving onstage bare-legged and bare-waisted; and more recently, by totally nude ballet dancers in John Neumeier's *Rite of Spring* (Hamburg Ballet, 1976). However, once a dancer's naked flesh is seen and talked about by everybody, the interest seems to wane and once again costumes are "rediscovered" as adding variety and attractive lines to the basically familiar human form.

In the early 1800s, Viganò returned to his native Italy to become ballet master of Milan's La Scala Opera House. Here he continued in Noverre's tradition of making unified expressive dance works, which moved audiences emotionally at the same time as they created beautiful pictures. This approach is known as **ballet d'action**, since it follows dramatic plots and imitates life scenes while including a few sequences of dancing just for the sake of beautiful motion or pure design. Viganò created dozens of ballets at La Scala, attracting the interest of Beethoven, who composed *Prometheus* for him, and the novelist Stendhal, who wrote often about the "immortal Viganò" with such praise as, "he is a genius who will make his art grow with him and who has no equal in France."

After this brief flare-up of ballet excellence in Italy, the Paris Opera again moved into center stage, having survived the revolution and the proud Napoleonic Empire by quietly carrying on in a rather uninspired manner under the direction of Pierre Gardel and Louis-Jacques Milon. Their choreography continued to take themes from ancient times and to treat them in a standardized manner, although occasionally audiences experienced worthwhile evenings because of exceptional dancing. Emilie Bigottini (1784 to 1858) impressed her viewers with dramatic interpretations. Auguste Vestris (1760 to 1842) shone as the star of Noverre's ballets, with brilliant technique, as his father Gaetan Vestris had done a generation earlier. Unfortunately, whenever we talk about a fine dancer from a past age, particularly before methods were invented to preserve performances on film or videotape, we have only verbal descriptions to go by. And it is very hard to re-create a dance personality from words alone.

Costume Changes

The only real development in ballet that we can point to during these years of political storms was in stage costume—not just the lack of it, as exhibited by Maria Viganò, but the simplification and softness into which her daring exposure fit logically. Costume in the theater reflected the extreme innovations that were taking place in fashion all over Europe. Seldom in history has there been such a thorough break between old and new clothing fashion, as occurred at the turn of the century, between 1790 and 1810.

The transformation in dress can be linked to ideas of human freedom and naturalism. These were expressed by philosophers like Jean Jacques Rousseau. And of course the ultimate expression was in the political revolutions in France and America that overturned the rule of kings in the name of the people. These revolts were inspired by the French revolutionary demand for liberty, equality, and fraternity. The new costumes can also be linked to influential painters like Jacques David, who presented Greek and Roman characters in authentic dress: simple flowing tunics and loosely gathered hairstyles, according to findings that were then being made in archaeology. This was in marked contrast to the way these characters were dressed in ballets as recently as Noverre's. His Medea, that hateful Greek queen who murdered her children, danced her fury onstage wearing a tight, long-waisted, low-cut bodice, joined to a stiff skirt that was distended beyond all reason to encase her bottom half in a tremendous, rigid cage of fabric. Topping this all off was an absurd pomaded, powdered hairdo, piled up perhaps a foot high on the ballerina's head. This was all merely carrying a little further the latest dress that was in vogue offstage.

Marie Sallé was described in the previous chapter as dancing her *Pygmalion* in a thin shift, as far back as 1734. But while she foreshadowed the trends that were to arrive at the end of the century, she did not seem to affect the practice in her own time. By 1790, all the exaggerated stiffness was giving way to loose-flowing, plain gowns, and relatively simple hairstyles. Thus Maria Viganò's nudity in 1793 was merely carrying a little further the latest statements in dress and undress that were in vogue onstage and offstage.

Thus is ballet touched by developments in the other arts, in philosophy, and in society at large. This last statement seems to contradict the point made early in this chapter that history "is made up of an unending quantity of separate activities." Well really, both these things are true, because: all events influence each other; each particular field—like ballet—has its own inner life that is partially independent; individuals like Marie Sallé often make unique creations that are a little like biological mutants, seemingly unrelated to what is going on around them.

Questions for Review

1.   Are you familiar with any dance compositions that have political content? Do you find them interesting or enjoyable?

2.   Discuss changes in ballet costume, from 1581 to 1789.

11 ROMANTIC BALLET

THE TAGLIONI INFLUENCE

Romanticism

A sigh of nostalgia for the Romantic ballerina has been echoed thousands of times, particularly after performances of *Giselle*, which has become one of the all-time favorites of the ballet repertory. If *Giselle* still has such great appeal 150 years after its premiere, then there must be something in Romanticism that speaks in a language more universal than that of the Parisian French of the 1840s. In fact *Romanticism* is the word historians use to describe much of European culture in the nineteenth century. Similar attitudes and ideas were expressed in poetry, novels, paintings, symphonic music, as well as ballet during that period. What united all these creations was their emphasis on the emotions. Imagination, flying free, was carried aloft by the supercharged feelings of excited artists.

    Emotion in Ballet. You may well ask: Isn't all art always concerned with imagination and feelings? And the answer would have to be yes. Any dance (or painting, poem, or play for that matter) expresses feelings, and they need not be happy ones. For example, both *Romeo and Juliet* and *La Fille Mal Gardée* are about the same thing. Two young people love each other, against the wishes of the girl's elders, who have plans for her to marry someone else. *Romeo and Juliet* in its many versions expresses dread, dismay, and needless, youthful death. The pantomimic movements in this ballet are seriously dramatic, the story has a tragic ending, and the music and many of the dance patterns are heavy with foreboding. On the other hand, in *La Fille Mal Gardée*, the pantomime is light and playful, even slap-stick. The story ends happily. The music and the dance patterns are light, bouncy, and folksy, arranged in symmetrical designs. Therefore this ballet always expresses feelings of carefree harmony and foolishness. We do not go to see either of these ballets—or any others—for information and intellectual stimulation, but rather for emotional experience.

The difference that marked the Romantic Age was not the discovery of emotion, but the central place assigned to it, both in the theme itself and also in its treatment. The Romantic artist was less interested in telling a story than in delving deeply into feelings, his own and those of the characters he described. And for the most part, these feelings were not the ones that accompany the daily routine of living, but those that arise in solitude, at night, or while daydreaming. The Romantic artist was introspective, and therefore often gloomy. Or else he dreamed about far-off places, fairy-tale settings for exotic adventures. Romanticism was fantasy that stemmed from a sense of dissatisfaction with the here and now; a longing for distance in either time or space; a wish to escape from present reality. Its themes were poetic love that could never be real, foreign exotic scenes, and spiritual creatures that resembled people, but couldn't be grasped by ordinary men. Historically, the Romantic movement reached its peak in the years following the French Revolution and the Napoleonic wars. Because of this timing, it has been explained by many historians as a disillusioned reaction against the excesses of war and politics; a desire to get away from the grim truth. However, even when reality is not so horrible, perhaps only fixed into boring routine, the idea of an imaginative escape is appealing.

It would be hard to find a more dreamy, sentimental image than that of the fairylike Romantic ballerina, floating as an unattainable figure of pure love, above mere mortal men. The steamy, hothouse climate of Paris in the 1820s turned the city into a breeding ground for exotic ballets, of which *Giselle* and *La Sylphide* later emerged as the shining examples. But *Giselle* still has top billing in the ballet repertory. And it is therefore Giselle who calls down through the ages from the spirit world, and awakens poetic longing in many hearts, especially in Act II when she dances after her death with her beloved prince.

Ballet and Opera. In 1800, the center of the ballet world was still Paris, although for a while during the Reign of Terror, London took over. There was also ballet activity as far north as Sweden, as far east as Russia, and as far west as the United States. The main setting for important new productions was the Paris Opera. This meant that ballets were often designed as amusing diversions in full-length opera productions. Even when ballet evenings were given separately, the choreographers, composers, scene designers, and performers were hired by the opera director.

Opera, like ballet, had its roots in elaborate Italian Renaissance spectacles. At first, both forms were related to theatrical drama, taking their plots from ancient Greece and Rome. To carry along the action, the opera substituted singing for dialogue, while the ballet substituted mime for speech. Also included were passages of just song, or just dance. Both depended for their appeal, to a large extent, on cleverly engineered scenery. And both were closely intertwined with the historical development of music.

Ever since their birth, ballet and opera have grown along parallel lines, first at the courts and then in the more widely attended public theaters. Today they share the honor of being the most expensive art forms to produce. At any rate, they have been reared together intimately, often sharing one opera theater and one management, supported by subsidies of royal courts, civil governments, or wealthy establishment patrons. When they are together like this, the ballet is the subordinate unit. After all, dancing is often found as part of an opera, but who ever heard of opera being only part of a ballet?

Ballet of the Nuns

This ballet appeared in the third act of the opera *Robert le Diable* in 1831, and at its premiere it scored immediately with the public. Now you have to suffer through a long list of credits, because many of the names connected with this work have relevance for the whole of our Romantic golden age. Of course, some are notable only because they are linked with this pace-setting opera. The music was composed by Giacomo Meyerbeer. The libretto (scenario) was written by Eugène Scribe. The scenery was designed by Pierre Ciceri and Henri Duponchel. The choreography was arranged by Filippo Taglioni. The leading dance roles were performed by Marie Taglioni as the abbess and Adolphe Nourrit as Robert. And the opera manager was Louis Véron.

We now consider the contribution of each of these people. Histories of music refer to Meyerbeer (German born) as the most successful practitioner of the form known as French grand spectacle opera. Naturally this form included ballet interludes. The music for the *Ballet of the Nuns* was described as diabolical and highly effective. *Libretto*, which means the word script to be sung, as well as the scenario, was by a playwright. Eugène Scribe was not only the most popular and prolific playwright of his day, turning out almost five hundred plays, he also merits a mention in our field as a scenarist.

We generally think of a scenarist as one who outlines the plot, charac-ters, and situations of a movie. The word is also used for one who does this service for a ballet. Before Scribe, during the 1800s, the choreographer had usually been his own scenarist. He would settle for following the outlines of a drama already written: as Noverre did with the Greek play *Jason and Medea;* or Dauberval, who choreographed *La Fille Mal Gardée* after a comic opera libretto of 1758. Scribe changed this approach in 1827, when he pro-vided a scenario for *La Somnambule (The Sleepwalker).* Four years before the premiere of *Robert le Diable (Robert the Devil),* *La Somnambule* was successful precisely because of Scribe's contribution. His subject of a sleepwalker allowed for suspenseful moments in movement as the sleeping heroine unknowingly made her way along a roof, in danger of falling to her death. This proved a welcome change from the ancient legendary heroes that had occupied the ballet scene for over two hundred years. Further, it foreshad-owed the aerial themes and the psychological mysteries that were to seep into so many Romantic ballets.

Now, with *Robert le Diable,* the opera-ballet made another leap from Mount Olympus into the airy, eerie vapors of wispy phantoms. Greek and Roman gods and mortals were dismissed from center stage, which was now crowded instead with figures of the German poetic imagination, both on the floor and hovering above it. You see, Romanticism started out as a literary movement—actually with German novels, poems, and plays. So when writers turned their attention to ballet, as Scribe and then the play-wright Saint-Georges and the poet Gautier did (these last two were later to provide the scenario for *Giselle),* the immediate effect was a complete shift in subject matter.

Writers brought with them the ideas and themes that were popular in their own fields. Goethe's novel *The Sorrows of Young Werther,* about a young man who wallowed in hopeless misery through a foredoomed love affair, had appeared in 1774 and had quickly become a runaway best-seller. Byron's poem about a prisoner of Chilton has this message, "I learned to love despair," a line that sums up Goethe's novel of self-pity, and many other popular works of the day. Another favorite literary character was the supernatural being—whether ghost or sylph—who was enough like a per-son to attract human passion, but who tended to fade away when touched by a love-sick mortal.

This last idea was to be featured in *La Sylphide* and *Giselle,* but some of the elements were present in *Robert le Diable.* Scribe's plot for the opera has Robert, a wicked knight, craving the love of Princess Isabelle. He can win her love with the aid of a magic stone, which he must seek from a statue of Saint Rosalie in the graveyard of a ruined cloister. The *Ballet of the Nuns* takes place at night, in the cemetery, where Robert is surrounded by spirits of dead nuns, who are damned because they broke their religious vows. They dance in wicked abandon, led by their abbess Helena, who tries to lure Robert to disaster. Finally, however, he reaches the statue, grabs the magic charm, and with its help makes his way safely through the group of nuns who weakly sink back to their waiting demons.

The tremendous impact made by this ballet scene came partly from the striking originality of the subject matter. Nuns in themselves were a departure from the usual. But wicked nuns! They were a real attention getter. The evil insinuations of the music also strengthened the drama. But a large share of the credit must go to Duponchel, who designed the scene, and Ciceri who painted it. We see a lot of ballets in the twentieth century that are performed on a bare stage, and so we sometimes forget what a prominent role ballet gave to stage settings in earlier years. For the *Ballet of the Nuns,* Henri Duponchel conceived the idea which Pierre Ciceri carried out, which was to create a mysterious night atmosphere, quite different from the ordinary bright or stormy landscape generally seen.

As visual artists, Duponchel and Ciceri would probably have been aware of the moonlit images in paintings by German Romantics like Casper David Friedrich. At any rate, they took advantage of the advanced lighting equipment that had recently been installed at the opera house by the new opera director Louis Véron to create a memorable poetic scene. Moonlight was exactly right for the Romantic themes of supernatural spirits, love-sick melancholy, and mystical charms. Ciceri caught this same atmosphere again later in *La Sylphide,* and it was to be taken up repeatedly by other ballet designers, as the moonlit landscape became a symbol for Romanticism.

What about those artists without whom there wouldn't be any ballet at all: the dancers and the choreographer? Wasn't there anything outstanding about the dancing in *Robert le Diable?* Yes, there certainly was. Marie Taglioni (1804 to 1884) triumphed in the part of the abbess Helena, which her father Filippo Taglioni had choreographed, and for which he had coached her.

Taglioni's Style

For many historians, Marie Taglioni's dance personality is synonomous with the whole concept of Romantic ballet. She had made her Paris Opera debut in 1827, four years before the premiere of *Robert le Diable.* But her appearance in the *Ballet of the Nuns,* with its dance of dead maidens, made a strong identification between Marie Taglioni and supernatural fantasy, an idea that was confirmed in *La Sylphide,* which we'll look at in a minute. In these two productions, Taglioni's personal style matched perfectly with that of the works themselves, and the combination suited the spirit of the times.

What Taglioni did was to revolutionize the approach to ballet dancing. She changed it in two ways: first of all, through her attitude toward technique; and secondly, through her performing manner. Taglioni's mastery of technical difficulties was outstanding, but she added to that an illusion of effortless grace that was in marked contrast to what had been usual before her appearance, when a performer swaggered before the audience as though saying, "Look how good I am in these almost impossibly hard steps!" Further, in performing style, Taglioni allowed the dance role to be the focus of attention, rather than burying the content of the choreography under her own feminine charms and flirting tricks. The fashion before Taglioni was called the *danse noble*, the classical style with its mannered poses, stiffness, stereotyped smiles. In 1840, a critic compared the state of ballet performance before and after Taglioni's arrival on the scene:

> Before her appearance, the sceptre of the dance was entrusted to the hands, or rather the legs, of Messieurs Paul and Albert. Theirs was a dance of the springboard and the public square, and the daughters of Terpsichore [old style] were founded in their image.
>
> No elegance, no taste; frightful pirouettes, horrible efforts of muscle and calf, legs ungracefully stretched, stiff and raised to the level of the eyes or the chin the whole evening long; tours de force, the grand écart, the perilous leap. All the male dancers were brought up in this school and built on this model.
>
> The female dancers dislocated themselves by imitating these muscular and semaphoric exercises.
>
> Then Marie Taglioni appeared and started a revolution against the rule of the pirouette, but a revolution that was gently accomplished, through the irresistible power of grace, perfection and beauty in the art.
>
> Marie Taglioni loosened the legs, softened the muscles, gradually changed by her example the tasteless routine and unstylish attitudes, taught the art of seductive poses and correct and harmonious lines, and founded the double kingdom of grace and strength, the most beautiful and most pleasing and rarest of kingdoms.

We have this and other detailed descriptions of all these matters, because no fewer than thirty-four newspapers and periodicals were printed in Paris with columns about ballet and opera. Many letters and memoirs from the period have also been preserved. The quotations in this chapter are found in Ivor Guest's *The Romantic Ballet in Paris*.

Marie Taglioni is also remembered for her gliding *en pointe*. Although Taglioni did not invent this use of the foot—rising up to, and moving on the very tips of the toes—she did popularize it by the light, floating quality she gave these steps. Thus Taglioni won her fame through the combination of great skill and attitude of ease. Along with this, she refused to empha-size her feats of technique; and maintained an air of aloof dignity that was a departure from standard ballerina conduct. For much of this we must thank her father Filippo Taglioni, who was her demanding private tutor. Not only did he put his daughter through a daily torturous physical routine, as severe as any ballet schooling has ever been, but he insisted on modest decorum in performance.

Ballet masters at the Paris Opera were known for preaching quite another line. Opera director Véron wrote in his memoirs, that along with pliés and pirouettes, teachers gave instructions to promote:

> elegance, seduction; they insisted on provocative smiles, poses and attitudes that were almost immodest and shameless. One was often heard telling his pupils, "My dears, be charming, coquettish; display the most alluring freedom in every move you make; you must inspire love both during and after your 'pas' and make the audience and orchestra desirous of sleeping with you!"

Véron went on to point out that Filippo Taglioni's instructions were exactly the opposite. Taglioni demanded graceful ease of movement, lightness and especially ballon; but he did not allow his daughter a sin-gle gesture or pose which might be lacking in decency or modesty. He told her: "Women and young girls must be able to watch your dance without blushing; your performance should be marked by restraint, delicacy and good taste." Accordingly, one woman in the audience wrote after Marie Taglioni's opera debut, "Here is a new style of danc-ing, graceful beyond all comparison. . ." And she was particularly charmed by the "decent dignity" with which Taglioni acknowledged the clapping and cheering that burst out at the end: "This was very unlike the leering smiles with which, in general, a danseuse thinks it necessary to advance to the front of the proscenium, showing all her teeth, as she slowly curtsies to the audience."

Filippo Taglioni carefully guarded his daughter's unique style, and when she was elevated to the position of first soloist at the opera, one of the conditions in the contract was that her father would arrange her pieces, and also be engaged as ballet master. Opera director Louis Véron's gen-erosity with both Taglionis was justified by the success of the *Ballet of the Nuns* in *Robert le Diable*, in November 1831. But when this was followed by the reception given to *La Sylphide* in March 1832, Véron not only won a place for himself in dance history, but he made money for the opera—and himself. When he retired in 1835, it was with a personal profit of about one million francs. Adolphe Nourrit, who danced the title role in *Robert le Diable*, is not important in our history for that reason, but because he was the scenarist for *La Sylphide*.

Carla Fracci in "La Sylphide" has been called the twentieth-century Taglioni.

La Sylphide

With *La Sylphide*, the Romantic ballet reached full flower. In the theater, it was a moment of complete triumph for a theme whose time had come, for the inspired designers of movement patterns, stage settings, and costumes, and above all, for a dancer who seemed born to embody a poetic image of Romanticism.

First, a note of caution. Don't confuse La Sylphide (singular) with Les Sylphides (plural). Les Sylphides, a scene of winged fairies dancing in a moonlit forest around a dreamy youth, was choreographed many years later by Fokine, who wanted to revive the spirit of Romanticism, when once again ballet had deteriorated into a free-for-all for acrobats and showoffs. You may have seen Les Sylphides which is given by many companies. You may even have danced in some of its Chopin-accompanied patterns in class. The chances are, however, that you have not seen La Sylphide, although there are some versions of it around, notably in the repertory of the Royal Danish Ballet and the American Ballet Theater. But if you were part of the ballet public in the 1830s, you undoubtedly would have seen La Sylphide—and more than once.

La Sylphide, 1832, tells the story of a winged sylph who falls in love with a mortal Scotsman, James. She comes to him with a kiss, on the night before he is to marry Effie, a fully human girl. Because of this beautiful vision, James cannot bring himself to go ahead with the wedding. Running out on Effie, he follows the sylph into a forest. Although she keeps fading out of sight, he catches up with her at dawn. When he finally reaches out to capture her, her wings fall off and she drops to her death. Grief-stricken, James is left alone, standing in the shadow of the trees as a wedding procession is seen passing in the distance. Effie has married another peasant lad, who loved her all along.

To understand the instant and continuing appeal of the theme, you must not think of the story literally. A man who abandons a flesh-and-blood, luscious bride, to chase after a dimly seen winged spirit, sounds like a dimwit. The fascination becomes acceptable if you look at the sylph as a symbol, which is the way she was viewed by the French public in 1832. A symbol of what? In a general way, the creature of flight stood for the spiritual half of man's nature. Victor Hugo, a French playwright who was a major spokesman for Romanticism, wrote in a preface to a play in 1824:

> Christianity told man "you have a double nature. You are composed of two beings, the one perishable, the other immortal; the one flesh, the other spirit." One is chained by appetites, needs and passions. The other is carried on the wings of ecstasy and vision. The former always falls towards the earth, its mother; the latter constantly shoots towards heaven, its father.

The sylph therefore became a dance symbol of the poetic fantasy which lifts people away from everyday physical reality.

The sylph represents a young man's dream, his ideal vision, whether of beauty, art, love, or politics. This can be carried over to the disillusionment after the French Revolution. How magnificent the concepts of liberty, equality, and brotherhood! Compare the dream to the bloody terror that became the reality. Specifically, the sylph is the vision of a perfect love. In real life, such a dream is never fulfilled. Hence, when grasped, the wings fall off and the vision fades away. You can consider more realistically the future of the happy couple Lisette and Colin in *La Fille Mal Gardée*. It is easy to imagine them both growing a little stout and quarreling about money. To the Romantic poet, such a future was totally unacceptable. Being forced to settle for prosaic affection and the ordinary ups and downs of a relationship would be an intolerable compromise with a man's search for love. If he couldn't have his perfect, spiritual, eternal love, he would choose lonely misery or even death.

The scenarist for *La Sylphide*, Adolphe Nourrit, was known in his day not as a poet but as a tenor in the opera. He took the male lead in *Ballet of the Nuns*. However, his literary interests were demonstrated several times after he did the plot for *La Sylphide*, with his name appearing on a number of ballet scenarios. For this most famous work, he had several literary models for inspiration, particularly the story *Trilby*, which was also set in Scotland. But instead of a peasant lad longing for a female sylph, *Trilby* tells of a young fisherman's wife who was lured by the advances of an unearthly male creature. Thrown into a deep, psychological conflict by her desires, divided between normal happiness with her husband and her dreamy longings for mystical experience as represented by the elfin Trilby, the heroine dies. Despite the reversal of sex roles, the resemblance between *Trilby* and *La Sylphide* is quite clear. It would seem that scenarist Nourrit also felt too deeply, within himself, some kind of conflict between reality and dream, because seven years after *La Sylphide* came out, he committed suicide by jumping from a hotel room in Naples.

La Sylphide symbolized for one viewer nothing less than political freedom. This interpretation was included in a ballet review in the newspaper *Le Constitutionel:* "For a sylphide, as for a people, liberty is life. Deprived of wings, she ceases to exist." This was a disappointed reference to the French Revolution of 1830, as much as it was an explanation of the ballet. A modern viewer will not associate the wings of a ballerina's costume with political revolution. However, whether he recognizes the reason or not, if he enjoys and gets a lift from a Romantic ballet, it is because he shares with the viewers of 1830 a response to a winged vision of some beautiful ideal, a sense of escaping from the gravity of earthly problems. Today, this theme proves its universal appeal time and again for audiences as far apart as Tashkent, Russia and Havana, Cuba.

Interestingly enough, the director of the opera, Véron, was given his job after the revolution in the summer of 1830. Changes in public opinion and in the new government's financial policy brought about the separation of the opera from the royal court, where both it and the ballet had been from their beginnings. This separation meant that a director would be chosen to run the opera as a private business for profit. As noted above, Dr. Louis Véron, the first director under the new system, so well understood the business side of entertainment that he made a lot of money. (Those who followed him did not.) It is instructive to read Véron's formula for success, which he later set down in his memoirs:

> Dramas and comedies of manners do not come within the choreographer's scope; in a ballet the public demands above all a varied and striking score, new and unusual costumes, a great variety, contrasting sets, surprises, transformation scenes, and a simple plot which is easy to follow and in which the dance develops naturally out of the situations.
>
> To all that must be added the charm of a young and beautiful dancer who dances better and differently than those who have preceded her. If one is aiming neither at the intelligence nor at the heart, one must appeal to the senses and most particularly to the eyes.

Véron's opinion of ballet as an art form whose main appeal was to the eyes was echoed by Gautier, a famous poet and dance critic who is best remembered in the dance world for inspiring the creation of *Giselle*. In a ballet review in 1837, Gautier wrote:

> Without a doubt, spiritualism is a respectable thing. But in making a dance, one does well to make concessions to materialism. The dance after all, has no other aim but to exhibit beautiful forms in graceful poses, and to develop lines pleasing to the eye...
>
> The dance is less suited to presenting metaphysical ideas. It only expresses feelings: love and desire with all their coquettries. The man is aggressive, and the woman modestly defends herself—the theme of all primitive dance.

Gautier loved ballet, but he limited its sphere to sex appeal and pleasing the eye, as did the opera director Véron. Needless to say, we can find a contradiction between Gautier's statement of 1837 that denies spiritualism in ballet, and his responsibility in 1841 for the theme of *Giselle*, which ranks with *La Sylphide* as a symbol of Romantic spirituality. It seems that both Véron and Gautier underrated ballet. It is true that many people go only for eye-filling spectacle or to be amused by a pretty girl (or boy). But there is often more to be found in a dance work, even if it is not easy to pin down exactly what it is.

A dance work presents ideal figures, in the person of dancers, carefully shaped by years of special preparation. It presents images, created onstage by the combined effect of these figures, their movement patterns enhanced by costume and scenery, ideas and music. These images can be compared to the statements made in poetry. They produce associations in the viewer's mind that awaken feelings and ideas. For example, a long, lifting leap can suggest flight, freedom, or ecstasy. When it is exquisitely performed, along with stirring music, it can bring the viewer an experience that is richer and more complex than simply visual pleasure. Even if the experience cannot be summed up in words, we know it occurs, because we have felt it. In this way, the excitement of the Paris audiences in 1832 at *La Sylphide*, and in the 1840s at *Giselle*, can be understood, as can that of audiences at hundreds of performances of Romantic ballets like these, down to the present. Therefore the statements of Véron and Gautier, along with those of certain twentieth-century producers, can be discounted. Very often, we find that people who themselves make important contributions to the dance art in practice, fall down quite clumsily when it comes to theoretical explanations.

At any rate, one reason for the tremendous reception given to *La Sylphide* came from a theme that was suited perfectly to the temper of the times. Of course, along with the theme, or idea, there was also the way it was carried out in dance, music, in stage setting, and costume. The music, composed by Schneitzhoeffer (the French ballet world had a terrible time pronouncing this name!) does not seem to have been one of the ballet's strong points. In fact, the Danish version that survives today is accompanied by a different score. There was a mixed reception for Schneitzhoeffer's original score, with some critics praising it and others complaining that it was weak. No matter. The visual atmosphere made up for whatever was lacking in sound. The setting by Ciceri, particularly the forest touched by dawn in the second act, when James pursues the sylph, was considered a masterpiece.

As for the costume, tradition credits this ballet with the introduction of the full, bell-shaped tutu that extends down to mid-calf, which is associated with all Romantic ballet. In fact, these ballets, with their endless yards of white gauze drifting about the legs of ballerinas, are also called *ballets blancs*, "white ballets," because of the popularity of this costume. Never mind that similar skirts were not that unusual in performances before *La Sylphide*, and that they only reached their full size quite a bit later. A number of ballet traditions rest on inaccurate information. Just as Marie Taglioni is mistakenly thought to have invented toe-dancing, she is also remembered incorrectly as appearing in *La Sylphide* in the first bell-shaped tutu. The persistence of these false traditions really means that Taglioni's strong impression in *La Sylphide* led to her being credited with inventing all the new developments that characterize the Romantic ballet. Because beyond the theme, the scenery, or anything else, it was Taglioni's dancing that made *La Sylphide* such a sensation. From her debut in 1827, to her interpretation of the abbess Helena in *Robert le Diable*, Taglioni had already won fame for her highly skilled, unassuming dancing, particularly her gliding *en pointe* and her ethereal manner.

As noted earlier, it is impossible to separate her own part in this from her father Filippo Taglioni's. It was he who trained his daughter, and Filippo was satisfied with nothing less than technical perfection. He was the one responsible for emphasizing dance in her performance, rather than sex appeal or personality. And finally, it was Filippo Taglioni who arranged the choreography for Marie, in which she shone so brightly. Unfortunately we have very little information about the choreography in *La Sylphide*. The surviving Danish version by Auguste Bournonville uses only the libretto—the scenario of the original. And we have seen that it uses another musical score. Not surprisingly, Bournonville created his own steps and patterns, rather than taking Filippo Taglioni's.

A brief comment from one spectator mentions an original effect in Taglioni's choreography in which the sylphs advanced from "the back of the stage, in groups of four, to form a delightful group in the very front." That is not much help in imagining the way the ballet proceeded! However, the audience does not usually observe the choreography very well, but tends to see the dancer who is physically before them.

Choreography often stands or falls on the performer's personality and ability. Marie Taglioni may have learned her art from Filippo, and was executing his steps. But Marie was onstage, not Filippo, and in the public mind she was *La Sylphide,* because the subject was perfectly suited to the Paris taste of 1832 and to Marie Taglioni's temperament. The ballerina once said of herself, "I have spiritual hands and feet." It is also true that she was not comfortable in the part of the abbess Helena, which included a seduction scene in the moonlit graveyard. Although she was highly praised in the *Ballet of the Nuns,* Marie asked to be replaced after three performances.

In *La Sylphide* she found the role of a lifetime. It was absolutely right as the setting for her ethereal, poetic style. While her father had helped form this style, he in turn was inspired by the magical quality of her dancing, and his choreography for this masterwork reflected it. The afterimage that Marie Taglioni left here was that of "a shadow condensed into a mist." One review raved:

> There is a sequence of furtive, aerial steps, something ravishing beyond all description....The irresolute flight of a butterfly, those round tufts which the mild wind of April plucks like down from the cups of flowers and balances in the air, these are the only points of comparison with the timid graces, the mocking abandon, and the artful modesty of the Sylphide.
>
> Really Taglioni is no mortal. God could not have imagined the cherubim better.

Earlier, when Marie Taglioni first became the darling of the public, the word *taglioniser* was used to describe a light, floating dance technique. After the premiere of *La Sylphide,* the word itself—*sylphide*—was heard everywhere to describe dresses, hairstyles, and moods. The ballet became such a fad that two periodicals with ballet and theater news came out, one called *Sylph* and another called *Sylphide.*

Relative Importance of Male and Female Dancers. If such titles were conferred in the arts as they are in beauty contests, Marie Taglioni would have been unanimously acclaimed Miss Sylphide and even Miss Romantic Ballet. Don't bother to look for Mr. Romantic Ballet. The ballerina Taglioni summarized the Romantic ballet style. Her eminence in *La Sylphide* was the origin of the one-sided feminine emphasis in ballet. This art form swings from one extreme to the other in its sexist attitudes. A hundred years earlier, when Louis XIV took the stage as the Sun God, you can bet that this glittering male peacock was the center of all attention and the focus of the action. In fact, it was considered improper for women even to appear onstage. Men, dressed in skirts, took women's roles. Then the situation reversed itself. George Balanchine has often been quoted as saying, "ballet is a woman." This idea can be traced directly to *La Sylphide* and to ballerina Marie Taglioni as the visual symbol of the mysterious, elusive, feminine ideal. The male dancer was demoted from a masterly, dashing figure, spinning around on strong muscular legs, to a servant who waited around at the ballerina's feet. His job was to lift her and extend the image of her weightlessness by carrying her through space as though suspended.

In his book on the theory and practice of dancing, Carlo Blasis had stressed multiple pirouettes in his training manual. The male dancers of the 1820s had brought multiple pirouettes to the height of virtuosity. (Emphasis on jumps for men was a later, Russian contribution.) Perhaps because the male dancers made too much of a good thing, they helped bring about their own downfall. They overdid pirouettes, dragging them in whenever possible in order to dazzle the spectators. These monotonous repetitions may well have been partly responsible for the decline in male importance through the 1800s. Certainly during the golden age of Romantic ballet, there was only one popular male dancer, Jules Perrot (1810 to 1892), while there were many favorite ballerinas in addition to Taglioni, as we shall see.

There is no doubt that by 1840 the ballet world was clearly a matri-archy, as mirrored in this typical reaction of one newspaper writer:

> You know we are hardly a supporter of what are called the "grand danseurs" [the male ballet stars]. The "grand danseur" appears to us so sad and heavy! He is so unhappy and so self-satisfied! He responds to nothing, he represents nothing, he is nothing.
>
> Speak to us of a pretty dancing girl who displays the grace of her features and the elegance of her figure, who reveals so fleetingly all the treasures of her beauty. Thank God I understand that perfectly. I know what this lovely creature wishes us, and I would willingly follow her wherever she wishes in the sweet land of love.
>
> But a man, frightful man, as ugly as you and I, a wretched fellow who leaps about without knowing why, a creature specially made to carry a musket and a sword and to wear a uniform. That this fellow should dance as a woman does—impossible!
>
> Today, thanks to this revolution which we have effected, woman is the queen of ballet. She breathes and dances there at her ease. She is no longer forced to cut off half her silk petticoat to dress her partner with it. Today the dancing man is no longer tolerated except as a useful accessory. He is the shading of the picture, the green box trees surrounding the garden flowers, the necessary foil.

All this came about after *La Sylphide*. A foreshadowing hint of this develop-ment can be read into the birth of Nourrit's scenario. As noted before, his inspiration is credited to the novel *Trilby*, which concerned a peasant woman and a male elfin creature. If Nourrit changed the male to a female fairy, it was partly to give Taglioni a suitable role. But the deeper reason was that the French public of 1830 was in a mood to elevate the ballerina above her male partner. While Nijinsky, Nureyev, and others have restored prestige to the male dancer, in many circles the art of ballet is still often considered effeminate. This prejudice can be traced to the Romantic ballet, and to *La Sylphide*—Marie Taglioni.

Questions for Review

1.   Discuss Romanticism as the spirit of an age, and in ballet.

2.   What has been the relationship between opera and ballet since the Renaissance in Europe?

3.   What are the elements that made *La Sylphide* <u>the</u> Romantic ballet?

4.   Discuss the relative position of the sexes in ballet before and after Marie Taglioni's starring position at the Paris Opera.

12 EXOTIC VOYAGES

THE IMPACT OF FANNY ELSSLER

Up to now, we have been looking at the Romantic ballet as all moonbeams and shadows. However, if you want to escape from reality, it isn't necessary to get lost in a melancholy dream. An imaginative trip to far-away places also fills this need. With Fanny Elssler (1810 to 1884) a ballerina who arrived on the scene in 1834, the opera public basked in the bright sunlight of exotic passions, and was soon divided in loyalty between her and Taglioni.

Spanish Dance. Even before Elssler, the ballet public saw dances that expressed the spirit of far-off lands. In fact, native Spanish dancers performed in Paris for the first time. Because civil war threatened to break out in their own country, and caused the theaters in Madrid to be closed, four leading Spanish dancers accepted a contract with Dr. Véron at the Paris Opera. Like audiences everywhere, down to the present day, the Paris of 1834 responded enthusiastically to the tricky Spanish footwork, the exciting sounds of the castanets, and the proud posture of the dancers. Nothing like this had been seen at the opera, and the reviewers raved, "brilliant, alive, poetic, strongly colored, captivating, full of charm, seduction, passion and fire." (Quotations in this chapter come from Ivor Guest's *Fanny Elssler*.)

At about the same time, Filippo Taglioni was adding foreign spices to the ballets he was arranging for daughter Marie, after *La Sylphide*. The exotic character that he put in his works was certainly not authentic—really a flavoring. But it answered a need in the Romantic public, similar to that filled by the genuine Spanish artists. One piece, *La Revolte Au Serail*, was set

Spanish dancers strike a pose from this ever-popular dance form.

in Granada, Spain during the Moslem conquests. It was complete with a ruling Moorish sultan, and a harem scene, with Marie as a slave girl, leading an armed revolt against the Sultan. Another, *Brézilia*, showed a primitive tribe of women in South America, pledging themselves to hate the male sex.

New Female Images. Interestingly enough, along with their exotic overtones, these themes reflected growing ideas of female liberation. Although often enough, the ballets ended with the men and women embracing in happy, traditional fashion, you can see a new, vigorous, female image, when there is a slave girl carrying weapons, or a tribe of women who band together against men. Perhaps because the instrument of the ballet art is the human body, from time to time sex roles are emphasized, and often inverted. As the male dancer constantly lost ground through the golden age of ballet, so women could be accepted as warriors, or as sufficient unto themselves without men. Fanny Elssler was to be partnered frequently by her tall sister. Therese, in a man's costume; and Fanny herself was to enchant audiences in a role where she was disguised as an army officer. And as you will soon see, the Wilis in *Giselle* had as their aim forcing men to dance to their death. Both in *La Revolte Au Serail* and in *Brézilia*, Marie Taglioni was acclaimed, but these productions didn't make ideal material for her understated reserve. It was in *La Revolte Au Serail* (1833) that her partner Jules Perrot received more applause than she did, enraging Marie. A stage personality who did not possess Marie Taglioni's spiritual dignity was called for to give audiences the glamour and thrills they seemed to want. Fanny Elssler appeared to answer this need.

Taglioni-Elssler Rivalry

After Véron had raised Marie Taglioni to a position of supremacy among the ballerinas at the opera, he deliberately introduced and promoted Fanny Elssler to rival her. About the same time, incidentally, he let Jules Perrot go—another sign of the lack of attention paid to male dancers. Perrot was a brilliant dancer, well above any other man around. Yet Véron wouldn't meet his demands, as he was prepared to do with Elssler. In her case, he had acted wisely. It was good business to let Elssler challenge Taglioni, because the competition interested people. They wanted to compare and judge the two stars, and so they came often to the ballet. In fact, the management encouraged the presence of claques, which were groups of people paid to applaud a particular performer. It was also good art. Variety and contrast are as desirable in performing styles as they are in choreography. Not only is it more interesting to see varied styles, it is necessary. After all, if ballet is to be considered a genuine art form, it must be capable of expressing a wide range of human feelings and ideas.

Fanny Elssler, who was born and trained in Vienna, had already toured as a solo dancer when opera director Véron saw her perform, and offered her a contract, together with her sister, Therese. While it was obvious that Fanny was the more talented, she would not come alone, without her older sister, who acted as business manager and also danced with Fanny. Just as any dealings with Marie Taglioni had to take her father Filippo into account, any dealings with Fanny Elssler had to include her sister Therese.

Elssler's Début. In 1834, Fanny made her Paris debut in *La Tempête*. Many of the names connected with this work have already appeared in our story, or will be heard again. Adolphe Nourrit, whose scenario for *La Sylphide* had been so successful, this time prepared a poor, dull scenario, based on Shakespeare's comedy *The Tempest*. The ballet was saved through fresh choreography by Jean Coralli, who is best remembered for his later work with *Giselle.* Another plus was the vigorous, pleasing music by Schneitzhoeffer, who had done the score for *La Sylphide*. The ballet was further enhanced through magnificent sets that were produced under Duponchel's direction (he had also been responsible for supervising the décor of *La Sylphide*); and there was a new effect of waves moving in a storm, so clever that it made one critic feel seasick.

But most of all, there was Fanny Elssler, who made a sensation at once. One critic wrote:

> There was not half a second's uncertainty over Fanny Elssler's first appearance yesterday....It is only by seeing her that an exact idea can be be formed of her, for no description could be adequate.
>
> The erudite call her style a "danse tacquetée," which signifies that it consists chiefly of little steps, rapid, precise, sharp, biting the boards, and always as vigorous and delicate as they are graceful and brilliant. *Pointes* play an important part in her dancing, commanding admiration and attention; she circles the stage with no apparent fatigue and without losing any of her incredible aplomb or gentle charm. There could be no more striking contrast with the justly appreciated talent of Marie Taglioni.

Spirituality versus Earthly Delights. Here it was, recognized from the first—Elssler's spirit was the opposite of Taglioni's. Refer back to the quote from Victor Hugo in the previous chapter which describes the double nature of man; the difference between perishable flesh, drawn to the earth, and immortal spirit, carried on the wings of vision. If Taglioni represented spirituality, then Elssler expressed physical passion. In addition to this personal sparkle, she proved to have considerable acting ability, which was slightly lacking in Taglioni. Thus taken together, the two dancers had an abundance of good qualities with which to please audiences.

The other side of this artistic blessing was a deep rivalry, which did not confine itself to words. During one special Taglioni evening in 1835, a tribute onstage was arranged to honor the star. Before their final dance, the corps de ballet was to circle the stage in a procession while the famous elderly dancer, Vestris, was to place a crown on Taglioni's head. But just when this was supposed to take place, the orchestra suddenly began the music for the lively finale. The corps had to scramble into place, while Vestris and Taglioni were forced to hurry offstage as best they could, in a rather undignified manner. It was never made clear who had given the conductor the wrong signal, but there was no doubt that it was deliberate. Taglioni was furious—chalk up a point for Elssler's fans!

Episodes continued. Over three years later (October 1838), when Elssler appeared in a so-called Taglioni role, there was actual physical violence:

> As she made her first entrance, two or three whistles pierced the air and were almost at once drowned by a wave of applause. Some minutes later, at the end of her pas, more whistling broke out, shriller than before.
>
> During the interval between the acts, Auguste, the leader of the claque, left the theater to seek reinforcements to counter the hostile demonstration, and during the second act his men set to with the utmost zeal.
>
> As soon as the demonstration recommenced, the "claqueurs" went into action, mercilessly assaulting anyone they suspected of breaking the peace. The tumult grew in intensity as the ballet continued; innocent and guilty suffered alike from the fury of the claque, suspected demonstrators were manhandled to the exits, and soon nearly everybody in the pit was on his feet. Fanny's appearance before the curtain at the end was a signal for a fresh salvo of whistling . . .

So that evening scored several points for Taglioni. But the fact is that by then, Taglioni's expensive contract was not renewed, and she moved to Russia, accepting an offer from the Imperial Ballet at St. Petersburg.

Cachucha. The field was therefore left to Elssler, who continued to bring her audiences great pleasure. Just as Marie Taglioni was thought of as *La Sylphide*, so Elssler became identified with her most famous dance. This was the *cachucha*, a Spanish character number that Fanny had arranged for the ballet *Le Diable Boiteux*, 1836, in which her role was that of Florinda, a Spanish dancer. Fanny had learned authentic techniques from the Spanish dancers who had delighted the Paris public in 1834. Up to this ballet, Fanny had proved herself to be an excellent actress and character dancer, in parts that had Italian, Gypsy, or Chinese local color. However, her Spanish cachucha was in a class by itself, and Paris went wild over it. The cachucha became an overnight craze, and whenever Fanny danced it, she had to give an encore immediately. Two months after the premiere, she danced the cachucha by royal command at the French court, and for years she repeated it to resounding applause and rave reviews.

Only one other number of hers came close to the cachucha in popularity. This was another character piece, the *cracovienne*, which is a Polish folk dance. It appeared in the melodramatic *La Gipsy* (1839), whose scenario was prepared by dramatist de Saint-Georges. Fanny played a noble Scottish girl, who is brought up by a band of Gypsies, a role that gave Fanny's acting talent full scope. Again, the hit of the ballet was her "folk" solo, again in an unusual, memorable costume. Gautier found her irresistible:

It was the most coquettish, roguish costume imaginable. Fanny's trim figure was encased in a white tunic, sparkling with three rows of buttons and gallons of silver braid, which enhanced the bright colors of her blue silk skirt and scarlet boots with their metal heels and tiny gold spurs. Two long plaits tied with red ribbon escaped from a black military cap, which was decorated with a cockade and a white feather...

This dance has a rhythmical precision mingled with a charming abandon, a tense and bounding nimbleness that surpasses one's imagination; and the metallic chatter of her spurs, which are a kind of castanets worn on the heels, accentuates every step and gives the dance a quality of joyous vivacity.

However, each champion is always forced to defend his title against newcomers. Elssler was clearly at the top of the heap in Paris in 1839. She was preparing for a tour in far-off North America when she found herself threatened by the gentle manner of Lucille Grahn, who had just signed a three-year contract at the opera.

Lucille Grahn. Grahn (1819 to 1907) had already won great acclaim in her native Denmark, under the direction of August Bournonville. But because she spurned Bournonville's romantic advances, the director turned against her and made life unpleasant for her at the Copenhagen Royal Theater. Accordingly, she managed to get hired in Paris, and one evening took advantage of Fanny Elssler's illness to dance in La Sylphide. Now the critics hailed her for qualities that reminded them of the absent Taglioni: modesty, reserve, and timidity. Elssler was furious that Grahn had been allowed to dance the role, and she tore up her contract, which really didn't matter much, because she was to accept an engagement in New York shortly. Meanwhile, Grahn drifted off to St. Petersburg. We'll meet her again soon in London. With Taglioni gone, and now Grahn and Elssler deserting Paris, you might expect to find that there was no ballerina of star magnitude left to shine at the opera. Not so. There were many reasons to call this the golden age of ballet. When we come to Giselle, you will meet Carlotta Grisi.

Questions for Review

1.   Why was there a strong rivalry between Taglioni and Elssler?

2.   What made the cachucha so popular?

3.   Have you ever been part of a claque?

13 GISELLE

TIMELESS ROMANTIC BALLET

A Romantic Classic

Neither ballerina Carlotta Grisi (1819 to 1899), who danced in the original *Giselle*, nor the ballet itself appeared suddenly from nowhere, like one of the Wilis in Act II. Rather, both the dancer and the work fused and reflected much of what we have already noted about the Romantic Age. Both were products of the highly experienced, brilliant, professional talent that shone at the Paris Opera for about two decades before the premiere of *Giselle* in June 1841. In fact, *Giselle* takes us back in spirit to the ballet that launched the romantic era, to *La Sylphide* with its ghostly creature flitting through the woods; and with its hero caught between duty to a flesh-and-blood fiancée and an obsession with an unattainable image of ideal perfection. Here once more is the dreamy face of the Romantic ballet, the image that keeps returning to haunt our theaters, dissolving like a drifting cloud, and yet remaining in our memories.

Romantic versus Classic. The contradiction of dissolving and yet remaining is mirrored in the phrase *romantic classic*. Words, like dance scenes, call forth images that are hard to pin down when they refer to a cluster of ideas, rather than a single, fixed object. The term *Romantic* has already been defined as referring to a specific period in European culture, as a label loosely describing the style of expression in the nineteenth century that accented feeling and imagination, with relative freedom from

Carla Fracci and Erik Bruhn, seen here in the American Ballet Theater's "Giselle," made a wonderful team.

rules. So far, the term *classic* has had an opposing meaning. Instead of emphasizing emotions, as do Romantic works, classic works emphasize traditional forms. When we speak of a classical period in the arts, we refer to the ancient Greeks and their fixed rules of proportion and harmony; or to eighteenth-century musicians who wrote classical symphonies that followed strict forms in creating and developing their melodies.

However, a *classic* also has come to mean a work that is a production of the highest caliber and best type, one that would rate an *A plus* in an academy, or from a critic (well, from most critics, since these people take pleasure in disagreeing with one another). Stemming from its excellence is the fact that a classic is a work that continues to be produced and appreciated long after its day. Of course, a particular classic does not appeal to everyone. Taste is always personal and individual. If someone finds the field of ballet at all appealing, the chances are that he or she likes *Giselle* because so many things about this work are typical of other ballets, yet at the same time, a little bit better. Which is why it is considered a classic and why it has been produced hundreds of times. On the other hand, it wouldn't appeal to someone who is not at all inclined toward the Romantic style. So we are back again with our Romantic classic, and we will start with the man who is credited with its conception: Theophile Gautier.

Theophile Gautier (1811 to 1872). Gautier was a poet and a journalist as well as a Romantic. He consciously helped in creating the intellectual atmosphere of his time. Further, he revealed personal romantic inclinations in the glowing descriptions of several ballerinas whose concerts he reviewed, and in his close relationships with some of them. He was a stage-struck man, quite carried away by theatrical visions, and quick to fall in love. It must be noted that Gautier's stated romantic preference was for sensuous, fleshy beauty rather than for spiritual nobility. He rated the full-bosomed, round-armed, bright-eyed, lively Fanny Elssler above the poetic, aerial, virginally graceful, colder Marie Taglioni. Once, in comparing them, he rejected Taglioni's "spiritual arms and aesthetic legs," claiming that "dance is basically pagan, physical, and voluptuous," as projected by Elssler. But when Gautier dignified his personal emotions by casting them into statements of artistic theory, he left himself open to charges of inconsistency. For in a conflict between what an artist actually does and what he claims are his beliefs, we have to give more weight to his actions. And when Gautier came up with the idea for *Giselle* it was certainly not sensual. Indeed, it called for "spiritual arms and aesthetic legs." And he followed his contribution to *Giselle* with a fantasy scenario for *La Péri*, a ballet which again was in the tradition of the moon-struck *Sylphide*. Like it or not, Gautier is identified with the Romantic movement, and particularly with ballets in that style.

In one of his newspaper pieces, Gautier described how the seed of *Giselle* was planted. He wrote about it in the form of a letter to Heinrich Heine, a poet who had just written a book about German literature and folk legends. You see, Gautier didn't dream up the idea for *Giselle* in some moony reverie. What he did was to take Heine's words and apply them to dance.

My dear Heinrich Heine, when reviewing your fine book, I came across a charming passage—the place where you speak of elves in white dresses, whose hems are always damp; of nixes who display their little satin feet on the ceiling of the nuptial chamber; of snow-colored Wilis who waltz pitilessly; and of those delicious apparitions you have encountered in a mist softened by German moonlight; and I involuntarily said to myself: "Wouldn't this make a pretty ballet?"

As we learn in *The Ballet Called Giselle* by Cyril Beaumont, Gautier put this imagery together with a poem by Victor Hugo. The poem tells of a young girl who was crazy about dancing. She became overheated at a ball, caught a chill on her way home through the dawn air, and died. (Earlier, Hugo was mentioned as one of the German poets who produced the Romantic climate of the 1800s with poems like this one.)

After Gautier had this double inspiration, he tried to plan a ballet. Luckily, he soon ran into Vernoy de Saint-Georges who was a very experienced theatrical writer. Up to that time Gautier's only writing for the dance world had been criticism, and he realized he would need help in putting together a decent scenario. (Criticizing a finished product calls for different skills from manufacturing one.) Vernoy de Saint-Georges immediately saw dance possibilities in the theme that Gautier suggested and within three days Vernoy de Saint-Georges came up with the scenario of *Giselle* that we are familiar with today.

Structure and Credits. Act I tells a tragic story in a straightforward dramatic manner: Giselle is a happy yet fragile peasant girl, very much in love with a lad who lives nearby. He fully returns her love. This ideal romance hides a dreadful secret, however. The village lad is none other than Prince Albrecht in disguise. Albrecht's royal blood would be enough of an obstacle to his marrying a mere peasant; but the situation is even more serious, because in his real noble identity, Albrecht is already engaged to Bathilde, a lady of proper background. The truth is bound to come out eventually. It is revealed with brutal suddenness by the jealous Hilarion, a peasant who also loves Giselle. The abrupt delivery of the painful news proves too much for the frail Giselle. She goes mad. Seizing the prince's sword, she rushes around with it in a frenzy until she drops dead of a failed heart, broken with grief and perhaps also pierced by the sword. This act of *Giselle* bears some resemblance to *La Fille Mal Gardée* in its portrayal of lovers beset by problems in an otherwise carefree village, complete with harvest festivals. The love story of *Giselle* turns into a tragedy of course, while *La Fille Mal Gardée* proceeds in a lighter mood to a happy ending. Nevertheless, the landscape and the background of custom and costume are the same.

It is Act II that makes *Giselle* into something else completely, with its

supernatural episode that can only be traced to *La Sylphide.* In a forest setting, a mystical band of sylphlike Wilis go through their nightly ritual. The
Wilis are ghostly female creatures: spirits of maidens who died before they
were married, betrayed by heartless men. Now they dance through every
night, getting their cold revenge against the male sex. Any man who wanders into the forest ballroom is forced to dance with them, and keep dancing until he drops dead of exhaustion. Giselle joins their cruel sorority and
when Albrecht visits her tomb he is trapped by their pitiless dance of
death. However, Giselle's love is so strong that even now she pleads with
the relentless Myrtha, queen of the Wilis, to let Albrecht go. Finally, he is
saved by the dawn which sends the Wilis floating away into the mist.

The Romantic similarities to *La Sylphide* are plain to see. The Wilis,
like the sylphs, are wispy symbols of the dreamer's desire for ungrasped
ideal love. Here the dreamer is Albrecht, who pursues the spirit of Giselle
in preference to the very tangible fiancée Bathilde, just as in *La Sylphide*
James passes by his fleshy betrothed Effie in favor of a shadowy nymph.
Obviously, such otherworldly ambitions cannot be successful on earth.
Hence the inevitable tragedies. But don't forget, suffering was considered a
more desirable condition than happiness in the Romantic philosophy.

We haven't even touched on the choreography, music, setting, or cast
of *Giselle*, and already four names have been mentioned: Theophile
Gautier, Heinrich Heine, Victor Hugo, and Vernoy de Saint-Georges. This
work is certainly an illustration of the process of collaboration which is
basic to the dance field. It shows how the effect of a dance work is created
not only by the movements and steps of the choreography, and of course
the interpretation, technical ability, and appeal of the dancers themselves,
but also by the music, sets, costumes, and stories, ideas, and emotions that
make up its content. The other important lesson in this large number of
helping hands is the appearance through history of golden ages in one art
form or another. It is no accident that creativity flowers in clusters. Artists
are by their nature highly receptive people with a strong urge to communicate. Accordingly, they stimulate and inspire one another not only through
what they create, but also in person when they get together to exchange
ideas, teach, or collaborate. That is why we come across sets of names from
time to time, such as the Elizabethan dramatists Shakespeare, Marlow, and
Jonson; the seventeenth-century Dutch painters Rembrandt and Vermeer;
and the Viennese composers Haydn, Mozart, and Beethoven. Our concern
is dance and we have already seen how it glittered at the court of Louis
XIV with Lully, Molière, and Beauchamp.

As we move through the passage of time we will notice other shining
examples like the Romantic Age, and the soon-to-be-encountered classical
brilliance in St. Petersburg, where Petipa, Tchaikovsky and Ivanov, burning with inspiration, strike sparks off one another. Now that we understand why there are so many names connected with *Giselle,* let's bring in

the rest. You will recognize some of the names in this list of credits from ballets already noted; others will be heard from again later in our story: scenario by Theophile Gautier and Vernoy de Saint-Georges (from an idea by Heinrich Heine and Victor Hugo); music by Adolphe Adam; scenery by Ciceri; costumes by Lormier; choreography by Jean Coralli and Jules Perrot; leading roles at the premiere danced by Carlotta Grisi and Lucien Petipa. Gautier keeps popping up, of course, and he was to become a life-long friend and admirer of Carlotta Grisi, the ballerina who will soon step into the spotlight. Vernoy de Saint-Georges, the actual scenarist, had earlier done the scenario for one of Fanny Elssler's biggest hits, *La Gipsy*.

Adolphe Adam composed the well-known music for *Giselle*. Although he had already done ballet music used by Marie Taglioni and Fanny Elssler, none was to achieve the stature of Adam's beautifully tailored score for *Giselle*. Perhaps it is not great music by itself. But it was not designed to be performed without dance, any more than a gorgeous dress is designed to appear by itself in a room. The score was written to bring out the imagery of a theatrical ballet, and this it certainly did—and does. Its appeal lies in melodies that are delightful and that also serve as suitable accompaniment to characters and action. For example, Giselle has her own melodic theme, which is used to great dramatic advantage. This motif is heard at her first appearance in a carefree, happy form. When she goes mad, the motif is heard again, but in a broken, discordant manner. Lovely melodic lines accompany Giselle's blissful flirtations with Albrecht. These same melodies sound with heavy, tragic overtones in the mad scene. Then again when Giselle and Albrecht dance in the forest in Act II, these same melodies are harmonized to make a mournful, ghostly impression. In all, the score is remarkably effective.

Scenery was the work of Ciceri, who had already made a tremendous impact on the public with his moon-drenched graveyard décor for *The Ballet of the Nuns* and his enchanting forest for *La Sylphide*. Ciceri did a similar job for *Giselle*, with the rustic village, featuring Giselle's cottage and one that Albrecht uses. Costumes were contributed by hard-working Paul Lormier, who had dressed Fanny Elssler for her debut in *The Tempest*. Jean Coralli (1779 to 1854) was assigned by the Paris Opera management to do the choreography because he was on salary as ballet master. We noted earlier that Coralli received favorable comments on choreographing *The Tempest* in 1834. Probably because of his official position, he was given sole credit on the program for *Giselle*. But another artist, Jules Perrot, was in fact responsible for many of the famous scenes that Giselle herself danced.

You met Jules Perrot as Marie Taglioni's partner, angering her by getting more applause than she did. Perrot was let go from the opera ballet company in 1835 because the director didn't want to meet his high salary demands, although Perrot was recognized as one of the best male dancers of his time. There was simply no great interest in male dancers in that age of sylphs, and the management didn't try too hard to keep him on. Now Perrot assumes other roles in our story, those of coach, choreographer, and lover. After he left the Paris Opera, Perrot went to perform in Italy. There, in 1836, he was attracted by a talented seventeen-year-old, Carlotta Grisi.

Perrot coached Grisi, then took her on tour as his partner, arranging some of her material. Jules was nine years older than Carlotta and they developed a relationship that was part love, part ambition, part mutual artistic admiration. They lived together as a couple, spending endless hours together day and night, most of the time in studio practice. While some writers claim that they married, *The Concise Oxford Dictionary of Ballet* states quite firmly that "they never married, though for some time Carlotta called herself Madame Perrot." This certainly accounts for the impression of marriage, even if there was no official registration and ceremony. In any event, Perrot was not rehired at the opera, but he was asked to arrange dance sequences for Carlotta's debut, and he continued to prepare her parts.

Step by step, there is almost no way of knowing how much is preserved of the original *Giselle*. Perhaps only the spiritual core regarding the way the shadowy Wilis resemble live peasant girls. Since that spirit was created by Perrot and Coralli, it is not surprising that it is a strong one, however. Perrot was outstanding for the way he combined expressive movement with dance steps. This may seem an obvious approach. But often in ballet history we find dance passages which stop dead every now and then for chunks of mimed action, in which the characters present their thoughts, feelings, and reactions to each other in sign language. For example, a couple in love can tell us about it this way. The male points to his own heart and then to the female. Then she does the same for him. Then they break into a dance that shows off their technical brilliance. But throughout *Giselle* there are fully emotional passsages that carry the story forward, clothed in dance gestures. For example, in the first scene between Giselle and Albrecht, flirtation, affection, and joy are all present. A charming moment occurs when Giselle sits on a bench and keeps shyly shifting away from Albrecht who also sits down, and keeps chasing her by moving closer each time she tries to evade him. Then there is the flower petal game of "he loves me, he loves me not." While these little scenes have strong elements of pantomime, they are not stiff signs, but rhythmic gestures, completely in harmony with the music and dance style, and strung together on connecting threads of danced steps.

In Act II, the Giselle-Albrecht duets lean to more "pure" dance. But the way he holds and sways her romantically, or lifts her tenderly and sets her down reluctantly—his manner of movement—expresses his feelings quite clearly. Undoubtedly, some of these ideas were introduced at a later date by another dance director. But there is no question that the approach was in the tradition set by Perrot's original version. We know this from reviews of the period which describe other ballets that he choreographed. *Giselle* also contains many bits of the other kind of pantomime: the conventional sign language. Right near the beginning, for example, the peasant Hilarion goes to the door of Giselle's cottage and announces in *dumb show* that this is the house of the girl he loves. These more ordinary passages are probably the work of Jean Coralli who, as we noted, was official choreographer of the Paris Opera and given sole credit for the choreography at the premiere.

This is not to say that Coralli lacked ability. In his long career he was occasionally credited with delightful, original choreography. More often, however, the critics regarded his work as undistinguished. For *Giselle*, Coralli was praised for many of his overall contributions, not for the mime parts, which were rather ordinary, but for the peasant *pas de deux* in Act I and for the ensemble dances in Act II. Gautier himself said that the Wilis' dances showed "exquisite elegance and novelty," and composer Adolphe Adam wrote: "There has never been anything so pretty in choreography as the groups of women which Coralli has arranged with so superior a skill." On June 28, 1841 the premiere performance took place at the Paris Opera with Carlotta Grisi as Giselle and Lucien Petipa as Albrecht.

Carlotta Grisi (1819 to 1899). The original Giselle, Italian-born Carlotta Grisi, came from a family better known for opera singers than dancers, and she almost chose to develop her promising voice as an instrument, instead of her body. However, uplifted by Jules Perrot's enthusiastic, energetic training, she landed a ballet contract at the Paris Opera. We learn from Ivor Guest's *The Romantic Ballet in Paris* that her debut stirred Gautier to write: "She dances marvelously. She has strength, lightness, suppleness and an originality of style which places her at one bound between Elssler and Taglioni. The lessons of Perrot are there for all to see. Her success is complete and lasting. She has beauty, youth and talent—an admirable trinity." As noted previously, Theophile Gautier became devoted to Carlotta both in the theater and in private life.

Lucien Petipa, brother of the more famous Marius Petipa, whom we will soon follow to Russia, was the first Prince Albrecht. Lucien was an elegant classical dancer, and he was to be Carlotta Grisi's regular partner. Then as now, the paths of well-known figures in the rather intimate world of ballet crisscrossed repeatedly. Also, ballet families pop up from time to time, like father Filippo Taglioni and daughter Marie, the brothers Petipa, and the sisters Elssler. Throughout the 1840s, Carlotta Grisi danced back and forth across the English Channel, appearing both at the Paris Opera and in London, in ballets by Jules Perrot. In the 1850s, separated from Carlotta, Jules Perrot went on to St. Petersburg where he married a Russian ballerina. Another Frenchman, Marius Petipa, first served under Perrot's direction in St. Petersburg and then on his own. You will soon hear more about their work.

Even without their activities in other European capitals, the names Carlotta Grisi and Jules Perrot would have a secure place in dance history because of *Giselle*. From the very first performance there was no question of the ballet's success. The public was most enthusiastic. While there was praise for the music, the choreography, and the setting (especially the effect of a sunrise which concluded Act II), all the critics wholeheartedly cheered the star Carlotta Grisi. One reviewer put it this way:

> The real queen of the festival was, beyond comparison, Carlotta Grisi. What a charming creature! And how she dances!...
>
> From one end of *Giselle* to the other the poor child is perpetually in the air, on her *pointes*...in the second act she must be a thousand times lighter and intangible, since she is a shade. No longer is the earth beneath her feet, no longer has she any support!
>
> She cleaves the air like a swallow, she balances on rushes, she leans from the treetops—this is actual fact—to throw flowers to her lover...Giselle is a Sylphide with not a moment's rest...Yes, for myself, I have no hesitation in proclaiming that the diverse qualities of Taglioni and Elssler are combined in Carlotta Grisi.

As a result of such reviews (quoted in *The Romantic Ballet* in Paris), Carlotta received a generous new contract, and with only one exception she danced the role of Giselle at the Paris Opera all through the 1840s. Note the comparison to *La Sylphide* which had captured the Paris ballet public nine years earlier.

Giselle repeated that triumph. Its performances kept the seats in the opera house full even during the summer, although this was the season when Parisians deserted their city for cooler air and usually caused box office sales to drop. Fans bought pictures and statuettes of Carlotta Grisi and arrangements of the ballet music. As the fashion industry had honored *La Sylphide,* so a silk material and a special millinery flower came on the market, both named *Giselle.* Those two ballets marked high points in the romantic era. From the viewpoint of a century and a half later, *Giselle* is rated above *La Sylphide* if only because of its long life. In fact, Giselle has remained in the repertory of great companies all over the world almost continuously since its premiere in 1841, while *La Sylphide* faded away after a few years everywhere but in Denmark, where other music is used.

Fifty-two years earlier, *La Fille Mal Gardée* had come out and it still has the honor of being the oldest ballet in existence. Yet contemporary versions bear almost no resemblance to the original, whereas *Giselle* sticks close to its premiere in music and choreographic outline. Further, *Giselle* is one of the most popular ballets ever created, both with the public and with the dancers as well. The role of Giselle is a favorite challenge for every ballerina. It calls for varied acting and mime, ranging from expressions of lighthearted playfulness, trusting love, and shocked horror in Act I, to otherworldly devotion for her earthbound lover in Act II. It also demands throughout the highest level of skill in classical ballet technique. So many traditions and memories of ballet are bound up with *Giselle* that familiarity with it is a must for anyone who wants to cultivate this field of art.

Questions for Review

1. What contributions to Giselle did the following people make: Gautier? Grisi? Adam? Coralli? Perrot?

2. Why do ballerinas covet the role of Giselle?

3. Have you ever seen *Giselle?* What impression did it make on you?

14 TRAVELOGUE

FROM BOURNONVILLE IN DENMARK TO COPPÉLIA IN FRANCE

The International Art World

Dancers always move around a lot, not just onstage, but from job to job and city to city. The collaborative nature of ballet has always had an international aspect. Artists from many countries and fields join together to produce a ballet. This art form in turn sends them out again to other places. We saw this in the 1500s, when the Italian musician Beaujoyeux followed Catherine de Medici to the French court and staged the *Ballet Comique de la Reine* for her. Then in the 1600s, Italian-born Lully traveled along the same route to play a major role in shaping French court ballet and opera under Louis XIV. Then in the 1700s, Marie Sallé took her original dance style in *Pygmalion* from Paris to London. Similarly, the French Noverre moved to the German Stuttgart court, where he choreographed his brilliant ballets and wrote his perceptive books. In the 1800s, the two most famous ballerinas of Paris were the Viennese Fanny Elssler, and the Swedish-born Marie Taglioni, whose father was Italian. Two other Italians, Carlotta Grisi and Fanny Cerrito and the Danish Lucille Grahn were the other best-known dancers to appear at this prestigious French opera. The French dancer Marius Petipa went to St. Petersburg to bring the Russianballet to a grand classical climax. And August Bournonville partnered the great Marie Taglioni for two years at the Paris Opera, before he went north to the Royal Danish Ballet and established the repertory and schooling that are still in force there.

Therefore when we speak of the golden age of Romantic ballet as being French, we can really think of it as almost international, as it is today. We will be reminded of this again when we reach the twentieth century and find the Ballet Russe de Monte Carlo more at home in Paris, London, and New York than in Russia or Monte Carlo; and the South-African-born John Cranko winning acclaim with his Stuttgart Ballet. A ballet audience always contains talent scouts, sometimes from far-away places. Good ideas and capable people are snatched up quickly by people like opera managers, who cater to the entertainment hunger of the world's elite. As it could today, "have tights, will travel" could have been a motto for the ballet world of the nineteenth century. We have seen that dancers were mobile in the time of Noverre and indeed as far back as the Renaissance, although tights weren't part of the scene until 1838, when the Frenchman Maillot introduced them at the Paris Opera.

After the middle 1800s the French scene itself dimmed. *Giselle* was followed by *La Péri*, 1843, another enchanting spinoff from the sylph theme with the addition of an exotic whiff from an Arabian opium pipe. Theophile Gautier did the scenario and the stars were again Carlotta Grisi and her admirable partner Lucien Petipa. Otherwise, nothing memorable occurred in Paris until *Coppélia* (in 1870) which we will look at shortly. The more interesting action was elsewhere, in London, for example.

London

During the 1840s, Jules Perrot was ballet master at Her Majesty's Theater in London. (Her Majesty was, of course, Queen Victoria.) There Perrot created fine new works, many in which Carlotta Grisi danced while making alternate appearances at the Paris Opera.

Pas de Quatre. This is a ballet you ought to know about. It is less significant for its choreography than for its tradition-making character. *Pas de Quatre* (1845) was just that—a dance variation for four—a plotless quartet. But what a quartet! *Pas de Quatre* was made for an ensemble of absolutely first-class ballerinas: Carlotta Grisi, whose triumph you just witnessed in *Giselle*; Marie Taglioni, who had launched the Romantic ballet with her roles in *The Ballet of the Nuns* and *La Sylphide*; Lucille Grahn, the gentle Danish dancer who had performed in La Sylphide at the Paris Opera in 1839, getting good reviews and infuriating Fanny Elssler who felt threatened by her talent; and the Italian Fanny Cerrito (1817 to 1909), who is new to our story, but not to the dance world.

While we have been attending the Paris Opera, Fanny Cerrito has been studying with dancer-choreographer Jules Perrot and with Carlo Blasis, already mentioned as the most famous ballet teacher of the nineteenth century, and writer of a manual on technique that is still valid today.

With such excellent training joined to her natural fiery brilliance, it is no wonder that Fanny Cerrito became a popular dancer, beginning with her debut in Naples in 1832, and going on to capture audiences in Vienna and London, before she did her star turn in Perrot's *Pas de Quatre* in 1845. Fanny then married the dancer Saint-Léon, who was to choreograph *Coppélia.* She continued her successes in Paris and elsewhere, often partnered by Saint-Léon, and finally concluded her dazzling career in Russia in the 1850s.

The idea for *Pas de Quatre* was soley contributed by the manager of Her Majesty's Theater. He decided that it would be a good box-office draw to assemble the top ballerinas of t arie Taglioni, Carlotta Grisi, Lucille Grahn, and Fanny Cerrito—on one stage at the same time. Of course he was right. With such a cast how could there be anything but success? Choreographer Jules Perrot arranged solos to music by Cesare Pugni that showed off the best qualities of each dancer: Grahn's controlled lightness; Grisi's sharp vibrancy; Cerrito's darting turns; and Taglioni's soaring leaps that paused in midair. The composition also included some duets and began and ended with the famous tableau preserved in a lithograph. All four ballerinas are graciously posed with the senior (forty-year-old) Taglioni forming the crown of the incomparable group.

Not surprisingly, the biggest problem facing the skilled choreographer Jules Perrot was a diplomatic one. When four reigning queens are all at one party, who takes precedence in order? The right of seniority was granted to Taglioni without question, since the other three ballerinas were all in their twenties. But after that generous gesture, each one claimed the next-best position. The theater manager provided the solution. He suggested that order should be determined by age. With sudden shyness—no one wishing to reveal her age—the three ladies giggled and allowed Perrot to place them as he saw fit, according to the needs of the choreography. The audience came to the theater loaded down with flowers, expecting a very special performance. They were not disappointed and showed their favor by showering the stage with bouquets. Each ballerina outdid herself; and the four repeated the triumph on three more evenings, at one of which Queen Victoria was present. But except for a brief revival in 1847, the *Pas de Quatre* was not kept in the repertory. That's not because the idea wasn't considered often, but the difficulties in getting such a cast together were overwhelming. However, the spectacular occasion survives in ballet tradition as a glorious peak in achievement. It also pointed up the cult of the ballerina. No male dancers were even considered! Today, there are often productions of *Pas de Quatre* with four characters named Taglioni, Grisi, Grahn, and Cerrito. This is not Perrot's composition, however, but one of several ballets created during this century in honor of that memorable event. Cesare Pugni's music is the same and the lithograph pose is always included. Otherwise, lacking records of the dance except newspaper reports, the choreographers have had to rely on their own imaginations to re-create the spirit of the original gala. In some interpretations, such as Anton Dolin's, 1941, when the ballerinas bow to one another in introducing each section, they display a sly ironic manner as though reflecting the thoughts of the original stars: "You think you're so great. Wait until you see what I can do!"

There is, after all, a large measure of competitive egotism among dance artists. Don't make the mistake of thinking that this is a totally negative quality. On the contrary, without a strong sense of self, no artist would have the drive toward expression in any medium. In fact, the dancer must have a particularly well-developed ego, because his instrument is his very own self—body and soul. Competition is a spur in the daily effort the dancer must make to keep his instrument in good working order, and *self-importance* is another name for the desire to be seen, which acts as a spur toward expressive communication. If we discouraged egotism completely, we would have no dance performances. Ego in the dancer is unfortunate only when it swells to the point where the performer is interested soley in showing off his abilities, to the detriment of the choreographer's ideas, the music, the other performers, or anything else that may divert attention from him.

The kindest label for this attribute is *artistic temperament*. We have witnessed Taglioni's sulks when her partner Perrot stole the spotlight from her; the nasty rivalry between Elssler and Taglioni; the fury of Elssler when Grahn danced "her" role in *La Sylphide*; and Perrot's problems in arranging the sequences of *Pas de Quatre*. You can be sure that such things, and worse, still go on all the time in our field. Later we will trace the striking ballet theme of Jerome Robbins's *Afternoon of a Faun* (1953) to dancers' self-love at the same time as his work recalls Vaslav Nijinsky's *Afternoon of a Faun* (1912). Thus again, we see how appreciation of a dance is increased when we are aware of the traditions and thoughts that have helped shape the choreography, a reminder that the main purpose of this dance history is to enlighten present experiences—not just to poke around in the dusty past. To continue our story we must close the curtain on the sophisticated capitals of France and England and move to the simpler tidiness of Danish society.

Denmark

When the curtain opens at the Danish Royal Theater, we hear the French professional ballet terms like plié and jeté pronounced with a different accent. By the 1850s, most creative dance was found in Copenhagen. We have already met one dancer from Denmark, Lucille Grahn. We noted that she accepted a position at the Paris Opera because the ballet director at the Copenhagen Theater was giving her a bad time. Grahn continued a fine career for many years, mostly outside of Denmark. For example, in London we found her in the illustrious cast of *Pas de Quatre*. It is her bossy teacher, ballet master August Bournonville, who now steps into our spotlight.

August Bournonville. Bournonville (1805 to 1879) deserves full recognition for shaping the Royal Danish Ballet into an outstanding company; and for contributing a technical method and a repertory that are both still very much alive today. Note that the name Bournonville is not Danish but French. Well, he was born in Denmark, but of a French father who studied with Noverre. His father then moved to Denmark to dance, to direct the Royal Danish Ballet, and to supervise the studies of his talented son August. Therefore August Bournonville was brought up in the ballet tradition, already a performer at eight years of age. When still a young man in 1820, he studied in Paris, where he realized that the available training back home in Denmark was unsatisfactory. He particularly admired the gifted star Auguste Vestris. Please note that this was 1820, and Romantic fashion had not yet reduced the male dancer to the role of a prop for the Queen Bee (*Bee* for *Ballerina*, that is).

It was a time of male virtuosity and Vestris was a fabulous technician who was considered the best of his day. Vestris's pirouettes, batterie (beating the legs rapidly against each other in the air), and elevation were all sensational. He was to teach not only Bournonville, but also Marie Taglioni and Jules Perrot. After August Bournonville became Director of the Royal Theater of Copenhagen Ballet in 1830, and continued in that position for almost fifty years, he held on to the image imprinted by Auguste Vestris of the male dancer as a lively, forceful figure. In the more than fifty ballets that Bournonville choreographed, the male continued to have an importance that he had completely lost in the French style. For example, even Bournonville's *La Sylphide* gave the role of James a prominence that it lacked in the French original.

You may remember that *La Sylphide*, in which Marie Taglioni had conquered Paris in 1832, was the work that led to the supremacy of the female image in the dance art. After that, the floating fairy figure in an airy net skirt became the symbol of ballet. However, when we see *La Sylphide* onstage today, it is not the original version. Papa Taglioni's choreography survives only as legend. What we see is a revival of the Bournonville version, which he staged in 1836, using the same Nourrit scenario, but to different music. In this country the American Ballet Theater presents it regularly. Bournonville's work has been preserved in the repertory of the Royal Danish Ballet, and has been performed in Denmark almost continuously since the premiere, when Lucille Grahn danced the title role and

Bournonville partnered Grahn as James. (Obviously, this was before Grahn had broken away from her despotic ballet master.)

Probably Bournonville's egotism had something to do with the way he emphasized James's part—and therefore his own—in the action. But the tremendous impression that Auguste Vestris had made on him, and the technical skills suitable for men that he had taught the young Bournonville, also affected his approach to the male figure in *La Sylphide*. Then too, his personal temperament and outlook led him to give the sexes a more balanced treatment than was the fashion in Paris. Denmark's artists were very much aware of French Romantic culture, but the influence was lessened by the nature of Danish society, which was more conventional, more solidly middle class, and less inclined to adopt passionate extremes than the French. Danish theater expressed a comfortable satisfaction with life, rather than the unhappy longing for perfection that ends in despair. In the middle 1800s, Copenhagen was a pretty, peaceful capital city, where on Sundays the Danish king would go sailing through the park canals among his friendly subjects. Despite his French heritage, August Bournonville was more at home with the modest, respectable Danish culture than he was with the supernatural, or the fiery passions that appealed to the sophisticated, stormy Parisians. His ideals were good taste and balance. These prevented Bournonville from losing his sense of proportion to the extent of elevating the female dancer and neglecting the male. You can find a complete portrait of this gentleman in *Bournonville and Ballet Technique* by Bruhn and Moore. Therefore even though the plot of *La Sylphide* concerns a young man, moon-struck by a female shadow, Bournonville at least gives James full scope for dance and mime.

After *La Sylphide*, Bournonville wrote his own scenarios for most of his ballets, where the themes were harmonious and usually led to happy endings. He once expressed his philosophy that "joy is strength; intoxication, weakness." He disapproved of giving in to passion or to self-indulgent misery and longing for the unattainable. He believed in respectable Christian morality. Therefore in his plots we find heroic boys who fall in love with pure, wholesome girls whom they marry, and live happily ever after. *A Folk Tale*, one of his ballets, ends with "The Bridal Waltz," a kind of hymn in praise of marriage and domestic harmony—an idea that the cynical Parisians would certainly have found naive. *A Folk Tale* is another of Bournonville's ballets still in the Danish repertory, along with at least a dozen others. This artist based his choreography mainly on classical technique, working in a skillful use of folk steps here and there. His ballets excel in passages that project high spirits, with movement combinations that dart through space to proclaim the joy of living.

Another Bournonville piece that we are likely to see is the pas de deux from *Flower Festival in Genzano*, 1858. The entire one-act ballet is not given outside of Denmark, but the popular pas de deux is in the repertory of the British Royal Ballet, and several companies in America and elsewhere. While this pas de deux is a favorite with knowledgeable dance fans, it sometimes disappoints the average viewer. The outstanding feature of *Flower Festival* is the illusion of joyful lightness. Bournonville uses delicate and fleeting transition steps and unexpected changes of direction that make the dancers seem to spring through space and skim over the surface of the stage. The Danish bounciness is less spectacular than the grand jumps, turns, and high lifts that the Russians developed later on. If the viewer expects the more acrobatic virtuosity of the Russian style, he will miss the lovely qualities of sweet, fresh gaiety that *Flower Festival in Genzano* pas de deux projects. In addition to leaving a danceable repertory, Bournonville created a method of training dancers that is still in use. The system is outstanding in its quality of ballon (light, bouncy, but strong elevation); and it is known particularly for turning out excellent male dancers who project a virile, happy energy.

You have seen how in the middle 1800s, ballet was part of the cultural scene as far north as Denmark and Sweden, and as far south as Italy. Soon we will follow it eastward into Russia, and in Part III, westward into America. Ballet had taken root in all these countries through transplants of French talent. Or else, in America for instance, it flourished briefly through local artists who had danced or studied in France, or through American tours of foreign performers, like Fanny Elssler.

Coppélia

Before we continue on to Russia, we will pay one last visit to the Paris Opera, for the premiere of *Coppélia* in 1870. This ballet was the work of Arthur Saint-Léon, (1821 to 1870), a good example not only of the traveling dancer, but of the kinship between music and dance, and of the egotist in art. Born in Paris, Arthur Saint-Léon's early studies in violin and in ballet were at the courts of Tuscany (Italy) and Stuttgart (Germany), where his father was ballet master. After young Arthur made his debut as a violinist at age thirteen in Stuttgart, and as a dancer at fourteen in Munich, he went on to study in Paris and in Brussels (Belgium). Saint-Léon then toured, choreographed, and was a partner and husband to Fanny Cerrito (one of the *Pas de Quatre* ballerinas) in several Italian cities, Vienna, London, Paris, and then in St. Petersburg (Russia), where he was ballet master from 1859 to 1860. Saint-Léon returned to Paris in 1870, and in this last year of his life staged *Coppélia*. By that time he had parted from Fanny Cerrito (which is not surprising, since he had a reputation for being an ambitious egomaniac who could stand neither criticism nor the success of his rivals).

When Saint-Léon staged many ballets all over Europe, he didn't

Patricia McBride as Coppélia and Shaun O'Brien as Dr. Coppélius were a fine comedic contrast in The New York City Ballet's "Coppélia."

hesitate to use the same choreography in different places, simply changing the titles. He composed the music for some of his ballets and in one of them, he appeared both dancing and playing the violin. In the temperamental dance world, character is less important than talent. Saint-Léon may not have been as great as he thought he was, but there is no question that he was talented. The survival of *Coppélia* is some evidence of this, although the choreography is very different in any version staged today, from the original production in 1870. Saint-Léon did the choreography and collaborated on the action scenario with Charles Nuitter (as they had collaborated earlier on *La Source*). Their scenario was in turn based on a tale by Hoffmann. This is what they came up with.

Swanilda, a village girl, loves Franz. But he is mad about the daughter of Old Doctor Coppélius, an eccentric wizard. Swanilda discovers that her rival, who has never been seen except through a window reading a book, is no girl at all, but only a lifelike doll created by her "father." She contrives to reveal the truth to Franz, whereupon he is happy to admit his error and wed his live, resourceful sweetheart. The ballet survives in part because it offers the ballerina a delightful dual role as a mischievous, charming female schemer, and also as a mechanical doll (when the girl takes the doll's place and pretends to come to life).

Coppélia is a comic variation on the theme of *La Sylphide* and *Giselle* where the male prefers an ideal love to a mere mortal. Classic ballet variations combined with mime express the characters of the besotted youth, the wily sorcerer, and the vivacious girl. Opportunities for exotic dancing are offered by other dolls found in the old man's workshop: a Chinese, a harlequin, a one-man band. The plot of *Coppélia* also serves as a frame, for gaily exciting Hungarian dances like the *czardas,* as the villagers celebrate a wedding or a harvest festival. By the way, this will give you some idea of the lack of importance of male dancers in the French ballet after the Romantic period. The part of Franz, the hero, was danced by a female. He-she was given very little dancing. The grand pas de deux between Franz and Swanilda that is today always part of the ballet is a later addition. As for the original Swanilda, the sixteen-year-old Italian Giuseppina Bozzacchi died during the Franco-Prussian War which broke out after the ballet's eighteenth performance.

Crucial to the ballet's survival is the score by Leo Delibes, whose ballet music for *Sylvia* and *La Source* is frequently heard today (especially as accompaniment for exercises in ballet classes). The composer was a pupil of Adolphe Adam, whose music for *Giselle* had featured the leitmotif, that is, the device of having special musical themes to accompany important ballet characters. Delibes was a kind of bridge between Adam and Tchaikovsky. He continued the leitmotif idea, and his keen dramatic sense led him to match heroine Swanilda's merry, pert, and self-assured actions with suitably fine music. The composer was also very successful in feeding the appetite of his day, a craze for nationalism in music, a fashion that Tchaikovsky was to follow so brilliantly. Delibes's Polish *mazurka* and his Hungarian *czardas* in the *Coppélia* score have that lift and gusto that make the viewer want to get up and dance, and are no doubt responsible for many popular productions of *Coppélia* that have been staged all over the world in the one hundred years since the premiere.

Time and again we see that good music plays a large part in a ballet's success. A fine score may not be necessary for an instant hit—which can also come from a novel idea or an excellent performer—but ballets with mediocre musical accompaniment seldom last long in the repertory. *Coppélia* was created by the Frenchmen Saint-Léon and Delibes. However, its Polish-Hungarian flavor owes more to Eastern Europe than to France. Moving in that direction a little farther, we now come to Russia.

Questions for Review

1. Discuss the original performance of *Pas de Quatre*. Why was it a commercial success?

2. Have you ever seen *Pas de Quatre*? Were the performers first class?

3. What was the ballet scene like in the United States in the 1840s?

4. Why is Bournonville remembered today?

15 IMPERIAL HEIGHTS

THE AGE OF PETIPA

Russia

During the first half of the twentieth century, the big stars in ballet came from Russia. In fact, if you wanted a ballet career, a Russian name was desirable. One of the top ballerinas of the middle 1900s on the English and American stages was born in London and named Alice Marks. But once she had embarked on a dance career she changed her name to Alicia Markova. She did this quite a few years after the Russian Ballet (by now Soviet) was quite hidden from Western eyes by a curtain of mutual distrust and had retreated from the center of the international stage. Markova's name change was a tribute to the prominence of Russian ballet in the last years of the nineteenth century and the first of the twentieth, when the best ballet was produced in St. Petersburg. It was also a nod toward the Russian dancers who had moved to France, England, and America, and revived the ballet in those countries from a long sleep. Therefore it is ironic to recall that during the heyday of the art form in St. Petersburg and Moscow, the big names were more likely to be French and Italian than Russian. Even the language of practice sessions was often French, and not just the professional terms like *port de bras* (arm motions) and *pirouettes* (turns) which have remained French everywhere. Instruction and conversation were also in French, because ballet geniuses like Saint-Léon and Petipa clung to their native language. We shall even see how in the case of Lev Ivanov it was a disadvantage to be Russian! Then too, among the upper classes of the

1800s, French was the international language used by everyone in "cultured" society, just as English is the international language today.

Ballet had a long history in Russia, with dancing masters at the tsar's court as early as the 1600s. From that time on, trained Russian dancers began to make their appearances. However, foreign performing stars, choreographers, teachers, and ballets continued to be imported from France and Italy right up until 1900. In addition to Marius Petipa, the best known, there were Marie Taglioni, Carlotta Grisi, Fanny Elssler, Fanny Cerrito, all of whom made a big hit with the Russian public, as did their famous roles in *La Sylphide, Giselle, La Fille Mal Gardée,* and *La Péri.*

Jules Perrot, whose work you are familiar with from *Giselle* in Paris and *Pas de Quatre* in London, became ballet master in St. Petersburg, where he staged his works from 1851 to 1858. Arthur Saint-Léon had this job from 1859 to 1869 before he returned to Paris to do *Coppélia.* The highest technical standards were established in Russia by Carlo Blasis, Christian Johansson, and Enrico Cecchetti. Carlo Blasis, whom you met as the author of a technique manual, taught in Moscow in the 1860s. At this time, Christian Johansson, who had been a student of Bournonville's in Copenhagen, became a teacher at the Russian Imperial Ballet School in St. Petersburg. Then in the 1890s, Enrico Cecchetti, who had made his debut in Italy, became second ballet master and teacher at the Imperial Theater and School.

Above all these names stands that of Marius Petipa (1818 to 1910), who was hailed as a top dancer in France before he moved to St. Petersburg in 1847. He lived and worked in Russia for the rest of the century where he achieved such prominence that this whole period of ballet history is known as the Age of Petipa. No mention has been made here of the great Russians Fokine, Diaghilev, Pavlova, Nijinsky, Stravinsky, Ulanova, and Plisetskaya (and Nureyev and Baryshnikov), because they were to grace the scene later, the first five in the early twentieth century and the others more recently. Apart from Paul Gerdt and Lev Ivanov, the only outstanding Russian names of the Petipa period are all in music. Paul Gerdt (1844 to 1917), the Russian-born dancer who was a pupil of Christian Johansson, appeared with great distinction in the leading male roles at the premiere performances of *The Sleeping Beauty, Raymonda, Swan Lake, The Nutcracker,* and *Don Quixote,* in short, in the most famous ballets of the era. And we shall see how Lev Ivanov made great contributions to these works in his position as assistant ballet master to Petipa.

The composer Pyotr Ilyich Tchaikovsky (1840 to 1893), above all, gets a lot of the credit for the overwhelming popularity of *Swan Lake, The Sleeping Beauty,* and *The Nutcracker.* It is ironic that all three of the great ballets of the Petipa era seemed unpromising at first. *The Sleeping Beauty* had only a passable reception, and *The Nutcracker* an unfavorable one. While *Swan Lake,* the third and greatest of them, received fine notices in 1895,

Tchaikovsky died some months earlier believing that this composition too was a failure. You see, he had completed the music for *Swan Lake* in 1877 and the first production got indifferent reviews, not only for the mediocre choreography (by a man named Reisinger, unimportant to our story) but even for the Tchaikovsky score which the public found boring. That's because the usual ballet music of the time was lively and light, although not very interesting. Much like a musical comedy, viewers could leave the theater whistling its tunes. Tchaikovsky worked differently. He approached ballet accompaniment like symphonic composing, and came up with much richer, more complicated music that audiences and critics found difficult to follow, although at least one reviewer thought in 1877 that the *Swan Lake* score was charming and predicted that a talented choreographer could make something of it. Before that happened, Hansen, another undistinguished choreographer gave *Swan Lake* a second try in 1880 and a third in 1882. These did not create any interest.

Classical Petipa ballets. Marius Petipa is credited with choreographing about sixty ballets, a number of which became the mainstay of the classical ballet repertory, down to this day. The word *classical* refers here, as it did in the case of *Giselle*, to works of the highest quality. However, unlike *Giselle*, these works were also classical, rather than Romantic, in spirit and style. Classical works are created according to formal rules, in contrast to the inventive freedom in Romantic works. An emphasis on technical virtuosity, rather than on emotional depth, is another characteristic of classical style.

Petipa's ballets were conceived in the grand manner. The typical Romantic ballet image was a wispy sylph, floating above a moonlit forest, pursued feverishly through the shadows by a love-sick youth. In contrast, the typical classical ballet image was a procession of elaborately dressed, jewelled noblemen, surrounding a reigning monarch, along with fanciful characters assembled for their entertainment, in a ballroom whose sparkling chandeliers were as bright as the sun. Classical Petipa ballets harkened back to dazzling, colorful Renaissance spectacle and to the impressive ceremonious Baroque grandeur that surrounded Louis XIV. It is no accident that Petipa's productions glittered in St. Petersburg, the home of the Russian tsar's imperial court, just as ballet under the direction of Lully and Beauchamp had graced the court of Louis XIV, the Sun King. There was a great resemblance between the French Baroque and Russian tsarist courts in the power of their absolute rulers as well as the life enjoyed by their privileged aristocracies who gave frequent sumptuous parties and attended ballet and opera evenings in expensive, jewelled clothing.

It is not surprising that ballets made under such conditions expressed devotion to the supreme monarch. When King Louis was on the throne, all was right with the world. So it was under the tsar. Tribute to royalty was paid in Petipa's ballets when he featured royal characters as heros and heroines. Their action was often set in palaces and followed orderly procedures, like court ceremonies. We saw earlier that at the court of Louis XIV, impressive spectacles were more likely to contain complicated, carefully engineered scenic effects than much interesting dancing. At the tsar's court there were also elaborate stage settings, but this time there was more attention paid to the actual dancing, which was very skillful. The object was the same at both royal courts: to produce dazzling visual entertainment for the upper classes. Therefore the resulting spirit was the same and the many differences between Petipa's productions and those during the reign of Louis XIV arose from two hundred years of developments in the performance of ballets.

By Petipa's time, dance technique had reached a high point, demanding years of devoted study for its mastery. By necessity, the ballet world was thoroughly professional, no longer the plaything of amateurs. True, a tsar might fancy a particular dancer, as did the young Nicholas before he became tsar in 1894, when he fell in love with ballerina Mathilde Kschessinka. But this action took place backstage and not in performance! Similarly, the Russian nobility might wish to show themselves at the ballet, but they had to confine their exhibitionism to the boxes in the audience, and not display themselves from the stage the way Louis XIV and his courtiers had done. Sexual roles had also reversed themselves. In the time of Louis XIV, not only were the males the central figures strutting in noble attire, ladies seldom appeared at all. Women's and girls' parts were taken by males in female costumes. Then gradually, women took their place on the stage, side by side with men until the romantic era, when females rose above the males to dominate the scene. Petipa's ballets continued in this line. His choreography always featured the ballerina, and left the male either to carry her around, or at least to stand slightly behind her, showing off her poses.

Along with the strides made in virtuoso technique and the emphasis on the female, many traditions had grown up in the ballet-music world with the passage of time, and were drawn upon by each new generation of producers. In short, the art of choreography had matured considerably since Louis's day. Petipa worked out a formula derived from elements already familiar to the ballet public. However, in a few works these elements were combined in such a skillful manner that they continue to be effective today, at least when they are refinished according to modern fashion. As always, we must keep in mind that when we see a production of *The Sleeping Beauty* or *Swan Lake*, we are not really watching a genuine nineteenth-century ballet, staged by a twentieth-century company. We are seeing a twentieth-century version of a nineteenth-century ballet. This is not necessarily because the original work has been forgotten. Detailed records were kept of the important Russian productions by ballet master

Nicholas Sergeyev, and after the revolution he restaged these in Paris and London, where they have been handed down from dancer to dancer.

However, styles change. Even when a work from an earlier period has a fine reputation as a classic, and a ballet director decides to show it to the modern public, he usually doesn't want it to look old-fashioned. He wants the audience of his day, and the critics, to enjoy it as a ballet, rather than as a museum relic. Therefore he gives it an up-to-date appearance. Then too, the dancers themselves have a different look from previous generations and their own ways of dancing ballets. By the way, this happens in any performing art: drama, music, or dance. It doesn't happen with painting, sculpture, or novels because they don't require anyone to give them life. A Rembrandt painting remains as it was in the 1600s; a statue by Rodin doesn't change; when you read a novel by Charles Dickens, it is the way he wrote it. However, when you hear a Bach concerto, it is not played exactly as it was in Bach's time. There are bigger alterations in drama. The words in a present-day production of *Hamlet* are Shakespeare's, but the actors and director interpret the play according to modern ideas of psychology and behavior. As for dance, since the very medium of this art form is human action—or behavior—ballets are presented quite differently as time goes by.

Again, we are faced with seeming contradictions. How can we speak about great *classic* works that live beyond their time, and also say that ballets change all the time? Perhaps an example will clarify the situation. Let's look at Petipa's ballet *The Sleeping Beauty*, and we will see how the overall spirit, the music, the theme, and the plot outline remain the same, while interpretations and details vary in successive productions. Just as the non-dancing writer Gautier and the director of the Paris Opera Louis Véron had a lot to do with launching the Romantic ballet, so another nondancer whose name began with *V*, Vsevolojsky, had an important role in the Petipa era.

The Sleeping Beauty

Ivan Vsevolojsky, director of the Russian Imperial Theaters, provided the seed that germinated into *The Sleeping Beauty*, in 1890. He chose the story from the Mother Goose tales of Perrault, and decided that the setting should be a palace of Louis XIV. This was quite logical, since the Frenchman Perrault lived during the reign of Louis XIV and wrote for his court circles. Vsevolojsky also included in his suggestions characters from other Perrault tales, which is why Puss in Boots and Red Riding Hood make their appearances in the entertainment pageant that takes place within the ballet. Incidentally, Vsevolojsky's choices demonstrate again the similarity of outlook between the courtiers of Louis XIV and those of the tsar.

What ensured artistic greatness in what we might call an almost childish scenario was the score for the ballet. Vsevolojsky approached Tchaikovsky, who responded enthusiastically to Vsevolojsky's outline of the action, and agreed to work on the music. The result was an excellent dance score. Tchaikovsky even took advantage of the location at the court of Louis XIV, and used for his model the music of Lully, who was the opera and ballet music director for the Sun King.

Now Marius Petipa entered the scene, to correspond with Tchaikovsky on details of the scenario. Petipa was accustomed to ordering music according to measure from inferior composers like Minkus, the official ballet composer of the St. Petersburg Maryinsky Theater who turned out ballets to order, among them *Don Quixote* and *La Bayadère*. Petipa wrote to Tchaikovsky with instructions for *The Sleeping Beauty* like these for the cat dance, which are reproduced in *Ballet Music* by Roger Fiske:

> "Repeated mewing. Caresses and blows. At the end, claws scratching and squawling. Start off three-four *amoroso*. End up in three-four with mewing, becoming quicker and quicker.
>
> For the Diamond Fairy he asked for 'Showers of diamonds, like electric sparks, two-four *vivo*.'
>
> "Not that Tchaikovsky always obeyed servilely. Sometimes he flouted the choreographer's wishes, or—more probably—talked him out of them...He did, however, follow Petipa scrupulously when an accompaniment to mime was required.

Tchaikovsky seems to have responded with fine examples of descriptive dramatic music, rather than the rage that one would expect from a brilliant artist whose creative independence was being stepped on. In any case, *The Sleeping Beauty* is generally considered to be one of the finest ballet scores ever composed.

The music contains two major leitmotifs (melodic themes that always accompany the same character). One is an angry theme for the wicked Carabosse, and the other is a pleasant theme for the good Lilac Fairy. Recurrence of these two themes makes the score (and the ballet) into a running conflict between good and evil. At the end, good wins out. Along the way there are lovely dance variations—waltzes, polka, and a mazurka; dramatic character parts for Puss in Boots and Red Riding Hood; and at the end an old French folk tune that Tchaikovsky obviously chose in recognition of Perrault's French folk tales.

While this is a dramatic fairy tale ballet, the closeness between the choreography and the music makes *The Sleeping Beauty* a kind of symphonic ballet. We learn from *Dance Perspectives*, Number 24 that a Russian critic wrote: "Each of its four acts, like the movements of a symphony, is closed in form and can exist independently, but each can be appraised at its true worth only in relation to the other acts." Most viewers are too busy watching the dancing to notice the musical structure. No matter. We call *The Sleeping Beauty* a great classic precisely because there are many different things to appreciate. In addition to working out the scenario with Vsevolojsky and making suggestions to Tchaikovsky about the music, Petipa's main contribution to *The Sleeping Beauty* was the choreography. Here's a brief summary of the plot, with some of Petipa's ideas.

The king and queen give a grand party to celebrate the birth of their daughter Princess Aurora. The choreography offers a grand procession of the royal parents, their courtiers, six fairy godmothers, and attendants. Each fairy presents a gift to the new princess in the form of a special solo dance. Suddenly the wicked fairy Carabosse crashes in. Angry at not being invited to the party, she pronounces a dreadful curse: one day the princess shall prick her finger on a spindle and die. The good Lilac Fairy has not yet presented her gift. She is not powerful enough to remove the curse completely, but she can modify it. The princess shall not die, but fall into a deep sleep until a prince kisses her awake. This episode is staged with dramatic pantomime, contrasting the horrid old Carabosse with the loving Lilac Fairy.

Time passes and the scene moves to Princess Aurora's sixteenth birthday party. Again we see an impressive entrance of royal guests, joined by peasants who waltz with flower garlands. The high point of the party scene is the famous *rose adagio*, danced by Princess Aurora and four princes who have come to seek her hand in marriage. One by one the princes partner her, supporting her in slow turns which she performs *en pointe* on only one leg, with the other lifted in an *attitude* pose.

Once again festivities are interrupted by tragedy. Carabosse's dreadful curse is carried out, with Aurora pricking her finger on a spindle and collapsing. The Lilac Fairy gently waves her wand and everyone in the palace falls asleep, joining Aurora in slumber.

One hundred years go by. The next procession is at a royal hunt, led by a handsome Prince Charming. Again the party is joined by peasants dancing merry folk steps. But now we hear an echo from the Romantic ballet. The prince is moody, and wanders alone in the forest as night falls. Into the moonlight glides the Lilac Fairy, who leads the melancholy young man to a vision of the sleeping Princess Aurora, with whom he falls in love. In a scene reminiscent of *La Sylphide* and *Giselle*, the prince pursues the vision of Aurora, who is surrounded by fairies so that he can never catch up with her. (You may well ask how this Romantic scene floated into the formal "classic" choreography of Petipa. A Russian dance critic suggests that this scene was largely the work of Lev Ivanov, whom we will meet in a minute.) Finally, Prince Charming gets to the palace, covered with weeds and spider webs, suitable to a palace that's been neither swept nor dusted for one hundred years. He enters the room where Aurora is peacefully sleeping, kisses her, and she awakens as everybody in the palace comes to life.

Their wedding gives one more opportunity to stage a splendid procession. The royal family and the courtiers parade pompously. Among the guests are the other Mother Goose characters told about by Perrault: Cinderella, Puss in Boots, Tom Thumb, and Red Riding Hood. They take turns performing for the court. Outstanding in the entertainment are two love duets: the White Cat flirting coyly with Puss in Boots, and the brilliant soaring Blue Bird pas de deux. And then Aurora and Prince Charming appear in a pas de deux that is gracious and technically magnificent. Now the whole court joins in a spirited mazurka and the ballet ends with a flourishing pose. As if there weren't enough courtly ceremony up to the finale, the choreographer created one final tribute to royalty. The god Apollo, dressed up as King Louis XIV, appears surrounded by the fairies and lit by the rays of the sun.

At the premiere performance the cast was first-rate, including the Italian stars Carlotta Brianza (Aurora) and Enrico Cecchetti, who doubled as the wretched Carabosse and the Blue Bird. Cecchetti, of course, became famous as a teacher of: Pavlova, Fokine, Nijinsky, de Valois, Danilova, Markova, and Dolin, all of whom will appear later in our story. Petipa's daughter Marie was the Lilac Fairy. Despite all this talent, the ballet was a sleeping beauty in more than scenario. At first, it received a lukewarm reaction and only gradually did it gain popularity. However, while the tsar and the general audience weren't duly impressed, *The Sleeping Beauty* had its effect on certain artists, such as Anna Pavlova, who was eight years old when she saw it, and then persuaded her mother to enter her in the auditions for the Imperial Ballet School.

Petipa's formula for choreography reached its high point with *The Sleeping Beauty*. If you want to include it in your recipe file, here are the ingredients:

1. This marks a return to the French court ballet, where such entertainments continued for many hours. It was a complete evening's entertainment which was based on a dramatic plot and alternated mime episodes with dancing. This formula is regarded as ballet in the grand classical style.

2. *Spectacle.* Elaborate stage designs usually including a dazzling palace hall and large casts in colorful elaborate costumes that together fill the stage.

3.   *Virtuosity.* Talented dancers trained to a high level of skill execute brilliant, tricky steps and poses.

4.   *Choreographic variety.* Each act contains mimed action, and ballet pieces for soloists, couples, small groups, and large ensembles. There are also character dance bits that include folk and national steps which are arranged in geometric groupings. All kinds of comedy parts are included, such as impersonations of animals, clowns, sailors, and bossy old people, all presented with bold, obvious gestures. There are one or more stately processions.

5.   *Grand pas de deux.* Often at the conclusion, but sometimes earlier, the leading ballerina is joined by an important male dancer in an elegant duet with a fixed form. This bit begins with a supported adagio, in which the female does difficult pirouettes and complicated poses with her partner's support. Here the male's function is to show off the ballerina by displaying her high in the air and helping her to balance in ways that she could not achieve alone. Next, the male exhibits his own high jumps, leaps, and fancy turns. Then the ballerina does a solo in which her movements are small and dainty, but precise and brilliant. Finally, the two together do their flashy specialties in technique, ending with the ballerina diving into her partner's arms in a daring position.

6.   *Finale.* The ballet closes with the whole cast onstage, the important characters in the front, all in lively motion that ends with everyone posed, framing the stars of the performance.

7.   *Classic style.* Body shapes are clear and elegant. Groups are designed in straight lines, circles, squares, and triangles, usually in perfectly symmetrical arrangements. Soloists are always placed in the middle or above the ensemble. The total expressive manner is noble and orderly. Formal beauty is the keynote.

In all, the Frenchman Petipa spent fifty-six years in Russia, where he created forty-six original ballets and made new productions of seventeen ballets by other choreographers, not to mention thirty-five dances that he put together for operas. Petipa's best known works after the Tchaikovsky trio *The Sleeping Beauty, Swan Lake,* and *The Nutcracker* are *La Bayadère, Don Quixote, Bluebeard, Cinderella, Raymonda,* (whose music composer was Glazunov) *Harlequinade,* and *Le Corsair.* You may have seen some of these in versions by the Russian Kirov Ballet, Balanchine's New York City Ballet, or a number of other companies. However, *The Sleeping Beauty* remains the queen of the Petipa repertory.

While these works differed from one another, certain elements are considered characteristic of Petipa; for example, the pantomime that was like sign language rather than expressive acting. Swan Queen Odette fears that Prince Siegfried will shoot her, so she says "You" (points to him with her right hand) "me" (places fingertips to her breasts) "shoot" (mimes aiming an arrow in a crossbow) "not?" (negative gesture). Then there are the arrangements of classical dance sections. These are simple, symmetrical formations with emphasis on technical display, and a clear development, usually A-B-A (fast-slow-fast or slow-fast-slow).

Two other ballets, *The Nutcracker* and *Swan Lake*, together with *The Sleeping Beauty* are all very much alive today. Mark the Age of Petipa as a great one. Yet in that annoying way of the past to refuse to fit neatly into the student's notebook, Petipa cannot be given full credit for either of these two ballets. Although he didn't want to, he must share the honors of *Swan Lake* with Lev Ivanov, and leave them almost completely to Ivanov for *The Nutcracker*.

Lev Ivanov. Ivanov (1834 to 1901) was officially Petipa's assistant ballet master. But while Petipa was egotistical and bossy (in the typical manner of Arthur Saint-Léon, Jules Perrot, and other directors who demanded the spotlight even when working behind the scenes), Lev Ivanov was quite modest and easygoing. Ivanov put up with it when Jules Perrot, who was ballet master in St. Petersburg from 1851 to 1858, held back Ivanov's performing career. He did this by *not* assigning Ivanov the leading parts which his superior dancing ability really called for. Why? Because the Frenchman Perrot was prejudiced against Ivanov's Russian nationality—in the Russian Imperial Ballet!

Similarly, as a teacher and director, Ivanov did not play the demanding tyrant. Only in private did he express feelings of frustration and annoyance with the dancers, telling his pupils *only in his diary* (as quoted in Cyril Beaumont's *The Ballet Called Swan Lake*):

> I am always surprised and astonished at your indifferent and careless attention towards your art. You do not show the slightest interest in your profession. You are not artists but robots.
>
> At rehearsal you are lazy and unwilling to strive, and you do not give your mind to your work. You are just the same at an actual performance. For these reasons our joint labors suffer.

By the way, even today this is a frequent criticism of dancers, whose thoughts are not always concentrated where sensitive artistic directors would like them to be.

Anyway, given Ivanov's habit of avoiding unpleasant arguments, it is not surprising that he went along with Petipa, when Petipa insisted on receiving full credit for any works that were produced under his supervision, no matter how much others helped. Therefore, for many years, audiences remained ignorant of Ivanov's creative contributions to Petipa's ballets, such as the Romantic vision scene described above in *The Sleeping Beauty*. At least in the case of *The Nutcracker* there was no question of ignoring Ivanov. Petipa was forced to assign all the choreography to his assistant because he was too sick to do it himself.

The Nutcracker

The Nutcracker (1892) has probably been performed more than any other ballet, particularly in the United States where it has become an annual winter holiday tradition. By now, Americans have come to associate Christmas with *The Nutcracker*, as dance companies large and small, led by Balanchine's New York City Ballet, produce it every December. These versions may differ from one another but they all bear some relationship to the St. Petersburg premiere of 1892 which featured Tchaikovsky's music, Ivanov's choreography, and E.T.A. Hoffmann's story.

Another tale of E.T.A. Hoffmann formed the basis for *Coppélia* and there are similarities in the two plots. Both have a grotesque old man, half evil wizard, half mechanical genius, and toys that come to life, along with human characters that fall in love with the toys. For fun you might read the stories that Hoffmann wrote. You will enjoy shivering through their scary events, and you will see what a different impression they make from the cheerful, juvenile ballets derived from them. In fact, both *Coppélia* and *The Nutcracker* are considered perfect dance entertainment for children, whereas the stories have heavy overtones of dark psychological forces that are rough going even for mature readers.

However, the original idea behind *The Nutcracker* was to stage an amusement suitable for the fashionable adult audiences of the tsar's St. Petersburg. Once again the Russian theater official with the unpronounceable name (Vsevolojsky) wanted to bring Tchaikovsky and Petipa together as he had in *The Sleeping Beauty* and he decided that *The Nutcracker* would serve as a starting point for their joint efforts. It is not quite clear whether Vsevolojsky or Petipa worked more on the actual ballet scenario, eliminating all the evil details from Hoffmann's story and ending up with an outline of inoffensive action that would also allow for the national (folk) dances, the character roles, and the sections of pure ballet dancing, including the grand pas de deux that were indispensable to Petipa's formula. In some reference sources, Ivanov is credited with the *book* (the scenario) as well as the choreography for *The Nutcracker*.

It seems more logical that he was presented with the completed scenario, because when he received Tchaikovsky's music, the plot was already part of it. This plot had been dictated to the composer in advance, just as the outline of *The Sleeping Beauty* had been.

Tchaikovsky's comments about doing the music for *The Nutcracker* should be taken to heart by anyone who is interested in composing either music or dance. "The subject pleases me very little," he wrote. He composed the music purely as a job that had to be done, and not from any great inspiration. It was a struggle. Yet he recognized that sometimes assignments, or fixed commissions, resulted in better music than that produced by inspiration. He considered it an artist's duty to discipline himself to create even when he wasn't in the mood. He put it this way: "Inspiration is a guest who does not care to visit those who are lazy." At least Tchaikovsky had the consolation of one special interest in the piece, to the extent that he was using it to introduce the *celesta* to Russia. It was a new instrument that he had recently heard in Paris. And Tchaikovsky sent for it secretly, to prevent his competitor Rimsky-Korsakov from getting hold of it first. Of course, whatever doubts he may have had about it, Tchaikovsky succeeded with *The Nutcracker*, a score that is immensely popular today with or without the presence of dancers.

Ivanov could not help but respond to the colorful music. The familiar close connection between dance and music is illustrated in the abilities of this choreographer. The story is told that composer Anton Rubinstein was playing a new ballet in the rehearsal hall. When he left, Lev Ivanov sat at the piano and repeated almost the whole thing just from having heard it. At any rate, while the classical Petipa was more interested in pantomimic drama and formal spectacle, Ivanov had a Romantic inclination to express music and emotion through dance patterns. However, while Tchaikovsky's music inspired Ivanov to create fine choreography, he was somewhat limited by the ballet concept that Hoffmann, Vsevolojsky, and Petipa had supplied. Indeed, Tchaikovsky himself had already been limited by the scenario. Here is more or less the material that Tchaikovsky had to convert into music, and Ivanov into movement.

The first act presents a Christmas Eve party and a fantastic dream, set in the respectable middle-class home of a little girl (called Clara in the American adaptations). At the party, children dance gaily, adults more sedately, and mechanical toys perform. The mysteriously wicked, but seemingly kindly old Drosselmeyer is also a guest, and he gives little Clara a Nutcracker doll, which she immediately treasures, even falls in love with. At last everyone leaves. The party is over and the house is dark and quiet. Clara comes into the living room and has a nightmare in which there is a battle between evil mice and brave soldiers. The soldiers triumph, led by the Nutcracker, who has come to life as a handsome soldier-prince.

Then the Nutcracker Prince escorts Clara to a pleasanter dreamland for delightful visions. On the way, he takes her through a snowy forest, and there she watches the snowflakes in a whirling dance. They travel to the Kingdom of Sweets, and here the tasty international entertainment includes: Spanish chocolate, Arabian coffee, and Chinese tea. There is also the Ginger Clown, a figure in a tremendous skirt under which tricky clowns are hiding; Russian acrobatic jesters; waltzing flowers; and the Sugar-Plum Fairy herself, supported in a classic adagio by the Nutcracker Prince. After a grand finale in waltz time, Clara departs with the prince, and wakes up from her dream.

The Petipa formula is evident. There are pantomimic scenes of celebrating children receiving presents and proper adults being polite. Tricky Drosselmeyer is making mischief. Mice fight and frighten Clara. National dance scenes include Spanish posture and quick footwork for the coffee couple and Russian squatting jumps for the buffoons. Balletic scenes feature waltzes for snowflakes and flowers, traditional grand pas de deux for the Sugar-Plum Fairy and Nutcracker Prince, and the crowded finale for the entire Kingdom of Sweets.

Ivanov's accepting nature did not allow him to make any changes in the conception of the work, although we have seen that by temperament he was more interested in emotional poetry than in spectacular fireworks. His outstanding choreography seems to have been "The Waltz of the

Balanchine created this image of snowflakes for the New York City Ballet, based on Ivanov's original 1892 production of "The Nutcracker."

Snowflakes." Reports of this scene, quoted in Roslavleva's *Era of the Russian Ballet*, call it a symphonic masterpiece:

> Ivanov did succeed in creating, through the type of classical steps used, and in the ever-changing dance pattern, an illusion of falling snow, with soft, large flakes drifting in the frosty air.
>
> The "snowflakes" carried in their hands wands with spherical flakes attached to quivering wires, while similar wires and small white balls were attached to their headgear...
>
> The "snowflakes" quivered and seemed to be floating through the air. The dancers formed now a star and then assembled into one huge snowball, and in the end stood still in a closed group, as if chased by the wind into one large heap of snow.

Of course we don't really know how much of the impressive illusion was due to the dance patterns and how much to the quivering wires. The rest of the ballet came off in a conventional manner, and many of the premiere reviews were not favorable: "The production is an insult"; "carnival-fair character"; "for art absolutely nothing." Perhaps the ballet would have been satisfying if Petipa himself had staged it after all, or if Ivanov had changed the scenario to a more Romantic fantasy. However, playing "might have been" is a waste of time. It is difficult enough to find out what really happened in the past without trying to figure out what might have happened if the circumstances were different. In any case, since 1892 *The Nutcracker* has been revived by well-known choreographers all over the world, and every sign indicates that its popularity continues to increase.

Swan Lake

At last we come to the 1895 version of *Swan Lake* by Petipa and Ivanov, whose choreography at last was first-rate and was immediately acclaimed. But recognition came too late for Tchaikovsky. In fact, the first performances of this *Swan Lake* were arranged as a memorial to him. Several conflicting reports on the ballet, coupled with the fact that Ivanov's name wasn't even mentioned on the program, raise questions about the creation of this famous ballet. But all accounts agree that it was Lev Ivanov who created Act II, the most poetic scene from this work.

Act II takes place at the lake where the swan maidens flutter and sway as the prince tenderly embraces Odette, the White Swan; and the four little cygnettes do their saucy routine. This act is often given by itself as a complete short work. For example, in the repertory of the New York City Ballet, *Swan Lake* consists only of Act II. An administrator of that company once told me, "When we are on tour and the box office is slow, we need only schedule *Swan Lake* to raise ticket sales immediately."

But as we have seen, Ivanov always played second fiddle to Petipa, and the assistant ballet master got no credit at the premiere for this. Petipa was listed as sole choreographer. From the very beginning, there has been confusion about who contributed what ideas to *Swan Lake*. The background of the ballet's conception is given below, not because it is important to learn all the names and detailed circumstances, but because they illustrate once again the process of communication that is central to ballet. This process takes place first of all among many people who create a ballet, even before the artwork is presented to an audience. In this respect, *Swan Lake* reminds us of *Giselle*, which blossomed from Gautier's personal contact with Saint-Georges, Carlotta Grisi, Jules Perrot, and many others. As in the Paris of the early 1800s, so in the Moscow and the St. Petersburg of the late 1800s, groups of artists and intellectuals gathered in *salons* (not to be confused with *saloons* where another kind of social life went on).

Salons were informal social courts in private homes which gave talented people a place to exchange ideas. It was the middle-class answer to the artistic life of royal courts. Such gatherings met in the house of V.P. Begichev, who was an official in the Moscow Imperial Theater where the Bolshoi Ballet developed, while the Kirov Ballet came from St. Petersburg. Another home where salons met was that of Vassily Geltzer, a dancer who excelled in mimed character roles. At the first performance of *Swan Lake* in 1877, Begichev and Geltzer were credited with the scenario. Tchaikovsky may well have had a share in the early conception of the action. He was part of their intellectual circle as a teacher in the Moscow Conservatory of Music and as a tutor of Begichev's sons. Ballet ideas were undoubtedly tossed back and forth at these salons, as well as the latest themes of literature and philosophy. This lively society would surely have spoken about Russian fairy tales and Russian folk culture, since these were carefully nourished in this period of strong national feelings and growing Russian national identity. Certainly, these enthusiastic artists were familiar with German Romantic fairy stories and their own Pushkin's tale of a White Swan who is saved from a wicked hawk by a prince and who afterward appears as a beautiful maiden.

The spiritual sylph figure which we remember from *La Sylphide* and *Giselle* was changed into a bird or a swan. But the same elements of magic spells, and even more important, of ideal females symbolized by flying creatures that can't be grabbed and possessed, recur in *Swan Lake* where they continue to strike a responsive chord in the ballet public. This presents us with another contradiction. Here we speak of the Age of Petipa as the period that saw the peak of the classical ballet repertory, when the standards of technical vituosity were set. Yet the favorite scene in the most famous of ballets is Romantic! Well, the more we investigate any particular stage of the dance art, the more we discover these contradictions; which is another way of saying once more that art is too complex to permit exact theories as if they were mathematical theorems. The romantic era, despite the emphasis on free emotional expression, saw the introduction of *point* technique (toe-dancing) as well as the first comprehensive manual on ballet technique (by Carlo Blasis). In the same way, the classic era, despite its emphasis on set choreographic forms and technical displays, also saw poetic emotional scenes. You need only look around you today to find groups which do not follow the prevailing modernistic trends to understand that an age becomes gradually identified by certain outstanding characteristics, while their opposites still hang about at the edge.

The scenario of *Swan Lake* allows for a variety of effective scenes and the music provides a stirring, memorable underpinning to the staged action. When we meet Prince Siegfried, our hero is reluctant to marry. He prefers dancing and drinking at village festivals or hunting. His mother, the queen, breaks in on his merrymaking to scold him for his irresponsible behavior and to inform him that she is giving a party the next day at which he must choose a bride. After the queen leaves, the merrymakers spot a flock of swans and they decide to hunt them down and see who is the best shot. At a lake, the prince and his friend Benno prepare to shoot the birds with their crossbows. But night has fallen and suddenly Odette, the enchanted Swan Queen, appears as her real self—a beautiful maiden—and she pleads with the prince to spare her swans. Siegfried agrees not to hurt them and at the same moment he falls deeply in love with Odette, who explains about her magic spell. She can only be saved if the prince remains true to her. Siegfried swears eternal love and Odette vanishes into the forest with the swan maidens.

Now comes the magnificent ball where eligible girls dance for the prince. None succeeds in catching his fancy until one special lady, Odile, dances for him. Odile is really the daughter of Rothbart, the wicked magician who had put the spell on Odette the Swan Queen. By wicked cunning, Odile is able to deceive the prince into thinking she is really Odette, his true love. Siegfried is uncertain at first, but the trick finally works and he embraces the wicked Odile and declares his love for her. With a nasty triumphant leer, Odile and her father leave, and the prince realizes too late that he has not been true to Odette, and has therefore condemned her to remain imprisoned as a swan. He runs to the forest to beg her forgiveness. Siegfried and Odette cling together in hopeless depair and prepare to die in the now stormy lake. Finally, peace descends upon the scene and the lovers kiss. In some versions this is presented as a happy ending. Siegfried's deep love and willingness to sacrifice his life have broken Odette's spell, and they will live happily ever after. In the original, however, they die, and the calm ending presents the couple united in a heavenly hereafter, sometimes gliding off together in a swan boat on the distant horizon.

Ivanov is generally credited with arranging the ending, as well as the famous Act II. But who knows how many suggestions he made along the way? Petipa's spectacular style is recognized at the ball and in the village festival because these resemble his approach to so many other ballets. In contrast to the classical Petipa, his assistant, the Russian Lev Ivanov can be seen as both a throwback to the romantic era in Paris and a foretaste of another Romantic Russian. That would be Michel Fokine, whom we will meet when we move into the twentieth century and watch the ballet spread out from Russia and back to the West.

Questions for Review

1.   How would you characterize the Age of Petipa?

2.   What are the elements in Petipa's classic ballets?

3.   Contrast Petipa's style with Ivanov's.

4.   Which of the three great Tchaikovsky ballets have you seen? Describe the performances.

16 EXPERIMENTS IN ENTERTAINMENT

SERGEI DIAGHILEV AND THE BALLETS RUSSES

Russian Artists after the Revolution

At last, with the brilliant artists who created Sergei Diaghilev's Ballets Russes, we arrive at the edge of recent memory. During the first decades of the twentieth century, these figures were to become the teachers of today's ballet stars and the creators of their modern ballet repertory. The story of the Ballets Russes began in Russia, where since the end of the nineteenth century, the finest ballet dancers were being trained. From there, the action soon shifted to Paris. Diaghilev and his cluster of outstanding, talented individuals were responsible for balletic entertainments as fine as anything produced during the reign of Louis XIV, the Romantic Age in Paris, or the recent Age of Petipa in Russia. Here are some of the prominent artists who were involved with the Ballets Russes.

Music. Igor Stravinsky, Sergei Prokofiev, Claude Debussy, Maurice Ravel, Richard Strauss, Erik Satie, Manuel de Falla, Francis Poulenc, Darius Milhaud, Constant Lambert.

Design of stage sets and costumes. Alexander Benois, Leon Bakst, Robert E. Jones, Pablo Picasso, Georges Braque, Henri Matisse, Juan Gris, Maurice Utrillo, Joan Miro, Georges Rouault.

Scenarios. Alexander Benois, Leon Bakst, Igor Stravinsky, Jean Cocteau.

Dance. Michel Fokine, Anna Pavlova, Vaslav Nijinsky, Bronislava Nijinska, Tamara Karsavina, Adolph Bolm, Enrico Cecchetti, Leonide Massine, Anton Dolin, Alicia Markova, Serge Lifar, George Balanchine, Marie Rambert, Ninette de Valois, Alexandra Danilova.

As for Sergei Diaghilev (1872 to 1929), he does not fit in any of the above classifications. Yet without him, it is unlikely that these (and other) ballets would have seen the lights of a theater: *Les Sylphides, Firebird, Coq D'Or, Rite of Spring, Petrouchka, Les Noces, Apollo, Prodigal Son, The Three-Cornered Hat, Parade.* Who was Diaghilev and what did he have to do with all this? Sergei was born an upper-class Russian with the ambition to make a name in the art world. After dropping his law studies, he tried unsuccessfully to compose music. Piaghilev then joined a circle of artists and got them to publish a journal that he edited, which discussed the latest developments in poetry and painting. He had a position with the Russian Imperial Theaters and supervised several productions. But his difficult personality made enemies who finally got him dismissed from the bureaucracy. For a while he exhibited the latest Russian paintings both at home in St. Petersburg and abroad in Paris. Then at last, he found a proper outlet for his energy, his administrative ability, and his enthusiasm for exciting new artworks—as an impresario-producer of ballets.

At the start, the idea (of Alexander Benois) had been to show Russian ballet in Paris. Although we know that French and Italian artists had originally introduced the ballet into Russia, by this date the art form was in a very poor state in Western Europe. Diaghilev's concerts were successful from their first performances in May 1909.

Since Diaghilev came to the ballet world from music, painting, and poetry, it is not surprising that these aspects of his productions often outshone the dance movements. In fact, as we find in Percival's *The World of Diaghilev*, Alexander Benois wrote later:

> It was no accident that what was afterwards known as the Ballets Russes was originally conceived not by the professionals of the dance but by a circle of artists, linked together by the idea of Art as an entity.
>
> Everything followed from the common desire of several painters and musicians to see the fulfillment of the theatrical dreams which haunted them.

The visual designs for the Ballets Russes had an immediate impact on fashion-conscious Paris. For example, the lavish colorful settings that Leon Bakst did for *Sheherazade* (1910) caused a new "Oriental" look in clothes and home decorating. Also, painters Benois and Bakst and composer Stravinsky conceived the ideas and scenarios for many of the ballets. In return, of course, the performers helped to acquaint the public with the cubism of Picasso and Braque and the expressionism of Rouault and Matisse, as well as with the new musical sounds of Stravinsky, Prokofiev, and Satie.

In Diaghilev, we meet a complex theatrical figure. Some insight into the man's magnetic force is given by Tamara Karsavina, one of the great ballerinas who starred in his company and at the same time continued as a soloist in the Imperial Ballet in St. Petersburg. In her autobiography, *Theater Street*, she writes:

> It was Diaghilev's will that set in motion every cog and wheel of the unwieldy machine. . . by a casual remark he could pull aside a curtain and open a lovely vista to the imagination. . . . He brought quick, unhesitating decision to every doubt.
>
> He had the sense of the theater to an uncanny degree...He was unerring in his judgement; artists believed implicitly in his opinion. It pleased him to divine a seed of genius where a lesser intuition would see eccentricity only....He enlarged the scope of my artistic emotions; he educated and formed me.

However, when Karsavina didn't fit in with his plans, Diaghilev made her miserable. Karsavina had signed up for a season with the London Coliseum and Diaghilev wanted her to cancel it so that she could appear in Paris for him.

> I was being literally tormented by Diaghilev. I dreaded the telephone, as it was not easy to resist Diaghilev's pressure. He would wear out his opponent, not by the logic of his arguments, but by sheer stress of his own will.

Fokine, the brilliant choreographer whose masterpieces had so enriched the Ballets Russes in its first four seasons complained bitterly about Diaghilev's betrayal. He claimed that because Diaghilev commissioned Nijinsky, his latest favorite, to stage *Afternoon of a Faun*, in 1912, he did all he could to wreck Fokine's *Daphnis and Chloe*, by having its premiere at the same time. Fokine accused Diaghilev of collecting old costumes from the previous season for his new ballet, something that had never happened before in his company. Then he interfered with Fokine's rehearsals. And as a final gesture of ill will, he scheduled the premiere of *Daphnis and Chloe* as a curtain raiser, something without precedent in the annals of ballet history.

Stravinsky, the giant of twentieth-century music whom Diaghilev "discovered" in St. Petersburg, made this comment on the impresario's conduct: "It is almost impossible to describe the perversity of Diaghilev's entourage—a kind of homosexual Guard." He reminded another musician of a "decadent Roman emperor—possibly even Genghis Khan." At this point, it would be easy to become bogged down in the mire of gossip. Diaghilev's private life was as sensational as his ballet productions, as you would soon find out if you were to poke around in the personal memoirs of Ballets Russes celebrities, or in Richard Buckle's *Diaghilev*. However, I do not raise this issue merely to spice up my story, but because Diaghilev's sexual preferences had a real influence on ballet development, not only in instances like the promotion of Nijinsky over Fokine as a choreographer, but in general. Through the Ballets Russes, the male dancer regained the ground he had lost during the ballerina-dominated romantic era.

First-rank male soloists and choreographers appeared on the scene, such as: Michel Fokine, Vaslav Nijinsky, Serge Lifar, Leonide Massine, Adolph Bolm, Anton Dolin, and George Balanchine. Incidentally, please do *not* conclude that all these dancers were personally linked to Diaghilev. His remarkable sense of theater and his ability to recognize fresh talent were equally responsible for the new look of ballet. In any case, these men were not only to make their mark with the Ballets Russes, but except for the ill-fated Nijinsky, they were to influence the art form enormously in France, England, and America, down to the present day. Further, the breakup of the female monopoly on dance imagery opened the door to many interesting choreographic possibilities. In three, Fokine's *Petrouchka*, Nijinsky's *Afternoon of a Faun*, and Balanchine's *Prodigal Son*, the central ballet characters were a tragic clown, a sensuous male animal, and a youth who rejects the path of righteousness. These provided a welcome change from male dancers who were merely strong arms serving to elevate females.

The Ballets Russes started out with an annual Paris season, arranged by Diaghilev for outstanding Russian artists who continued to dance and choreograph in St. Petersburg, under contract with the Imperial Ballet. At first, there was even official Russian sponsorship from people like Grand Duke Vladimir (the tsar's uncle). Gradually, because of personal and artistic conflicts and later because of political ones when the revolution of 1917 trampled on the old artistic establishment, Diaghilev and many ballet people cut their ties with Russia. The Ballets Russes took up its residence in the Chatelet Theater of Paris and an impressive body of Russian soloists moved westward. Some of them joined the Ballets Russes which Diaghilev ran from 1909 until his death in 1929. Others started their own companies.

In any case, audiences in London, Paris, New York, and elsewhere were treated to fine ballet performances of a quality not before seen. The ground was prepared for a flowering of ballet in Western countries, particularly when excellent Russian dancers settled in them permanently. They brought with them the great nineteenth-century classics from *Giselle* through *Swan Lake*; and in addition, exciting works by Fokine, Nijinsky, Massine, and Balanchine that emerged from Diaghilev's company to lay the foundations of modern ballet.

Michel Fokine

The first choreographer of the Ballets Russes, Fokine (1880 to 1942), was graduated in 1907 as a fine dancer from the St. Petersburg Imperial School. For a while, he went along with the tired-out conventions regulating the ballet, but he was not happy about them. In a pas de deux he performed with Anna Pavlova, he was Apollo and she was Flora. In his *Memoirs of a Ballet Master*, he wrote: "The choreography for these we mostly staged our- selves...We did whatever we felt we could do best. There was no connec- tion whatever between our 'number' and the ballet into which it was inserted. Neither was there any connection with the music . . . Pavlova would say to me, 'Take it easy, we still have a great deal of music left,' or 'Hurry, hurry!'" Fokine began to ask "Is this all necessary? What does it mean?" He particularly objected to the numerous interruptions of applause. "Is a separate success for each small number in the ballet neces- sary?...Artists do not feel their roles, do not grasp the relationship between characters, but at all times are conscious of the audience . . . I realized that the audience couldn't possibly believe in any sincerity of interpretation from artists, who, portraying a couple in love, acted as though completely oblivious of each other, focusing their gaze at the balcony, looking expec- tantly for applause from that source."

Interestingly enough, the early stirrings of another reform, called *modern dance,* were part of the Russian scene during this same period. Isadora Duncan first appeared in Russia in 1905 and ran a school in that country for several years. Karsavina describes Isadora's impact:

> The great sensation caused in the artistic world by the first appearance of Isadora Duncan was still fresh when, in the spring of 1907, Fokine produced his *Eunice.*
>
> Isadora had rapidly conquered the Petersburg theatrical world . . .
>
> I remember that the first time I saw her dance I fell completely under her sway. It never occurred to me that there was the slightest hostility between her art and ours. There seemed room for both, and each had much that it could learn to advantage.

However, while Fokine, like Duncan, was interested in making the art form more expressive, he didn't intend to destroy the old order completely as she did.

Fokine favored the classic ballet technique, with its straight back and turned-out legs, as the best training for a dancer; and he built his theories and his choreography on solid ballet traditions. His manifesto for reform could have been a quotation from Noverre's *Letters on Dancing and Ballets* written about 150 years earlier. Fokine believed that:

1. "The ballet should be staged in conformity with the epoch represented."
2. "The dance pantomime and gesture should...be of a kind that best fits the style of the period."
3. "The ballet must be uninterrupted—a complete artistic creation and not a series of separate numbers."
4. "The action must not be interrupted with applause and its acknowledgement by the artists."
5. "The music should not consist of waltzes, polkas and final galops—but must express the story of the ballet and, primarily, its emotional content."

Don't these suggestions which Fokine wrote for his directors in 1904 seem quite tame today? But at the time they were revolutionary.

Of more interest to us than his theories are the dozens of works Fokine created, a number of which are still being danced. These include *The Dying Swan, Les Sylphides, Spectre de la Rose, Sheherazade, Firebird, Petrouchka*, and several more that are revived on occasion, but these six are the ones most frequently staged. Perhaps the most famous is the solo *The Dying Swan* (1905) which Fokine composed for his former classmate and partner Anna Pavlova. Fokine suggested the music by Saint-Saëns and he later wrote:

> The dance was composed in a few minutes...A high degree of technical perfection is necessary, but the technique serves only as the means of creating a poetic image, a symbol of the perpetual longing for life by all mortals.
> The dance aims not so much at the eye of the spectator, but at his soul, at his emotions.

This last sentence was a restatement of the Romantic philosophy that led him to stage *Chopiniana* (1907), the forerunner of *Les Sylphides*, for a charity benefit in St. Petersburg, before he joined forces with Diaghilev. Fokine reports that with *Chopiniana* he set out to prove that:

> I did understand the toe dance, but I understood it differently from my contemporaries...In the pursuit of acrobatic feats, ballet and the toe dance had lost the very important purpose for which they were created.
> Looking at the ballerinas of the Romantic period, like Taglioni, I clearly saw that theirs was not a demonstration of physical strength but of pure poetry.

(The above quotation is found in Fokine's *Memoirs of a Ballet Master*, as is most of the material on the great choreographer.) Fokine tried to revive this poetic Romanticism which ballet dancers had lost in their race for circus-type tricks. And indeed, he succeeded with *Les Sylphides* which has been called the most poetical of ballets of the twentieth century and perhaps of all time.

In *Les Sylphides* (1907), many echoes of the romantic era reach us. The title itself is the plural form of *La Sylphide*, the work that you remember as inflaming the Paris ballet public in 1832. The Polish composer Chopin had lived in Paris from 1831 until his death in 1849, the period that coincided with the years of the Romantic ballet. Chopin is thought to have been inspired by Taglioni's dancing. He must at least have been aware of the outstanding events in her art form, even though his own close associates were not dancers but the musicians Liszt and Berlioz and the writers Balzac, Dumas, and Heine. His great love was a writer, Baroness Aurore Dudevant, known to us by her pen name George Sand. Chopin's personal story was quite romantic. His long love affair with Sand was passionate and stormy. He died two years after their separation, at the age of thirty-nine, of tuberculosis and some say a broken heart.

But even without such biographical memories, the moody emotional tone of his music is enough to mark him as a Romantic. Needless to say, his preludes, waltzes, and mazurkas make ideal accompaniments for ballet steps, whether in classroom exercises or in such works as *Dances At a Gathering* (1969), which was choreographed to his music by Jerome Robbins. In fact, *Chopiniana*, Fokine's first version of *Les Sylphides*, was designed to be a dance portrait of the romantically unhappy composer himself. The nocturne scene presented a very ill Chopin seated at a piano in a gloomy monastery where he suffers a nightmare of dead monks rising to torment him (much like the dead nuns in *Robert le Diable*). A female in white appears to chase away his morbid fantasies and to comfort him.

There is a Polish ball (the "Polonaise"), a wedding at which the bride runs out on her elderly bridegroom to join her young lover (the "Mazurka," surely reminiscent of James running out on Effie in *La Sylphide*), and a scene in Naples (a "Tarantella"). The waltz is a pure dance duet for a Taglioni-like ballerina and her partner.

This suggested the final form of *Les Sylphides*, premiered during Diaghilev's first Ballets Russes season (1909), which does not tell a story at all, but rather weaves an atmosphere of poetic mist, free from dramatic mime. But while it has no specific plot, *Les Sylphides* resembles *Giselle* and *La Sylphide* in that it presents the image of a young man haunted by dreams and searching for wispy, ideal, feminine beauty. Visually also, *Les Sylphides* was set by the artist Benois back in the shadowy moonlit forest of *La Sylphide* and *Giselle's* Wilis. The ensemble of female sylphs was costumed in the long (mid-calf) tutu of the Romantic ballet. Fokine wrote: "I was surrounded by twenty-three Taglionis. I inspected their coiffures to make sure that they all had their hair parted in the middle, and of course they all wore dainty flower wreaths, copied from Taglioni lithographs."

The specific movement patterns were quite traditional: simple leaps, balancés, bourrées, that is, simple to stage, not simple to perform well. There were gently rounded arm positions like those in the lithographs of *Pas de Quatre* (1845) and harmonious, often symmetrical groupings of dancers that shifted in an orderly manner from one geometrical design to another. Thus with this ballet's style, Fokine looked backward to the romantic era. But at the same time, by arranging *Les Sylphides* as a series of dances united by mood rather than story, he was also an advance messenger of the plotless ballet that George Balanchine was to develop so fully later on in America.

In addition to *The Dying Swan* and *Les Sylphides*, one other of Fokine's ballets reminds us of the romantic era: *La Spectre de la Rose* (1911). Here the symbolic figure is not a bird nor an enchanted wood nymph, but the spirit of a flower, a rose. Also, the rose's spirit is danced by a male, while the dreamer this time is a female. A young girl returns from a ball, holding a rose. She falls asleep to relive the raptures of the evening's dancing, partnered by the spirit of the rose, who at dawn leaps from her window, leaving her to awaken in her chair. This leaping exit of the rose, performed at the 1911 premiere by Vaslav Nijinsky, imprinted on dance tradition an image of a flight of such unbelievable height and breadth that it is a technical feat as supernatural as any sylph or fading Wili. Fokine regretted this because his intention had been to create a poetic dance that was "expressive at all times" and "contained no dances staged to display technique." However, because of Nijinsky's remarkable elevation and the desire of the public to see a dancer stretch the bounds of human accomplishment, the memory of this leap looms larger than anything else about the short ballet to Weber's music "Invitation to the Dance."

Fokine's inspiration for this elusive dream came from a poem by Theophile Gautier, whom you met as one of the moving forces behind the Romantic ballet of Paris in the 1830s and 1840s. The romantic era, as we noted, had two different faces. In addition to the moony, sentimentally sad one which Michel Fokine recalled with *The Dying Swan*, *Les Sylphides*, and *La Spectre de la Rose*, there was the look of strange, foreign adventure, seen, for example, in Fanny Elssler's cachucha. Fokine did not neglect this area either. He used Rimsky-Korsakov's lush musical description of Oriental splendor to create the exotic, sensuous *Sheherazade* (1910), aflame with boldly colorful scenery and costumes by the painter Alexander Benois. The ballet *Sheherazade* presents harem women who take advantage of their royal master's absence to enjoy an orgy of drunken excitement and sexual passion with Nubian slaves. Unexpectedly, the monarch returns and in a towering rage he orders everybody killed, including the stars of the piece, his favorite wife Zobeide and her dearest slave.

At the premiere in 1910, Nijinsky's black slave gave an impression of brilliant excitement as unforgettable as his soaring leap was to be the following year in *Spectre de la Rose*. A sculptor was quoted in Paul Magriel's book *Nijinsky, Pavlova, Duncan*: "Nijinsky is filled with the dark effluvium of free animals. He is abrupt, but naively more than human, and he has something of the sacred animal." Fokine's movement style in *Sheherazade* was not authentically Oriental. Rather, he featured rippling, sinuous motions of the torso and arms that suited the music and the scenario, again in a way that conventional, academic ballet technique would not have done.

The melodrama was choreographed so that the action swept along through the dance, with no artificial interruptions. That is, the story was told through expressive movements of the whole body, woven into solo and group dancing. Today we take such an approach for granted. But really to appreciate Fokine's inventiveness, you have to consider the ballet conventions and formulas that were accepted before he discarded them. In Petipa's Russia, the plot was carried forward with artificial sign language of the hands that stopped the dancing dead in its tracks. Fokine also changed the flat face-front use of stage space. As he wrote in his memoirs:

> Trying to give a meaning to everything in ballet, I could not reconcile myself to the idea of having the dancers perform facing the audience . . .
>
> When my dancers had to address their movements to someone, I tried to have them face that person . . . It is now difficult to realize to what a degree dancers once feared to show their backs to the audience. This had its origins in the court ballets, built on the servile approach of constantly facing some exalted personage in the audience.
>
> My new ballet began to dance for itself and the surrounding people. This not only enriched the dance but freed it from the ugliness inescapably connected with the necessity of walking backwards and side-stepping.

Always building on this drive to be expressive, Fokine was especially fortunate in having Stravinsky's fresh musical genius to lead him in two major ballets. Diaghilev introduced Igor Stravinsky to the dance world when he asked the composer to do a score for *Firebird* in 1910. Like Fokine, Stravinsky respected classical forms and traditions, but he was endlessly inventive. Therefore while his rhythmic patterns and tonal relationships were daringly new, his approach to structure was traditional and, at least during this period, he was content to follow the narrative line of a ballet scenario. In fact, he worked very closely with Fokine, the two of them exchanging ideas for scene after scene.

Firebird was based on a combination of Russian fairy tales in order to serve a specific national purpose. After all, the original idea behind the

Ballets Russes had been to acquaint Europe with Russian artistic achieve-ments. And the first season had produced no ballet with a Russian theme. The Firebird was a familiar figure in Russian folklore, appearing in a vari-ety of legends. And as we have seen in *Swan Lake, Giselle,* and *La Sylphide,* a flying creature is particularly suitable for ballet. Fokine fashioned the sce-nario with help from Stravinsky and the painter Benois (although another artist, Golovine, was to do the sets and costumes).

As in *Swan Lake,* the plot begins with a prince (Ivan) aiming an arrow to shoot a radiantly beautiful bird. He misses, but then succeeds in captur-ing the magic Firebird in his arms. She struggles to get away, but can't free herself from his embrace. Finally, she offers him a magic feather in return for her freedom. Ivan lets her go and then comes upon a group of maidens, led by one more richly dressed who is their ranking princess. He falls in love with the royal maiden (not with the bird this time!). Suddenly, the evil magician Kostchei appears, along with his enchanted monsters. Kostchei is about to put Ivan too under a magic spell, but Ivan waves the magic feath-er that the Firebird had given him just in time. The Firebird flies in and forces the demons to dance until they fall asleep. Then she shows Ivan where an enormous egg is hidden, one which turns out to contain the soul of the wicked Kostchei. Ivan smashes the egg, thus killing the wicked Kostchei. With the death of the villainous enchanter, the noblemen and noblewomen regain their real shapes from the demon appearances that Kostchei had cast on them. In the finale, there is a procession to crown Ivan as the most powerful lord who will soon marry the beautiful maiden-princess.

As with other ballets, a bare outline of the plot makes *Firebird* seem childish. Dance is not, after all, a literary art form. Movement, music, and visual spectacle are needed to create imagery, to give life to the ideas and symbols contained in the action. The original production starred Tamara Karsavina as the Firebird, the choreographer Michel Fokine as Ivan, and his wife Vera as the beautiful maiden. It was a great success. Down through the years the ballet has been revived innumerable times with many changes, sometimes by Stravinsky and Fokine themselves, and more frequently by other choreographers like Adolph Bolm, George Balanchine, Serge Lifar, John Cranko, and Maurice Béjart. In 1945, Marc Chagall paint-ed the scenery for an American Ballet Theater version.

The second and last ballet that both Fokine and Stravinsky worked on was *Petrouchka.* This time Diaghilev and Stravinsky both had a hand in the scenario, as did Benois. Petrouchka is a clown-puppet based on a familiar character in travelling Russian shows that were staged at village fairs. Entertainers—whether actors, acrobats, or puppeteers—wanted to attract as big a crowd as possible for their performances. Thus they would arrive in a town with a splash of noisy confusion. For example, two of their troupe would wear makeup so as to appear dark skinned. They dressed in

Rudolph Nureyev interprets Fokine's "Petrouchka."

gold and velvet and beat each other energetically with sticks. These theatrically rowdy players were called *balagani*. The word describes the colorful
disorder that is often found among theatrical entertainers. Benois wrote,
"The dear *balagani* were the great delight of my childhood and had been
the delight of my father before me." He was fascinated by Diaghilev's suggestion that they be a subject for a dance. Stravinsky too found inspiration
in this street theater, and even before he worked on the ballet itself, he

composed a "Russian Dance" and "Petrouchka's Cry," which in turn provided more fuel for Benois's imagination.

The ballet opens in a large public square during a carnival, where the crowd is entertained by a puppet show. In Acts II and III, we are reminded of *The Nutcracker, Coppélia,* and other works where toy soldiers and dolls come to life. As *Coppélia* had Dr. Coppelius, a kind of evil magician who could create lifelike toys, so *Petrouchka* had the Charlatan. The Charlatan, as the puppeteer, rules over the puppet Petrouchka, Columbine the frivolous doll-ballerina whom Petrouchka adores, and the Moor, a powerful figure of black magic with whom Columbine is in love. In addition to controlling the onstage behavior of Petrouchka, Columbine, and the Moor, the Charlatan also controls their offstage destinies. After the show, he shuts them up in their boxes, where they play out their private drama. When Columbine and the Moor make love, Petrouchka rushes in, wild with jealousy, and tries to separate them. The Moor first pushes Petrouchka away, and then chases after him with a sword and kills him. An odd twist occurs at the end. Act IV is back outside at the fair. People in the crowd hear noises of a struggle and the cries of a dying puppet (or person). But then, the Charlatan picks up the lifeless clown and shows the crowd. See, it is just a puppet! However a final turnabout occurs with the sad appearance of Petrouchka's ghost. So maybe it is a human after all.

In choreographing the solos, Fokine gave Petrouchka sunken gestures and turned-in poses to express his pathetic introversion: head hanging, arms drooping, hunched-over torso, knees and toes turned in, sometimes actually touching. In contrast, the Moor's cruel self-confidence is expressed in widely spread legs, hand resting on well turned-out knee, head high, chest out. Fokine was obviously a sharp observer of what psychologists today call body language. In addition to these personality gestures, Petrouchka and the Moor must at all times keep a mechanical, puppetlike attitude. In the case of the Ballerina, Fokine pictured simply "an attractive, stupid doll."

As a clear and interesting contrast to the puppets, Fokine tried to make the crowd as alive as possible. He wrote: "I wanted all the dancers strolling at the fair to dance gaily, freely, as if the dances were not staged but arose spontaneously from an overabundance of emotional gaiety, arousing the crowd to wild improvisation." His approach was exactly the one that Noverre had favored in his treatise on choreography. Fokine peopled the scene with a variety of characters: nurses, coachmen, organ-grinders, soldiers, ladies, gentlemen, children, policemen, drunken peasants, and so on, and gave each type suitable motions, the way a play director would stage a scene in a realistic drama. The premiere of *Petrouchka* in June, 1911 made a brilliant impression largely through the fantastic dance-acting of Nijinsky as Petrouchka and Karsavina as the Ballerina. Less impressive was the crowd scene. Fokine complained that he had only a two-hour rehearsal to set it.

In its first three seasons (1909, 1910, and 1911), the Ballets Russes had presented a number of fine dances by Fokine in fresh, expressive styles; outstanding performances by Nijinsky and Karsavina; and brilliant compositions by Stravinsky. Vivid stage designs by artists like Benois and Bakst had set new high standards for ballet productions. For Parisians in the know, continuing offstage dramas provided many entertaining scenes for them to chew over. For example, Benois found that Bakst, who had offered to repair part of the *Petrouchka* set that had been damaged in travelling, had substituted a painting of his own instead of repairing one by Benois. Benois shouted, "Take it down immediately, I shall not allow it!" and he rushed out of the theater to submit his resignation. Of course there was more to it than that. Like most of the bad feelings among the Ballets Russes people, Benois's fury stemmed from Diaghilev's high-handed manner in showing favoritism toward one temperamental artist over another.

Inevitably, these plots and intrigues had their effects on the productions of the company. For the fourth season (1912), Fokine was working on an ancient Greek legendary love story, *Daphnis and Chloe*. Maurice Ravel was commissioned to compose the music. Although *Daphnis and Chloe*, danced by Nijinsky and Karsavina, was well received and has since been restaged frequently by first-rate companies, it was overshadowed at its premiere season by another premiere, the notorious *Afternoon of a Faun*, which Nijinsky both choreographed and performed in. As was pointed out previously, Diaghilev deliberately slighted Fokine's new work in costumes, rehearsal time, and advance publicity in favor of Nijinsky's. The impresario was determined to promote his pet Nijinsky as a choreographer and he claimed that Fokine was played out and already old-fashioned. Fokine left the company but continued to choreograph profusely in Europe and the United States.

Nijinsky. As for the Ballets Russes, Nijinsky, who was still the star male dancer, now became chief choreographer, for one year only. In 1913, he followed *Afternoon of a Faun* with *Jeux* and then *Rite of Spring* and went with the company on tour to South America. While on tour, he married one of the dancers, Romola de Pulzky. Word reached Diaghilev, who had remained back in Europe, and in a fit of furious jealousy, the impresario dismissed Nijinsky by cable. This proved to be the beginning of the end for the brilliant young dancer. Bad luck, illness, and finally insanity hunted him down and forced him into a mental institution by the time he was thirty. He never recovered and died in 1950.

Nijinsky choreographed and performed in four ballets. Two of these created shock waves both for their daring sexual attitudes and for their nonballetic motions. One was *Afternoon of a Faun* (1912), a dance to music by Debussy which was in turn an impression of a poem by Stephen Mallarmé. The slim scenario concerned a creature, half animal, half human, enjoying a summer day by eating a bunch of grapes and playing a flute. His desire is awakened by a group of passing nymphs. They run from his advances except for one beauty, a little bolder than her sisters. She moves close enough to touch but then she too runs off, leaving behind a scarf. The faun takes the scarf and caresses it tenderly, as though making love to it.

In arranging the ballet, Nijinsky created a flat, two-dimensional moving picture, as though a Greek frieze were to come to life with the figures still remaining in the shapes into which they had been painted. The dancers in *Afternoon of a Faun* keep their heads and feet in profile and their torsos facing front. This is an extremely artificial position. In ancient Greece and Egypt, figures were painted in this manner in order to give a sense of motion and at the same time show most of the body, not because people moved like that. Of course, the very fact that the position is unnatural can in itself create interest. Don't make the mistake of thinking that dance is ever really "natural." Very often an original effect delights an audience that is looking for something new. Just as often, however, people in an audience can be very irritated when they see things that are strange to them.

Added to this forced body position, the dancers in *Afternoon of a Faun* were given a peculiar run from one side of the stage to the other, landing on the heels and the whole foot, rather than first on the toes, in the accepted manner. Thus for its dance movements alone, the ballet would have made a strong impression on the Parisian viewers of 1912. But the concluding action created such a sensation that it, and not the choreographic style, became the focus of all discussion in the press and at social gatherings. When Nijinsk yembraced the scarf, he thrust his body upon it in such a way that left no doubt of his meaning .The faun had released his sexual longings through a private act with a scarf on a lazy summer afternoon. *Afternoon of a Faun* is the only Nijinsky ballet that survives in anything like its original form, although the shocking end was modified.

Two of his other works, *Rite of Spring* (in French: *Le Sacre du Printemps*), 1913, to a Stravinsky score, and *Jeux*, 1913, to a specially composed score by Debussy, have also been restaged frequently. However up until the Joffrey production of *Rite of Spring*, in 1987, these have been presented in versions totally different from the original, with only the title, the music, and the general theme remaining, so that they don't count as Nijinsky's. *Rite of Spring* was Nijinsky's most famous—really, most notorious—production. The memory of the premiere lives on in many accounts. The piece caused a riot. Not only were there shouts and whistles of disapproval, but people actually hit each other in violent disagreement about its artistic merit. This time, the shock was caused by the style of the composition rather than by the subject matter.

Stravinsky's score created the mood both for Nijinsky and for the audience. The composer had set out to create an exciting image of pagan Russia in its annual reawakening from the frozen sleep of winter. His explicit scenario describes an ancient rite of fertility in which tribal elders choose and dedicate the tribe's fairest virgin, who must then dance until she dies of exhaustion. As we discussed in detail in Part I, this sacrifice is intended to ensure fertility, both for the people in the primitive village and for their spring crops. Stravinsky's stupendous music fulfills this idea. In 1913, the score was truly a revolutionary masterpiece, and has become a landmark in the history of that art form. Today, the striking rhythms of pounding intensity, the complex broken meter, and the bitonal sound do not send listeners into an uproar. But nothing like it had ever been heard before its premiere. The music seems to have been equally responsible with the dancing for outraged reactions on opening night. Words like these occured in reports of the new work: "harsh," "bitter," "raw," "brutal," "coarse," "seriously ugly."

The dancers were seen in strange, spasmodic, quivering motions, with their knees and toes turned in, and their heads leaning sideways on one arm which was in turn supported by the other fist. Bodies were rigid or bent awkwardly. Groups appeared in a mass, rather than in geometrically clear patterns. It took over one hundred hours of rehearsal time for the classically trained dancers to learn their parts. You can imagine how hard they found these unfamiliar positions. Keeping time to the music proved to be a major problem, which is not surprising when you note that one short section had the following metrical arrangement: 3/16, 5/16, 3/16, 4/16, 5/16, 3/16, 4/16. In the end, Nijinsky's *Rite of Spring* was performed only six times.

The last ballet credited to the ill-fated Nijinsky was the short-lived *Tyl Eulenspiegel* (1916) which was danced to Richard Strauss's tone poem. Some critics have held the opinion that the brilliant dancer showed signs of being a fine original choreographer as well as an astonishing performer. However, his mental state prevented him from proving this one way or the other. Nevertheless, Nijinsky's place in ballet history is firmly secured by the glowing descriptions provoked by his dancing. Comments like these by critic Carl Van Vechten have been echoed by many others who saw Vaslav Nijinsky dance:

> His dancing is accomplished in that flowing line, without a break between poses and gestures, which is the despair of all novices and almost all other virtuosi. His dancing has the unbroken quality of music, the balance of great painting, the meaning of fine literature, and the emotion inherent in all these arts . . .
> I have not been able to discover flaws in the art of this young man. It seems to me that in his chosen medium he approaches perfection.

The above quotation is found in the book *Nijinsky, Pavlova, Duncan*, edited by Paul Magriel.

The Avant-garde Parade

In 1915, with Fokine and Nijinsky out of the picture, you might think that Diaghilev's Ballets Russes was finished. Not so. The magician still had aces up his sleeve: Leonide Massine, Bronislava Nijinska (the sister of the unfortunate Vaslav), and George Balanchine, not to mention the artistic avant-garde. Diaghilev hired Leonide Massine (1895 to 1979) in 1915 in Moscow to dance the title role in Fokine's *Legend of Joseph* to music specially written by Richard Strauss. The ballet was memorable only because of Massine's performance in the title role. He proved to be technically good and dramatically outstanding. Massine continued in the company as a lead performer, and began to choreograph some minor works. Then he arranged the movements for *Parade* in 1917. *Parade* is not important as a choreographed ballet. It earned its place in our history because three artists of the international avant-garde were involved: poet and playwright Jean Cocteau, painter Pablo Picasso, and Erik Satie, a leading spokesman for a group of antiestablishment composers. These are famous names in the twentieth-century avant-garde, and they created a sensation with *Parade*.

Definition of Terms. A brief note on the terms *avant-garde, revolutionary*, and *modern* is now in order. They are all important in any discussion of twentieth-century dance styles. Although we can't pin them down exactly, and they do overlap, it is still useful to try to distinguish among them. In all three cases, it is always necessary to consider a particular work in the context of what was accepted and usual at the time it appeared.

The term *revolutionary* is used for large stylistic changes made by one or more artists. Fokine was a revolutionary when he arranged gestures for the Ballets Russes. In these repertory works he chose special movements to express his dance themes. These movements were outside of the generally accepted dance vocabulary. And Fokine was also a revolutionary when he strove for unity of theme, music, and décor. Nijinsky was a revolutionary both in staging controversial situations and gestures and in arranging unfamiliar movement patterns.

The term *modern dance* describes the works of Isadora Duncan, Ruth St. Denis, Mary Wigman, Rudolf Laban, Martha Graham, Doris Humphrey, and other Americans and Germans. It is obvious that these artists were also revolutionary in their approach to movement. But they went beyond Fokine and Nijinsky to change movements not only in specific dance works but in overall technical method. Their basic attitudes toward the art itself were new. Fokine applied the theories of Noverre to ballet choreography in the interests of realism and expression, but he never considered changing the academic ballet technique that had been developing in a straight line since the Renaissance. Because Duncan, Wigman, Graham, and others sought totally different concepts of body use and expression, they form a separate branch of our art called modern dance.

Modern Dance is a confusing and unfortunate term. The art form has undergone so many changes in its ninety or more years that some of its practitioners work in ways directly opposite to others. However, we are stuck with the term because of common usage. Perhaps the one trait that unifies all modern dancers is their rejection of the academic, classic ballet as the basis of the dance art. In any case, this group has made so many important artistic contributions in the twentieth century and has drawn from so many sources other than the ballet and Renaissance courts that it deserves its own special treatment, which it will soon receive in this history.

As for the term *avant-garde*, this literally means the front ranks of a battle formation. It refers to the type of artistic movements common in this century, whose practitioners thumb their noses at accepted, conventional styles. Members of the same avant-garde share an ideology. Because novelty is a major characteristic of the avant-garde, new artistic ideologies tend to follow one another rapidly, and to cross from one field to another. In painting, some avant-garde labels are surrealism, Dada, pop, and constructivism. Music can be atonal, serial, or electronic. In dance and theater, we have happenings, chance, theater of the absurd, and mixed media. Avant-garde dance often brings in experimental artists from other areas who are responding to similar stimuli. Always remember that ours is a collaborative art form. Thus in an avant-garde dance work the focus may be on the unusual effects of décor or sound, with the dancing the least important part.

This is exactly what happened in *Parade.* Jean Cocteau, who was later to make his mark on experimental theater, film, and literature as well as ballet, supplied the ideas for the piece, which was inspired by Diaghilev's command to him: "Shock me!" Pablo Picasso designed the costumes (some were constructions rather than clothing!) and Erik Satie contributed the music, including the sounds of a motor and a typewriter, along with snatches of jazz. Oh yes, as already noted, Massine did the movements.

Parade is about entertainment. The *hows* and *whys* of entertainment are subjects that often fascinate people in the arts. The title *Parade* refers to the procession of circus performers around their tent at a carnival in a bid for the attention and the paid attendance of the public. We think back to the *balagani* in *Petrouchka* and the Renaissance processions that heralded a day of festivities in an Italian town. Well, here was the same idea, but treated with a mixture of exaggeration, surprise, and deadpan self-mockery, in a sequence of absurd events. The ballet's characters and action include: a

Paris show-business manager wearing an eight-foot-high Picasso construction of a dress suit; a New York manager whose equally elaborate costume includes a skyscraper; and a manager who rides on a horse made up from the old trick of dancers inside the head and rear of a horse costume. These managers introduce various acts of magic, acrobatics, and hints of American movie scenes. All this is accompanied by a lighthearted musical smorgasbord.

In the 1990s, it is hard to understand the tremendous impact of the premiere of *Parade*. We have become so accustomed to avant-garde shows with "startling" effects that almost nothing surprises us. But in 1917, there had never before been a ballet that refused to take itself seriously in this way, nor even a concert score that included jazz. *Parade* marked out one approach to avant-garde choreography whose details are still being filled in. It was billed as a "realistic" ballet. As we have seen, it did treat specific themes, although in a style we would call *surrealistic* rather than *realistic*.

A few years later in Germany, an avant-garde path led in the opposite direction, toward abstraction. Oskar Schlemmer (1888 to 1943) produced the *Triadic Ballet* in 1922 to demonstrate relationships of bodily forms to their surrounding space. Although Schlemmer was intrigued by dance, he never studied it. Instead, as a teacher at the Bauhaus School of Architecture and Design, he treated dance as an activity of colored geometrical figures. His performers' costumes were exaggerated constructions of cubes, spheres, and cylinders. These were so heavy that the dancers needed to rest frequently. They moved along exact straight and curved lines. The dance aspect of works like *The Triadic Ballet* was severely limited, and the interest lay in sculptured costumes and colored lights. More importantly, however, the ideas behind both *Parade* and the *Triadic Ballet* were picked up again later and developed further, mostly by modern dancers.

Further Developments

In Diaghilev's time, the Ballets Russes continued to be the center of developments in dance. Massine went on to choreograph many works for them, all more conventional than *Parade*. These were characterized by strong, individual roles. Two Massine ballets which were very popular were *La Boutique Fantasque* (1919) and *The Three-Cornered Hat* (1919). In *La Boutique Fantasque*, we again meet dolls that come to life. But here, the toy shop contains dolls in love, who revolt against being sold to separate households. There is a pleasant dose of good humor in Massine's witty characters, underscored by Rossini's melodic music.

The Three-Cornered Hat is based on a Spanish play by Martinez Sierra about a devoted couple, a miller and his attractive wife, and a senile official who has the miller kidnapped and then tries unsuccessfully to seduce his charming woman. The ballet combines the comedy action for which Massine had a special flair with the always popular Spanish dance steps and style. The work is heightened immensely by Manuel De Falla's music, which the composer specially arranged at Diaghilev's request to suit the ballet.

Both in and out of the Ballets Russes, Massine choreographed a large number of other works. Outstanding in his varied output are symphonic ballets to famous works of Tchaikovsky, Brahms, Berlioz, and Beethoven. Because of wide-spread exposure, his choreography for the films *The Red Shoes* (1946) and *Tales of Hoffmann* (1951) helped tune in the general public to the pleasures of ballet.

The next Ballets Russes choreographer after Massine, who was dismissed in 1921 because of quarrels with the imperious Diaghilev, was Bronislava Nijinska (1891 to 1972). Her masterpiece was *Les Noces* (1923), a Russian wedding presented in the ritualistic, unglamorous manner of *Rite of Spring*. In fact, the idea came from Igor Stravinsky, who was inspired while he was writing the score for *Rite of Spring*. *Les Noces* portrays a Russian bride and groom in their peasant homes, being prepared for the ceremony. They are escorted together to their joint wedding bed while the villagers share the wedding feast. Bronislava Nijinska staged *Les Noces* with massed groups, designed to convey what she found in the overwhelming music: deep drama, interspersed with occasional splashes of joyousness and the true feeling of Russia.

A mixed reaction, with strong opponents and strong defenders, was provoked by: the somber colors designed by Gontcharova; the lack of virtuoso ballet passages; the ensemble forming blocklike structures; the harsh sounds and disturbing rhythms of Stravinsky's score as performed by a singing chorus "chanting, wailing, crying, and shouting"; and a percussionist ensemble and four "banging, thumping, tickling," pianists. Diaghilev was surely delighted by the controversy.

Nijinska made many other ballets for Diaghilev. The most interesting was *Les Biches* (1924, music by Francis Poulenc), which is a view of the flirtations that occupy fashionable guests at a house party. Like Massine, Nijinska had a long career as a choreographer after leaving the Ballets Russes, contributing works to companies in Europe and America.

Balanchine. Beginning in 1925, George Balanchine was the last of Diaghilev's major choreographers. He arranged ten works for the company. Two of them are still performed: *Apollo* (1928, to music by Stravinsky) and *The Prodigal Son* (1929, to a Prokofiev score).

Apollo is considered by some to be one of the most important ballets of this century. Again it was Stravinsky who provided the work's underpinnings. He had been commissioned to write the music for an American production which was choreographed in Chicago by Adolph Bolm, a former

Ballets Russes performer. After the premiere, Stravinsky presented the score to Diaghilev, who assigned it to Balanchine. With *Apollo*, Balanchine arrived at his influential *neoclassic* style, and he credits Stravinsky's score with pointing the way. Balanchine wrote in his book, *New Complete Stories of the Great Ballets*: "In its discipline and restraint, in its sustained oneness of tone and feeling, the Stravinsky score was a revelation. It seemed to tell me that I could, for the first time, dare not use all my ideas; that I too could eliminate."

That was the *neo* part in *neoclassic*: restrained, sculptured lines, with bent, straightforward (rather than turned-out) limbs. The *classic* part was the use of strict, sharp, brilliant steps in the academic tradition of Petipa, one that Balanchine had absorbed and loved at the St. Petersburg Ballet School from which he graduated in 1921. After years of emphasizing novelty and characterization in movement, instead of classical technique, the Ballets Russes returned with *Apollo* to virtuoso steps and patterns. However, Balanchine had not therefore stepped backward, but rather developed a fresh treatment for traditional material. Stravinsky's music as a stimulus and inspiration for Balanchine's entire choreographic approach is yet another example of the deep relationship between the arts of music and dance. And as we shall see, these two Russians continued to work together on and off over the next forty years.

The action of *Apollo* followed Stravinsky's scenario. A prologue presents Leto giving birth to the god Apollo. The god takes his first baby steps and proceeds to more skillful motions. When he is given a lyre, he teaches himself to dance. In the body of the work, Apollo appears in full divine authority and three Muses come for his approval, one by one. Calliope demonstrates poetics, Polymnia mime, and Terpsichore dance. Apollo reveals his own talents as a heroic athlete, and then chooses Terpsichore for his partner. After their pas de deux, Apollo harnesses the three Muses to his chariot, and finally, with him in the lead, they all ascend toward Mount Olympus, and glory.

While there are specific characters and sketched-in scenes, the dance celebrates the glorious qualities of Apollo and the Muses rather than works out a plot. *Apollo* moved toward Balanchine's later plotless ballets. This neoclassical ballet made a great hit, in part through the dancing of Serge Lifar (1905 to 1986), who also performed the title role in *Prodigal Son*. With décor by Rouault, *Prodigal Son* looks different from *Apollo*. It is a strongly dramatic work that expresses the very human emotions found in the biblical tale (the New Testament in the Gospel according to Luke). A young man leaves home, rejecting the moral values of his father and sisters, to seek excitement in the world at large. He falls into the company of depraved, drunken boors. He is tossed about and robbed. A glamorous woman seduces and humiliates him. At the end, he crawls home, where his father embraces him with tender forgiveness. In *Prodigal Son*, Balanchine moved closer to Fokine than to Petipa. In any case, both works show his extraordinary gift for choreography even at this early stage. When we get to America, we will hear a lot more about this artist.

Legacy of The Ballets Russes. We now part from Diaghilev. He died in 1929 after having set a standard for excellence in every phase of ballet. Diaghilev proved that this art form is worthy of the efforts of the foremost artists in music, painting, and writing as well as in movement. He enriched the field with seventy-two dance productions, of which at least sixteen have entered the permanent repertory. These ballets were carried to countries all over the world by a host of choreographers and dancers who had been involved, however briefly, with the Ballets Russes. In addition to the magnificent dancers like Nijinsky and Karsavina who appeared in leading roles, the company gave opportunities to many young people who came into their own after Diaghilev's passing, as well as to already proven artists, who paused to absorb some of the excitement before going elsewhere.

In addition to the names that have appeared frequently in this text, here are only a few of the important personalities that appeared on Ballets Russes programs at one time or another: Ida Rubinstein, Anna Pavlova, Enrico Cecchetti, Vera Nemchinova, Anton Dolin, Alexandra Danilova, Alicia Markova, and Ninette de ValoisIn the next chapters we shall see how Marie Rambert and Ninette de Valois in England, George Balanchine in America, and Serge Lifar in France, among others, revitalize the ballet art form internationally, as part of the heritage of the amazing Sergei Diaghilev and his illustrious Ballets Russes.

Questions for Review

1. How would you describe Diaghilev's part in the great Ballets Russes?

2. Discuss Fokine's choreographic style.

3. What was so shocking about Nijinsky's *Rite of Spring*?

4. How do you think Oskar Schlemmer's *Triadic Ballet* would be received today?

5. What was Anna Pavlova's contribution to the art of dance?

6. What kinds of work did Massine choreograph?

7. What is the significance of the Ballets Russes for the contemporary dance world?

17 INTERNATIONAL REGROUPING

EUROPEAN BALLET FROM 1929 TO 1945

Dispersal of the Ballets Russes

After Diaghilev's death, Ballets Russes dancers spread out to a number of countries where they had a tremendous influence on the dance art. Serge Lifar (born in 1905, in Russia) for example, one of the last major soloists in the Ballets Russes, went to the Paris Opera to stage *The Creatures of Prometheus* to a Beethoven score in 1929. This work was so well received that Lifar was appointed choreographer and principal dancer at the opera in 1931. Although Lifar did not create ballets that were to find a lasting place in the repertory, he did bring the Paris scene to life by producing and starring in good productions of the classics. He also reorganized the Paris Opera ballet, which had declined sadly since its great period one hundred years earlier.

Lifar's efforts paved the way for a number of talented native French dancers like Roland Petit, Jean Babilée, and Janine Charrat, all of whom contributed to the international ballet scene. Roland Petit (born in 1924) and Jean Babilée (born in 1923) started out at the Paris Opera and then went off on their own. Both men were outstanding performers as well as choreographers and both of them married dancers whom they partnered. Roland Petit and Renée Jeanmaire (born in 1924) made a stunning couple in *Carmen* (1949, to music by Bizet) which Petit choreographed in a daring sexy style that was highly theatrical.

Jean Babilée's outstanding role was the Artist, a character in another of Roland Petit's sensational creations, *Le Jeune Homme et la Mort* (1946). Babilée's wife Nathalie Philippart portrayed the Artist's sweetheart, who comes to his attic and by her scornful rejection drives him to hang himself. The girl returns to visit the attic again, this time wearing a death mask, and she leads the young man away over the rooftops of Paris. This ballet (in English: The Young Man and Death) was outstanding for its scenario by Jean Cocteau and also for the striking use of Bach's *Passacaglia in C minor* as accompaniment, although the rehearsals were conducted to jazz music!

Janine Charrat (born in 1924, a vintage year for French dancers) performed often with Roland Petit in the 1940s, in duets that she composed. Charrat went on to choreograph for companies in France and elsewhere, in a modernistic dramatic style. She did works like *Les Liens* (1957, music by Semenoff), in which hanging bands enmesh the dancers in a hostile fate; and *Electra* (1960), an interpretation of the Greek legend to music by Pousseur.

At the same time that French dance took on new life, frantic attempts to keep the Ballets Russes company alive were plagued by a death struggle between René Blum and Colonel de Basil over who should inherit Diaghilev's crown of leadership. They also had conflicting ideas about choreographers, dancers, and other artists. For three decades, a series of companies carried on with names like The Ballets de Monte Carlo, Colonel W. de Basil's Ballets Russes, the Original Ballet Russe, the Covent Garden Ballet Russe, and Les Ballets 1933. It is more important to remember that there were a lot of companies than to try to straighten out the identity of each one. Even if you were able to follow the scenario of shifts in personnel and drawn-out legal battles, it would be an exercise in understanding psychological plotting and social history, and would yield no insights into the art of choreography.

From our point of view, the significance of these machinations lies in the interesting productions that emerged from time to time, particularly during the first decade, the 1930s. Bursts of quality were not surprising when you consider that first-rate choreographers like Massine, Fokine, Balanchine, Nijinska, and David Lichine had a hand in these productions. Unfortunately, many of these survive only in dance reviews or history books. The instability of the performing organizations stood in the way of their permanence, no matter what the artistic merit may have been; and many well-received works were lost to us forever. It is still worth noting the outstanding ones, because having entered the traditions of the ballet world, they have appeared or will appear in other versions.

Here's a brief look at works that made their mark in the 1930s, many of which were characterized by visual chic—resembling the latest fashion collections of Paris designers—or else by a clever idea. Few of them seem to have been noteworthy in their movements, the basic medium of dance. After all, these groups were continuing in the footsteps of Diaghilev, who had been preoccupied with scenic design by avant-garde artists, or the latest musical experiments, rather than with choreographic depth. For example, in 1932, Massine's *Jeux d'Enfants* (music by Bizet) returned to the cliché of toys coming to life. The one unusual feature of this ballet was the surrealistic decor by Joan Miro. In 1933, Balanchine choreographed *Mozartiana* to Tchaikovsky's *Mozart Suite* (an example of the way music composers, like choreographers, base a new work on one that is part of the traditional repertory). This was one of Balanchine's first experiments in plotless ballet, whose only subject is the accompanying music.

During the same season, Massine came up with his symphonic ballets which got the music world in an uproar at the idea of using masterpieces by Tchaikovsky or Brahms as dance accompaniment. *Les Présages*, which was choreographed to Tchaikovsky's *Fifth Symphony*, was not a visualization of the music in Balanchine's style. Although there was no story, there was a definite theme. Man was portrayed by a dancer, struggling with Destiny, portrayed by another dancer. Along the way, he meets up with characters like Frivolity and Passion, also portrayed by dancers. In *Choreartium* (also 1933) to Brahms's *Fourth Symphony*, Massine arranged each movement around an emotional idea, a Lamentation, a Frolic, and so on. Massine also restaged *Le Beau Danube* which he had first done in 1924. This was to become immensely popular with its accompaniment of Johann Strauss's famous waltz. It presents a lighthearted tale of a dashing officer and his charming fiancée. The couple's engagement is almost broken off by the appearance of a street dancer from the soldier's past. In the end, true love triumphs and even the discarded high-spirited dancer adds her good wishes for the couple's future.

In 1934, Massine's *Union Pacific* marked the first of many attempts to create an "American" ballet in the way that *Firebird* and *Petrouchka* had been created as "Russian" ballets, and were being performed in the United States as "Russian," despite their origins in France. The premiere of *Union Pacific* was in Philadelphia, home of the American Declaration of Independence. Nicholas Nabokov's musical score was woven from familiar American tunes, and the scenario by the American poet Archibald MacLeish told of Mexican, Irish, and Chinese frontier railway workers and of a brawl over the favors of a popular beauty. However, this ballet did not succeed in expressing an American spirit as Agnes de Mille's *Rodeo* and Eugene Loring's *Billy the Kid* were to do. *Union Pacific* was memorable chiefly for the role of a cocky bartender, danced by Massine himself. Indeed, his own dancing gave a special flavor to many of Massine's works.

In 1936, Massine was outstanding as the lead in his own *Symphonie Fantastique* (music by Berlioz, designs by Christian Berard). This ballet takes the hero on a drugged trip during which he is executed for murdering his beloved. Later, as a corpse, he is caught up in a witches' ritual, and again meets his beloved. This time she is one of the witches. In 1938, Massine went on to create two more symphonic ballets. First, *The Seventh Symphony* (Beethoven) which combined the biblical episode of creation with pagan gods and destruction by fire. Then, *Rouge et Noir* (to the *First Symphony* of Shostakovich), which featured complex movements by a group in colorful yet rather depersonalized costumes, and décor by Henri Matisse. Again the themes are large and world shaking: Man and Woman tormented by brutal forces and evil spirits; temporary joy; surrender to destiny. Also in 1938, Massine staged a spiritual work about Saint Francis, to music by Hindemith.

Bacchanale (1939) was one of three ballets that Massine arranged according to scenario and décor by the irreverent surrealist Salvador Dali and music by Wagner. As might be expected, the choreography was a minor feature of these productions. More satisfactory for most audiences than either the pretentious Dali "jokes" or the heavy philosophical symphonies are Massine's bright, witty pieces like the previously mentioned *Boutique Fantasque* and *Le Beau Danube*. In this class belongs his *Gaiete Parisian* (1938), a series of lighthearted flirtations in a nightclub to music by Offenbach. Equally popular for its happy appeal is David Lichine's *Graduation Ball* (1940, to music by Johann Strauss), which presents a lively party at a girls' school with the invited guests from a neighboring military academy.

Like Massine, Fokine first made his reputation with Diaghilev, for whom he did major works like *Sheherazade, Firebird,* and *Petrouchka*. Later he continued to contribute to a number of companies, but he never again reached the heights he had with Diaghilev. In 1936, Fokine choreographed *L'Epreuve d'Amour*, a danced version of a Korean fairy tale, and *Don Juan*, to music which Gluck had written for a ballet in 1761! Fokine followed these in 1937 with *Le Coq d'Or*, a one-act ballet to music by Rimsky-Korsakov which Fokine based on his own 1914 staging of the three-act opera. His 1938 treatment of *Cinderella* (music by d'Erlanger) was only one of many ballets on this story by Perrault (who had also written the story *Sleeping Beauty*). In 1939, Fokine created *Paganini*, which presented the struggles of the musical genius to a score by Rachmaninoff. Then he did *Bluebeard* (1941, to music by Offenbach) and *Russian Soldier* (1942, to music by Prokofiev).

In the same way, Bronislava Nijinska, who had staged for Diaghilev the impressive Russian wedding *Les Noces*, went on to choreograph ballets. She created *Les Cent Baisers* (1935, to music by d'Erlanger) and *Pictures from an Exhibition* (1944, to music by Mussorgsky for groups in America and Europe. Thus Massine, Fokine, and Nijinska, among others, wandered around after Diaghilev's death. Although they missed the focus of a great company, which he had certainly provided, they nevertheless continued to create.

Massine's "Graduation Ball" is in the repertory of the American Ballet Theater.

At the same time, as interim Ballets Russes companies introduced these works to the public, they also acted as finishing schools for a new generation of dancers like the three "baby ballerinas" Irina Baronova, Tamara Toumanova, and Tatiana Riabouchinskaya; as well as Alicia Markova, Anton Dolin, Andre Eglevsky, Igor Youskevitch, Frederic Franklin, and Mia Slavenska. Most of these people were born in Russia, but got their ballet schooling in Paris from famous dancers who had left Russia after the 1917 revolution. Their performing was then divided between Europe and America. All this activity not only created new audiences for our art form, it also helped bring first-rate ballet to countries where there had been little or none before. As this next generation of Russians began to put down roots in the West, ballet blossomed in South America and Europe, as well as England and the United States.

We turn our attention now to London, and later to cities in America, where the main action was taking place apart from any of the Ballets Russes offshoots. Yet through much of this present century, the repertory, the dancers, the teachers, and the choreographers of internationally acclaimed ballet owe as large a debt to Diaghilev's Ballets Russes as the nineteenth century ballet world owed to the Romantic Age in Paris.

Questions for Review

1.   Discuss the wandering nature of history's dance artists.

2.   What were the developments in French ballet in the middle of the twentieth century?

3.   What happened to Ballets Russes choreographers Massine, Nijinska, and Balanchine after Diaghilev's death?

18 BRITISH TASTE AND MANNERS

BALLET IN ENGLAND FROM 1910 TO THE PRESENT

England's Dance Artists

In an earlier chapter, we noted that the English Puritans with Cromwell at their head put an end to the lively dance spectacles that Queen Elizabeth I used to enjoy so much. From then on, into the first decades of our century, the ballet seen in that country was almost all staged by visiting artists. Yet today, England's Royal Ballet is one of the world's finest companies. In addition, the Ballet Rambert, the London Festival Ballet, and several other fine companies make their home in England. Three great names dominate the story of this transformation: Ninette de Valois, Marie Rambert, and Frederick Ashton. Margot Fonteyn, Antony Tudor, Hugh Laing, and Robert Helpmann also figure prominently in the action. These names are referred to today with a sense of awe, as befits royal personages. Indeed, their queen Elizabeth II recognized the noble deeds they performed, and accordingly, five of them now bear titles such as Dame Ninette de Valois, Dame Marie Rambert, Sir Frederick Ashton, Dame Margot Fonteyn, and Sir Robert Helpmann. Antony Tudor and Hugh Laing were not similarly honored. This was not because of lesser artistic merit, but because they left England in 1939 to grace the American scene thereafter.

In the 1920s and 1930s however, these noble artists did not rule a kingdom, but interacted in a small society that was rich in imagination, but quite poor in material resources. When we read accounts of their dance activities, we are struck by the way things were patched together in a most uncomfortable and rather undignified manner. Lack of money as well as heat probably occupied their thinking as much as barre exercises and choreography. At the same time, they were by no means free of self-serving maneuvers and temperamental clashes. Once more, we are reminded that artistic determination in choreographers, directors, and performers is accompanied by a strong ego—which means a difficult personality. There are many detailed accounts of these early London struggles. For the liveliest reading, see Agnes de Mille's *Dance To The Piper*. Although de Mille made her reputation in America, she was in Rambert's Ballet Club for a number of years, and she brings it to life with words like these:

> The walls sweated. The gray damp of English winter steamed and thickened on the pale windows. On arrival a girl would vigorously pull off her woolen dress and standing in her woolen undershirt, hold her damp black tights over the oil stove while her pale flesh quivered at the exposure.
>
> In the center of the room darted Mim [Marie Rambert], her little legs in wrinkled black tights, her childlike body in a shapeless baby-pink garment ruffled at the hips, a veil around her little dark head, she went from side to side in the room, pulling, pushing, poking, screaming and imploring.
>
> Now and then she would stamp her foot and literally howl with distaste: "Freddie! [to Frederick Ashton] pull in your great bottom. You flaunt your bottom like a banner."

We also hear that just as there once had been rival factions at the Paris Opera, there now developed in London fanatical followers who championed either Tudor or Ashton. The Tudor group praised his psychological drama, but the Ashton group was in favor of his decorative, musical approach.

A National Style. Particularly in the case of England, it is surely more helpful to discuss the creations and theories of the artists rather than to dwell on anecdotes about them and their personal quirks. The make-up of the English character and the style of the English ballet dictate a more objective, rational approach than might the French and the Russian. This is because of the very nature of artistic style. When we speak of a national style we really mean something like a national personality. Now obviously, individual Englishmen are not all the same. Nevertheless, we always refer to English reserve and scientific detachment, as well as to English etiquette and good form, because these qualities are so often present in the people of that country. Therefore, since art is an expression of people's emotions and attitudes, we can expect to find these same qualities in their national ballet—and we are not disappointed.

British dance is known to be clean and precise. Attention to detail is always apparent. The feet of the Royal Ballet dancers are outstanding for their beautiful precision in *point* work, as well as the dancers' posture and arm positions. If there is ever a choice between full emotion and correct technique in British ballet, the academic rules always win. In choreography, we shall see how Tudor and Ashton, each in a different way, express English reserve and concern with manners and good taste. Above all, we will find the British insistence on high standards in the philosophy of Ninette de Valois who, more than anyone else, is credited with establishing Britain's Royal Ballet.

Forerunners of the British Ballet Revival. Before we go into more detail about these artistic giants, we will glance briefly at a few dancers who prepared the way for them. Danish-born Adeline Genée (1878 to 1970) began her ten-year stint in 1897 as a ballerina at London's Empire Theater, and helped build a warm audience for dance. Adelene Genée was also one of the founders in 1920 of a dance association which was to be granted a royal charter in 1936 as the Royal Academy of Dancing (R.A.D.). The aim of this institution was to set standards for teaching classical ballet technique. It has been so successful that today R.A.D. courses and qualifying examinations are given all over the British Commonwealth and in a few other countries to many thousands of teachers and students. Genée was the first president of the R.A.D. and in 1954 she was succeeded by Fonteyn.

Then we must take note of the great Russian dancer Anna Pavlova. After Pavlova had received her schooling at the St. Petersburg School of Ballet, and performed in the Russian Imperial Ballet where she reached the highest rank of prima ballerina, she was inspired by Marie Taglioni's life story and decided to tour abroad in the footsteps of that famous dancer. Eventually, Pavlova was to travel farther than her Romantic predecessor, performing for millions of people all over Europe, North and South America, and the Far East. Pavlova, whose dream of a ballet career had started during a performance of Petipa's *The Sleeping Beauty*, was in turn responsible for implanting the same dream in the hearts of countless young girls who watched her perform—to mention only two, Agnes de Mille and Doris Humphrey.

At the very least, Anna Pavlova helped build audiences for ballet where this art form had never taken root, or even been seen. (She often performed in a high school auditorium in towns or villages which lacked a theater.) Certainly in England, which became her permanent residence in 1912 and where she opened a school, Pavlova attracted an immense new public for ballet. Further, she imparted a strict respectability to what had been considered a rather cheap pursuit.

Pavlova did not join Fokine or Diaghilev in revolutionary experiments. Rather, she remained quite conservative in her choice of choreography and music, presenting variations from old classic ballets. However, all reports agree that through her great artistry she deeply moved her viewers and achieved an unprecedented success whenever she appeared. Her own ideal of the function of dancing was "to give men a sight of an unreal world, beautiful, dazzling as their dreams." However, she by no means approved of exhibiting technique for its own sake, pleading instead for expressive grace, passion, joy, wonder, and delight. In her own dancing, she seems to have fulfilled this exalted image of her art.

Both de Valois and Ashton expressed their love for and admiration of Pavlova. When de Valois was a teenager she saw Pavlova in London. Ashton saw her when he was a young boy in South America. They were in complete agreement that there had never been anything like her. Pavlova was not alone in bringing Russian ballet to the British public. During the same 1910 season when she first danced in London, stars and full supporting casts from St. Petersburg and Moscow staged both *Swan Lake* and *Giselle*. Then in 1911, Diaghilev's Ballets Russes held a gala as part of George V's coronation festivities, which presented "more glitter than the coronation itself."

English audiences were to give the Ballets Russes their best box office. One critic spoke of a "love affair" between the British public and their beloved Russian dancers. Two of the most important names in British ballet, Marie Rambert and Ninette de Valois, had been associated briefly with the Ballets Russes. Marie Rambert, a pupil of the Dalcroze system (that used movement to analyze musical rhythms), helped Nijinsky to count the dreadfully complex rhythms in Stravinsky's score for *Rite of Spring*. Ninette de Valois was a soloist in Diaghilev's company from 1923 to 1925. However, the Ballets Russes influence does not seem to have been decisive in the subsequent achievements of either woman.

Moving from the background into the main story, a date to mark is 1926. That year, Ninette de Valois (born in 1898 as Edris Stennus, too plain a name for the dance world) opened a dancing school in London. She also began work at the Old Vic Theater, which led eventually to her position as director of the Sadler's Wells Ballet, which later became the Royal Ballet. Also in 1926, Marie Rambert (who was born in 1888 in Poland as Cyvia Rambam, and died in 1982) started a company made up of London pupils from her school, which had been holding classes since 1920. The Ballet Rambert remained small in size, unlike the Sadler's Wells-Royal Ballet of de Valois. However, the Ballet Rambert was responsible for promoting a tremendous amount of choreographic talent, including Antony Tudor, Norman Morrice, and above all, Frederick Ashton. Ashton, who along with de Valois and Rambert headed the cast of British ballet founders, staged his first ballet, *A Tragedy of Fashion*, for Marie Rambert's company in 1926. Ashton was to go on from there to create the bulk of the English repertory.

Ninette de Valois

Of these three founders, it was Ninette de Valois who used a talent for choreography, a gift for teaching, and administrative ability to fulfill a daring vision: the creation of a national English ballet company. In the words of American choreographer Agnes de Mille:

> This achievement is without precedent. Previously it required one or two centuries and the resources of a monarch to build a first-class ballet company. Sadler's Wells [later the Royal Ballet] was built in twenty years, all but unaided. The British government took it over, a finished product.

Ninette de Valois wisely used the talented people that were available in the England of the 1930s, such as Alicia Markova and Anton Dolin. They both had appeared as soloists with Diaghilev, although they were born and trained in England (she as Lillian Alicia Marks and he as Sydney Francis Patrick Chippendale Healey-Kay). For Markova and Dolin, classics like *Giselle*, *Nutcracker*, and *Swan Lake* were revived with the aid of the Russian ballet master Nicholas Sergeyev. He had recorded in dance notation twenty-one ballet productions during his fourteen years as director at the St. Petersburg Maryinsky Theater. In Alicia Markova the young English company had one of the great ballerinas of our century. In the English publication *Ballet Annual*, Number 10, Markova's many unforgettable performances in *Giselle* led one critic to write:

> How often the contemporaries of Marie Taglioni paid tribute to her superhuman lightness: for instance that poetic allusion to "a cloud with two feet." Was this a far-flung flight of fancy? I think not, because Markova proves beyond question that such phantom lightness is within the bounds of a ballerina's achievement.

When Markova and Dolin left to form their own company in 1935, de Valois daringly featured unknown dancers like Margot Fonteyn, whom she had patiently developed on her own. From its beginnings, the English company was solidly rooted in a traditional classical repertory.

At the same time, de Valois herself created dramatic ballets that clearly showed their stylistic kinship with the great theatrical heritage of England, which was, after all, the home of Shakespeare and Ben Jonson. She also worked using themes taken from English visual art. Blake's paintings inspired *Job* and Hogarth's *The Rake's Progress*. This fulfilled her philosophy that the true aim of modern ballet is to expand the possibilities of the classical ballet in harmony with the other arts of the theater. At the beginning she was understandably concerned with only the basics in order to establish a tradition. She knew that from there, dancers would branch off in experimental work of their own. And of course they did. De Valois saw the essence of ballet as the discipline of natural, ordinary, everyday movement that was formalized to the peak of perfection. In her own choreography, she thought of herself as a stage or a theatrical producer. Her method of working was to arrange dance movement to a written scenario and a musical score that were already prepared on a given theme. De Valois's most important works that have been presented by English and foreign companies are *Job, Haunted Ballroom, The Rake's Progress*, and *Checkmate.*

Job. This work (1931) is known as a masque for dancing, rather than a ballet because it features the biblical drama and scenic design. Indeed, the idea for the piece and the synopsis of the action were supplied by Geoffrey Keynes, inspired by his studies of William Blake, the eighteenth-century painter-poet who had made twenty-one engravings illustrating the Book of Job. Keynes asked Vaughan Williams to prepare a musical score, following the narrative line, and Gwendolyn Raverat to design scenes and costumes based on Blake's pictures. Only after the piece was presented in concert as a musical selection did Ninette de Valois become involved as the choreographer. She made effective use of the scenario, with its contrasting scenes of calm spiritual beauty and the horrors of disease and sudden death. The ballet's central role is that of Satan, successfully portrayed at the 1931 premiere by Anton Dolin. In style, de Valois leaned towards the expressive dance being seen in Europe at the time. Over four decades later (in 1975), the ballet was to be rechoreographed for British television by Robert Cohan, a former Martha Graham dancer who was to export Graham's technical approach from New York to London.

The Rake's Progress. This ballet (1935) served as animation for a visual subject: pictures by another eighteenth-century artist, William Hogarth. Gavin Gordon outlined the action and wrote the music, and once more, this was as much a mimed play as a ballet. *The Rake's Progress* presents a young man from a rural area who inherits a lot of money and goes to London to live like a gentleman. But he takes up with gamblers, indecent women, and drunks who take advantage of his money and his naiveté. He loses all his money and sinks increasingly lower until finally he ends up thoroughly broken in an insane asylum, where he dies in a hysterical fit. Again Ninette de Valois entered the picture after the scenario and music had been written. Rex Whistler did the scenery and costume design.

Checkmate. Arthur Bliss wrote the scenario and musical score and E. McKnight Kauffer did the decor for this 1937 symbolic piece that presented a struggle between the evil force of Death and the lighter power of Love in the guise of a chess game. Love's side is represented by the red pieces;

Death's by the black. Black wins. De Valois created patterns for her chess pieces that combine classical *point* work, folk dance steps, and an overall group style that showed the influence of expressionistic modern German Dance.

Haunted Ballroom. With music and scenario by Geoffrey Toye, *Haunted Ballroom* (1934) takes us back once more to the Romantic world of gloomy spirits. The setting is an ancient, haunted ballroom in a Scottish castle, where the hero and his father are doomed to share the fate of their ancestors: they will dance to their deaths, hypnotically led on by ghostly creatures. Once again the elements sound familiar, reminding us of the Scottish James in *La Sylphide*, the dying Chopin shown playing the piano in *Chopiniana*, Fokine's first version of *Les Sylphides*, and the dance to the death caused by female spirits (the Wilis in *Giselle*).

In her choreography, de Valois used classical ballet technique. But by adding mass movements of the German school, she departed from the conventional ballet style. In a way, Ninette de Valois followed the practice of those ballet choreographers who regarded their jobs somewhat the way we think of a stage director's. That is, in her works, she would arrange movements that gave life to the drama and emotions created by a scenario writer and a music composer, who were usually one and the same person. When de Valois borrowed from the German modern dance, she was also following the practice of ballet choreographers who have often sought interest and novelty by adapting other dance styles to their own needs.

Robert Helpmann. Although Alicia Markova and Anton Dolin starred in de Valois's ballets as well as in the traditional classics, new dancers were also making names for themselves. For example, Robert Helpmann was outstanding as the doomed Scotsman in *The Haunted Ballroom*. When Markova and Dolin went off to form their own company in 1935, Helpmann shone in Dolin's former role of Satan in *Job*, and in the title role in *The Rake's Progress*, and as the Red King in *Checkmate*. Robert Helpmann (1909 to 1986) was born in Australia and when Pavlova visited that remote continent, he studied with her company. He then came to London where he was a starring male dancer in the Sadler's Wells Ballet from 1933 until he left in 1950. Helpmann's dramatic ability struck de Valois from their first meeting when she decided that something must be done to use his marvelous face. He went on to bring out dramatic possibilities not only in De Valois's own characters, but even in classic roles like Albrecht, in *Giselle*.

Beyond Helpmann's strength as a performer lay a talent for highly theatrical choreography. He contributed two major works to the English repertory: *Hamlet* (1942, music by Tchaikovsky) and *Miracle in the Gorbals* (1944, music by Arthur Bliss). His successfully realized *Hamlet* is not a full-scale staging of the play without the words. Rather, it presents a flood of memories in the mind of the dying prince of Denmark, arranged like dreams of psychological intensity and exaggeration. Hamlet himself (originally played by Helpmann) sometimes watches the action and sometimes moves as part of it. The extent to which this is a theatrical work is shown by the fact that Helpmann called in a producer of drama to direct the final rehearsals of *Hamlet*. In fact, Helpmann also did this for *Miracle in the Gorbals*, which is an unusual modern-dress version of the Jesus story. Jesus pays a visit to the slums of Glasgow in Scotland, where he brings to life a young girl who had committed suicide. His action arouses the primitive fears of the tough slum dwellers and Jesus is put to death once again—by a local person. The work is outstanding for its three-dimensional characterizations.

Margot Fonteyn. In many ballets after the Diaghilev period, the leading figures were male. This was certainly true of most de Valois works. However, in the school that she had established for her ballet company, de Valois was patiently developing a host of fine dancers, many of them female. Margot Fonteyn (1919 to 1991), of course, heads the list of de Valois's female dancers. Fonteyn was relatively unknown when she stepped into the shoes of the departing Alicia Markova as star of the English company. (In 1935, it was still called the Sadler's Wells Ballet. Over twenty years later, Queen Elizabeth II issued the charter that turned it into the Royal Ballet.)

Ninette de Valois had been teaching in her own ballet school since 1926. In 1931, she moved her private pupils to the Sadler's Wells Ballet School which was constantly expanded until it became a boarding school, responsible for a future ballet dancer's complete education in academic subjects as well as training in dance and music. (This was modelled after the famous Maryinsky Academy of St. Petersburg.) De Valois saw that a school was necessary to ensure a decent company. One reason that the Diaghilev ballet had not survived the death of Sergei Diaghilev had been the lack of a school or any organized means of maintaining a well-trained company and a source for new dancers. Through this schooling, Margot Fonteyn started to grow into one of the finest ballerinas of her time. Although very different in style from Alicia Markova, Fonteyn too was superb as a classical dancer. First-rate in the Petipa ballets, she also proved outstanding in the neoclassic creations of Frederick Ashton which dominated the repertory in the late 1930s.

Frederick Ashton

Ashton (1906 to 1988) began to study dance in the 1920s, after a standard (nondance) English education. Almost immediately, he did some performing, and then choreography, which increasingly held his interest. He produced many works for Marie Rambert and then for Sadler's Wells, where he was appointed associate director in 1952 (together with de Valois) and sole director (1963 to 1970) of the company, which had by then been named the Royal Ballet. Ashton created the bulk of the repertory of the Royal Ballet in a style quite unlike de Valois's. While her works were dramatic and literal, his were musical and mood pieces. She used modernistic groupings and expressive movements, but he leaned toward classical harmony and the beauty of academic dancing. She featured strong emotions, whereas he produced restrained, lyrical, elegant works with touches of wit.

Ashton's tremendous output ranged widely and included: restaging old ballets like *La Fille Mal Gardée* (1960); lighthearted variations on a theme like the meetings and partings in *Les Rendezvous* (1937); balletic versions of a literary work like a Shakespearean play in *The Dream* (1964); plotless musical works like *Monotones* (Erik Satie, 1965); historical flashbacks like the Romantic, eerie *Apparitions* (1936), and a royal tribute, *Homage to the Queen* (1953) in honor of Elizabeth II's coronation.

Whatever his theme, however, Ashton concentrated heavily on the music. He was more concerned that there be a harmonious relationship between music and movement, for example, than that the movements in themselves should communicate ideas or feelings. In his musical approach, Ashton was stimulated and aided by Constant Lambert, who was not only a conductor and composer, but who was one of the moving spirits behind the creation and development of the Sadler's Wells Ballet, where he was musical director until his death in 1951. Lambert arranged or wrote music for many Ashton ballets. Further, his artistic taste and experience with music for ballet, which began with his 1926 score *Romeo and Juliet* for the Diaghilev company choreographer Bronislava Nijinska, were significant in shaping Ashton's choreographic philosophy. We will look briefly at four Ashton ballets, selected arbitrarily from dozens: *Façade, Les Patineurs, Symphonic Variations*, and *Ondine*.

Façade. This ballet (1931) was choreographed to music that William Walton had composed to accompany a group of poems by Edith Sitwell. Although the choreography was not based on the poems at all, but on the music, it is hard to accept the statement of one writer (Balanchine) that "the ballet has nothing to do with the poems." If the movement reflects the music, and the music was written to the poems, then there has to be some connection, at least in mood. Anyway, *Façade* doesn't pretend to be more than a light frothy entertainment. This very early Ashton ballet is made up of a series of dance diversions, such as a Scottish dance, a polka, and a waltz. One scene features a milkmaid serenaded by three yodelers. Another has a couple dance a tango while the male makes passes at his partner. There is a mocking air about all the scenes, which take place outside the facade of a Victorian house, designed by John Armstrong. For the finale, the cast swings into a lively Tarantella.

Les Patineurs. This ballet (1937) was choreographed to musical pieces which Constant Lambert arranged from Meyerbeer's works. (You may recall Meyerbeer as the composer of the opera *Robert le Diable* in which appeared the "Ballet of the Nuns" that marked the beginning of the Romantic ballet.) Again Ashton created a series of frolicsome dances, this time variations on the theme of ice-skating. Audiences still enjoy this transference of the virtuoso spinning and gliding ice-skating tricks to the ballet stage, and the way that Ashton took advantage of the unsteady tripping and fearful gestures of awkward beginners—miming, but in dance patterns. William Chappel costumed the skater-dancers in bright colors and set them on a frozen pond beneath snowy branches decorated with lanterns. It is a most attractive winter scene.

Symphonic Variations. In this work (1946) Ashton dispensed with all references to specific situations, designing plotless dance movements to music. The ballet reflects the texture and phrasing of Cesar Franck's musical composition for piano and orchestra, *Symphonic Variation*. This is a fine example of Ashton's lyrical, flowing sculptured style. The plastic effect of his patterns is based on classical position but softened by the gentle lines of the dancers' heads and arms. This effect is heightened by the spare abstract lines of Sophie Fedorovitch's backdrop and the supple simplicity of the girls' tunics and the boys' draped blouses. There are only six dancers in the work, three male and three female. They begin and end in the same poised meditation, and in between, they perform in varying combinations and moods.

Ondine. In this ballet (1958), Ashton moved away from abstract patterns and short works and applied his supreme craftsmanship to a more common ballet idea: the staging of a fairy tale as a full evening's production in several acts. An echo of the Romantic past is found in Ashton's use of a story that had served as a ballet scenario a century earlier. Heinrich Fouque, a German novelist, in 1811 wrote *Ondine*, about a nymph who had no soul. This served as a subject for several ballets, the most famous by Jules Perrot (whom we remember for his work in *Giselle*) who used the idea to supply Fanny Cerrito with a good role in 1843. Ashton made a completely different version, constructing his own scenario and ordering music for it from Hans Werner Henze. His notes to the composer were quite detailed, reminding us of Petipa's instructions to Tchaikovsky. For example: "Solemn dance, interrupted by Ondine in frenzy—fright of Bertolda, all exit—two minutes"

The plot shows clearly its German Romantic origin, and, with a touch of *Romeo and Juliet*, easily takes its place next to *La Sylphide*, *Giselle*, *Swan*

Lake, and *Firebird*. Outside a castle, the advances of the hero Palemon are rejected by Berta. Then Ondine, a water sprite in the form of a maiden, appears and immediately captures Palemon's love. In a mysterious forest, the lovers come upon Terrenio, King of the Sea, who warns Palemon that he will die if he is unfaithful to Ondine. Bravely defying the curse, the couple gets married and Ondine gains a human soul. Next, the newlyweds go sailing on a ship where Berta, who is now jealous and wants Palemon for herself, hides. Terrenio creates a storm, wrecks the boat, and drags Ondine into the sea with him. Back at the palace again, Palemon and Berta are preparing to celebrate their wedding. Terrenio arrives to fulfill his threat. Berta is dragged away. Ondine appears and Palemon regains his true love, and kisses her, and falls dead at her feet. She takes his body back to the sea with her for eternity. Lila de Nobili designed appropriate settings particularly for the scene at the sea, where greens and browns filtered through sunlight on the rippling waves highlight the drama.

It sounds like a typical nineteenth-century ballet, with the substitution of water for air as the element inhabited by supernatural beings. However, Ashton did not emphasize the narrative itself, and one critic described it as a three-act ballet of mood rather than a three-act drama. As David Vaughan tells us in *Frederick Ashton And His Ballets*, Ashton himself explained that he molded the movements of nature into this ballet: "I spent hours watching water move. All the choreography, especially that of the corps, moves in surges of movement like the swell of waves...I wanted the movement to be fluid like the rhythm of the sea, rather than set ballet steps." Ashton also sought to create an interlude between the more intense first and third acts. "I wanted it to rest the audience as it were."

After the premiere, a critic wrote that "Margot Fonteyn's Ondine belongs already to the gallery of great ballet interpretations." However, even before the first rehearsal, Fonteyn had a hand in the ballet. In fact, she helped choose the theme. Ashton often conceived his ballets directly for Fonteyn, and then she collaborated with him all through the creation. As reported by Van Praagh and Brinson in *The Choreographic Art*, Fonteyn described how she devised a change in a bit of business that seemed fake to her:

> In the original version Ondine was attracted by Palemon's amulet and snatched it away. When he took it back she became petulant and angry. But when we did that scene it seemed false, especially musically. So now Ondine replaces the amulet around Palemon's neck. . .
>
> At that moment he presses her hand to his heart. She is frightened by his heartbeat [Ondines don't have hearts, you know] and jumps back with surprise. Then overcome by curiosity, she puts her hand over his heart to feel it beat again.

The authors comment:

> Ashton has used Fonteyn's personal qualities [of fluidity of movement combined with exceptional control and discipline] to great effect in many of his ballets. Her quality of emotional restraint has appealed so much to Ashton that he has used it constantly. It represents an emotional discipline corresponding to the discipline of her movement. So exactly does it reflect the English character that it makes her a personification of the English school as well as its model.

Ashton's works were influenced by other dancers who were available to him as well. For example Van Praagh and Brinson write:

> The steadiness and security of Michael Somes, as a long-term partner of Fonteyn, and his noble presence onstage have been used in Ashton's works to contrast and highlight Fonteyn's lively femininity. In return, Ashton's large output became the mainstay of the growing English company and therefore helped shape its character.

De Valois has called Ashton the Petipa of Great Britain for the volume of lasting works that he created. Above all, in Ashton's style we can see the British connections. Words like *neat, gracious, tasteful,* and *distinctive* apply to Ashton, never words like *stormy* or *passionate.* One writer even spoke of his "party manners" in choreography. Thus the Royal Ballet developed a style of its own. It was a combined expression of the British nation in general, and in particular of the personalities of Ninette de Valois, Frederick Ashton, Robert Helpmann, Margot Fonteyn, and Constant Lambert, along with Antony Tudor and others who worked under Marie Rambert, with whom we will now pause.

Marie Rambert

Rambert served in a way as the Diaghilev of ballet in England. Without dancing or choreographing herself, she directed a ballet club. She discovered and guided so many choreographic talents including Frederick Ashton, Antony Tudor, Walter Gore, Andrée Howard, Norman Morrice, and Christopher Bruce that her club, which was really a performing company, has been called the cradle of British choreography. The old rebuilt parish house which contained her company and school became the first permanent home of ballet in England.

In 1926, we noted that Ashton did his first piece for Marie Rambert's group, *A Tragedy of Fashion,* as part of a theater revue. For a number of years he benefited from her advice, a kind of continuing guidance that

Rambert saw as necessary for every young choreographer. Rambert once said at a symposium:

> What is really needed is a guide who must encourage the artist to search for the most perfect expression, rejecting every too facile invention. To make last-minute corrections or to impose advice and directions may save a ballet but not an artist...
>
> Real guidance is work of great patience, and faith in the ultimate value of the artist whom one wishes to help.

Sometimes this guidance appears to be very casual. For example, David Vaughan reports in *Frederick Ashton and His Ballets* that Rambert told him:

> One evening after a performance, dancer Andrée Howard came out of the dressing room on her way to a party, wearing a beautiful evening dress in the Edwardian style. It was black with a flower at her hip. Fred and I were in the studio and I said, "Fred Ashton, you must make a dance for Andrée wearing that dress."
>
> The music was to be a French popular song that I sang to him.

Ashton called the dance *Pompette*, a slang term for being a little drunk. Many such incidents like this in choreography remind us that ballet is often concerned with lighthearted entertainment, rather than "serious art."

Rambert's company never reached the size and stature of the Sadler's Wells, partly because of its small stage and theater space. As a result, dancers and choreographers were always leaving Rambert to join de Valois's more "official" company or to work abroad, where there were better opportunities. Yet just because of its limited size and low production costs, the organization allowed for constant experiment. Agnes de Mille, the American dancer who was part of the struggling Rambert scene in the 1930s, gave another reason why artists went elsewhere: "Rambert drove them nuts," she claimed, telling of Rambert's eccentric personal behavior. How she might suddenly turn cartwheels in the studio when an "important" visitor came to watch a lesson. Her lack of organization, her temperamental outbursts and cutting remarks which often had dancers crying through their pliés. Yet even her "victims" agreed that she did a great deal for English ballet.

Antony Tudor

Born in 1909 as William Cook (died 1987), Tudor was the most illustrious of Rambert's circle. He did not come to ballet until a youth of twenty, when he approached Marie Rambert. Rambert wrote of Tudor in *Quicksilver*: "He had fine eyes and looked like a poet. He told me he could not come to classes before 4 P.M.. as he worked from 5 A.M. to 3 P.M. in an accountant's office." Rambert immediately took him in as a pupil and also employed him around the studio so that he could devote all his energies to dance. From the first, he was interested primarily in being a choreographer, although he did perform for a number of years, mostly in his own works.

Like Fokine, Tudor built on a foundation of classical technique, and at the same time created expressive movements that were appropriate to the idea of each dance. But while Fokine had been interested in the broad dramatic sweep of a story line, and took his themes from fairy tales and folk legends, Tudor, on the other hand, was tuned in to subtle psychological case studies of ordinary people. His characters are believable and reveal themselves in precise gestures, even when he chose to do a scene from the exotic past, like *Romeo and Juliet*. Tudor was known to spend hours working with a soloist, seeking the exact right motion for a certain personality. For example, the arrogant shoulder shrug of the hero in *Undertow* and the spinster's nervous pulling of her collar in *Pillar of Fire* mark this collaboration.

Major roles in Tudor's ballets are identified with a chosen few dancers, particularly Hugh Laing (first in England and then the U.S.) and Nora Kaye (only in the States), who became known as Tudor dancers.

Hugh Laing once explained how he changed his type of shoe, needing one kind to move with Romeo's ardent youthfulness, and another to walk with the vulgarity of the seducer in *Pillar of Fire*. Laing was quoted in *Dance Perspectives*, Number 18: "You can't be a dancer in Tudor ballets. The technique is basically classical but it must look nonexistent. He may want four pirouettes as part of a phrase saying 'I love you, Juliet', but you must not interrupt the phrase to take a fourth position in preparation because then you are paying attention to yourself as a dancer and not to Juliet." Nora Kaye added: "One critic wrote that I was a fine actress, but he would like to see me dance. He didn't realize that technically the role is fiendishly difficult. The way Tudor choreographs, it doesn't look like technique."

Tudor's choreographic career spans five decades. However, again like Fokine, he created his masterpieces during a fairly short period of time, about ten years. Those of us who are interested in what makes ballet tick may speculate about why this happens to some choreographers. In Tudor's case, it may be that his natural environment was England, where his talent came to full flower. Transplanting him to America's more lusty cultural environment may have overpowered this artist who was molded by British restraint. Look how Tudor's works reflected British culture. He began in 1931 with *Cross-Gaitered* based on Shakespeare's *Twelfth Night* for Rambert's Ballet Club, and continued through the 1970s in the U.S. and elsewhere. In England, he produced his first great works such as *Lilac*

Nora Kaye created the role of Hagar, the spinster-heroine of Tudor's "Pillar of Fire."

Garden, Dark Elegies, Judgement of Paris, and *Gala Performance.* Then in America, he followed these with *Pillar of Fire, Romeo and Juliet, Dim Luster,* and *Undertow.*

Lilac Garden. This Tudor ballet (1936, to music by Ernest Chausson) presents an image of romantic frustration. At a party on the eve of her arranged marriage, Caroline tries for a private parting farewell from her true love. However, Caroline does not succeed because of interruptions from her proper husband-to-be, his former mistress who seeks reassurance, and other guests. Hugh Stevenson, who helped Tudor with the scenario, designed costumes and scenery that placed the action in the Edwardian era. This was a time when social conventions dictated the restrained, inhibited conduct which Tudor brought to life with compressed motions of heads, arms and hands, and subtle pauses.

Dark Elegies. This work (1937) is a lament. There is no specific story, but the accompaniment—Gustav Mahler's *Kindertotenlieder* (Songs for Dead Children), Nadia Benois's costumes (dark, unadorned dresses for the women, plain trousers and shirts for the men), and the backdrop of a somber coast—establishes the situation of villagers in mourning in the wake of a catastrophe that befell their children. Tudor's patterns are simple: the group steps solemnly as a community, linked in lines and circles that remind us of folk dances. Solo figures occasionally break out in phrases of wild or quiet grief, while others reach out in sympathy. Finally, the group forms a calm procession and the dance ends on a note of resigned acceptance.

Judgment of Paris. This ballet (1938) reveals Tudor's lighter side, which is composed more of biting wit than of jolly laughter. Hugh Laing did the scenario and the costumes as a parody on the ancient Greek legend, in which the Trojan prince Paris is asked to decide which one of three goddesses should receive an apple inscribed "To The Fairest." The action was moved to a shabby twentieth-century French cafe, the prince changed into a Parisian drunk, and the goddesses into three aging prostitutes who competed for the drunk's attention. They go through their tired routines with disinterested boredom to accompanying selections from Kurt Weill's satiric masterpiece *The Threepenny Opera.*

Gala Performance. This Tudor work (1938, to Prokofiev's music) also satirizes the antics of three women competing for the spotlight. However, this occasion is less pathetic and more familiar to Tudor, and by now, to us. An Italian, a Russian, and a French ballerina appearing together (remember *Pas de Quatre?*) try to get the better of one another with showy technical tricks during the performance, and also backstage with spiteful exhibitionism.

Pillar of Fire. In 1942, *Pillar of Fire* premiered in New York, where Tudor and Hugh Laing had settled two years earlier. This work established Tudor as an artist of the first rank in the eyes of the American ballet public. He had made the move to America because his earlier fine works did not earn for him the status to which he was entitled in English ballet. The main attention in England was on the growing national ballet establishment, rather than on the activities of Rambert's company and its offshoots. Agnes de Mille flatly states that "de Valois thought Antony had no talent and refused for twenty years to let him near her. When she did it was to be long after his American success." For his impressive *Pillar of Fire*, Tudor did the scenario (and, of course, the choreography) to Schoenberg's *Verklarte Nacht*. Schoenberg had composed *Verklarte Nacht* after a nineteenth-century poem about a woman who confesses to her lover that in her search for emotional security she has betrayed him with another man. Her lover forgives her in full understanding and acceptance. Jo Mielziner, a well-known theatrical designer, did the costumes and decor. The scenario was based on the narrative idea that had originally inspired the music.

In the ballet, the setting is changed from a moonlit German forest (remember *Sylphide*, *Swan Lake*, and all the other Romantic woodlands?) to a small American town in 1900. The woman Hagar's actions are explained by the jealousy of her flirtatious younger sister, and the fear of becoming a dried-up spinster like her older sister. Townspeople and groups of couples are added, together with a young man who uses Hagar's emotional turmoil merely to serve his own sexual pleasure. With Nora Kaye as Hagar, Hugh Laing as the young man, and Antony Tudor himself as the sympathetic, loving friend, the work won immediate overwhelming praise. *Pillar of Fire* marked the high point of Tudor's creative career. Although premiered in New York, it was still fed by British discoveries.

Romeo and Juliet (1943, music by Delius) received mixed notices as did *Dim Luster* (1943, music by Richard Strauss), which is also about a couple meeting at a ball. However, this time the possible romantic involvement is thwarted not by other people as in *Lilac Garden*, or by fate as in *Romeo and Juliet*, but by neurotic self-involvement. Each half of the couple remains immersed in past memories and never fully relates to the other.

Undertow (1945, music by William Schuman) went even further in psychological probing. Playwright John van Druten suggested the idea and Tudor plotted the action, which became a dramatically powerful case history of a young man who commits murder. The Transgressor (again Hugh Laing) is presented sympathetically. He is a lonely figure whose feelings of rejection and disillusionment grow into a hatred of women that finally pushes him toward this horrible deed. Murder is not an attractive dance subject, and this ballet did not become popular.

Tudor continued to choreograph and to influence a generation of artists at Juilliard, one of America's leading academic dance institutions. In *Dance Perspectives*, Number 18, Jerome Robbins had this to say: "Tudor brought psychological motivation into ballet; he conveyed through movement emotions that could not be put into words. He had a great influence on my early work and a great influence on all contemporary ballet."

Other Developments in England. Before we follow Tudor as he settles down in the American scene, there are a few more people to touch on briefly back in England. South-African-born John Cranko (1927 to 1973) joined Sadler's Wells in 1946, where he immediately turned to choreography. His ballets include *Pineapple Poll* (1951, music by Arthur Sullivan), *The Lady and the Fool* (1954, music by Verdi), and *Prince of the Pagodas* (1957, music by Benjamin Britten). In 1961, Cranko became director of the Stuttgart Ballet, which he developed into a first-class company. (It had gone down considerably after Noverre's leadership in the eighteenth century.) Cranko was particularly successful with full-length dramatic works. While at Stuttgart, Cranko created among other ballets: *Jeu de Cartes* (1965, music by Stravinsky), *Opus One* (1965, music by Webern), *Taming of the Shrew* (1969, music by Scarlatti), and *Ebony Concerto* (1970, music by Stravinsky).

Kenneth MacMillan was born 1929 in Scotland, and joined Sadler's Wells in 1946 when Cranko did. Like Cranko, he shone in choreography. His *Romeo and Juliet* (1965, music by Prokofiev) was filmed with Margot Fonteyn as Juliet. MacMillan became chief choreographer of the Royal Ballet in 1963 and succeeded Ashton as co-director in 1970. Walter Gore (1910 to 1977), also born in Scotland, appeared with the Rambert dancers and the Vic-Wells Ballet before he formed the London Ballet in 1961. His best-known work which he choreographed as ballet master in Frankfurt is *Eaters of Darkness* (1958, music by Benjamin Britten). It portrays a young bride who is driven mad after she is viciously committed to an insane asylum by her husband. After Gore, the English scene continued to be a lively one, down to the present. But remember, it all started back in the early days of this century when Ninette de Valois and Marie Rambert were first smitten with balletomania, and they went on to create a British branch of this noble European art form.

Questions for Review

1.   Why is Marie Rambert called the Diaghilev of British ballet?

2.   How would you characterize the choreography of Ninette de Valois? Why didn't she create more works?

3.   Describe Ashton's *Ondine* in relation to the terms *classic* and *Romantic*.

4.   Did you ever see a Tudor ballet? What do you think of his style?

19   REPRISE

EUROPEAN BALLET AFTER FOUR HUNDRED YEARS

The Convergence of Past and Present

Today in the 1990s, the ballet form is rounding out four centuries of existence, especially if you date its birth arbitrarily at 1581 with the presentation of the *Ballet Comique de la Reine*. A superficial comparison between
that court entertainment and, let's say, the premiere of a John Neumeier
work in 1979 for the Hamburg Ballet, makes you wonder whether these
works can honestly be treated as belonging to the same art form.
Neumeier's *Don Quixote* includes football and disco movements as well as
feudal knights. In one scene, it presents the hero, naked to his trunks, in a
boxing match. However, a closer look reassures you that they do indeed
have many things in common.

Both productions were elaborate spectacles that combined movement, music, unusual scenic effects, and varied costumes arranged for the
amusement of privileged people. (Of course, in our day, privileged people
are those who have a certain cultural background, rather than an aristocracy that claims a birthright.) The two productions were unified loosely by a
dramatic theme, that of a noble, courageous man who is opposed by dangerous forces. Their compositions were arranged to allow contrasting
scenes of action and of harmonious beauty. And both presented dance patterns that were adapted from social dancing, court forms in the earlier one,
and disco dancing in the recent one. The differences between the two productions were primarily in their costumes, personal behavior, and man-

ners. These differences stemmed from the distinctive modes of clothing and behavior acceptable in two societies that were separated by four hundred years of history.

The immensely more difficult dance movements in the 1979 production reflect the developments of a dance form that have been described in this study as evolving from a pastime of noble amateurs into a demanding life's work for professional virtuosos. Of course, at the same time, we can find in Neumeier's work, and indeed in the work of most present-day choreographers, manners that are quite foreign to the Renaissance courts that fathered ballet. In fact, echoes of primitive and ancient societies, as well as traces of modern dance creations that came into being in direct opposition to the ballet style, are familiar to today's audiences to a greater extent than the stately measures stepped by European nobility. For a look at various expressions of contemporary ballet, we will now make a brief tour of various companies, both far and near.

Hamburg Ballet. In a way, the entire repertory of the Hamburg Ballet illustrates the central objective of this to acquaint you with the major events of ballet's past, and to aid you in your appreciation of its present. Consider these works that the company performed during the season of its *Don Quixote* premiere: *Sleeping Beauty, Les Noces, Petrouchka, Variations, Sacre du Printemps, Daphnis and Chloe, Les Sylphides, Firebird, Le Train Bleu,* and *Parade.* Some of these were revivals of the original choreography by Petipa, Ivanov, Fokine, Bronislava Nijinska, and Jerome Robbins. Others were completely new creations by John Neumeier, but to the traditional music scores. And Neumeier obviously kept in mind the spirit and circumstances of earlier versions, as when his *Don Quixote* was at least true to the character of a man following irrational dreams and ideals.

In fact, that same July 1979 season at Hamburg contained two direct historical memorials. One evening was totally devoted to a verbal monologue which brought to life people like Diaghilev and Nijinsky in "conversations" that quoted their own words. The performer was Anton Dolin, himself one of Diaghilev's discoveries! Then there was an evening presented as a Nijinsky gala, which included re-creations of Nijinsky's famous roles as well as a piece called *Vaslav,* which Neumeier worked out according to a choreography plan by Nijinsky that the ill-fated dancer never carried out. As a viewer of dance, you could not have fully enjoyed these evenings without some knowledge of their past associations.

Ballet's International Character

Just as in 1581 when the dancing master at the French court, Beaujoyeux, had originally been Italian, so the international character of ballet continues to prevail. American-born John Neumeier (1942) studied in the United States and in England. He did choreography for the Royal Winnipeg and the Royal Danish companies before he became director of the Hamburg Opera Ballet Company in Germany. In fact, this movement across national borders is an outstanding feature of ballet today. In this respect, the most dramatic episodes have been the leaping of barriers that formerly divided the communist Eastern bloc from Western nations. This movement was led by Rudolf Nureyev in 1963 and followed by Baryshnikov in 1974, along with others like Valery and Galina Panov, Natalia Makarova, and Alexander Godunov. These dancers continue to make a strong impact on the West through their sensational technique, both in physical skills and in interpretive acting.

Ballet in Russia did not come to a halt with the revolution of 1917, even though wave after wave of top-flight dancers have fled from the former Soviet government. The academies in Moscow and St. Petersburg continued to excel in producing superb ballet dancers. For a while, it looked as though experimental choreography might have a chance, but cultural commissars soon denounced such attempts as bourgeois decadence and these experiments were not allowed to continue. Soviet ballet directors contented themselves with magnificent productions of classic standbys like *Giselle* and *Swan Lake*. They brought these to a pitch of virtuosity, and when their star dancers like Maya Plisetskaya appeared in the West, they became idols of the public. At the same time, they set a new standard to aim toward for the dancers of England, America, and elsewhere.

Less sensational, because it lacked political implications, has been the international career of Erik Bruhn, who was born in 1928 and trained in Denmark, where he became a soloist in the Royal Danish Ballet. Bruhn was considered to be one of the world's best male dancers in elegance of style, partnering, and forceful dance-acting. A lot of the credit must go to the ballet education system that August Bournonville established in Copenhagen, along with the repertory he created there. A century after Bournonville's great period of creativity, another choreographer emerged from the combined sponsorship of the Danish and Swedish royal companies: Birgit Culberg.

Birgit Culberg, who was born in Sweden in 1908, started her career as a student performer of modern dance. With such a background, it is not surprising that her works, which she created as resident choreographer for the Royal Swedish Ballet and later for the Royal Danish Ballet and the American Ballet Theater, were dramatic and emotional. The best-known is *Miss Julie* (1950, music by Rangstrom). Birgit Culberg based *Miss Julie* on the play by Strindberg, which tells of a young noblewoman who is thoroughly shamed when she succumbs sexually to the virile attractions of her father's valet. Culberg was inspired by the contrasting styles of the two leading characters: the aristocratic, refined, but degenerate Miss Julie, and the primitive, vigorous, and brutal servant Jean. She decided to use the hard, precise speed of ballet *point* technique for Miss Julie, and the manly, more weighty movements of modern dance for the lower-class servant Jean.

Other well-received Culberg ballets are *Medea* (1950, music by Bartók) which tells the same story of the ancient queen's dreadful revenge that Noverre presented in a ballet in the eighteenth century; and then *Moon Reindeer* (1957, music by Riisager), which is based on a Lapland legend of the familiar *Giselle* variety. A girl rejected by her beloved turns into a white reindeer when the moon is full. She charms hunters to follow her until they fall over a cliff to their deaths. Sooner or later most choreographers seem to come forth with their own versions of a Romantic love-death ballet, bathed in moonlight. This is surely one of the most persuasive ballet traditions of them all.

Erik Bruhn danced in Culberg ballets in Denmark and in the United States. His Jean in *Miss Julie* set an unforgettable standard for a male role in modern ballet, combining all the brilliant nobility of classical ballet with overpowering modern drama. Artists like Bruhn, Nureyev, and Baryshnikov have all been active in staging solid productions of the works they learned in their native schools. In this way, they have contributed to the ballet scenes in the United States, Canada, Italy, Australia, and elsewhere.

As I have mentioned several times, when one of these classical works is revived, you do not ever get to see the ballet as it was first performed. Memory losses and inadequate notation systems are only partly to blame. The ballet master usually makes some deliberate changes, either to suit the taste of a different audience or to take advantage of the skills in the available company. Or perhaps this is done according to some personal idea or interpretive difference of a star performer. For example, when Bruhn staged *Swan Lake* for the National Ballet of Canada in 1967, he enlarged the part of the prince from a colorless nobleman into a brooding type like Hamlet, who exhibits a tender Freudian admiration for his mother the queen. In any case, you can see that these artists contribute to the vigorous expansion of the ballet world, as they move about from place to place.

The Russian Kirov and Bolshoi Ballet Companies and the Royal Danish Ballet are usually numbered among the most important international companies, along with the British Royal Ballet, the New York City Ballet, and sometimes the American Ballet Theater. However, the scene changes constantly, and companies in unusual places frequently capture the public's fancy, which they hold for longer periods as they get stronger with an outstanding director-choreographer or a brilliant star. For example, the Ballet of the Twentieth Century, in Brussels, Belgium was founded in 1960. Director Maurice Béjart has been responsible for most of its unconventional repertory. Béjart draws his ideas from a variety of sources and usually mixes several dance and theater styles in vivid arrangements. His versions of *Sacre du Printemps* (Rite of Spring, 1959), *Les Noces* (1962), *Romeo and Juliet* (1966), *Firebird* (1950), and Ravel's *Bolero* (1960) are only a few of his works that have been presented by impressive ensembles, especially strong in male dancers. Béjart's central idea, as you can see in the name of his company, is to update ballet to the twentieth century. It is no accident that he, and many other important contemporary choreographers, have incorporated much modern dance and jazz into their creations.

In the subsequent decade, equally important developments took place in the Netherlands. At the end of the 1970s, director-choreographer Jiri Kylian brought the Netherlands Dance Theater to new heights. In repertory, he created for them a series of plotless works like *Symphonetta*, characterized by long passages of breathlessly driven energy and an open friendliness.

The Netherlands dancers are barefoot more often than not, but they exhibit remarkable virtuosity which clearly stems from classical technique as they skim along the stage floor, moving close to the ground but incredibly fast through space. They are as precise and elegant in their control and line as their counterparts in a company like the New York City Ballet, where toe shoes are very much in evidence. The two companies resemble each other further in that they do not feature individual stars, but instead appear as a beautiful, complete, functioning dance ensemble. What identifies the Dutch group with a ballet, rather than a modern dance heritage, is the emphasis on external line and visual spectacle along with the basic classical training. Admittedly, however, the distinction is not as sharp as it might be.

The Netherlands Dance Theater, established in 1959, was the first European ballet group to include modern dance classes in its daily training. But there are many ballet choreographers who have studied modern dance, to name a few: Jerome Robbins, Robert Joffrey, Gerald Arpino, and John Neumeier. At the same time, conventional ballet companies still attract enthusiastic audiences in places as far apart as Australia, Cuba, Holland, Canada, Israel, and Sweden. In fact, many of these countries are represented by more than one first-class group.

Don't forget that a performer's career is pretty well over by the age of fifty, a time of life that is just right for teaching, directing, or choreographing. Particularly in the U.S. and England, once the stars of the 1930s, 1940s, and 1950s left the stage, a large body of talent became available for launching and strengthening new companies. To take one example, Robert Helpmann left the Royal Ballet in London to direct and choreograph for the Australian Ballet. Dancers too are constantly moving around, offstage as well as on. Canadian Brian MacDonald started out in the National Ballet of Canada and then turned up directing the Royal Swedish, the American Harkness, and the Israeli Batsheva companies. I could go on and on.

It is my hope that you have acquired from these pages a foundation for appreciating the ballet art. It is a fair assumption that dance artists will continue to build on the rich traditions that have developed over the past four hundred years. Of course, we cannot predict the original turns they will take along the way. That unpredictability is one of the fascinations of the dance, and adds to the pleasure of those of you who are interested in following this art form. In the next chapters, we will see what happened to ballet when it migrated to the United States. We will also consider other dance art forms that are clearly American in origin.

Questions for Review

1.   What is similar about the art of ballet in the 1990s and the court ballet of the 1500s?

2.   What is different?

20 IN THE BEGINNING

AMERICAN DANCE UP TO THE 1900s

Variety of Forms

Walt Whitman wrote "I hear America singing." Isadora Duncan responded "I see America dancing." This is a vigorous nation and dance has always been present in its culture—actually its many cultures.

Native American Dance. Because dancing is an integral part of tribal life, we find it among our own tribal populations. For many centuries, Native Americans have practiced dance rituals in connection with hunting, planting, puberty, marriage, and war. When the United States government settled these tribes on reservations, we learn from Reginald and Gladys Laubin (in their book *Indian Dances of North America* (1975) and their article in Anatole Chujoy's *Dance Encyclopedia*) that dancing was suppressed. This happened presumably because the white rulers feared that "war dancing" would cause uprisings. By the time this policy was reversed, although the practice of ritual dancing had never really died out, many dances had been lost.

Reginald and Gladys Laubin are a couple who worked to foster Native American dances. Although they themselves are not Native Americans, the Laubins devoted their lives to performing Indian dances. In preparation, they lived for many years on Native American reservations in North and South Dakota, among the Sioux, Crow, Cheyenne, and other plains tribes. They were adopted by the Sioux who gave Gladys the name

Wiyaka Wastewin (Good Feather Woman), and Reginald the name *Tatanka Wanjila* (One Bull). This is the way the Laubins describe the style of Native American dancing. In body stance, backs are straight; knees are bent. Arms are not used a lot, but there is a great deal of head movement. The simple steps feature sudden, subtle shifts of weight. Dancers perform in a vigorous, but never frenzied manner. They are dignified and controlled, but at the same time, relaxed. Men do most of the dancing and wear the spectacular costumes. Women have their own dances, which are less showy than the men's.

That Native American dance in its original form has not disappeared entirely was demonstrated by the performance of the American Indian Dance Theater in 1989, at a New York theater. Doris Hering made these comments in *Dance Magazine* (January 1990):

> The company of twenty-three dancers, singers and musicians representing twenty tribes was thrilling . . . The atmosphere of the entire production was both honorable and engrossing . . .
>
> In the incredibly complex *Hoop Dance*, in which Eddie Swimmer manipulated no fewer than forty-two hoops, one became involved not in the "how" but in the "why," as the hoops seemed magically to come together in the shapes of animal creatures...
>
> The role of women in American Indian dance is decidedly secondary, but there was charm in the *Mother Earth Round Dance* with its small criss-crossing steps.

We hear of another phase of Native American dance from Erika Bourguignon who describes in "Trance Dance," (*Dance Perspectives*, Number 35) the *Ghost Dance* that swept through the tribes of the western United States in the 1880s. The Ghost Dances were an expression of hopeless pessimism. Bourguignon, who did field work among Native American tribes, reports:

> The essential theme combined ideas of the imminent end of the world and the return of the Indian dead and the buffalo with a special pattern of dance and ecstatic visions. . . . It was a simple circle dance in which as many as five hundred men, women and children might join.
>
> With clasped hands and intertwined fingers, the dancers moved slowly, with dragging feet from east to west . . . . As the dance continued, some persons might go into a trance, falling rigidly to the ground. Afterwards they related visions they had seen.

Folk Dance in America. Folk dancing is a popular tradition among the many groups that make up our immigrant nation. What we know as barn dancing or square dancing is an imported mix of English reels, Irish jigs, and other European dances. In the United States today you can watch or take part in folk dances from all over the world. There are international clubs that practice dances from many nations. There are also clubs that represent individual countries, or large geographical areas. Social dancing (sometimes called ballroom) is widely enjoyed. Its origin is twofold: aristocratic European (court) dancing, and African American vernacular dancing. Dance is also present in a number of other areas: dance therapy; sacred dance; rhythms for children; gymnastic and acrobatic exhibitions; ice skating; and physical education programs in colleges and high schools. The university curriculum offers a training ground for professional careers in dance history and criticism as well as performing and choreography. These subjects, however, fall beyond the scope of this book.

Our central interest is the history of dance as an art, that is, the presentation of art images with the body as the medium, in a theatrical setting. America has made two great contributions to this dance world, jazz and modern dance. Jazz dance was developed by one part of the American immigrant population: black Africans. Of course, they were not voluntary immigrants, but forced to come here as slaves. Nevertheless, they brought with them a love for dance and African movement styles that evolved into jazz and tap dance. Presently, we will see how these forms developed, conquered the hearts of Americans, and then spread throughout the world. We will confront the beginnings of modern dance in the next chapter. But first, we go back to the early days of the American colonies. How did the traditions of dance fare in the brave new world?

The American Gentry. As happened in England, there was almost no home-grown classical ballet in America before 1930. In the case of America, at first glance we are not surprised that this dance form hadn't taken hold. Didn't the art of the United States reflect its unique cultural mixture of frontier pioneering, a classless economy, democratic politics, black slavery, and an ever-quickening tempo of industrial growth in crowded, energetic cities? Ballet, which originated as the expression of unhurried, aristocratic European courts, would not seem to fit as naturally into this environment as it did in England, where a traditional monarchy continually kept before the public the royal imagery of a more leisurely society. However, as Victoria Huckenpahler points out in "George Washington Dances," an article in the bicentennial issue of *Dance Magazine* (July 1976), the eighteenth-century social ideal was far from open and democratic. There was an aristocratic group composed of landed gentry and wealthy merchants that made every effort to maintain class distinctions. As one means of accomplishing this purpose, they had dancing masters and dancing assemblies that remind us of courtly balls across the ocean.

> The institution of the "dancing assemblies" several decades before the revolution afforded the colonists a socially acceptable way to meet and mate . . .

In Virginia while its landed gentry patronized the elite City Dancing Assembly, where one might properly execute a minuet or *contredanse*, its craftsmen were relegated to the General Dancing Assembly where one could see the more plebeian jig . . . .

A socially prominent Virginia woman . . upon marrying a goldsmith, immediately had her membership to the City Assembly revoked.

To learn the proper way to do the dances, the Virginia gentry engaged dancing teachers for their families. We learn that the first president had a lifelong involvement with dance and deportment. Washington even wrote a list of rules for proper behavior which Huckenpahler compares to the rules set down by Thoinot Arbeau in *Orchesography*, his sixteenth-century instruction book for courtiers. In addition to frequenting balls, George Washington was a patron of theater dance. Whether the setting was Pennsylvania, New York, New Hampshire, Rhode Island, the Carolinas, or indeed any of the colonies, America had an upper class even if it lacked the titles of nobility. For example, in Connecticut a "polite society" known as the Standing Order derived its wealth and power from trade. Joy Van Cleef notes, in "Rural Felicity: Social Dance in 18th-Century Connecticut" (*Dance Perspectives* Number 65):

At formal balls and assemblies every effort was made to observe the same etiquette and display the same elegance as might have characterized a similar affair in London . . .

As dancing became increasingly important as a social skill, people looked upon it not only as a pleasant pastime but also a means of personal display and social advancement . . .

All through the eighteenth century, a fine carriage was much sought after by both men and women . . . Such importance was attached to "deportment" that dance retained its place as a basic element of genteel upbringing.

The dance steps came from England and France as did the music and many of the dancing masters.

Van Cleef makes interesting observations about the place of dance in the Revolutionary War. Military commanders like General Washington and General Rochambeau regarded dancing as essential for both the physical exercise and the morale of their officers. Accordingly, they spent money and effort to organize balls for their officers even under the severest conditions. At Valley Forge, a John Trotter was hired by the hospital staff to conduct dancing classes every afternoon!

Recreational Dancing in the California Gold Rush. In 1948, California became a state. In 1949, the gold rush was on. If we look at the social life of the miners as expressed in their dancing, we find a development from barbarism to the trappings of civilization occurring in less than a decade. Our source is "Pigeon Wings and Polkas: The Dance of the California Miners" by Gretchen Adel Schneider (*Dance Perspectives*, Number 39). When the first miners arrived in Spanish California, they lived in mining camps and spent six days a week in back-breaking, usually fruitless, labor. Sunday was for "hell-raising." Schneider tells us:

> The miner sought pleasure fiercely, in gambling, cockfights, horse racing, foot racing, bear and bull baiting . . . In their voracious desire for culture and vigorous living, the mining camps were not far behind San Francisco where "more music was performed and more murder committed during this decade, than in any other city in America."

Within a very short time, the miners were enjoying fandangos. We met the fandango as a spectacular Spanish dance, in Chapter 5. Schneider tells us that in Spanish California, among lower-class Mexicans, the fandango was:

> "a rude native dance" combined with gambling to produce the "fandango house". . . . The miners indiscriminately attached the term fandango to any dancing . . . including an 1853 Digger Indian festival in Placerville to celebrate "the green fields and pleasant weather without rain."

In the first mining camps, decent women were so scarce that they were idealized and idolized. The men, left to their own devices, enjoyed their "fandangos" by dancing together and combining the dancing with smoking, drinking, gambling, and fighting.

As the months passed, however, miners married and settled down. Their women worked hard, but they also acted as a restraining, civilizing force in the camps that gradually grew into towns complete with schools, newspapers, churches, hospitals, sheriffs—and dancing teachers! Lodges of Odd fellows and Masons made their appearance and also had a restraining effect on behavior. By 1853, the fandango had become a ball, often held in a hall built for one of the lodges. Schneider writes:

> At the ball "learned" dances, unabetted by prompting, separated the true gentlemen. Ideally the floor manager at a ball made appropriate introductions to the fair sex, and courtly manners were assumed to insure the magic, civilized dignity of the affair . . . The dynamic of the dancing school consumed the exuberance of the five years past; men became self-conscious in the new social order.

No doubt it was a while before the California balls approached the decorum of the more traditional East Coast affairs. But they never returned to the rough, unbridled merrymaking of 1849, when brawls and even fatal stabbings were a familiar feature of the fandango.

Religious Censure of Dance and Theater. In the art and entertainment of early America, there was another importation of European attitudes: a conflict between religious opposition to theater and dance, and the secular pleasure taken in these pastimes. This led not only to sermons, but also to legislation, such as a motion passed by the Continental Congress in 1778, declaring that anyone attending theatrical entertainments was morally unfit to hold political office. Not everyone took this declaration seriously, and performances continued in many theaters. In Boston, however, there was no public theater after 1750, when the Commonwealth of Massachusetts passed an Act to Prevent Stage Plays, until the act's repeal in 1792. In "Boston Goes to the Ballet, 1792–1797," (*Dance Magazine*, July 1976) Iris Fanger tells us that sometimes producers got around the law by billing their productions, for example, as "Moral Lectures." John Durang, whom we'll meet very soon, appeared in such a company when he was fifteen years old.

Even among religious figures themselves, opposition was not total. During the late 1600s and early 1700s, individual preachers like George Whitfield, a fiery prophet of a dissident sect known as the Great Awakening, thundered denunciations of dancing in any form as lewd, and certain to bring hellfire to the participants. However, Van Cleef points out that back in England many "conventional" young Puritans were sent to social dancing classes as a road to proper, civilized behavior. In New England, dancing and watching theater spectacles were more likely to be condemned for wasting time that could be put to more industrious use than for their wickedness. One form of dance always received unanimous religious censure: maypole dancing. You remember from our discussions of tribal ritual and folk festivals that the maypole dance originated as a pagan rite of spring, celebrating fertility. Religious authorities never forgot this connection, even when the common folk did.

Professional Theatrical Dance. In addition to providing pleasure and training in decorum, the ballroom dancing of the gentry also prepared them to be appreciative audiences for theatrical dance performances by professionals. In fact, enterprising dancers, who taught classes as well as directed and appeared in performances, sometimes gave their better students an opportunity to perform also. Such a professional was the popular William Francis, described in "A Chronicle of Dance in Baltimore 1780–1815" (*Dance Perspectives*, Number 66). The writer, Chrystelle T. Bond tells us about this versatile trouper:

> . . . affectionately called "Old Francis," who would dominate the Baltimore scene . . . at the Holliday Street Theater, between 1794 and 1826, as a talented and prolific choreographer, dancer, director, actor and dancing master.
> The bills suggest that Francis was a master of fast costume and make-up changes, and speedy switches from the role of actor to that of dancer as he

whipped from play, to dancing interlude, farce to pantomime, all in a night's work.

As this last passage suggests, the dancing on colonial stages was a real commercial "show biz" mix. It was made up of interchangeable specialty dances that could be inserted into a comic opera, a farce, a melodrama, or a circus program. There were also full-length pantomimes that centered on a plot and moved along with songs, musical interludes, acrobatic tricks, dialogues—and yes—dancing. These pantomimes were a European form, descended from the Italian *Commedia dell'Arte*, which in turn reached back to ancient plays and pantomimes in Rome. You can trace this lineage most clearly in the continuous presence of stock characters like Harlequin and Columbine. In another important respect these shows resembled the spectacles of Renaissance Italy in that they placed a major emphasis on scenic marvels. The public especially liked "transparencies." These were drop scenes and moving scenes that created optical illusions with special lighting effects. (You can think of them as a little like slide shows.)

During the same years that William Francis graced the scene, we hear of John Durang (1768 to 1822) , considered the first American professional dancer. Durang had the honor of performing for George Washington on more than one occasion. Another Jack-of-all-trades, Durang learned his craft by closely observing contemporary (mostly foreign) dancers. He made a specialty of country dances like the hornpipe. Durang had a long, successful career as an entertainer. He performed in Philadelphia, New York, and Boston, with Hallam's Old American Company, and with Alexandre Placide, a former Paris celebrity who formed his own company. Durang also did a Native American dance in one of the earliest American operas, John Hewitt's *Tammany*, or *The Indian Chief* (1794).

After she arrived from Santo Domingo, Madame Anna Gardie frequently appeared as Durang's partner, receiving good notices in the press. During the 1795 season in Boston, Durang danced the Clown, and Gardie the Columbine, in *Harlequin Restored*, a pantomime-ballet which featured a gladiator scene, a leap through a lion's mouth, and Harlequin's escape on the prongs of a pitchfork. They also appeared in *Harlequin Gardener* and *Harlequin Shipwrecked*, and in *La Forêt Noire*. *La Forêt Noire* (The Black Forest) a full-length pantomime set to music was, according to Lillian Moore (in her article on "Ballet in America" in Chujoy's *Dance Encyclopedia*), the first serious ballet given in this country. It had been premiered the previous year in Philadelphia, with Madame Gardie making her American debut as the female lead. The complicated plot concerns a kidnapping and includes a grand battle, a rescue, and a military procession. Durang went on to stage pantomime ballets for a Philadelphia circus troupe, and then at the Chestnut Theater. These included *The Country Frolic* (1796) and *The Western Exhibition* (1797). He raised his children to be dancers. Charles Durang in particular went on to become a ballet master, and the author of several guides to dancing.

Way back at the court of Louis XIII, we saw that ballets with patriotic and militaristic themes were not tremendously popular with the French courtiers, who preferred lighter subjects in their entertainments. In the new nation of America, however, at the end of the eighteenth century, Selma Jeanne Cohen tells us in "The Fourth of July," in the bicentennial issue of *Dance Magazine* that the patriotic pantomime became fashionable. Designed as a July Fourth celebration, Cohen believes that the form marks independence not only politically from Great Britain, but also artistically. Here are scenes Cohen describes from some Independence Day pantomimes:

> Once the exclusive domain of Harlequin . . . the pantomime was now free of subject restrictions. . . .
>
> In 1798, the Placide company presented...*America and Elutheria* in which the Geniuses of Tyranny and Pride were defeated by the American forces assisted by the Genius of France and the Spirit of Science—the latter in the guise of Benjamin Franklin, who brandished an electric rod to vanquish the foe. . . .
>
> Another widespread favorite was *The Death of Captain Cook*, which Placide's company presented with enactments of South Sea Indian ceremonies, human sacrifice and assassination!

Alexandre Placide was only one among many French dancers who came to these shores to escape the turmoil that followed the revolution in their native land. Olga Maynard tells us (in *The American Ballet*) that Placide and other French dancers dominated the American dance scene, particularly from the 1820s on. Francisque Hutin, for example, enchanted audiences with the latest techniques of French ballet: toe-dancing, multiple pirouettes and so on. In 1828, Charles and Ronzi Vestris arrived and toured for a year, increasing the popularity of ballet in America. Charles and Ronzi were members of that great French ballet dynasty whose family included Gaetan and Auguste Vestris, the most famous male dancers of their day.

Later came the Ravels, a troupe of ballet dancers and acrobats. They presented Leon Espinosa, who had been a pupil of Coulon and Taglioni, (teachers of the renowned Marie Taglioni), and then a member of the Bolshoi Ballet. Espinosa, although very short, was renowned for his ability to leap into the air. These two traits caused him, while on tour, to be captured by a group of Native Americans who were charmed by Espinosa's miniature figure, and his balloon. This was not the only piquant anecdote to combine Native Americans and ballet dancing. Maynard opens her book *The American Ballet* this way:

> On December 14, 1767, by command of his Excellency the Governor of New York, an entertainment called *Harlequin's Vagaries* was presented for ten Indian warriors newly arrived from South Carolina. There is no record of

how these first Americans responded . . . but ballet had begun in the American colonies.

Before we get back to our native born ballet artists, we pause with Fanny Elssler, the foreign dancer who made the most outstanding impression on the American stage. As Olga Maynard wrote: "A ballerina was a theatrical divinity in the United States, and public adulation culminated in the 'Esslermania' inspired by Fanny Elssler." You met Fanny Elssler previously as a prima ballerina of the romantic era in Paris. Now we look at her from this side of the ocean, where for a time during the 1840s, there was an outbreak of feverish excitement surrounding her appearances that we are more familiar with today in the presence of sports heroes or pop music figures. Ivor Guest, in *Fanny Elssler* reports that in New York her performances were constantly interrupted by deafening roars of admiration. There was such a fight to sit or stand in every corner of the theater where she appeared, and such a crush around the stage door after her performances, that the police were called out in force to keep the peace. Also, boats and horses were named after her. In the stores were Fanny Elssler boots, stockings, garters, corsets, shawls, parasols, fans, as well as cigars, boot polish, and shaving soap! In Philadelphia, the demand for seats was so enormous that there was a traffic jam of carriages and people around the theater. In Washington, she was received by President Van Buren and during her performances the House of Representatives couldn't master a quorum for a vote. In Baltimore, when she emerged from the stage door, the crowd unharnessed the horses and a pack of men pulled her carriage through the streets. In Boston, Ralph Waldo Emerson's companion admired Elssler's dancing as poetry. "No," replied Emerson, "it is religion." And Henry Wadsworth Longfellow wrote a play in which the heroine was a cachucha dancer. (You remember cachucha, the Spanish dance that became Elssler's signature piece.) Elssler's triumph brought in its wake a wave of religious sermons against her immodest dancing, to which Ivor Guest quotes the response of the *New York Herald*: "The parsons have preached, the old maids have clicked their tongues, the moralists have shaken their heads, but nothing has been able to calm this excitement."

American Ballet Stars By the time of Elssler's tour, there already existed ballet schools and trained dancers as well as theaters for dance performances in the major cities. This is what made it possible for Elssler and other visiting stars to travel to the States without the expense of bringing with them from Europe a large ensemble of dancers. They were able to recruit local dancers and teach them supporting roles. Another Frenchman who had danced at the Paris Opera came to America in the nineteenth century, and settled in Philadelphia. His name was Paul Hazard. Hazard enters our story as the teacher of three famous American Ballet dancers:

Augusta Maywood, Mary Ann Lee, and George Washington Smith, Augusta Maywood (1825 to 1876) and Mary Ann Lee (1823 to 1899) made a joint debut at the Chestnut Street Theater in Philadelphia in 1837. The piece they chose was an English version of a French opera-ballet, *Le Dieu et la Bayadère*. Lee, like Taglioni, was a lyric dancer. In contrast, Maywood was impetuous and vivacious (like Elssler). Unlike Taglioni and Elssler however-er, Lee and Maywood never became rivals.

That's because Maywood, who was born in New York and first made a name for herself there and in Philadelphia, soon left America to gain fame and fortune in Europe, never to return. At age fourteen, she won acclaim in Paris from Gautier, among others. She decided to stay on in Europe where she studied in Paris with Jean Coralli, one of the creators of *Giselle*. She married (and divorced) dancer Charles Mabille, and toured through the major European cities with great success in roles like Giselle. When she retired from the stage, it was to open a school in Vienna. Therefore, although Maywood was an American, she did little for the audiences of her own country.

Mary Ann Lee did more. An orphan whose dancer mother and acro-bat father had brought her up in the tradition of a trouper, she supported herself as a singer and dancer, touring America with the P.T. Barnum Circus and appearing in burlesque. At the same time, she studied classical ballet with James Sylvain, who had been one of Fanny Elssler's partners. From Sylvain, Mary Ann Lee learned Elssler's roles, including the Spanish cachucha. Then Lee went to Paris where she too studied with Coralli. However, she did not stay, but sailed back across the ocean and produced the first authentic American *Giselle*, which premiered in 1846 in Boston. In addition to teaching all the parts to the company, she danced the main role with great skill. Supporting Mary Ann Lee's *Giselle*, Albrecht was danced by George Washington Smith, who had been one of Elssler's partners dur-ing her historic American tour. The Lee-Smith partnership didn't have a very long run. Unfortunately, Lee wasn't strong enough to continue with such demanding work. At the age of twenty-four, she retired in poor health.

When Lee exited the scene, Julia Turnbull (1822 to 1887) became the unchallenged American prima ballerina, partnered by Smith. Turnbull was born in Canada, but came to the United States when she was three years old, with her actor father. She made her ballet debut as co-star with Mary Ann Lee in *The Sisters* at New York's Bowery Theater. During Elssler's tour, Turnbull also danced important roles in her company. Then, like Lee, she studied with Sylvain. She went on to make a hit with the American public in *Giselle*, in *Esmeralda*, and especially in *The Naiad Queen* (1847), and also appeared in acting parts.

Olga Maynard tells us that Turnbull's success in *The Naiad Queen* was scorned by Céleste, (one of the visiting French ballerinas who had married and settled in America). Céleste wrote a friend that Julia Turnbull had copied the ballet outright from *Ondine*, which Jules Perrot had created in 1843 in London for Fanny Cerrito, to rave reviews. You can well understand why a dancer might not worry about such a theft, so many miles away from the original. And, in fact, American audiences, with no Cerrito for comparison, declared Turnbull a sensation. However, American ballet was not so far away from European ballet in the matter of rivalries and backstage jealousies. When George Washington Smith chose to dance with Giovanna Ciocca, an imported Italian ballerina, instead of with Julia Turnbull, Maynard reports the occurrence of a "backstage riot." This was certainly one cause of Turnbull's retirement at the age of thirty-five.

George Washington Smith (1820 to 1899) was the first American *danseur noble*. Like Mary Ann Lee and Julia Turnbull, he studied with Sylvain. He had no rivals as a male dancer, and his career was long and successful. In his day, he partnered all the prima ballerinas in the States. Smith also toured with the notorious Lola Montez, whose reputation is based more on her succession of love affairs (causing a government crisis when in 1846 she became the mistress of King Ludwig I of Bavaria) than on her dancing. Smith was not only an adept *danseur noble*. He also staged ballets for his partners, and choreographed a major original ballet, *The Magic Flute*, (1848) as ballet master at the New York Bowery Theater. In 1859, Smith joined, as dancer and choreographer, the Ronzani Company, which included members of the illustrious Cecchetti family. Later, Smith opened a school in Philadelphia, where he taught until his death. His son Joseph Smith (1875 to 1932), became one of the best known American choreographers of musical theater.

The Mormons. In the middle 1800s, we take note of theater dance that thrived in the isolated Western community of Salt Lake City, Utah where the Mormons took wholeheartedly to dancing. The Mormons were (and are) a sect whose life is governed by religious belief. In their case, however, religious authority condoned and even encouraged, rather than forbade dance movements. In *Dance Chronicle* (Volume 1 Number 2) there is an article by Debra Hickenlooper Sowell, called "Theatrical Dancing in the Territory of Utah, 1848–1868." Here we learn that both Joseph Smith, the founder of the Mormon Church and Brigham Young, his successor, believed (unlike most religious ministers of their day) that dancing—in balls and also on the stage—was a desirable form of recreation for the members of their hard-working congregation. In 1849, Young backed the organization of The Deseret Musical and Dramatic Society, a company established to perform plays and dances for audiences in the Salt Lake City area.

There were, understandably, restrictions. The waltz and other "round dances" were discouraged, since they supposedly led to loose moral conduct. Brigham Young cautioned his followers: "When you go to amuse. . . if you cannot enjoy the Spirit of the Lord then and there, as you would at a prayer meeting, leave that place; and return not . . . until you may have the Spirit of the Lord in any situation in which you may be placed." Young also emphasized education and morality in entertainment. For example, plots had to show the triumph of Good over Evil. (Melodrama, the popular fare of the day, answered this demand very well.) Educational theater did not mean shabbiness to the Mormons. In fact, they built a theater in Salt Lake City that was equal in size and equipment with any in the nation. Nor did they lack adequate costuming, scenery, props, and music.

Sara Alexander, a convert to the Mormon Church, after she had been a performer in local theatricals, taught solo theatrical dancing, gymnastics, and fencing in Brigham Young's own home. Ten of his daughters who were all about the same age (from his many wives) formed their own little dance company known as The Big Ten.Susa Young Gates, one of the daughters, recorded a description of their roles as "fairies" in an 1864 production of *The Mountain Sylph*. (Since the heyday of the Romantic ballet, when so many ballets were cluttered up with sylphs and fairies flying about the stage, lesser dancers were often referred to as "fairies.") *The Mountain Sylph* was mounted by Mr. and Mrs. Selden Irwin, two touring stars from the East, and may have been similar to a dance presented by Julia Turnbull and George Washington Smith. Gates said little about the choreography, except that the fairies: "with their shapely ankles exposed, while their blue tarlatan skirts fell midway between knee and ankle...bowed and pirouetted and flung their flower hoops as they tripped lightly in the mazy figures of the dance . . . and danced in unison with the darting steps."

Sowell tells us that for the most part, like their professional colleagues throughout the country, the Salt Lake City dancers performed a ballet pantomime; or a couple of incidental dances in a play, such as a Gypsy dance; or a specialty number between the acts, like a jig, a hornpipe, or a Highland fling. With the completion of the intercontinental railroad in 1869, more and more stock companies appeared at the Salt Lake Theater, which had a management independent of the church. Finally, the Mormons could not compete with the touring stars for use of the well-equipped stage. But during the twenty years from 1849 to 1869, they must be credited with building and keeping alive traditions of theater dance, for the local audiences. They also paved the way for the three Christensen brothers, who were to help make Utah the important ballet center which it still is today. We will meet the Christensens when we discuss the modern ballet scene in America.

Art versus Entertainment. In the major cities of America, after the brief flurry of talented ballet stars in the middle 1800s, "elaborate but vulgar music spectacles" dominated American theater for the rest of the century. The best-known of these spectacles was *The Black Crook* (1866), a lavish extravaganza tied together by a silly, melodramatic plot. Directed by David Costa, and performed by a French ballet troupe starring Rita Sangalli and Marie Bonfanti, *The Black Crook* was restaged all over the country, into the first decade of the twentieth century. The reason the show became so widely imitated was simple. The original production ran continuously for over a year, grossing almost a million dollars—a lot of money in those days. Its appeal lay in many features: the spectacular dancing; the magnificent stage sets and wondrous scenic effects; the motley crew of characters, Satan, demons, an alchemist, an artist, a fairy queen; and the shocking costumes which revealed bodies more explicitly than ever before (in a respectable theater).

The Black Crook is considered a major source of developments in the American theater during the last half of the nineteenth century. This period saw mainstream dance and drama less and less as art, and more and more as entertainment. While there is no clear line dividing art from entertainment, we can speak of art forms as activities whose purpose is communication. In contrast, entertainment forms are designed primarily as social pastimes and diversions. The music hall, variety theater, vaudeville, and burlesque all flourished. So did the Minstrel Show, a form originating with the dance and song of Afro-Americans.

Minstrel Shows. Marshall and Jean Stearns, in their book *Jazz Dance*, tell us: "The story of minstrelsy is the story of the increasing influence of the Afro-American style of song and dance . . . Minstrelsy was the most popular form of entertainment in the United States from 1845 to 1900 approximately, and it soon spread to many parts of the world." The ironic phrase in that statement is *Afro-American*. You see, while the subject of the shows was the Afro-American and his music and dance, the performers were white men in blackface! Starting back at least as far as John Durang, each entertainer had his own repertory of characters: dwarfs, Indians, drunks, sailors, clowns, and so on, with music and movements to suit each type. Then someone hit on the black man as a character. Marian Winter wrote in *Chronicles of American Dance* (edited by Paul Magriel): "By 1810 the singing and dancing 'Negro Boy' was established . . . These blackface impersonators simply performed jigs and clogs of Irish and English origin. . . By 1820, white dancers in blackface imitating Negroes were all the rage." The swinging rhythm came later. Minstrelsy's most famous dance, The Essence of Old Virginia, was firmly based on the untutored dancing of plantation blacks. The Essence came from the Shuffle and led to the early Soft Shoe. So, of course black men danced. However, partly because white entertainers didn't want their competition, and partly because racial prejudice kept blacks away from respectable theaters, black dancers performed mostly in low-class dives, associated with brothels and saloons.

At least there was one black minstrel dancer of note. In fact, he became the most famous of them all, achieving the distinction of being the only black dancer to receive top billing with four white minstrel men. William Henry Lane (1825 [?] to 1852) was a freeborn black. He lived and worked in the dance houses of a dilapidated section of New York City known as the Five Points District, inhabited by free blacks and newly arrived Irish. Here the blacks easily picked up the Irish musical idiom, and their dance—the jig. Stearns tells us that Lane probably helped change the term *jig* from the name of an Irish dance to the general style of Afro-American dancing. Wherever he went, he made a tremendous impression. In 1848, when Lane danced in London, reviewers raved about his extraordinary dancing and his astonishing rhythmic facility.

William Henry Lane was always billed as Master Juba, after a famous dance step known as *juba*. The Stearns tell us that the juba step is found in Cuba:

> using steps and figures of the court of Versailles combined with hip movements of the Congo. . . . The juba step itself is described as going around in a circle with one foot raised—a sort of eccentric shuffle . . . the words and the steps are in call-and-response form, and the words must ring out rhythmically as a drummer's solo. . . . "Juba! Juba!". . .
>
> Patting Juba, which started as any kind of clapping with any dance to encourage another dancer, became a special routine of slapping the hands, knees, thighs, and body in a rhythmic display. [In Africa of course, this function would be performed by drums, but in the United States, where drums had been frequently forbidden for fear of slave revolts, the emergence of patting seems to have been inevitable.]

Later, we will see how juba and other Afro-American motions evolved into tap dance and modern jazz dance. In the meantime, although American ballet declined as a serious art form until its revival and steady ascendency beginning around the 1930s, Modern dance arrived.

Questions for Review

1. What are the prospects for the survival of Native American dances?

2. In what ways did early American social dancing resemble European?

3. Discuss ballet in the United States in the mid-1800s.

21 MODERN DANCE CREATIONS

ISADORA DUNCAN AND FORERUNNERS

Creeds and Manifestos. In the early 1900s, a revolutionary army invaded the dance field. Their intention was not just to innovate and refresh. It was to tear down the old ballet regime and create a new free dance. In the advance guard was a woman who strode onstage barefoot, in a red chiffon tunic, exposed one breast to the audience, and sang the "Marseillaise." Isadora Duncan was protesting in the name of the oppressed masses of the world, in which she included downtrodden workers, corseted women, and dancers imprisoned by the strict rules of ballet technique.

We have already met many artists in the chapters on ballet who were known as reformers, who worked hard to make their art form more alive. In the 1700s, Noverre had called for expressive dance that "reflects nature." Then, in 1904, Fokine wanted to make reforms in the worn-out conventions of ballet. To that end, he used undulating torso movements in *Scheherezade*; and pathetic, turned-in gestures in *Petrouchka*. Then, in 1913, we watched Nijinsky arrange twisted spasmodic gestures for *Rite of Spring*, and Massine use acrobatic movements in *Parade* (1917). However, these artists took for granted the basic technical training built on fixed positions of the legs and arms that had developed continuously since Beauchamps set and described them in the time of Louis XIV. Although Noverre, Fokine, Nijinsky, and Massine wanted to make their works very expressive, they still arranged them for ballet companies, and although they needed more hours of rehearsal to get their dancers to move according to their ideas, they stuck to a "ballet look." That is, their basic approach remained ballet-ic: For example, they regarded the proscenium arch as a picture frame for ballet scenes and poses.

But then this new breed of dancers came along. Defiantly, they remained *outside* of ballet companies to express the spirit of their times. Just as we have seen how Romantic ballet was related to Romantic expressions in music and literature, so we now meet modern dancers who shared in the same impulses that drove modern painters like Van Gogh and Cezanne; modern composers like Debussy and Ravel; and modern writers like Walt Whitman, Émile Zola, and August Strindberg to explore new ideas and techniques. In dance this meant: exploration of the middle body, the torso, to start waves of movement; the use of the bare foot; the free, swinging motion of the whole body; the treatment of space as three-dimensional; and the importance given to the expression of feelings and ideas.

However, modern dancers not only rejected ballet, they also claimed the freedom to be different from one another. Every major modern dancer was to create a special technique to train dancers for his or her company. One should really say *her* company, because almost all of the important early new dancers were women. In other words, modern dancers were individuals who spurned the restraints of traditional, ready-made dance forms, and the dictatorship of established ballet companies. *Individual* is the key word. Modern dance cannot be approached as one revolution with common goals. Rather, it was the contribution of self-willed, dynamic dancers, possessed by strong, inner drives and visions.

The major artists—Isadora Duncan, Ruth St. Denis and Ted Shawn, Martha Graham, Doris Humphrey and Charles Weidman, Mary Wigman, and Hanya Holm, and later Merce Cunningham, Alwin Nikolais, and a host of followers—created a succession of varied personal movements and styles. We will see how some of these artists appeared singly (Isadora Duncan), and others as families. For example, Martha Graham, Doris Humphrey, and Charles Weidman all started their careers with Ruth St. Denis and Ted Shawn in the Denishawn Company, until in turn, each one left to create a separate group. Each major artist was to found a school and a company. Each one was at the same time the star performer, the chief choreographer, and the company director. And each was to attract pupils and a separate audience that would spurn the other artistic chieftains.

At the same time, there were characteristics that loosely united these diverse revolutionaries. For one thing, they all looked upon the classical ballet as sterile, restrictive, and not relevant to the needs of twentieth-century audiences. That's because they were all aware (consciously or subconsciously) of changing attitudes toward the world, behavior, and the body. This is what we mean when we speak of the spirit of an age, whether the Renaissance, the age of Louis the XIV, or the Romantic Age. Artists and philosophers sense that times are ripe for a new way of looking at things, and in turn they get their audiences to see the world differently.

In the late nineteenth century, there was fomentation everywhere, with new ideas pushing through layers of convention in Western civilization. Along with theories of nationalism, communism, and socialism, the exciting ideas of freedom and equality were spreading. New nations were born (Italy, Germany), black slaves fought for freedom, and women demanded the vote. Dance, the art of the body and of behavior, could not help but be affected. Even within the ballet, we noted how Fokine and Nijinsky reacted.

Against this background, we should note that in the Prologue of this history, the claim was made that two characteristics cling to the dance field: tradition and creativity. There is more than enough evidence of creativity in modern dance. But can we still claim that these artists followed tradition? The answer is yes, in the sense that they trod new paths in the interests of freshness and life, just as ballet artists have always done. And also in the sense that they sometimes looked to the past for inspiration. For example, many modern dancers created "primitive" works. Nevertheless, like all revolutionaries, modern dancers clashed with defenders of tradition. Ballet fans attacked the modern dance as distorted, ugly, and amateurish. For a long time, the dance world was divided into two camps, each side determined to drive out the enemy and hold the field alone.

In the 1990s, we can look back and see that both sides won. On the one hand, ballet has absorbed many of the teachings of modern dance; and on the other hand, choreographers and performers who consider themselves modern dancers accept the classical ballet as part of their schooling. We can now speak of a Western theater dance. The mainstream of contemporary dance has a rich, varied form, fed continuously from both the modern and the classical streams. As historians, we must now back up a century, to meet and move around with the striking figures of modern dance.

Forerunners. The hindsight of history always reveals the existence of forerunners who contributed to the grand work of revolution. Out of many possibilities, I've chosen two men whose life's work preceded and influenced the thinking of modern dancers: Delsarte and Dalcroze. It is the fate of so many free-thinking revolutionaries to have their discoveries solidified into academic dogma, the very idea of which had made them rebel in the first place. This was to happen to François Delsarte (1811 to 1871), but fortunately not until his genuine discoveries made a strong impression on the artists of his time. Delsarte was a successful singer at the Paris Opera until he lost his voice because of bad training. This misfortune led him to search out a method of conveying feelings and ideas from the stage to the audience, through the body. Thus he developed precise theories of pantomime, and a detailed set of exercises for learning effective gestures of the torso and the limbs.

Delsarte's work caught on like wildfire in Europe, where bodybuilding and gymnastics to music were very popular, and it soon spread across the Atlantic to the States. That's when dozens of fans took to the lecture circuit with dramatic monologues, which they rendered with stock gestures lifted from Delsarte's exercises and performed by rote, in a stilted manner exactly contrary to the master's philosophy. Contrastingly, neither Ruth St. Denis nor Isadora Duncan studied at a Delsarte school, but they both absorbed the genuine basis of the technique. Instinctively, they used their arms and their torsos theatrically to project emotions in the manner prescribed by Delsarte. Later on, Ted Shawn incorporated Delsarte's exercises—like his series of spiral falls—into his own teaching. Shawn's book, *Every Little Movement*, discusses Delsarte's principles.

Musicians are indebted to Émile Jaques Dalcroze (1865 to 1950) for his system of rhythmic analysis, and for the effective method he devised for teaching it. This was a physical method. Students were (and are still) taught to respond to musical phrases with the body, on command. For example, to a given phrase of music, one steps on the beat; then runs twice as fast; then twice as slowly; then stops; then reverses direction; then skips; then slides. Every change is done at the teacher's word of command: "Hop!" Meanwhile, the arms are conducting to the beat, or in counterpoint.

Dalcroze was a pupil of Delsarte, but he never claimed his system was anything but a strictly disciplined approach to music theory. There were gestures, yes, but these were deliberately conventional, representing different time values. Unlike Delsarte, Dalcroze had absolutely no interest in the emotional possibilities of body movement. In fact, he went so far as to laugh at Marie Rambert, one of his trained teachers, whose first love was the dance. He criticized her as too balletic, and provoked her to shouting arguments by insisting that there was no such thing as an art of the dance independent of music. In this respect, Isadora Duncan might have agreed with him. Have you ever danced to music, just for your own pleasure, moving about freely in response to feelings you get from the music or maybe your own private emotions? If so, you have shared in Isadora Duncan's legacy.

Freedom Fighter: Isadora Duncan

Born in San Francisco, Isadora Duncan (1878 to 1927) would have been right at home among the hippies and flower children who thronged to her native city in the 1960s. Isadora's naive, idealistic, undisciplined lifestyle resembled theirs, and she and they spoke up for many of the same things. Isadora Duncan rebelled against the corseted coquettish art which consti-

Noted Russian ballerina Maya Plisetskaya interprets Isadora Duncan.

tuted ballet at the close of the nineteenth century. She threw off the restraining clothes and the sterile clichés that bound the dance, and made herself a symbol of the powerful new vision of expressive movement. Not only did she stand for a natural dance style as opposed to the artifices of ballet: she also called for the education of children in order to build a free society, for the dignity of men and women, for the unfettered movement of the body, and for free love. In 1900, America was not ready for her. She shocked audiences with her see-through costumes. Even those who could accept her uninhibited moral conduct, and her flimsy dress, could not tolerate her open admiration of the new Soviet state. She indulged herself in the custom of speechmaking, which was tiresome even for her friends. Stepping up to the footlights and waving a flaming red scarf, she might have shouted: "This is red. That is what I am. Don't let them tame you!" It is not surprising that she found herself performing in Indianapolis with four large, brass-buttoned policemen sitting in a row on the stage.

In Duncans's battles, she did at least have the sympathetic support of two brothers, a sister, and her mother. Isadora was the fourth child of a music teacher and an older man who was variously a journalist and a banker accused of forgery; he left Mrs. Duncan when she was pregnant with Isadora. From Mrs. Duncan, Isadora absorbed a love for music, a philosophy of humanistic atheism, and a bias against marriage, although Isadora was certainly not anti-men or anti-romance. At a young age, Isadora developed a belief in herself as a natural-born dancer and a free spirit. Her activities outside the theater—many romantic, sexual affairs; two unmarried pregnancies; constant declarations about the recent Soviet revolution as the answer for downtrodden mankind—were to be as much a part of Isadora Duncan's public image as her dance appearances.

To seek her rightful place, Isadora's family went abroad. She gave recitals at private parties and a few public concerts in London and Paris. Very soon, this beautiful girl in her early twenties was taken up by the sophisticated Parisian art world. Duncan made a tremendous impression on artists, who endlessly painted, sketched, took photographs, made statues, and wrote about her. She gave solo concerts in 1901 and 1902 in Germany and Hungary that were wildly popular. Gradually her fame spread, and she inspired a craze for barefoot dancing which swept across Europe and then America. Her approach to dance was completely personal. At first, she took rhythms and shapes from nature such as trees in the wind and rolling waves. Sometimes she pantomimed an idea or a scene. She always danced to great music, piano pieces by Chopin, and the majestic, symphonic scores of Beethoven. Then she and her brother Raymond were both smitten by the classical simplicity of ancient Greek art, wandering for days among the ancient statues in the Louvre Museum of Paris, and then visiting Greece itself.

Raymond Duncan put on sandals and the costume that Athenian men had worn over two thousand years earlier (he wore these for the rest of his life). He encouraged Isadora to keep the ruins of ancient Greek temples as the source for her vision of dance. This is what she sought, according to Irma Duncan in *Duncan Dancer*: "The dancer of the future will be one whose body and soul have grown so harmoniously together that the natural language of that soul will have become the music of the body. The dancer will not belong to a nation but to all humanity."

In *My Life*, Isadora later wrote about the way she felt when she danced:

> At the first sound of the orchestra, there surges within me the combined symphonic chord of all the instruments in one—the mighty reverberations run over me and I become the Medium to condense in unified expression the joy of Brunhilde awakened by Siegfried, or the soul of Isolde, seeking in death her realization.
>
> Voluminous, vast, swelling like sails in the wind, the movements of my dance carry me onward—onward and upward and I feel the presence of a mighty power within me which listens to the music and reaches out through all my body, trying to find an outlet for this listening.

Unfortunately, there is not one foot of film in existence of Isadora Duncan dancing, although she did not die until 1927. To understand her work and its appeal at all, it is necessary to read the words of those who saw her. Here is what Ilya Ilyich Schneider wrote (in *Isadora Duncan, The Russian Years*) after he saw her dance a Chopin mazurka:

> A kind of cloud ran over Isadora's face and I had a feeling that everything had grown dark. Why, of course, the girl had entered a dark forest. Here's the tree she nearly stumbled against . . . the girl tried to shake off the panic that had suddenly got hold of her.
>
> She was successful, and humming a tune, she joyfully rushed towards the light and again ran against a tree . . . standing silently in her way, a still higher, more enigmatic, more terrible tree...it was getting darker and darker . . . alas, a last timid and feeble attempt to break through the implacable tree trunks that barred her way on all side . . . an anguished pause . . . the girl fell to the ground like a blade of cut grass.

In *My Life*, Isadora quotes an art editor's description of herself:

> It is far back, deep down the centuries, that one's spirit passes when Isadora Duncan dances...
>
> When all the fervor of religion, of love, of patriotism, sacrifice or passion expressed itself...when men and women danced before their hearthstones and their gods in religious ecstasy, or out in the forests and by the sea because of the joy of life that was in them.

In *Isadora Duncan, the Russian Years*, we read what an American wrote of Isadora's first performance in St. Petersburg in December 1904:

> These first performances in Russia constitute one of Duncan's greatest contributions to dance, and they influence, not modern dance, but the ballet which she despised. She met the nation's greatest ballerinas, the designers Bakst and Benois and the impresario Sergei Diaghilev.
>
> Her work was seen by the choreographer Fokine who, as noted, found a use for many of her ideas, including the notions of dancing to Chopin. The use of Greek themes and costumes, the insistence on a flow of movement and on symmetry, the realization of the beauty of simple movements and of romantic music, all evidenced in the work of Fokine, are a legacy from Duncan. . . .
>
> In the *Marche Slav* of Tchaikovsky, Isadora symbolizes her conception of the Russian moujik, rising from slavery to freedom. With her hands bound behind her back, groping, stumbling, head bowed, knees bent, she struggles forward, clad only in a short red garment that barely covers her thighs.
>
> With further glances of extreme despair she peers above and ahead. When the strains of "God Save the Czar" are first heard in the orchestra, she falls to her knees and you see the peasant shuddering under the blows of the knout. The picture is a tragic one, cumulative in its horrific details.

Finally comes the moment of release and here Isadora makes one of her great effects. She does not spread her arms apart with a wide gesture. She brings them forward slowly and we observe with horror that they have practically forgotten how to move at all. They are crushed, these hands, crushed and bleeding after their long serfdom; they are not hands at all but claws, broken, twisted, hideous claws! The expression of frightened, almost uncomprehending joy with which Isadora concludes the *Marche*, is another stroke of her vivid imaginative genius.

In Paris, Isadora Duncan danced at one private gathering, where a sculptor saw her. What he wrote later was quoted in Paul Magriel's book *Nijinsky, Pavlova, Duncan*:

> It seemed to me in my mind, as I watched Madame Isadora Duncan sitting or reclining, that with each of her pauses she was offering me an antique marble throbbing with eternity . . . when she danced there was no break; it was like the seasons that follow one another in due course . . . Miss Duncan was like an eternal priestess; evoking all the masterpieces of the noblest and highest antiquity, through her superbly human heart.

Conventional music lovers were shocked when Isadora danced to great classical music. The American conductor, Wilfred Damrosch, came to her defense, and agreed to do a concert with her, featuring music by Bach. This passage appears in Magriel's book:

> The stage setting was what it usually is at a Duncan séance. Green curtains depended from the heights of the stage and fell in folds at the back and sides, leaving a semicircular floor in the center on which dim, rose colored lights flitted here, contrasting with shadows there. When Mr. Damrosch came to the conductor's desk and raised his baton all the lights in the auditorium were extinguished. The orchestra played the prelude to the suite and then Miss Duncan appeared.
>
> She wore, as she always does, some drapery of diaphanous material. She stood for a moment in the shadow at the back of the stage while the orchestra began the air, the celebrated slow movement in the suite, which violinists play on the G string. Miss Duncan waved her arms and posed during this movement but did not do much of what is conventionally called dancing.
>
> In the two pieces and the gigue which followed, however, the dancer was seen at her best. She flitted about the stage in her early Greek way and gave vivid imitations of what one may see on the spherical bodies of Greek vases.

And so Isadora, like many modern dancers who followed her, found inspiration in classical music. In this description of her dance to a Bach suite with its gavotte, gigue, and bourrée, we hear echoes of preclassic dance that was performed in the Renaissance courts, when these forms were heard in music and seen in the ballrooms, as the court dancing masters arranged fast and slow steps for the courtiers.

From all descriptions we gather that Isadora Duncan was one of those rare interpretive artists who are capable of stirring an audience deeply through sheer emotional magnetism. The specific motions and techniques which she used, as described in her own books and those of her pupil and disciple, Irma Duncan, are rhythmic sequences of simple natural movements: walking, running, skipping, rising and falling, twirling, and familiar combination steps like the waltz and the polka, along with gestures of pantomime and facial expressions. There is no characteristic stylization in the exercises. This helps explain why her imitators were so seldom impressive. Even in teaching, it was Duncan's inspired, charismatic creativity rather than her material that gave her pupils their special graceful appeal.

In 1904, Isadora founded a school in Germany with her sister Elizabeth. But Isadora was always preoccupied with her many lovers and her personal dancing career, performing in far-flung cities of Europe, and North and South America. She lacked the discipline necessary to stay in one place and concentrate on her pupils. One of her young pupils, Irma Duncan (not a relative; she took Isadora's name to indicate a spiritual relationship), wrote of how she suffered as a child, as did many of the young dancers, from Isadora's casual neglect of those who were dependent on her. The inspired dancer left her schools in inept and unkind hands so that she could carry on her personal triumphal tours, or engage in her celebrated love affairs. The children who remained behind to sample the glories of a pure approach to education in flowing tunics and sandals found that only lip service was paid to the founder's theories. In practice, harsh and restrictive measures were applied by those who were left in charge. As with all utopias, this one proved no better than the human beings who controlled it.

Despite the many flaws in its implementation, the Duncan method does seem to have been suitable for children. Look at this report from a Berlin newspaper review of 1905:

They appeared this time as angels in long white gowns and wreaths of flowers in their hair, striding gravely about. Then followed a very frolicsome dance, an animated swarm of colors and small shapes, as if a storm wind had tossed the flowers in a meadow together.

And then in the next dance the girls would break up into orderly groups, those in the foreground seemingly to paraphrase the melody, while the tallest girls in the background indicated the accompaniment.

Every now and then the set figures gave way, and the little ones would skip about spontaneously. It is important to remark that every form of affectation was avoided. The whole thing gave the impression of having been worked out with the characteristic naturalness of expression peculiar to children.

To compare this description with the stilted patterns and artificial tensions which are even today features of too many children's dance recitals is to realize that we can still improve dance training of the young along the lines set down by Isadora Duncan.

In 1921, when she was forty-three years old, it seemed as though the main threads of Isadora's life—art, politics, children's education, and love—were being gloriously tied together. She opened a school in Moscow, the chief city of Soviet Russia and she met a Russian poet, Sergei Essenin, who had blue eyes and curly golden hair. Although she had once vowed never to marry, she married Sergei after a romantic affair in which she danced and spoke English, French, and German, and he made love to her, drank a lot, and spoke Russian. Neither understood a single word the other said and nothing turned out the way Isadora hoped, not her school, not her poetic marriage.

When she was the honored guest at a party of Russian officials, she was shocked into making a flaming speech against the capitalistic decadence of the elaborate food, wines, and splendid antique furniture she found there. The marriage deteriorated rapidly, as Sergei indulged his wildly moody nature, swinging from hysterical joy to surly depression. He also indulged in drunken orgies with other women (he finally committed suicide). At the same time, Isadora's Russian school ran into conflict with the illogical bureaucracy, and suffered continually from lack of money. But she did get a school. It lasted for a number of years, and Isadora did have an influence on Russian ballet. Fokine and Diaghilev both admired her.

Isadora Duncan was invited to dance at the Bolshoi Theater on November 7, 1921, the fourth anniversary of the revolution. After her *Marche Slav* piece, Lenin himself rose from his seat crying, "Bravo, bravo Miss Duncan." But Lenin's cheers could not alter the situation in Russia. In the winter of 1921, Moscow had only half of its former inhabitants; and the population subsisted on two ounces of bread a day and a few frozen potatoes. There was no money for dancing. Duncan tried to find her own money for the school by dancing in the West. But if there was one thing America feared in 1922, it was bolshevism. And here was Isadora Duncan, who had gone of her own free will to the land of the Reds, and brought back a Russian husband.

Boston was a disaster. Essenin, wanting a bit of attention for himself, sat in the audience dressed like a Cossack, but Isadora's oration caused the real trouble. She informed her audience that her art was "symbolic of the freedom of woman and her emancipation from the hidebound conventions that are the warp and woof of New England Puritanism." She told them that she did not appeal to the lower instincts of mankind "as your half-clad chorus girls do." She denounced the women's costumes of the day, contrasting the beauty of her honest nudity with the vulgarity of other people's studied nakedness. Then she tugged off her red scarf and waved it at the crowd, saying, "This is Red. So am I. It is the color of life and vigor." Then, ripping the tunic to bare one breast she informed Boston, "This is beauty!" Isadora also danced with one breast bared in New York City, and while it left an impression on viewers there, it didn't cause a major scandal. Boston was different. The moralists were outraged. The headlines proclaimed, "Red Dancer Shocks Boston." Isadora left for Europe again. She danced in Berlin, but the contracts were fraudulent and she received no money. American friends collected some money to get her to Paris.

We will pass quickly over the sad last years of her life, which Isadora spent running up bills, drinking, and searching for enough money to start a school again, after the ones in Germany and Russia were lost. Her children were drowned. Essenin was gone. America had no use for her. Her death is legendary. She got into a glamorous sports car and waved to her friends, *"Adieu, mes amies, je vais à la gloire"* (Farewell, friends, I go to glory). Characteristically, she tossed a long scarf around her shoulders. When the car started the scarf caught in the wheel and broke her neck.

Isadora Duncan was a remarkable personality. She was a woman who lived fully in the vanguard of her age. Isadora was a free thinker, a pagan, who declared, "I believe in the beauty of the human foot." She left a deep impression on many famous artists whom she touched personally as friend, lover, wide-eyed, naive philosopher, and dancer. These included Stanislavski, Gordon Craig, Wagner's son Halle, and Ellen Terry. All histories of dance acknowledge the tremendous role played by Isadora in the origin of the form we call modern dance. However, if we are talking about the spirit of a time, we can expect to find more than one person as its figurehead. In a moment we will come to Ruth St. Denis. But first, let us here take brief note of two women who knew of both Duncan and St. Denis, and who took the stage from similar impulses: Loie Fuller and Maud Allan.

Loie Fuller 1862 to 1928. Like Isadora, Loie had no formal education in dance. Her movements were open and free: striding across the stage; lunging while arching her torso; and swinging her arms in large, sweeping gestures. Also like Isadora, Loie Fuller clothed herself in soft, gauzy fabrics, with bare or sandaled feet. She founded a company of girls, whom she called the Muses (after Isadora and the Greeks). In 1902, Fuller and Duncan made joint plans to tour, but Duncan left after a few performances.

Although Fuller claimed that she was reviving a primitive dance art that could be traced back thousands of years, her interest and talent lay less in the expressions and rituals of dance than in theatrical effects. She made a tremendous impression with numbers like *Fire Dance* and *The Butterfly*. These featured a flamboyant circling of rainbow draperies, under her own arrangement of the colored spotlights and footlights that were just then replacing gaslights on the stage. Fuller became so identified with fabric in motion, with the yards-long skirts and sleeves that she trailed and whirled as she danced, that she is called a skirt dancer. Many performers followed the fad. These shows were in Europe. In America, Fuller found very little interest in her aesthetic experiments. Artists like Rodin called her a genius. Parisian students adored her. They carpeted her stage with flowers, and drew her carriage through the streets in scenes that recalled the hysterical adoration of Romantic ballerinas.

   Maud Allan (1883 to 1956). Maud Allan was another Greek revivalist. She studied music and Greek art, and like Isadora, decided to restore Greek dancing to the world. She appeared in flimsy tunics and danced barefoot, often to music by Mendelssohn. Allan was a big success on world tours. Her greatest appeal was not, like Fuller's, in the mastery of fabric and lights, but rather as a dramatic artist. Her public's favorite piece was *The Vision of Salome*, for which she bedecked herself in costume jewelry, but otherwise wore only transparent chiffon. The first viewing of this number was a scandal, not just because of the near nudity, but also because the dancer pressed her lips to the severed head of John the Baptist. Once it caught on, however, *Salome* was a great hit. Allan's engagement at the London Music Hall ran for four years. No doubt King Edward the VII's compliments and sponsorship were a bit of a help.

   In any event, whether they stressed sensational costumes, theatrical lighting, musical training, or the language of gesture, all of these creative people were stepping out with a sense of freedom, and they were all aware of one another's existence. Since the subject is the dance art, however, we start and finish this chapter with Isadora Duncan. When Ruth St. Denis recalled her performances she said, "Isadora was dancing God right in front of you." As we will soon see, it was Ruth St. Denis herself who dreamed of dancing God.

Questions for Review

1.   What did all early modern dancers have in common?

2.   What contributions did nondancers François Delsarte and Emile Jaques Dalcroze make to the art of the dance?

3.   Why was Loie Fuller called a "skirt dancer"?

4.   Discuss Isadora Duncan's outlook on dance and life, as it related to the spirit of her times.

5.   What was there about her work that brought fame to Isadora?

22 DENISHAWN

FROM SACRED DANCE TO JACOB'S PILLOW

Ruth St. Denis and Ted Shawn

Together and separately they were to touch several generations of American dancers. Miss Ruth gets top billing as the first lady of the American dance world. She was the beautiful magnetic performer of the couple. Ruth St. Denis was born in Newark, New Jersey in 1877 or 1880, she was never too specific about the year. She died in 1968. Ruth St. Denis's early years resembled Isadora Duncan's. Both little girls had sympathetic families and danced freely at home and outside in the fields or near the water. They each had a few ballet lessons with the same retired ballet dancer from New York (Marie Bonfanti); and both recognized immediately that this style wasn't for them. Like Duncan, St. Denis strongly disapproved of the female ballet costume, which was tightly corsetted. Both were influenced by the work of François Delsarte. In fact, it was Genevieve Stebbins, a Delsarte pupil, who adopted the fabric and poses of Greek statues, and whose dancing inspired the teenage St. Denis with an image of beauty that lasted a lifetime.

Like Isadora, Ruth was driven by a combination of worldly, sensuous passions and spiritual visions. And like Isadora, Ruth was a sensationally popular performer. However, Ruth was disciplined, while Isadora was not. Ruth started out by spending ten years in commercial theater as an actress who danced and sang (the way a girl might work today in musical comedy or television). Then one day in 1904, she saw a poster that suddenly pointed out to her the career she had subconsciously been seeking. The poster advertised a brand of Egyptian cigarettes and it showed the majestic goddess of ancient Egypt, Isis, serenely seated in a temple. Ruth St. Denis spent the next years reading, researching, and raising money to produce dramatic dance scenes of Oriental life, which gradually changed from Egyptian to Hindu. Very early in the twentieth century, Miss Ruth developed a lifestyle that combined worship of a spiritual god (in her own version of Christian Science) with worship of the gods of art and physical love.

In some respects she was a forerunner of the young mystics of the sixties, who turned to the Orient for religions that placed human sensuality on a par with human spirituality. Unlike the hip generation, however, she suffered a guilty sense of conflict among these allegiances, feeling faithless to one when she served another. Miss Ruth's story is an inconsistent one only if it is scrutinized as the reflection of a systematic intellectual mind, which hers was not. If she is instead approached as a sensitive, original, driven, magnetic, egotistical personality, she is revealed simply as a magnificent artist, in whom contradictions are beside the point.

Like Isadora Duncan, Ruth St. Denis reacted to her own strong emotions and to the world around her by creating powerful dance images that moved her viewers deeply. If music was the stimulus and model for Isadora, for Ruth it was the exotic Orient, with its mixture of sensual splendor and inner serenity. In 1906, she managed to interest a group of society ladies and a theater manager in sponsoring an all-dance program. It included the famous pieces *The Incense, The Cobras,* and *Radha.* We know what the society ladies saw, because St. Denis danced these numbers down through the years. Each dance was a scene of life in India.

In *The Incense*, a woman made a ritual of prayer. Moving about in slow, quiet steps, she held a tray of smoking incense. As the smoke rose into the air, her body mirrored its flow with gentle ripples. A wavelike motion began in the shoulders and passed outward through the arms and the fingers, finally spreading to the torso, which took up the hint of sinuous motion. The high point of the ceremony was reached when the woman lifted the tray slowly, curling it around her body and close to her head, a solid reflection of the rising smoke. Finally, she extended it high upward to the heavens as an offering.

In *The Cobras*, Ruth was at once a ragged snake charmer and two reptiles. Her slithering arms became the snake's bodies and her hands darted and struck out as the snakes' heads. In *Radha*, she was a goddess who looked on unmovingly from a dais as priests paid her homage. Their ceremony found favor in her eyes. She descended from her platform to dance the lesson of physical pleasure and renunciation. Ruth stroked her own body with flowers, then raised a bowl to her lips and drank wine. She gave herself over to the scenes, twirling and reeling around in ecstasy until she fell to the ground. At the end, she rose to sit serenely in her temple.

Each scene was theatrically stunning. The dim lighting, smoking incense stands, and Ruth's gray sari all created an atmosphere of prayer amidst the incense. For *The Cobras*, Ruth stained her body brown. She painted her fingers blue and wore many rings to create snakes' eyes in her angled hands. For *Radha*, her brother Buzz invented a cage in which she could sit high up above the stage and change the colors of the spotlights to highlight mood changes. Ruth wore a great golden skirt which flew outward as she spun into the climax. The magnetic force of Ruth's personality, combined with the exotic and dramatically contrasting pieces and the spectacular staging, made this program a great success. Although her vision was as daring as Isadora's, it was unthinkable for Ruth to preach at people. She understood how to entertain audiences as well as uplift them with mystical devotions, and they responded fully.

There were exceptions. Again, Boston audiences were always a special problem. During her career, Ruth St. Denis made dozens of appearances in the Boston area, many of which were marked by controversy. Her first one, at the Fenway Court (now the Gardner Museum), occurred in May 1906, when for a charitable cause she entertained Boston society with her personal vision of Oriental dance. A contemporary newspaper account began this way:

> Cold roast Boston sat up and took notice for about an hour yesterday in Fenway Court and rubbed its eyes at the spectacle presented by a bare-waisted and bare-legged maiden, who put the Persian dancers on the midway in the shade, as Ruth St. Denis burst on Boston after her triumph in New York.

Needless to say, what Boston saw as her nudity was motivated by a desire to create for Western audiences a sense of the spiritual peace and poise of the Orient through theatrical reproductions of Eastern themes and costumes. Even ten years later, when her art was enthusiastically accepted elsewhere, Boston continued to raise the issue of proper clothing. In February 1916, during her engagement at the Keith Theater, Ruth St. Denis was confronted with the city ruling prohibiting the appearance of bare legs on the stage. With characteristic spirited humor, she told the press:

> I prefer to comply with the absurd ruling, since I am here for one week only, under someone else's management. But next year when I am here with my full company and under my own management—well, just wait and see if I don't lead Mayor Curley a dance!

But for the most part, Ruth was so enthusiastically received that she was booked to tour abroad. She remained in Europe for three years, dancing successfully in Great Britain and on the Continent. German audiences took her to heart, as they had Isadora. She could have stayed there, with her own school and theater, but she chose to return to the U.S. Until 1913, Ruth continued to tour, adding Oriental pieces to her repertory: *The Nautch* (a street-dancing girl) and *Yogi* (a religious figure invoking the presence of Buddha or a Hindu god). In 1910, she finally did *Egypta*, the serious religious dance drama inspired by that famous poster of Isis. It was an expensive, full-length work and it didn't last long, although parts of it were added to the repertory in separate pieces. In 1913, she added a Japanese dance.

By then Miss Ruth's "show biz" sense told her that the momentum was draining from her career as a solo concert dancer. It was time for a change. A male partner might be the next step. She advertised, and came up with Ted Shawn, who became her husband, and the co-founder of their Denishawn Company and Dancing School.

Now we skip ahead to the 1930s, when Miss Ruth, separated from Ted as a single act once more, was inspired to dance her personal vision of Christianity. Ironically, some of the biggest battles fought by this dancer accused of immoral exposure stemmed from her strong religious convictions.

Sacred Dance. In 1934, St. Denis presented the first ritualistic dance seen in America, in a Christmas pageant at the New York City Riverside Church. She was embarked on the work which would occupy her until her death in 1968, although she did take time out in 1938 to found the dance department at Adelphi College. Miss Ruth drew partly on Hindu teaching, and also on material from Hebrew and Christian sources. She completed a dance play about David, made interpretations of Gregorian chants, and did a study of the Madonna.

Her first New England demonstration of dance as worship took place in December 1957 in the Church of the Epiphany, Winchester. She returned in 1964 to give a series of lecture demonstrations on sacred dance in the Boston area. During this series, she remarked:

> Anyone who dances is momentarily in harmony with the great cosmic order of the universe. This has always been recognized in the East, but only a little in the West. It is time to give attention to Christianity. To be a little startling, I would like to say that my plans for the future include a vision of the parking lots of all denominations being turned into dance floors for rhythmic choirs.
>
> My entire life has been spent learning to think good instead of evil. Scholars of metaphysics are taught to do this, but artists have not used this approach until I began to shout: "Man is responsible for his own universe!"
>
> What kind does he want to live in? All phases of dance are the unfolding of the individual. There is no such thing as physical health—there is only spiritual and mental therapy which manifest and express themselves through the body.

Miss Ruth never lost her sense of theater, despite her spiritual dedication. In 1941, she undertook a tour of nightspots, like the Rainbow Room in New York City, in order to obtain money to build her cathedral of dance. In 1942, she appeared at the Cape Cod Playhouse in Dennis on behalf of Russian war relief, in a novel concert of exotic Oriental numbers in "swingtime." This sense of theater stayed with her through old age. At a lecture demonstration in 1964, smiling, she opened her talk: "And I can just hear some of you whispering 'Isn't it remarkable? They tell me she's over ninety.'" The answer is yes, she was remarkable. Again that evening, as throughout the dance career which spanned six decades, Ruth St. Denis gave evidence of the inspiring personality which made her the first lady of the dance world. One went to see the elderly Miss Ruth perform out of respect for a legend, not expecting to be moved by her dancing. But surprisingly, even at that stage, there were poignant moments that provided glimpses of beauty and theatrical intensity. St. Denis's dancing still evoked a sense of the magnificent artist she had been at the peak of her career. Although it was painful to see her totter unsteadily, there was an admirable air of graceful dignity about her head and arm movements. Miss Ruth danced her own message: the belief in the development of the human being, and in the body as the instrument of the individual spirit.

Ted Shawn (1891 to 1972). Ted Shawn was twenty-two years old when he asked Ruth St. Denis whether she would give him lessons in dance. Then and there she auditioned him, and invited him to be her partner, after an all-night talk session. Isadora Duncan, Ruth St. Denis, Ted Shawn—this new breed of dancers loved to talk. They were high on dance, which was for them art, revolution, religion, and the meaning of life all in one. They saw themselves as missionaries, practicing a true artistic spiritualism. Their spiritual flame was fed by talk.

In fact, Ted Shawn started out to be a conventional man of God, studying for the Methodist ministry. He began dancing as physical therapy for his paralysis, which followed an illness during his junior year at the university in 1911. He studied ballet and went on to do exhibition ballroom dancing with a couple of different women. Along the way, Shawn saw Miss Ruth dance *The Incense* and he was smitten. But they didn't meet for a few years, during which time he dropped his ministry studies, continued to perform, gave lessons, worked on choreography, and made a film in Los Angeles about dance.

Finally, in 1914, he found himself in New York, where he set out to study Oriental dancing with the leading artist in the field—Ruth St. Denis. It was just at this time that St. Denis, who was aware of the craze for ballroom dance, and also of a falling box office, decided to employ a male dancer somewhere in her program. Within a short time, Ruth and Ted were dancing together and then they were married. A year later in Los

Angeles, they opened the Denishawn School, from which a company developed.

Ted Shawn was a well-organized worker with wide-ranging abilities. He set up the school's curriculum, and taught stretching exercises, a ballet barre, and free movement. St. Denis taught her personal Oriental techniques, including yoga meditation, as well as music visualization, which was inspired by Isadora Duncan's work. They soon added a teacher in the Delsarte system of pantomime. This combination of techniques formed the Denishawn style and was passed on to thousands of pupils, including Charles Weidman, Martha Graham, Doris Humphrey, and Jack Cole. Each of these masters was to create in a different way from Ted and Ruth, but the original Denishawn approach continued to have a large following of its own.

Skipping ahead to 1970, Marion Rice, a woman who taught Denishawn in Massachusetts for over forty years and was presenting a concert, said:

> While there are certain positions you're supposed to be in, we have many, many variations of the steps, and the style is so free and flowing—truly a joyous thing! Denishawn must be something that lives. I have in my classes grandchildren of my first concert group.

A guest artist at the concert was Marion Rice's daughter, Carolyn Brown, who through the 1960s and 1970s was a female lead in Merce Cunningham's company. Soon we will meet Cunningham as an avantgarde dancer who split away from Martha Graham and from Denishawn. What is interesting about Carolyn Brown in this part of the story is her appearance in an old-fashioned Denishawn work. On this occasion she performed *Graduation Dance*, a piece by Ted Shawn. Her mother said:

> Carolyn thinks it is divine to dance to music again. The sounds in a Merce Cunningham concert are terrible. Once at a performance where the loudspeakers were right on stage, Carolyn became really ill from the noise.

Once again, we are reminded that dance styles rise and fall in popularity according to the mood of a society. The "latest thing" may well be a slightly disguised revival of something from your mother's day—or perhaps your grandmother's. We also note that first-rate dancers dance in many different styles. Carolyn Brown loved doing the movements of Merce Cunningham as well as those of Ted Shawn. Rudolf Nureyev was brilliant in Petipa ballets as well as Martha Graham's. It is indeed hard to shut a dance artist into a neatly labelled file drawer.

In its day, which spanned the years from 1914 to 1927, Denishawn was highly successful in concert and on the vaudeville circuit. In 1916, they were invited to be the first dancers to perform in the University of California's Greek theater. An audience of ten thousand people watched *A Dance Pageant of Egypt, Greece and India*, an ambitious program based on three ancient civilizations. Ruth and Ted arranged it for a cast of 170 as well as for a symphony orchestra and a chorus. During this period, talented people joined the Denishawn organization: Louis Horst as musical director, and Pauline Lawrence as piano accompanist; in addition to Martha Graham, Doris Humphrey, and Charles Weidman. In 1917, Ted Shawn choreographed *The Doxology*, a religious service which he performed at the First Interdenominational Church of San Francisco. Ted and Ruth toured with the company sometimes together and sometimes separately. Shawn did a work based on the *Arabian Nights*, and one on an Aztec legend, *Xochitl*, which featured Martha Graham as the emperor's serving maiden. St. Denis took Doris Humphrey and a group on tour in plotless movement designs of Schumann and Beethoven scores.

Striking theatrical effects in lighting and costumes always made a Denishawn production expensive, but undoubtedly added to the appeal. They didn't forget that audiences were not prepared for their new, strange approach to dance as a serious art. But unlike the modern dancers who followed them, Ruth and Ted always kept an eye on the box office and on spectacle. Also, their movement style was fluid. They were well received as a result. Even on their tour of the Orient in 1925, these Westerners won much applause for dances that they composed about Oriental civilizations. This was a high point for Denishawn. They returned to America with new choreography and fresh costumes picked up in the Far East, and with ambitious plans to build a permanent Denishawn house.

The house was built, but at about the same time the best dancers of the group—Martha Graham, Doris Humphrey, and Charles Weidman—left to develop their own creative lines, and the differences between Ruth and Ted led to a complete separation. What differences? Maybe one should say *similarities*. Both were tremendously talented, creative, ambitious, and made grandiose plans, many of which they carried out. And both were very egotistical. We have already met artists of the dance world with these characteristics, and have seen the wreckage in human relationships, most recently of the marriage between Isadora Duncan and her Russian poet. Perhaps you also remember the disagreements of Bournonville and Lucille Grahn back at the Royal Danish Ballet. When they met, Ruth St. Denis was a famous dancer, fourteen years older than Ted. It was understandable that she gave herself top billing in their first performances. But to continue this fourteen years later, to the point where she announced to a cheering audience in New York's Carnegie Hall that she was going to build a Denishawn house and school—without mentioning Ted at all, who stood in the wings and watched her claim his idea as her own—was a bit much.

Years later, Ruth gloried in admitting in print that she was a selfish, egotistical woman. But this did not help at the time. At least if Ted were a shrinking violet they might have worked things out, but the opposite was true. In 1927, he and Ruth called a meeting at the finished Denishawn house, which had put the company in debt. They demanded that Doris Humphrey and Charles Weidman raise money, as Ted and Ruth had been doing by touring America in vaudeville shows and the Ziegfield Follies. Doris Humphrey, who together with Weidman had kept the New York school together while Ruth and Ted were on the road, objected to cheapening their art form in this manner. Listen to the dialogue, as quoted in Selma Jeanne Cohen's biography of Doris Humphrey.

Ted Shawn: "Is Jesus Christ any less great because he addressed the common people?"

Doris Humphrey: "No, but you are not Jesus Christ."

Ted: "I am the Jesus Christ of the dance."

This last remark is hardly the statement of a modest man. So while gossips speculated for years about the Denishawn marriage, we are not surprised to hear that two such egotists broke apart, or that after this meeting Doris and Charles left to open their own studio which we will visit soon. For a time, Ted and Ruth still came together once a year to give joint performances at New York's summer series at Lewissohn Stadium. The final one was in 1931, at which Ruth St. Denis did a solo called *The Prophetess* which foretold her devotion to religious dance for the rest of her career.

Jacob's Pillow. As for Ted Shawn, he went on to found an all-men's dance troupe, which performed successfully for seven years, demonstrating that men had an important part in modern dance. His first program offered themes of American Indians, European workers, Japanese coolies and warriors, Negro spirituals, and a movement visualization of a Brahms rhapsody. This was typical of his men's repertory, and gave clear evidence of Denishawn roots. The men's group rehearsed at Jacob's Pillow, a farm in Lee, Massachusetts, which Ted acquired in 1931. He converted a barn on the property to a dance theater, which survives to this day. When this group disbanded in 1940, Ted Shawn used Jacob's Pillow to realize another great dream. He founded and directed a summer school and concert series. They embodied his philosophy: "The art of the dance is too big to be encompassed by any one system, school or style. On the contrary, the dance includes every way that men of all races in every period of the world's history have moved rhythmically to express themselves." Jacob's Pillow presented a summer concert series in which America's foremost dance stars as well as visiting artists performed. Each program included ballet artists, ethnic dance representatives, and modern dancers.

Ted Shawn's even-handed acceptance of all dance styles was sometimes put to the test from the swinging sixties onward. This was because

Ted Shawn's all-male group is seen here at Jacob's Pillow.

the modern ballet pas de deux evolved from a decorous courtship ceremony, to a free-for-all of the most contorted, erotic, and sexually explicit positions imaginable. In a Jacob's Pillow interview one summer, Ted described to me a duet in which the male held the female between her legs, aloft on his hand. At the climax, she slid down his arm until her crotch struck him in the jaw, causing a loud *click* from his ill-fitting false teeth. "That's not what we had in mind," he concluded with laughing indignation, "when we set out to reform the dance art!"

The Jacob's Pillow University of the Dance, which Ted ran until his death in 1972, offered courses in ballet, modern dance, ethnic dance, dance composition, anatomy, kinesiology, principles of movement and rhythm, mime, backgrounds of American dance, elements of performing, as well as a stage workshop, and a series of lectures in dance appreciation, one each Sunday evening by visiting authorities. Since Shawn's death, Jacob's Pillow has continued as the scene of performances and classes under the direction of various people, including writer and manager Charles Reinhart, critic Walter Terry, and dancer-choreographer Norman Walker. Many dance fans were gratified when Ruth St. Denis and Ted Shawn came together for a dance program at Jacob's Pillow in 1964 to celebrate their fiftieth anniversary! Yes, Denishawn had real style.

Questions for Review

1. Do you see any contradictions in the artistic aims of Ruth St. Denis?

2. What were the religious elements in Miss Ruth's sacred dance?

3. Why did Ted Shawn found an all-men's group?

4. What contributions did Denishawn make to the field of modern dance?

23 GERMAN DETOUR

EUROPEAN MODERN DANCE

You have seen how Isadora Duncan, who represented the spirit of free, modern America, lived in Europe and had her greatest success in Germany. This is not surprising if you can picture Germany before 1933. Hitler had not yet come to power, and the German people had not yet accepted Nazism, suppressing all that was good in themselves and their culture. Since the beginning of this century, German artists have been feverishly creating new forms in music (Berg, Hindemith, Schönberg, Richard Strauss), in theater and film (Brecht, Max Rinehart, Lubitsch), and in painting and architecture (Kandinsky, Klee, Gropius). These men were at the Bauhaus with Oskar Schlemmer, whose work was mentioned in Chapter 16. At the same time, Germany was the center of a dance revolution, led by Rudolf Laban and Mary Wigman.

Rudolf Laban

Rudolf Laban (1879 to 1958) was more important as an educator and a theoretician than as a dancer. Born Rudolf Von Laban in Hungary to a noble military family, he left the army and went to Paris, where he dropped the Von, and moved in the bohemian world of artists and cabaret philosophers. Dance and movement excited him. In 1910, he founded a school where he inspired Mary Wigman, Kurt Jooss, and others to be modern dancers. Then, in the 1930s, Rudolf Laban staged mass productions for groups of laymen, who together interpreted emotional themes. This is a semi-improvisational approach, kept in bounds by a conductor, or leader. In 1936, he directed three thousand people in *movement choirs* for the opening celebration of the Berlin Olympics.

In the section on tribal dance, we described Labanotation, the method that Rudolf Laban devised for recording physical movement. At that point, we were interested in the system as a tool in cross-cultural studies. For dancers, Laban's analytical theories led to a thorough exploration of varied movement possibilities for every part of the body. There has always been an interest in finding methods of preserving dances. Other systems of dance notation go all the way back to Thoinot Arbeau's *Orchesography*, which was discussed in Chapter 6. Nikolas Sergeyev used the Stepanov system to note the Petipa ballets. Recently, Alwin Nikolais developed a method, as did Noa Eshkol in Israel. The methods of dance notation most commonly used today are *Choreology*, devised by Rudolf and Joan Benesh for the British Royal Ballet, and Labanotation.

Mary Wigman

Although Isadora Duncan and Ruth St. Denis were both very successful in Germany, modern dance in that country had a character very different from the American. We have already seen how ballet acquired, in turn, Italian, French, Danish, Russian, and English accents as it moved around from place to place. The same thing is true of modern dance, except that here we are concerned with only two national personalities: the American, as represented by Isadora Duncan, and the German, as represented by Mary Wigman (1886 to 1973).

These two dancers started out with the same basic idea: to rediscover the fundamental laws of human movement, so that once again dance might become the medium for fresh artistic impulses. Once they got down to business, however, they stood in direct contrast to one another. Isadora Duncan strove upwards. Her works were upbeat. Her style was graceful, optimistic. Her ideal was the harmonious Greek figure. She moved to great, familiar musical scores. She was open to the point of being naive. In contrast, Mary Wigman stayed rooted to the earth. Her images were dark, brooding, mysterious, those of death, witches, and war. Her style was heavy and tense. She moved to the sounds of primitive percussion, or in silence. Her works expressed a fatalistic abstract outlook on man's place in the universe.

Mary Wigman, the most famous European modern dancer, started out to be a musician. You may have noticed that many dancers begin this way. After she earned a teaching certificate at the Dalcroze School, Wigman went to study with Rudolf Laban. She was soon performing her own compositions and also teaching at Laban's school. Mary Wigman's works included these titles: *Death Call, Witch Dance, Dance of Death, The Seven Dances of Life, Celebration, Dance Fairy Tale, Space Shape*, and much later, *Rite of Spring*.   The following excerpt from *The Language of Dance* by Mary Wigman (translated by Walter Sorell), gives you an idea of Wigman's thought processes in her own words.   She spoke of the piece *Death Call*:

> There was from the beginning something like a feeling of being called that came from afar, emerging from a deep darkness, relentlessly demanding.   It forced the glance of my uplifted eyes to turn towards the depths and made me spread out my arm like a barrier which rose up against an onrushing power...
>
> There it was, an opposite pole, a point in space arresting eye and foot.   This probably self-created and space-reflected tension, however, forced the body into a sudden turn and twisted my back down into a deep bend in which the arms spread out again, helpless and hopeless this time...
>
> Tremendously large black banners began to fly and to rustle.   They were neither sinister nor threatening.   They were of a sober, swinging magnitude; to the rhythm of these banners the once arrested feet could begin to unshackle themselves and move sweepingly in a sequence of big steps.   Thus the dance unfolded in a succession of static, monumental poses and hugely conceived movements through space.
>
> At the conception of this dance I did not start with the image of death by any means!   At a certain point of the dance I began to shiver.   And I suddenly knew; Death is speaking to you.

Mary Wigman was a great artist.   The main sources of her style were Émile Jaques Dalcroze's work in rhythmic motion, and Rudolf Laban's attempts to discover a universal, ruling harmonic law in the spirit of dance. Beginning in the early 1920s, Wigman had a school of her own in Dresden, and this soon became the center of German expressionist dance.   Her gifted students were also in her company, including Hanya Holm, Yvonne Georgi, Gret Palucca, Margaretha Wallman, Max Terpis, and Harold Kreutzberg.   Mary Wigman and her company toured widely, appearing in London beginning in 1928, and in the United States beginning in 1930.   The measure of Wigman's success is demonstrated by the fact that in the early 1930s, there were two thousand pupils in the branches of her school that were set up all over, including the United States.

All this time, since the middle 1920s, an increasing number of dancers inspired by Mary Wigman and Rudolf Laban were performing alone or with their companies.   Serious critical writing appeared, and there was great interest in German dancers' congresses.   Kreutzberg and Giorgi, and later Wigman, toured to enthusiastic notices in America.   In 1932, the first international choreographic competition was held in Paris, and Kurt Jooss won first prize for *The Green Table*, which you will hear more about in a few pages.

Gertrud Kraus

Gertrud Kraus (1901 to 1977), born in Vienna, studied music at the university. She was attracted to dance when she accompanied a dance class. A year and a half later, she got up the nerve to hire a hall and give a solo concert. She attributed her instant success to the mood of the times, and to Isadora Duncan, who had showed some years before that dance should express the emotions of the dancer. At the Munich Dance Congress of 1930, where there were 1,400 participants from all over the world, Gertrud Kraus's work, *Songs of the Ghetto*, impressed one dance critic above everything else that was presented. Kraus used Hasidic hand gestures and traditional biblical themes in this work. She herself took the part of a little boy in yarmulke and side locks. Some of the dances in this first program remained permanently in her repertory, including her own version of *The Dance of Death*, *Tired Death*. The image is one of a figure still claiming victims—but a figure dispirited, exhausted from the endless parade of World War I dead.

Kraus burned with energy—an excitement about dance, art, and life—the kind we find in all our great modern dancers. Mia Slavenska was one artist for whom Kraus opened up many avenues of creative thought in Europe. In Israel, Zeeva Cohen was another. When she moved to pre-state Israel in 1935, Gertrud Kraus carried the flame of German dance inspiration with her. She continued to dance and to choreograph; but now the entire country was her inspiration, stage, audience, and classroom. Kraus took part in productions of the Palestine Folk Opera, of Habima, of the Symphony Orchestra of Kibbutzim, and of holiday festivals. She performed in an army corps of entertainers. She founded a company in consultation with Jerome Robbins and Talley Beatty; but it was short-lived. After 1951, Gertrud Kraus took up an entirely new career in painting and sculpture.

Kurt Jooss: The Green Table

The importance to this story of Kurt Jooss (1901 to 1979), is confined to one great work. *The Green Table* still is a successful piece, having entered the international repertory in thousands of performances. For example, you may have seen it danced by the Joffrey Ballet, the Batsheva Company, or the Chilean National Ballet. A close-up of *The Green Table* shows us what German modern dancers were thinking about in the early 1930s. (It also shows us what makes a good composition at any time.) First of all, art could portray serious social and political ideas: war, social problems, poverty, and scenes of the common people. In fact, *The Green Table* started out as a dance of death (remember Wigman's *Death Call*?). Kurt Jooss, with

Kurt Jooss's The Green Table is in the repertory of the Joffrey Ballet.

composer Fritz Cohen, planned a solo based on medieval drawings and legends of Death as a dancing figure. But he needed a group dance to enter the Paris International Competition. When Jooss read prophecies of another war and of the Nazi regime, suddenly there was the place for his Death figure. In a few days, he and Cohen created the masterwork.

The title *The Green Table* refers to the bargaining table of international diplomacy. What a cartoon The Gentlemen in Black make with their grotesque face masks, and their pointed gestures of pompous, useless argument, all to witty tango music. (Unfortunately, the bitter satire is more apt today than ever before, when our daily TV news brings us pictures of endless quibbles at international meetings while millions of the common people starve or kill each other.)

This diplomatic dance opens and closes the piece, providing a most satisfactory structural frame for a series of contrasting scenes with the common—and some not-so-common—people. The soldier goes courageously to battle; mothers and sweethearts tearfully stay behind; refugees huddle; a war profiteer and a prostitute sell their wares—and who is everywhere? Death. The treatment of this central role is highly interesting. Death's character varies from the spirited voice of patriotism that lures men to battle, to the tender nurse who puts an end to suffering. But no matter what, he is the ever-present conductor of human fate. This is all expressed through movement. Death lurks in a crouch, his arms stretched wide, fists clenched; his legs are extended in open positions, fixed in a bridge. Then his legs snap tightly closed—a final trap. A profiteer slinks and creeps. A heroic resister stamps at the enemy. The diplomats routinely go through their motions. At each point the music heightens the effect.

Back in 1932, other European dancers were experimenting with social commentary. However, in too many cases they got carried away with the ideas and the artistry got left out. *The Green Table*, like *Giselle*, *Swan Lake*, and *Petrouchka*, fulfills the standards that Noverre set in the eighteenth century and that Fokine set in the twentieth. Therefore, it endures, and when talented dancers perform it, the viewer is gratified. The high point of expressive dance was reached with this composition by Kurt Jooss.

Nazi Dance Gap. But these were the years of Hitler's rise to power. The 1936 Olympic Games held in Berlin, when Laban used Wigman and her pupils in a mass dance ceremony, was the last event of this kind. The Nazis closed the Dresden school, although they allowed Wigman to teach at the Leipzig Music Academy. Once Hitler came to power, the upheaval in German society destroyed the growth of modern dance along with so much else. Wigman stayed on quietly, surviving in obscurity. Kurt Jooss and later Rudolf Laban fled to England, where they worked together on Laban's theories. Some dancers left Germany because they were Jewish; others because they wanted to make political statements through dance and knew that the Nazis would not permit this; and still others because they simply could not work under the Nazi regime. After the war, Mary Wigman once again rose to dance and to head a school in West Berlin, which attracted modern dancers from all over the world. She also choreographed first-class productions like Gluck's *Orpheus and Eurydice*, Orff's *Carmina Burana*, and Stravinsky's *Sacre du Printemps* for various opera houses. Who can say what place Wigman would have had in our story, if not for Germany's Dark Age?

Hanya Holm

Hanya Holm (1893-1992) brought the German modern dance to America. The most famous torchbearer from German creative fires, she had already gone to the U.S. in 1931 to open a Mary Wigman School under the sponsorship of Saul Hurok. By 1936, the dancer disassociated herself from Hitler's Germany and called her New York school The Hanya Holm School of the

Dance. She soon became part of the American scene, joining the summer faculty at the Bennington School of Dance, along with Martha Graham, Doris Humphrey, and Charles Weidman.

It was at Bennington in 1937 that Hanya Holm created *Trend*, which was hailed as a modern dance classic. The music was by Wallingford Riegger. A program note explained: *"Trend* expresses the rhythm of our Western civilization, in which social confusion dominates, but cannot eradicate, the timeless creative forces that persist beneath the surface of contemporary existence." The first section depicted the joyless routine of jobs and daily life. Other sections showed the bored life of the idle rich, the worship of money, and escape into drugs. The final section, "Resurgence," to music by Edgar Varese, showed the mass stirring of hope that would allow good to triumph over evil. *Trend'*s colossal theme was carried out in the ebb and flow of group movement, and it made a tremendous impression on dance audiences of the day.

In a 1946 interview in *The Journal of Health and Physical Education*, Hanya Holm summed up for me the principles of German modern dance which she followed, in this way. The first principle is the study of body movement according to certain laws of motion. These are coordination, gravity, momentum, and progression, and are intrinsic in all dance. They become varied through dynamics, tempo, understatement or overstatement and the like, which change the proportions of a movement. In this way, although certain patterns recur, such as the turn, the leap, and the swing, the modern dancer may take liberties with the forms in the ways just mentioned to suit the needs of the composition. This is in opposition to the ballet, which has arrived at certain set standards and can vary only insofar as the personality of the dancer imposes slight changes on the execution of a step.

The second principle concerns the movement of the dancer in relation to the space in which he moves. This emphasis on space consciousness, one of the greatest contributions of the German dancers, forms the basis for an approach to dance composition. Dancing then becomes the discipline and organization of power within the body, and the release of this power into space.

The third principle is that the dancer must be challenged as an individual, rather than made to accept something alien, something imposed by the teacher. Only fundamentals are stressed, so that the pupil is given every opportunity to develop his own dance personality. The genuine artist who has anything to say can therefore use such training as a starting point for evolving his own particular mode of expression.

By the 1940s, Holm had already modified her work to suit American conditions. She explained that the teacher seeks to satisfy the needs of her pupils. American students have certain problems which do not take the same form in the minds of German pupils. In Germany, for example,

Wigman found group improvisation to be an important means of expression. There seemed to be a need to dance with the consciousness of others in simultaneous motion (as in Laban's movement choirs). Holm found this need lacking among professional dancers in America. She felt that the layman found his mass activity in other forms, such as sports or folk dancing. Just as Holm had adapted her teaching to suit American culture, she similarly modified her choreography to please the audiences' tastes in the U.S. Beginning in the late 1940s, Hanya Holm did her choreography on Broadway for musical shows, such as *Kiss Me Kate* and the long-running *My Fair Lady*. She never stopped teaching, however, and her famous pupils included Valerie Bettis and Mary Anthony.

Questions for Review

1. How did Mary Wigman's approach to choreography differ from that of the early American modern dancers?

2. What elements make Kurt Jooss's *The Green Table* a classic?

3. Discuss Hanya Holm's philosophy.

4. What is the need for dance notation?

24 TOWERING GENIUS OF PSYCHODRAMA

MARTHA GRAHAM

Now we come to Martha Graham (1894 to 1991). For a young person there is often one figure who seems to embody all cherished ideals, and whose life presents the image toward which he or she aspires—first in fantasy and perhaps later in actuality. The dancer gives shape to female aspirations the way the athlete embodies those of the male. Those who argue that sex roles are changing must also note that the dancer's image has also undergone change. Picture the difference between Isadora Duncan, Ruth St. Denis, Pavlova, and Martha Graham. Yet each of these dancers had a devoted following that was largely female. In art and in lifestyle, they all symbolized what uncounted women longed for. (The situation changed later, when the leading modern dancers and choreographers once again were men.)

No one held center stage in this role for more years than Martha Graham. Thousands of her students keep poignant memories of their contact with this fascinating woman. I am one of them. Studying with Martha Graham was a most unsettling experience. You never left her classes in an indifferent mood. You either sailed out in a surge of elation, or plodded home in a heavy, self-destructive cloud of despair. When she was in a mood to give, Martha got amazing results. "Don't say, 'I want to,' *thus*!" sticking out her chin, "but, 'I want to,' *thus*," she insisted as she moved across the floor as though propelled by an inner demon. And sure enough, she would have the whole group moving with a concentrated intensity that they did not know they possessed. Once, by talking quietly in her throaty, hypnotic voice, she had the entire intermediate class in a perfect 180-degree turnout. This should impress dance students who constantly batter them-selves against the wall of human anatomical limitations.

Graham inspired students with her absolute belief in individual dig-nity and courage. "Great artists must reach beyond themselves, to the point of defying death!" No artistic snob, she held up the circus acrobat as a worthy model. Hence her work *Acrobats of God*, in which the dancer per-forms daring feats to curry favor with a whip-cracking circus-master Muse. She preached against moving in fear, against making the tentative gesture out of concern for avoiding mistakes. "If you will be wrong, be magnifi-cently wrong!" Gene Kelly was one dancer who won her admiration for his wholehearted abandonment to movement.

There were frightening, stormy sessions too, that you learned to dread. Graham's displeasure was as unequivocal as her respect for inner discipline. In bitter disgust, she might stop the class to burst out, "I wouldn't bother at all with any of you, but I must buy my time to dance!" Individuals were often targets of hostile criticism, brooding in private anguish over remarks like: "You're too mental," "You'll never dance," "Your thighs are too fat!" All her classes were ritualistic, almost religious. Everyone prepared for the daily instruction with great attention to person-al appearance. This did not mean gaudy handkerchiefs and earrings; but rather every hair in place; no ornaments and no runs in the austere black tights and leotards. Graham demanded that students regard the studio as both theater and temple.

You came in early and sat on the floor to stretch your legs and back. All of Graham's classes began on the floor. Suddenly, a figure in long black tunic would walk in quietly and sit purposefully on a small bench at the front of the room, hands clasped, back straight with poised authority. The students took up the prescribed opening position, and Miss Graham, in her low, husky tones, pronounced the one-word starting signal "and—" For the next fifteen or twenty minutes, the pianist would lead the class through a series of exercises for torsos, legs, arms, and heads, performed in solemn devotion, without further instruction. After the first few weeks of a new term, each class knew an entire set of identical movements that began every lesson. The rest of the hour proceeded with sporadic injunctions: "Take the exercise on six—four on twelve, four on six, and two on eight." There were interruptions, of course, for corrections. But the overall atmos-phere was one of ritual, rather than education. Martha, like Isadora Duncan, was a zealot.

The Formative Years. Martha Graham was born to a stern Presbyterian family in Pennsylvania. When she was fourteen, they moved to California, where freedom and openness overwhelmed her at first, but to which she gradually responded. When at seventeen, she attended a Ruth St. Denis concert, she saw on the stage an exotic, flowing vision of what she wanted to be. When she was twenty, Martha enrolled in the recently opened Denishawn Los Angeles school. Martha was a bit over-weight, short (five-foot-two), but very strong. Ruth St. Denis was turned off by this plain-looking, serious, determined student. But Ted Shawn caught the flaming inner intensity in every movement Martha made even then. That same year, they gave Martha Graham her first professional role in *A Dance Pageant of Egypt, Greece and India.*

When Ted Shawn enlisted in the army, he invited Martha to live and teach at the Denishawn studio, and in 1920 he created a solo for her. In *Xochitl*, Graham danced for the Emperor, played by Shawn. When he tried to rape her in a fit of drunken lust, she resisted him with fury. Through her long career, Martha Graham threw herself completely into any part, body and soul. Shawn later complained of bruises he got performing *Xochitl*.

Martha stayed with Denishawn until 1923, teaching and touring with the company across the United States. In a series of one-night stands she learned to be a trouper. She also learned about costumes, lighting, spacing a group of dancers on stages of different sizes, and performing in all kinds of weather for all kinds of audiences. In short, she learned the trade of the-ater dance. At Denishawn, she also met and had an affair with her life-long advisor and musical director, Louis Horst. Horst was married and Martha went around making speeches about the glories of free love. Close to twenty-nine-years old, she played to the hilt the part of an emancipated woman, along with the role of an artist, whose creative life exempted her from conventional controls. Frequently, Martha gave vent to her explosive temper, obviously relishing the experience of a violent scene, both offstage and on. The discipline in which she believed concerned only dance, where it was fanatical. Otherwise, she permitted her artistic temperament any indulgence.

The lead couple of Denishawn could not tolerate the presence of an egotistical star in the company—other than themselves. Ruth St. Denis made her attitude clear when she insisted on doing Martha's solo in *Xochitl* for a cross-country tour, even though Ruth already had several featured solos and this was Martha's major role. Then Ted Shawn lectured Martha on flaunting her affairs with Louis. This occurred on the last stop of the tour in New York City. During the two-week run at Town Hall, Martha Graham's special personal quality attracted the producer of *The Greenwich Follies.* He offered her a job. Martha obviously felt there was no place for her burning ambition in Denishawn, and accepted the offer. Shawn bitter-ly noted that she gave him absolutely no credit for the Spanish-style solo, *Serenata Morisca,* that he had choreographed for her at Denishawn, when she went out to perform it in the Follies.

In 1925, after two years in the Follies, which was further training in show business, Martha joined the faculty of the new dance department at Rochester's Eastman School of Music. Again, she found herself staging entertainments, and not the serious art dances that were taking shape in her imagination. But we learn from Don McDonagh's biography, *Martha Graham*, that there were three young women, Thelma Biracree, Evelyn Sabin, and Betty MacDonald at the Eastman School who wholeheartedly accepted Martha's fanatical dance aesthetic, which meant following any command or whim of their leader, including rehearsals on bleeding feet. They were early disciples in a zealous cult. When Graham left Eastman, the three followed her to New York City. Musician Louis Horst became Graham's working partner. In April 1926, with her three dancers and with Louis Horst at the piano, Martha gave her first concert.

Graham was to create close to two hundred dance compositions over the next fifty years. The earliest ones showed her origins with Denishawn. They were musical pieces, such as *Chorale* (to a Cesar Franck score) and *Intermezzo* (to Brahms). However, Louis Horst got her to use contemporary composers like Erik Satie; and Horst himself wrote the music for *Three Poems of the East*, *Scene Javanaise*, and other dances over the next fifteen years. Note that these two Oriental titles show the influence of Horst's long association with Denishawn as musical director. We will digress for a moment to discuss Horst.

Louis Horst (1884 to 1964). Louis Horst was not a dancer, but he was an important presence in the modern dance scene. For ten years he was Denishawn's musical director. Then he went to Europe to observe Wigman and the art scene in general. When he returned to the States, he began his twenty-year role as Graham's adviser on music and choreography. He founded the monthly *Dance Observer*, the first journal devoted exclusively and seriously to modern dance. Horst also developed a method of teaching choreography. Three principles governed Horst's approach:

1. A choreographer must choreograph something daily, even a short passage, with or without inspiration. Only that way can he learn the craft, and be ready when inspiration does strike.

2. Form is musical, based on the classical A-B-A structure. A is the first theme introduced and developed; B is the second contrasting theme introduced and developed, but in the same style; A is the return of the first theme but with a slight difference, leading to a resolution.

3. Style should be fresh, original, and modern. Again, it should parallel the developments in music and all the other arts: distorted gesture, asymmetrical shapes, and uneven rhythms.

In the preclassical part of his course, his students had to prepare for each session a gigue, a sarabande, a pavan, and so on, in an A-B-A form of eight measures each. But the idea was not to re-create an authentic, preclassical dance like the ones described in Chapter 6, but to compose a modern version. For example, a minuet might be a fussy, mincing portrait of a spinster; a pavan might show the cool, pompous anger of a bossy figure. The students showed their pieces, after which the other students and Louis himself would comment. The more advanced courses in modern forms offered a similar approach to other musical subjects, such as whole-tone scales, jazz, and primitive music. The biggest sins, according to Louis, were pretty, sentimental bits in balletic poses. And, of course, Louis Horst put this modern aesthetic and his critical intelligence completely in the service of Martha Graham's choreography, although hundreds of other modern dancers were to study with him and also show the influence of his teaching.

The Development of Graham's Psychodrama

By 1928, Graham had broken completely with her Denishawn past and was finding her own grim style. Movements were supported on bare feet that travelled in straight lines, parallel to each other. There was no turnout in the hip or leg. The foot was bent sharply at the ankle. There was no airy lightness. There were no softly curved lines in the arms or at the waist. The dancers worked low to the floor. Their shapes were angular; their dynamics were percussive; sharp and strong, lacking follow-through. Martha designed the costumes, which were made of dark-colored, heavy-knitted jersey. The subjects she chose were harsh: *Revolt, Immigrants, Resurrection*. In other words, the whole was as unballetic as possible.

In 1930, Leonide Massine asked Martha Graham to dance in the New York premiere of his *Rite of Spring*, to the Stravinsky score that had its scandalous Ballets Russes premiere in 1912. They finally got the piece onstage, but the dancer fought with the choreographer all the way. Massine wanted her to be airborne, to leap as all ballet dancers learn to do. As we know, Martha Graham was not trained to do such a step. However, she wanted to do the role because of the prestige attached, so Graham practiced with her superhuman concentration until she mastered a very acceptable split leap. As she had hoped, her appearance in this work by a world-famous ballet choreographer did add to her reputation.

No doubt, the ballet also influenced her first great work, *Primitive Mysteries*, (1931). Here the word *primitive* denotes movement style, in the sense of simple and naive. It means that religious ritual (the theme of prayer) is performed in formal designs, alternately gravely ceremonial and fervently ecstatic. The word *mysteries* refers to the Christian Mass, with its worship of the Virgin Mary, the suffering of the crucifixion, and the exaltation of worship. It is Christianity grafted onto tribal religion. Only from Louis Horst's score do we get the specific tribal association with the Spanish Native Americans of the American Southwest.

At the time, the critic John Martin wrote:

> *Primitive Mysteries* is a profoundly moving translation of ritual into the forms of art. At the conclusion of its first presentation, the entire audience burst into shouting, not so much by way of conscious praise as of an involuntary release of pent-up emotion.
>
> With this performance it became evident that there was a large Graham audience, in spite of her austerity, of her refusal to conform.

It was also at this time that she locked horns with another world-famous choreographer, Michael Fokine, exchanging harsh words with him at a demonstration of her movement theories. As a result, New York dance fans were divided into Graham supporters and Fokine supporters through the 1930s. This was a clear sign that Graham had come into her own. Fokine certainly would not have bothered to be her enemy if she were a nobody. "I'm nobody, who are you? Are you nobody, too? Then there's a pair of us." These are lines from a poem by Emily Dickinson. Graham used them in her dance, *Letter to the World*. Neither Graham nor Dickinson was a nobody in the eyes of our society, and Graham, as we know, did not act like a nobody. Yet the dancer responded to the poet's whimsical thoughts about a woman's identity, and in 1940, she created a masterpiece. Hunter Johnson composed the music and Arch Lauterer designed the sets.

By the late 1930s, Graham was warmed up and had reached full stride in her unique branch of theater dance. She produced only one or two new works a year, but each premiere was an exciting artistic occasion. In 1938, *American Document* was produced. Erick Hawkins, a handsome, bare-chested man, strode onstage, and later did a dignified but sensual duet with Martha, who played a Puritan maid. They gestured of desire, accompanied by the words of a fanatical clergyman who promised eternal damnation. Stirring words from America's past echoed through the voice of a narrator. Native American figures did a dance about belonging to the land before the white man took over ("my blood remembers"). The group sternly paraded as proud Puritans, and then, as pioneers, they leaped with joy and love of country. *American Document* featured the use of words, a male dancer, a patriotic theme, and a pas de deux of love. All these marked a new openness that invited the audience to share and understand, a vision of life in America that was not sentimental but definitely upbeat. Ray Green wrote the music and Arch Lauterer did the sets.

Every Soul Is a Circus followed in 1939 to a score by Paul Nordoff. Words by Vachel Lindsay provided the theme: "Every soul is a circus, every mind is a tent, every heart is a sawdust ring, where the circling race is spent." Graham was the foolish star of her own show, who submitted to the dominating male, Erick Hawkins, who cracked the whip of a ringmaster. But at the same time, Merce Cunningham, as the Acrobat, raised romantic longings in the foolish woman's soul. It was all done in a delightful mock-serious mood. Similarly, *Punch and the Judy* (1941) presented marriage as a puppet show. Again, Graham's female was subservient to Erick Hawkins, a pompous, blustering male who knocked her about. She dreamed of the love of brave, heroic men while her neglected children got along as best they could.

Balancing these two satirical views of women in relation to men, Martha Graham produced a work derived from Christian legend, *El Penitente*, another that ranged from dark to light, *Letter to the World*, and one in a somber mood, *Deaths and Entrances*. *El Penitente* presented Martha in contrasting roles as the Virgin and as Mary Magdalene. Erick Hawkins was cast as the Flagellant, and Merce Cunningham as the Crucified One. In *Letter to the World*, Graham split the central characters into two different bodies. Jean Erdman, a talented dancer-actress, spoke lines from Emily Dickinson's poems. Martha, dressed the same way, danced the poetic scenes beginning with the lines quoted above when Jean and Martha greeted each other as the two nobodies. This time, the woman lost her deep love, not through her own or a man's foolish behavior, but to the figure of Death, the tall, statuesque Jane Dudley, all in black. Jane Dudley was unforgettable in her stern cruelty as the Ancestress. There were joyous scenes, too: "Come in dear March" when windblown Merce Cunningham jumped through the sky.

Deaths and Entrances, music by Hunter Johnson and sets by Arch Lauterer, ware somber and dark throughout. There were no words either, although the inspiration was in part literary. There were three female figures, the Bronte Sisters, locked together in brooding frustration. As the central figure, Martha stormed through the past and present struggles and crises with them and others. Her Dark Beloved was Erick Hawkins and Merce Cunningham again played the romanticized Poetic Beloved. At the end, Martha made a triumphant, grand gesture. She stood over the two sisters who were seated, and lifting high her arm, she cut between them and firmly planted a symbolic chess piece on their table.

Then in 1944, Martha Graham created a beautiful portrait of mating, *Appalachian Spring*, with the beloved musical score by Aaron Copland and a fine set by Isamu Noguchi. In *Appalachian Spring*, a pioneer man and woman marry and move into their new home. The husband, Erick Hawkins, does a handstand and slaps his legs joyously, but he also bows formally to villagers and prays quietly. The wife Martha adores the husband, and walks next to him with obedient little bows. She projects anxiety about the future: will she be a good wife and mother? But she also looks forward with happy self-possession, and she and her husband receive the welcoming community with warm dignity. The humorous side is the preacher's. Merce Cunningham danced of hellfire and sin, but he was a bounding, light fellow, amusing rather than frightening, especially with his chorus of four adoring little village girls, fluttering around him devotedly.

In 1946, Martha Graham produced *Dark Meadow* and *Cave of the Heart*, transitional expressions of a maturity that led to increasingly dark visions with the passage of time. Rituals of primitive sex, and myths and plays of ancient Greece and of the Bible that dealt with fear, jealousy, rage, and despair became the content of Graham's work from that time on. Many of them were masterpieces: *Errand into the Maze, Night Journey, Diversion of Angels, Clytemnestra, Embattled Garden*, and *Acrobats of God*.

The Graham Approach

Because Graham's approach influenced several generations of dance and theater artists, we are familiar with it by now. But in her heyday she was totally original. Martha Graham found a way to treat all the elements of dance so that each one reinforced the others to produce vivid, forceful compositions. Let's look at the movement, the music, the costumes and sets, structure and content, and performance in Graham's work.

The movement is tense. Even on the lighter side of the dynamic scale, there is never a relaxed swing or easy follow-through, but abrupt little motions. No limb of the body falls free, but is held in position or moves in fixed paths. Graham's dance works are all built upon the Graham technique, and the Graham technique consists of exercises made up of phrases from Graham's dance works.

The music is composed for the dance. When Graham has a new idea, it takes root in her mind, and grows, develops, and nags at her for months or years. When she is ready to use it, she writes a brief scenario which she gives to a composer (always a well-known artist whose contemporary sounds and rhythms reflect her own tense, disciplined approach). Only when she gets and absorbs the finished score—by listening to it for hours— is she ready to put movement sequences together.

Visually, her stage is sculptured with figures holding still in foreground or background as others move. The décor is designed by contemporary sculptors and set designers, known for spare, symbolic shapes, always functional to her imagery. In the beginning, Martha designed her costumes in weighted, fluid, or stiff materials.

When we come to structure—the actual composition of the work, the construction of each scene, and the arrangement of the parts—we find Graham's method to be absolutely ingenious. In each piece, she plays around with time and memory the way films, or stream-of-consciousness literature do. As an example of her method, let's consider *Dream*, done in 1974. In every way this follows the pattern Graham set in the 1940s. Her themes, taken from literature and legend, were used as a vehicle for exploring human emotions and behavior. Graham has said, "Myths are the psychology of an earlier time."

Thus, *Dream* is based on Jacob's struggles, first with his brother Esau, and then with the Angel of Destiny, who calls on him to accept the glory and the responsibility of Israel. Once she has her subject matter, Graham's treatment in her unique form departs from literal continuity of plot. The work proceeds in a series of movement recitatives—solo revelations or duos of conflict or love—linked by a Greek chorus of men or women, who file prophetically through the action. The stage becomes a landscape of memory or emotion, and every theatrical device is used to create symbolic images. In *Dream*, the back curtain opens to reveal a ladder, extending up and out of sight, on which near-nude angels entwine and climb, and which Jacob mounts at the end with his Angel of Destiny, as a sign of ascent. His mother removes a cloak from Jacob's body, and unites it with the angels' totem of Israel. A doorlike structure opens and closes to frame a pagan goddess, a symbol of what the tribe must finally reject.

Graham's movements are rooted in gestures that denote pain, love, or fear—but they are not pantomimic. Encased within her own technique—a highly controlled, stylized vocabulary of body positions and pulses stemming from the central torso—they create in the dancers, and through kinetic empathy in the viewer, a continuous build-up of tension. As Graham told a gathering of student choreographers in 1952:

> No movement is completely representational that a dancer makes. There is a very old symbolism behind movement. The arabesque is not to show off a girl's or a man's body in flight. It goes to the meaning of flight—anything cleaving through space.
>
> The audience does not have to be aware of the symbolism. What the spectator has to be aware of is something within his own body. He does not have to analyze what flight means, but he should have the feeling or sensation of flight.

By the time she created *Dream* in the 1970s, Graham was no longer dancing. But years earlier, in an interview, she told me: "I do not do choreography. I create vehicles for myself." Digging deeper, we find a core in much of Graham's work that is exactly what she says it is—herself. Her dances were personal visions of a wildly emotional woman. You can bet that she fully experienced anger, jealousy, anxiety, need for approval, fear, sexual attraction, humiliation, and all the other emotions that the rest of us have. But unlike most of us, she recognized no conventional limitations, and gave free rein to these emotions. Also unlike most of us, she thought and read continuously, ranging over the philosophers, the poets, and the theologians of Oriental and Western religions. Then, when she was working on an idea, she seized on words that struck her as fitting.

Many women's minds and feelings work this way. They are able to relate what they see and hear personally, and to find connections between ideas and their emotions and physical sensations. That may explain why the great early modern dancers were women, and why their audiences were largely female. That was, of course, during the period when modern dance was expressive and emotional. We will soon meet the less emotional and the more impersonal avant-garde choreographers, led by the male figures of Merce Cunningham and Alwin Nikolais.

To get back to Graham, however, it might interest you to read the notes she made when she was planning *Dark Meadow*. They are included along with hundreds of others in *The Notebooks of Martha Graham*, introduced by Nancy Wilson Ross:

> The place of transformation is really the place of the uterus. Absorption with oneself (introversion) is an entrance into one's own uterus, and also at the same time, aesceticism.
>
> In the philosophy of the Brahmins the world arose from this activity among the post-Christian Agnostics. It produced the revival and spiritual rebirth of the individual, who was born into a new spiritual world. The Hindu philosophy is considerably more daring and logical, and assumes that creation results from introversion in general, as in the wonderful hymn of Rig-Veda, 10, 29..."What was hidden the shell, was born through the power of fiery torments," Jung, 416.

Brahmins? Post-Christian Agnostic? Rig-Veda? Jung? That's pretty heavy stuff, but typical of her thought processes. She boasted:

> I am a thief—and I glory in it—I steal from the present and from the glorious past, and I stand in the dark of the future as a glorying and joyous thief...

All artists feed on the cultures around them, but Graham's appetite was larger than most. Needless to say, she did not arrive at a reasoned or consistent synthesis of these varied sources. However, she did come up with dance works which were deeply moving because they were enriched with all these associations.

Finally, we come to performance. The whole was welded together in performance, first by the creator and secondly by a group that was trained in her technique and rehearsed in her ascetic creed of aware concentration. One season, Graham brought her group to a small Ohio college. As a resident teacher, I conducted her backstage through an irrational maze of halls, stairways, and passages in an unused building annex to reach a remote dressing room. When I offered to escort her back later, she dismissed the idea: "I never lose the way once I've gone over it." Martha demanded the same awareness from company members. Not only did they focus their gazes on an abstract horizon, they had to be aware of their own positions in relation to every other dancer on the stage, every prop, the manipulation of unfamiliar costumes, and even the way the stage wings were placed. Woe to the dancer whose arm or leg brushed a curtain on entrance or exit!

Unlike Isadora Duncan, Martha Graham handed down to thousands of students a unique, concrete, teachable technique of movement based on the contraction and release of the torso. Exercises emphasized the torso as the emotional center, with movements stemming from pelvis and lower back and travelling outward to arms, legs and head. Percussive beats, uneven phrasing, and twisted shapes all conveyed internal discord. However, many of the exercises and the daily class ritual were built on phrases that Martha had put together in past performances of choreography. Exercises were not therefore designed systematically to stretch and strengthen all the parts of the body. Rather, they were designed to train dancers to move in Martha Graham's personal style. Therefore the Graham technique reflects a world-view based on inner psychological conflict and dramatic challenge.

Company members were all trained at the Graham school. In fact, the Graham technique classes ensured a constant supply of dancers well versed in Graham's style and phrasing, and also accustomed to her stern single-mindedness. That's why the Graham company was always excellent, even though the personnel changed from year to year. Many of the stars of Graham's companies grew into well-known modern dancers, choreographers, and teachers in their own right, among them: Anna Sokolow, Martha Hill, Jane Dudley, Sophie Maslow, Bessie Schoenberg, Gertrude Shurr, Jean Erdman, May O'Donnell, and Pearl Lang. Among the men there were: Merce Cunningham, Erick Hawkins, Robert Cohan, Bertram Ross, Paul Taylor, Glen Tetley, Gus Solomons, Jr., and even Nureyev, although in his case, his fame preceded his appearance in Graham's group in the 1970s.

Erick Hawkins: Conflict Amidst Triumph

Graham's choreography and therefore her technique classes changed through the years. In the 1950s her technique became more fluid, and not only did company members go out of the studio for ballet classes, Erick Hawkins taught a ballet class in the studio itself. No men were on the scene in the beginning. The first was Erick Hawkins, featured in *American Document* in 1938, followed in 1939 by Merce Cunningham. By 1950, Robert Cohan and Bertram Ross were Martha's leading men. But when the thirty-year-old Hawkins came into the all-female Graham group and was immediately given a starring role and then became the priestess's lover, it shook things up quite a bit. A number of the women left, to do things their own way.

Then Louis Horst left Martha in the late 1940s, walking out on her simply because she reprimanded him at a rehearsal in front of dancers and instrumentalists. Louis continued as a teacher and critic until his death in 1966, but his break with Martha was total. Of course, the public reprimand was not the real cause of his desertion. It was the presence of Erick Hawkins.

Horst was a father figure in modern dance, a portly gentleman, complete with wife and ambitions to write music. Louis Horst was an artist of his times. Along with the bohemians of Europe and America, he mocked the conventions of "bourgeois mentality." He would subject countless young women to private lectures at a cafe about having the courage to be free, while he conferred with them on writing assignments for the *Dance Observer*, or discussed with them their choreography and their future plans in the dance world. Of course, money wasn't involved at all. Whether in 1928, 1948, 1968, or 1988 you were in the modern dance field because of passionate dedication, not for fame or fortune.

Louis (he was always referred to by his first name, just as Martha was by hers) opened Martha's eyes and ears to the world of modern art. He encouraged her to use contemporary composers and to have music written for her dances. It was he, the musician, who insisted that the dance should be the dominant art. The music and décor were there only to serve the choreographer's vision. He was personally present to criticize, to encourage, and to demand that Martha give nothing but her best. Thus, from 1926 to 1938, while she was the genius, the priestess of her cult, his position as the dominant male and the artistic director was unchallenged. Remember, Martha always played to the hilt her offstage role. In 1938, she was at the height of her career. Hers was the one name in modern dance that was familiar to a wide public. Subsidy money was beginning to come in from Baroness de Rothschild, from Katherine Cornell who raised money from theater people, from Elizabeth Sprague Coolidge, from a Guggenheim Fellowship, and from many others.

At forty-four, she was truly glamorous. Great dancers—ballet or modern—have a special look. This comes first of all from technical training. During practice sessions they actually shape the contours of their bodies and faces by the repetition of formal motions never made in ordinary living. Thus in concentrated rehearsal and performance of compositions, a person's expressive qualities are brought to the surface. Martha's face was molded in exotic lines around a strong chin and high cheekbones. She held her head at a slight tilt; her eyes shone and her mouth was slightly open. She wore subtle make-up, simple dramatic clothing, and her hair was pulled back tight and wound in a chignon. Her voice was low and breathy. All this produced the image of a striking theatrical star who made her presence felt. Onstage, she projected magnificently. Critic Edwin Denby called her "an actress of magnificent power; a dancer of astonishing skill—elegant, womanly, controlled." Merle Armitage wrote, "There are moments in Martha Graham's dancing when the poignant meaning is projected with the velocity of a pitched ball." John Martin spoke of her "inner stillness, whether she is active or in repose, commanding power over an audience."

The Graham group was fine, but there was a period when their leader outshone them. She did not confine herself to the exact pulse and shape that she demanded from them, but allowed herself a curved shoulder, or a slight retard in tempo, in other words, a spontaneity that belonged only to her, and she used it brilliantly. Remember, she was dancing her own inner life. The upbeat period in choreography that continued for about two decades after 1938 reflected first of all what may have been the most gratifying time of her life. She was the love object of the handsome young Erick Hawkins. She had a full-time involvement in her own company and choreography, and recognition in the form of prizes, fellowships, subsidies, excited audiences and critics—who would not be high?

There were problems with Hawkins, who struggled with her for dominance of artistic policy. And he undoubtedly struggled with her personally. As noted before, because of the presence of Hawkins, there were problems with women in the company and with Louis Horst. You can imagine the gossip and the rivalry in the intense, temperamental world that was the Graham company. This filtered down even to the intermediate students who were jockeying for front-line position in the studio—and at the mirror in the dressing room! However, bright side, dark side, any emotion was grist for Martha's mill. Sexual love was certainly the subject (at least in part) of all her works once Hawkins stepped onstage. *Letter to the World*, *Every Soul Is a Circus*, *Deaths and Entrances*, *Punch and the Judy*, and *Appalachian Spring* were all aspects of Graham in love and sex.

When Horst left her and then Hawkins, she found other males in real life and onstage. However, it must be noted that Hawkins's desertion affected her profoundly. She underwent psychoanalysis, delving even deeper into herself. By the way, the split with Hawkins was only personal. For a while, he continued to dance in her company. She cast herself in furiously emotional roles. Jocasta, in *Night Journey*, hangs herself because she had sex with her son Oedipus. Medea, in *Cave of the Heart*, kills her two children in a jealous fever when her husband Jason turns to a younger woman. As the title role in *Clytemnestra*, she murders her husband Agamemnon, again in jealous revenge.

Final Curtain Call. In the end, both the dancer and her audiences paid a price for Martha's magnificent ego. In the 1960s, as she approached seventy years of age, Martha's body and her creative energy could no longer meet the insatiable demands of the dance art. Yet she continued to perform and to choreograph. It was embarrassing to watch her onstage,

Martha Graham and Paul Taylor in a dramatic monent from "Clytemnestra."

where she knelt and rose with difficulty; all the more obvious in contrast to
the fabulous technical ease of the younger women performing with her.

It was even more embarrassing to see the new theater pieces she
turned out, like *A Time of Snow* (1969), with music by Norman Dello Joio.
Cloaks figured prominently in this dramatic dance. *A Time of Snow* was a
translation into movement of the romance of Abelard and Heloise, complete with a castration scene. The form followed Graham's usual approach

to legend, starting near the end and proceeding in flashbacks. As an elderly nun, Miss Graham's Heloise thought back to her days of loneliness. At such performances I always felt sorry that the young people in the audience were obviously thinking: "This is the great Martha Graham? What's all the fuss about?"

Martha was not unaware of the ravages of time, and increasingly sought consolation in alcohol. At least she did revive some of her best works, giving the roles to soloists whom she had developed, such as Ethel Winter in *Appalachian Spring*, and Mary Hinkson in *El Penitente*. To a woman who "did not do choreography, but created vehicles for *herself* to perform," this was punishment. In fact, she left the job of re-creating these roles strictly to the company, boycotting the rehearsals that were so painful for her. Finally, she stopped performing and continued to produce and to gather beautiful dancers as well as stars around her . She did a work called *Lucifer* for Rudolf Nureyev in 1975 to music by Halim El'Dabh. There were still rewards to be had from a Graham company concert.

In 1984, when Martha turned ninety, she directed a two-week season of her company, for which she created a version of Stravinsky's *Rite of Spring*. At the premiere, the choreographer received a standing ovation, but it was not for the dance piece. Rather, it was a tribute to a great artist and dedicated to the memory of her past glories. When Graham died, at her request there was no funeral. Two months later, however, luminaries and followers of the dance world packed New York's City Center where her company gave a performance in her memory, and the audience responded with tears and cheers. The program closed with Martha Graham's first masterpiece, *Primitive Mysteries*, which had been choreographed sixty years earlier with a score by Louis Horst. Her staged figure of the Madonna, crowned with a shining halo created by the stage lighting and the group's adoring hands and fingers, made a fitting memorial to the dedicated artist, who stood apart in the dance world.

Questions for Review

1. Why do we use the term *psychodrama* in connection with Martha Graham's work?

2. Describe this artist's approach to music and décor in choreography.

3. Discuss the Graham technique as a system of dance training.

4. What was the role of Louis Horst in modern dance?

5. Consider Graham's remarks about "flight" in relation to the entire field of dance.

25 HUMANISTS

HUMPHREY AND WEIDMAN

Doris Humphrey

In this constellation of early modern dance stars, one glittered in a space apart. Doris Humphrey did share with the others a great talent, a unique vision of dance art, and a wholehearted dedication to achievement. But unlike the other women, Doris Humphrey never became a cult figure, nor was her name a really famous one outside the field. Humphrey never lashed out at her company, nor did she demand from them bonds forged from loyalty and guilt. She never displayed her personal life in public like a mink stole. She married quietly, bearing and raising one child. This is not to say that the artist was above the fray of human emotions. A little later on we will hear about family problems. As for her career, she was not unaware of the rivalry with Martha Graham for "first place" in the modern dance hierarchy. Especially at the Bennington Summer School of the Dance, where Martha's fans had crucial staff positions, Doris Humphrey knew that in their eyes she didn't measure up.

Because Graham and Humphrey were so totally different in personality, it is not at all surprising that they came up with opposite theories both of dance and of styles of choreography. To return to Kurt Sach's distinction between ecstasy and harmony: we can think of Martha's technique and her dance works as representing the height of passionate excitement, of dark, personal storms; while Doris represents the harmonious, balanced, noble side of humanity. The best example of their contrasting natures is the way each reacted when she could no longer dance. We have seen how Martha escaped by drinking and by refusing to help company members learn her roles. Doris, while still in her forties, was hit with a degenerative crippling disease that not only kept her from dancing but made it painfully difficult for her to walk. But she went on to choreograph her finest works, using José Limón, Pauline Koner, and other younger dancers.

Above all, Doris Humphrey's distinction lay in a fine, rational mind that could organize theories and express them clearly in speech and writing. In addition to her letters, we now have personal details of her early life which Doris put down on paper at the very end of her "day on earth" while confined to a sickbed. The style of her writing, like the style of her choreography, reflects a dignified, caring personality. By the way, *personality* is a very serviceable one-word definition for the concept of style in art as well as that of a person's characteristics. During her lifetime, the dance world knew Doris Humphrey as a Denishawn dancer, than as Charles Weidman's working partner, and finally as a magnificent choreographer, teacher, and artistic director of José Limón's company.

The Denishawn Years. Born in a Chicago suburb, Doris Humphrey was in her twenties when she went to Los Angeles to study at the newly opened Denishawn School at the urging of Mary Wood Hinman. Hinman, a devoted dance educator who studied gymnastics in Sweden and folk dancing in Europe, was Doris's teacher for many years at a private elementary school. She recognized Doris's talent and encouraged her to study seriously. Doris took lessons from ballet dancers in the Chicago area and then for five years she taught her own classes to support her parents. In 1918, Doris left the Oak Park, Illinois school in other hands and auditioned for Ruth St. Denis in California. St. Denis immediately invited her to join the Denishawn company and Doris's modern dance career was launched.

Like Martha Graham, Doris Humphrey learned the professional dance trade with Denishawn. Ruth St. Denis taught her how to apply stage make-up and how to manipulate Oriental costumes. Most of all, she inspired Doris through endless talking about her hopes and plans for theatrical dance. The bright, alert, excited young Doris picked up everything else as a member of Denishawn while on a vaudeville tour. They crossed the country, giving two, sometimes three performances a day of numbers with Native American, Spanish, East Indian, or Japanese subjects. It was also at Denishawn that Doris met Pauline Lawrence, who accompanied classes, and Charles Weidman, who was eager to be a dancer. When Ruth St. Denis began her concert group with a program of music visualizations, she helped Doris to choreograph *Soaring* for five girls and a huge scarf to a piece by Schumann.

Doris went on to create a few other group pieces and solos for herself, all in the mode of Ruth St. Denis—and Isadora Duncan before her—that is, dances that interpreted the spirit of a music score. In the 1920s, such dances were called *music visualizations*. Today they are called *plotless ballets*. When Isadora Duncan and then Denishawn performed them, there were outraged purists who objected to using great music as dance accompaniment. Attitudes seem to have changed. There has been no public outcry in recent years. In fact, a good many people have become accustomed to the harsh sounds of Stravinsky, Bartok, and Mahler because they have heard them at modern dance concerts.

Through the ten years she studied at Denishawn, Doris was never fully satisfied. Alone, and with Pauline Lawrence and Charles Weidman, she began to search for a dance vocabulary that was more authentic for an American woman than the combination of Oriental gestures on which Ruth St. Denis largely relied. However, the ethical young woman did not leave Denishawn for that reason. Doris Humphrey was actually voted out of Denishawn because she refused to spend a year performing in the Zeigfield Follies to raise money for their new building in the Bronx. It was a beautiful building. In the late 1930s, one of the teachers was Klarna Pinska, who directed a spring recital that was a fairly literal visualization of Schubert's *Unfinished Symphony*. Students represented the musical instruments, swaying in time with their melodic passages. The big girls were "cellos." Little "violas" (I was one) knelt on one knee and wiggled their fingers as that instrument was heard in a contrapuntal theme. By the time of that recital, Doris had departed completely from Ruth St. Denis's methods of choreography. When she left Denishawn in the summer of 1928, her two close companions, Pauline Lawrence and Charles Weidman, went with her to form their own company. Like other great pioneers, they invented new approaches to all the elements of theater dance.

Humphrey's Company

Pauline Lawrence (1900 to 1971). Pauline Lawrence had studied music and costuming. For the new group, she not only played piano accompaniment as she had at Denishawn, she also took care of music choices, costumes, lighting, and management. Margaret Lloyd (in *The Borzoi Book of Modern Dance*) described the way Pauline "brewed" a costume:

> She would stroll through the yardgoods section of a department store, humming the music of a dance, until the right material called out to her, "I am it." With the material popped ideas for cutting. Hems were left unfinished, but not only because there was no time to finish them, but because they moved better so. Movement and music, lighting, make-up, and dance idea were active ingredients in the costuming, which came out in unusual, sometimes ravishing color combinations.

The sets were in the manner of Gordon Craig or of the Bauhaus school. The company acquired giant boxes of various sizes and shapes, ten screens that were eighteen feet high and five feet wide, and a low platform. These were always combined differently so that in each dance, the viewers' eyes took in a fresh impression of lines and shapes to point up the particular idea.

In March 1928, they gave their first concert. The company included Gertrude Shurr and Eleanor King, both of whom later made names for themselves. Louis Horst was one of the accompanists. The works were mostly St.Denis-type music visualizations, except for Humphrey's *Color Harmony* in which she worked out different modes of motion: cool blue for slow; yellow for vivacious; and red for strength. Charles Weidman contributed two comedies: a trio and a more successful solo, *Scherzo*, in which he juggled invisible items. From the very beginning, Doris Humphrey's work explored wide possibilities of the dance art.

In 1928, *Water Study* was an experiment with unaccompanied movement that portrayed natural forces. It was as though the dancers were pushed and pulled by the tidal forces that mold water into waves and send it rushing up onto the shore, drag it out again, and fling its spraying drops into the air. As we learn in Selma Jeanne Cohen's biography, Doris Humphrey explained in a program note this attempt to make dance independent of music:

> Probably the thing that distinguishes musical rhythm from other rhythm is the measured time beat, so this has been eliminated from the Water Study and the rhythm flows in natural phrases instead of cerebral measures. There is no count to hold the dancers together in the very slow opening rhythm, only the feel of the wave length that curves the backs of the group.

Water Study worked with the gesture of a curved back. In stage space, it used vertical up-and-down patterns. The dancers' breathing and the noise made by their feet on the stage were the sounds that the audience heard. At this time, Mary Wigman was also experimenting with body rhythms as separate from rhythms in music. However, Doris did only a few such pieces before she returned to musical accompaniment.

In *Life of the Bee* (1929), she spread the dancers' arms out horizontally and used diagonal floor patterns to portray a conflict of forces. This time, the natural forces were those of biology instead of physics: the old Queen Bee fighting in vain to defend her ruling position against the challenge of the new Queen Bee while the Worker Bees hovered about them worriedly. Pauline Lawrence arranged an ingenious accompaniment: a voice chorus, humming through combs covered with tissue paper. This not only suggested an insectlike buzz, but lent a fittingly ominous tone to the melodramatic struggle as the old Queen was deposed.

The Shakers. Between the spring of 1928 when she left Denishawn and the beginning of 1931, Doris choreographed over two dozen dances that played with designs in movement, space, rhythm, and the relationship between movement and sounds, and movement and silence. Then, in 1931, already a mature choreographer, she created *The Shakers*, a modern dance masterpiece. In *The Shakers*, Doris portrayed a religious sect that practiced communal living and rituals of purification. They gathered together to shake their bodies free of sin and to make open confession. In addition, the Shakers were more fanatical than most puritanical religious groups. They not only believed that sex was sinful, they totally forbade its practice.

The dancers dress in costumes that resemble those of Quakers, and in reference to the traditional sexual division, the women dance only onstage right and the men onstage left. Their movements—clapping, swaying, and marching—reflect the actual religious gestures of this sect. An insistent rhythmic beat which gradually increases its tempo is suddenly broken, and climaxes with a woman's outcry. *The Shakers* builds from quiet devotion to fervent emotionalism, and finally reveals the ecstasy of communal rever-

The José Limón Company in Humphrey's "Shakers."

ence. So although there is an ecstatic outburst, the choreographer controls it with great formality.

The Shakers has been presented may times, and by a number of companies, particularly because this dance had been notated in Labanotation. In revivals, unfortunately, while the motions and the structure are faithful to the original choreography, the central quality is missing. This quality is passionate feeling, without which the dance becomes a meaningless performance of mechanical puppets. This happens because unlike the "good old days," increasingly more modern dancers have been trained to be fine virtuoso technicians, with no attention whatever to emotional motivation or dramatic content. Shortly, we will see how developments and outlooks in modern dance and ballet changed in the 1950s to bring this about. At this point, we note only that it is difficult to get a proper rendition of a dance piece from another era, particularly in modern dance where everything was so personal.

Humphrey's Choreography: An Expression of Her Worldview

During the 1930s, Doris Humphrey was hard at work devising a movement technique suitable for her own vision of dance (which Martha Graham was doing at about the same time and which Ruth St. Denis and Isadora Duncan had done previously). Doris too, wanted to find the basic springs of human movement in the name of truth and of realism. Isadora Duncan had located the seat of human emotions in the solar plexus, and Martha Graham had located them in the central torso. Isadora and Ruth St. Denis (like François Delsarte) found that the arms, head, and upper torso were the emotionally expressive areas of the body. Doris Humphrey came up with a technique known as *fall and recovery*. She wrote (in *Dance, A Basic Educational Technique*, edited by Frederick Rand Rogers):

> I conceive movement for the dancer's purpose to be basically one of equilibrium. In fact, *my entire technique consists of the development of the process of falling away from and returning to equilibrium.* This is far more than a mere business of "keeping your balance," which is a muscular and structural problem. Falling and recovering is the very stuff of movement, the constant flux which is going on in every living body in all its tiniest parts, all the time.
>
> Nor is this all, for the process has a psychological meaning as well. I recognized these emotional overtones very early and instinctively responded very strongly to the exciting danger of the fall, and the repose and the peace of the recovery.

Doris used this technique in the service of her vision of mankind. Characteristically, Doris's vision was intellectually clear in her mind. In a letter she wrote to John Martin, she expressed her philosophy by defending her choice of Bach's music as accompaniment in a program that consisted entirely of Bach pieces. These quotes come from Selma Jeanne Cohen's biography, *Doris Humphrey*. In answer to an article of January 17, 1943, in which Martin objected to her choreographing to music that was intended for listening, he said, "Perhaps Miss Humphrey is dancing to this music because she loves it." However, while she did love Bach's music, she had a different, stronger motivation for using it:

> It seems to me that the motivation behind all my dances, from *The Shakers* to the *Choral Preludes* (fifteen years) has been the same to the point of monotony—and can be epitomized in the Shaker faith that "ye shall be saved when ye are shaken free of sin."
>
> In fact this seems so obvious to me that I am surprised and also pleased to find myself uncriticized for evangelism, and a general paucity of fresh ideas. Perhaps that can be attributed to the limitless possibilities of the theme and my skill and imagination as a choreographer.

By the way, Doris Humphrey never accepted an orthodox religious outlook; nevertheless, as you can see from her words, she was a very moral person. The date tells us that this letter was written in the middle of World War II. Doris continued:

> Now is the time for me to tell of the nobility that the human spirit is capable of, stress the grace that is in us, give the young dancers a chance to move harmoniously with each other, say, in my small way, there is hope as long as corners remain where unity prevails.
>
> Perhaps I am not succeeding in expressing these ideas—however, this is the intention. I picked Bach for music because I still think he has the greatest of all genius for these very qualities of variety held in unity, of grandeur of the human spirit, of grace for fallen man; not only this, but I sincerely believe the music has movement in it, based on dances of forgotten men or women who are the unknown authors of much of the music of this or any other age.

In 1935 and 1936, Doris set a new standard for excellence in modern dance with a masterwork—actually three compositions—that she finally saw as a trilogy. But because the three pieces together—*New Dance, With My Red Fires*, and *Theater Piece*—took about three hours to perform, they were never presented on one program. *New Dance* was the first modern dance of its length and stature. It is symphonic in structure. A man and a woman each dance a theme of identity and moral conviction. The themes interweave as does their relationship. A group of women and a group of men take up the themes and the development proceeds as in an orchestral score. There is rivalry and pettiness along the way, but finally a satisfying, triumphant resolution. Wallingford Riegger did the music, as he did for *Theater Piece* and *With My Red Fires*. *Theater Piece* was specific, where *New*

Dance was abstract. It presented a surrealistic view of hucksters in the relentless pursuit of money; of women on the make for men in "Hunting Dance"; and of sportsmen and politicians out for glory. Finally, *The Race*, which was composed by Charles Weidman, throws all kinds of people into a greedy, feudal competition for the goodies of life. In the epilogue, a strong female figure gets everybody's hushed attention and directs them to a meaningful statement of cooperation.

If you are interested in Doris's real-life conflicting roles of woman versus artist, *With My Red Fires* is a most interesting reflection of her innermost feelings. It portrays the hindrances to humane morality that lie in destructive personal relationships. The villain of the piece is the Matriarch, who opposes the loving union of a young couple. The Matriarch whips the group up into a frantic hunt for the lovers, to prevent their mating. Here is what Doris's husband wrote to her when he saw her perform *With My Red Fires* in 1942:

> I'm afraid that I was so overwhelmed by your performance in the murder that for the rest of the evening I was unreceptive—numbed—or shall we say, just plain scared. Of course, I am not obliged to accept you in your characteristic role, but I usually do.
>
> My living with you makes me perfectly aware that you have a drop of everything—saint and sinner—God and Demon. But, to see one of the less acceptable elements brought out, exaggerated, dramatized, given all the trappings of authenticity and performed with such power and vigor, is, to say the least of it, overpowering. Yet the character is not by any means repulsive. Quite the opposite. The body under that beautiful, vivacious face is full of fire and grace, serpentine in its fascination—vulgar yet hypnotic.

Marriage and Collaboration with José Limón. By then, Doris and Charles Woodford had been married for ten years, and their son, Charles Humphrey Woodford, was nine years old. Doris had been against marriage and its blotting out of the wife's identity, no less than had Isadora or Martha. But she fell in love with a British navy man eight years her junior, and finally yielded to Woodford's proposal when she was thirty-seven years old. She bore a child when she was thirty-eight. Marriage and motherhood made tremendous problems for Doris. She was never free from the guilty self-doubts with which so many women have become familiar in the 1980s and 1990s. Was she giving too much to her career at the expense of her family? (Her mother was another for whom Doris felt responsible and guilty of neglect.) But she never doubted that dance was her real calling.

Fortunately, her husband Charles Woodford was away at sea most of the time. Further, he was an unusual man in that he recognized Doris's genius and understood her absorption in dance. Fortunately, too, for their son, Doris was blessed with caring friends like Pauline Lawrence and José Limón. Limón was not only Doris's most talented company member, he

married Pauline Lawrence and the two became a second set of parents for
the boy, who spent summers at their farm. Pauline Lawrence Limón,
because of concern both for her husband José and her good friend Doris,
was also the matchmaker responsible for one of the great artistic alliances
in modern dance. When Doris was in the depths of despair, in 1945, her
dancing days at an end, it was Pauline who insisted that she continue to
choreograph; that she work out her ideas by using the willing body of José
Limón, who had been recently released from the army and was not quite
sure how to get moving again.

Their first collaboration, *Lament for Ignacio Sanchez Mejias* (1946, music
by Norman Lloyd), is a great work, perhaps the crowning achievement of
Doris Humphrey's life. When Doris Humphrey created *Lament*, she started
with a scenario that was already in existence. This was a poem of the same
title by Federico Garcia Lorca which told of a bullfighter's death in the ring,
and of his beautiful nobility in life. Lorca used repetition of the line, "At
five in the afternoon" to strike home the awful finality of the bullfighter
passing from life to death at a precise moment. Humphrey choreographed
the poem for three figures: one woman as the powerful Guardian of the
Bullfighter's Destiny who repeatedly announces the phrase, "At five in the
afternoon" and directs all the action; another woman as the Witness and
Mourner who cries out her passionate caring for the Bullfighter; and the
Bullfighter, who does not speak, but through dance movements, confronts
his mortal fate with splendid bravery.

José Limón certainly contributed a great deal to the role of Ignacio
and not only through his brilliant dancing. He went through the process of
choreography with Doris from the start. With words and arm motions, she
described her ideas for each rhythmic phrase. José, who had been a leading dancer in her company for many years, understood what she wanted
and gave it back in complete movements. This is not uncommon in our
field. When a choreographer has a strong, individual style and directs a
company for a number of years, there are always company members who
understand in their bodies exactly what the choreographer wants. Mary
Wigman and Martha Graham both used their solo dancers as clay from
which to mold a part—but living clay with a mind of its own. José Limón's
talent and mind followed magnificently under Doris Humphrey's direction. He was the perfect instrument for her last works.

Any of you who are interested in coming to grips with choreography
are fortunate in the wealth of material on *Lament for Ignacio Sanchez Mejias*.
Walter Strate made a film of the dance with José Limón in the title role.
The poem by Lorca is available in English translation. Doris Humphrey's
scenario is reproduced in Selma Jeanne Cohen's biography of the choreographer. Humphrey discusses *Lament* as an example of several points in her
book *The Art of Making Dances*. Those of us who saw the original production of *Lament* never forgot its beautiful portrait of the heroic bullfighter

"with all his death upon his shoulders." Using a cast of only three, it was a tragedy of Greek proportions.

Last Works. Working through others, Doris Humphrey continued to turn out fine dance works that illustrated her principles of composition, as well as her uplifting view of the world. *Day on Earth* went even further than *Lament*, this time with only four figures: a man, a younger and an older woman, and a child. In a work of under an hour, Humphrey gave us nothing less than a rich distillation of birth, life, death, and regeneration. The action takes place in a number of scenes: First, a man is at work. He has a playful, amorous meeting with a carefree young woman, who rejects him because of his desire for permanence. Second, the rejection wounds the man, whose consolation lies in a return to work. Third, a second woman joins him. They share a home, work side by side, and produce a child, danced by an eleven-year-old girl whose unformed motions both add variety and contrast, and are touching in themselves. Fourth, the family is close and happy, until the child escapes to achieve independence, leaving the parents twisting in tense agony. Finally, they slowly pull their lives together again. At the end, the three adults lie down onstage, and the child sits above them, ready to accept the future.

Humphrey used an oblong box as a bed, table, and coffin; and a cloth as another inventively suggestive prop. She based the movements on gestures of work and play. At the same time, she designed them in interesting shapes and rhythms that alternately contrasted and harmonized. This was composition at its best. It satisfied the spectators with the pleasures of artistry at the same time that it involved them in tender, human interplay. Aaron Copland's score complements the dancers' actions without overpowering them.

And so it went: with *Ritmo Jondo*, a vigorous group-courtship ritual of men and women, meeting and parting, to a commissioned score by Carlos Surinach; and with *Ruins and Visions*, a grim look at harsh reality, based on a poem by Stephen Spender, to a Benjamin Britten score. Both of these were performed in 1953. Doris Humphrey, however, did not lack a keen sense of humor. In 1938, she did a riotous *Race of Life* (music by Vivian Fine) and succeeded in the difficult task of matching James Thurber's comic worldview. In 1946, she staged *Story of Mankind*, a *New Yorker* cartoon series by Carl Rose, again leaving the audience happily laughing.

As you can see, inspiration hit Doris Humphrey everywhere. It didn't matter whether or not the ideas were popular. Humphrey maintained that in art, the audience is comparatively indifferent to the subject matter. She wrote:

> The blunt fact is that subject matter is mostly of concern to the choreographer, and whether it takes the form of narrative, symbolism, or a conviction about

style, is of no importance. The enthusiasm for it and innate talent is what keeps it alive...what audiences see is mostly the result in movement, which is exciting or not as the case may be.

The above words are in Humphrey's book entitled *The Art of Making Dances*. Before putting her early life on paper, Doris finished a book that she had been trying to write for a great many years. In fact, she had received a Guggenheim Fellowship to do so a decade earlier. The book contains thoughts about choreography, and is still the best work ever written on that subject.

Unlike Louis Horst's approach, Doris Humphrey's applies to dance companies of any kind. The elements that she deals with—gestures, rhythm, shape, and dynamics—are present in all movement phrases. When a series of phrases are combined so that a theme or subject matter, a structure, accompaniment, and stage design are also present, then we have a dance composition. Critical viewers as well as choreographers benefit from thinking along the lines that Humphrey drew. In her day, she taught many hundreds of students at Bennington, Connecticut College, Juilliard, and the Ninety-second Street YMHA in New York City. Doris's course at the YMHA was unusual in that she used simple explanatory words in discussing choreography. Too many dancers, when asked questions about their art, reply, "If it could be said in words, I would not have danced it."

It's certainly true that words are not a substitute for experiencing a dance or any artwork. But words can add a great deal to the appreciation of that experience. Everybody learned much from the brief talks that Doris gave, and also from her patient comments about their attempts at choreography. When Doris suggested in a demonstration class that a stout girl, who fulfilled a class assignment by doing a study of a starving European child, might choose a more appropriate theme, she did not allow a trace of sarcasm to mar her friendly tone.

Doris Humphrey was a great artist. Through an unfortunate combination of circumstances having to do with her illness and her never-ending battle with a lack of money, most of her works have been lost. She lives on, however, through her considerable influence in the field, (especially on the work of José Limón) and in her writings.

Charles Weidman (1901 to 1975). During the classical period of modern dance, from 1930 to 1950, critics put Charles Weidman on the same high plane of greatness with Doris Humphrey and Martha Graham. Looking backward, however, he recedes, taking second place to Humphrey as he did in their Humphrey-Weidman Company. Of course, it is impossible to measure exactly the impact each of these artists had on other dancers or on their audiences. But in retrospect, the golden age of modern dance shines forth as a matriarchy, dominated by the theatrical visions of Martha and Doris. It was not that Charles's talent was less than the women's. Both as a dancer and as a choreographer he was first-rate. But two factors worked against him. First, Weidman did not devise his own technical system, nor did he leave us any written works. Secondly, his approach to the world, the very facility with wit and humor that was his strong point, assures Charles Weidman a lesser role in history.

In the very first Humphrey-Weidman concert, in 1928, Charles contributed two comedies. This displayed an interest that never left him. Dance comedy is rare, and audiences are always very grateful for its presence, especially on a program of modern dance where grimness is a common ingredient. Dance comedy is rare because it is hard to do funny movements with any originality. Weidman was to become one of the few dancers with a great talent for comedy, both as a creator and as a performer. But if you think about comedy for a moment, you will see that by definition it is "light." It does not carry the weight of serious drama, with its passionate commitment. We may prefer comedy to tragedy, we may seek entertainment over meaningful experience, but in the last analysis, comedy and laughter do not win our deepest respect. Don't forget, modern dancers started out in opposition to the ballet, which they dismissed as frivolous.

Now let's take a look at the man himself and at the many accomplishments in Weidman's long career. Born in Nebraska, Charles studied dance with a local teacher. Although his father thought he would make a good cartoonist, Charles was inspired by photographs of Isadora Duncan and Ruth St. Denis, and he went to Los Angeles to Denishawn, where they soon sent him on tour with the company. He stayed with Denishawn for eight years, leaving in 1928 with Doris Humphrey and Pauline Lawrence. From then on, he proceeded to fulfill his father's vision. Charles became a cartoonist in the medium of movement. Here is a description of Charles's style by the perceptive critic Margaret Lloyd:

> What he did do, he did without waste, with clear-cut pointed immediacy. He delighted in incongruities, in fragmentary, mercurial movement, in abrupt changes of tempo, rhythm and dynamics. . . .
> He jested in stroke and curlicue, lampooning right and left with his pencil-slim body, making jokes with his fingers and witty observations with his bare toes. His mouth was a cave of comedy in itself.

Weidman's first major work was *The Happy Hypocrite* (1931), with music by Herbert Elwell. It was based on a humorous piece by Max Beerbohm, and it told the story through pantomimic gestures that were enlarged into dance phrases. In this and other compositions, his choreography reminded people of commedia dell'arte, with its casual air of improvisation, which was, of course, deceptive, because all the details of movement were planned very carefully.

Charles found material for his witty pieces all around him, starting with his own life. *Quest* (1936, music by Norman Lloyd) depicted the artist trying to realize himself, and along the way confronting ostentatious, insensitive critics, and adoring society ladies. Here, as elsewhere, serious ideas were combined with foolish satire, leading the audience from laughter, to the recognition of reality, and back again.

Also in 1936, he did *Atavisms*, to music by Lehman Engel. In its first section, "Bargain Counter," the audience was amused by a floorwalker trying to hold off a group of females who were feverishly fighting over the items on sale. Less funny was "Stock Exchange," a sour portrait of a bloated capitalist facing the stock market crash of 1929. Not funny at all, but most impressive, was the concluding "Lynchtown," in which a mob full of blood lust advanced on a jail.

Charles danced his autobiography, *On My Mother's Side* (1940, the music was popular songs), followed by *And Daddy Was a Fireman* (1943), with a score by Herbert Haufrecht. Again, these pieces were done in the style of gently sophisticated cartoon strips. *Flickers* (1941, music by Lionel Nowak) was a clever representation of silent movies.

In 1945, after Doris became too ill to perform, Weidman continued composing for his own company. One of his most popular works was *Fables For Our Time* (1947), in which his style proved perfect for putting James Thurber's zany world on the stage. It was accompanied by Freda Miller's score for two pianos, as well as by a narrator, who appeared onstage and wandered through the cartoonlike scenes. Weidman continued turning out fine works for his company and also choreographing for the New York City Opera Company and on Broadway, where his carefree wit was well received.

In the late 1950s, he combined forces with sculptor Mikhail Santaro to produce a mixed-media form called the Expression of Two Arts Theater, in their own loft. Santaro, who spoke in a free-association jargon while he painted large brush strokes on paper or moved around wooden shapes, was not enthusiastically received. One reviewer said he lacked dignity and purpose. No one made such accusations against Weidman. During these evenings he performed his old solos and some new pieces in his well-known, modest, meticulous manner, with respect for the music to which he danced. Right up until his death in 1975, Charles Weidman continued to involve himself in new projects in the art of dance.

Questions for Review

1.   What view of the world did Doris Humphrey project in her choreography?

2.   Why did Humphrey claim that the audience is indifferent to the subject matter of a dance? Do you agree?

3.   How is it possible for an artist to choreograph from a wheelchair?

4.   Discuss Charles Weidman's contribution to the Humphrey-Weidman Company.

5.   Why is dance comedy difficult to perform?

26 IMPRESSIVE FIGURES

TAMIRIS, HORTON, AND LEWITZKY

In the foregoing pages I have tried to introduce you to the major figures who brought forth the modern dance from the turn of the century up until the 1930s and 1940s. During the same early period, there were other artists who created imaginatively. However, their place in this history concerns the impressions that they made on others rather than the nature of their own artistic contributions. Among the most important were Helen Tamiris in New York, Lester Horton and Bella Lewitzky on the West Coast, and Katherine Dunham who paved the way for serious black theater dance.

Helen Tamiris

Helen Tamiris (1902 to 1966) starred in exciting scenes of New York City life in the 1930s and 1940s, when the Great Depression and World War II brought despair and tragedy to many who lived through them. It was also a time of hope and idealism, which artists and intellectuals of the day both reflected and helped to shape. As a vibrant, dynamic woman with an attractive personality and a strong social conscience, Tamiris made her presence felt both within and outside of modern dance.

Tamiris's social responsibility led her to be active in the cultural life of her day. She attempted to do something about the problem that has always plagued American artists—poverty. She organized the Dance Repertory Theater, which in 1930 presented joint performances by her own group and those of Doris Humphrey and Charles Weidman, Martha Graham, and in

1931, the second and last year of the project, Agnes de Mille. The public liked these joint concerts, but the artists, plagued by another problem we have frequently encountered in these pages—vanity—were unable (aside from Tamiris herself) to bend their egos to Tamiris's vision of sharing.

Then Tamiris was the organizing force behind a National Dance Congress and the American Dance Association. As the president of the American Dance Association, she went directly to Washington, D.C. and made sure that dance became a part of the Federal Theater. The Federal Theater was an exciting social and theatrical experiment, undertaken as part of Franklin D. Roosevelt's New Deal, and Tamiris became the chief choreographer. Before the theater was closed for lack of funds, all the leading modern dancers had taken part and the public had enjoyed their work immensely. After the shutdown, Tamiris began a new career in the 1940s as the most successful modern dance choreographer on Broadway. She added greatly to the appeal of shows like *Annie Get Your Gun* and *Showboat*. In 1944, she also took part in *The People's Bandwagon*, an interracial review organized to help elect President Roosevelt for a fourth term.

Born to Russian immigrants, dance attracted Helen Becker (who later took the name Tamiris) in her very early years. To keep her from dancing in the streets, the family sent her to take classes at a settlement house when she was eight years old; and at sixteen she got herself accepted into the Metropolitan Opera Ballet. She spent two years under the direction of Rosina Galli, dancing in a rigid Italian style, and then set out to look (in vain) for something less restrictive and more satisfying, as in the styles of Michel Fokine and Isadora Duncan. Finally, like Humphrey and Graham, she was forced to find what she wanted on her own. In 1927, she began her concert career in New York with *Dance Moods*. Louis Horst was her accompanist and she presented performances that were danced to modern American composers, one to Gershwins's *Rhapsody in Blue*, one called *Subconcious*, to Debussy, one without music, and *Impressions of the Bull Ring*, to a piece by Calleja.

In 1928, her second program included *Joshua Fit the Battle of Jericho*, with choreography inspired by a Negro spiritual. This type of dance became her hallmark. In that year she also gave a concert in Paris, where her warm, magnetic dancing and her fresh approach to repertory were immediately successful. Like Isadora Duncan before her, Tamiris was surrounded by artists of every description. But while she found the Parisian atmosphere very stimulating, she knew she needed to create in the United States. Her philosophy (as quoted in John Martin's *Book of the Dance*) was clear: "Art is international, but the artist is a product of nationality. No artist can achieve full maturity unless he recognizes his role as a citizen, taking responsibility to act . . . The validity of modern dance is rooted in its ability to express modern problems and further, to make modern audiences want to do something about them."

These beliefs led Tamiris to create dances with human significance, using themes of antimilitarism, the cry of oppressed peoples, and the need for social justice. She won a public wider than the usual modern dance audience, especially for her biggest successes which incorporated Negro songs of protest. These included *How Long Brethern?* (the 1930s saw innumerable lynchings in the South). *Abelante* was made up of scenes choreographed to poems from modern Spain to express her identification with the loyalists. They were troops fighting a losing battle against General Franco, who led an army to victory in Spain in 1937, and then ruled as a dictator until shortly before his death in 1975.

Through her work with such shows, and through the company that she directed along with her husband and dancing partner, Daniel Nagrin, Tamiris affected the development of a number of dancers. Some who danced under her direction and went on to make their own reputations include: Klarna Pinska, Dorothy Bird, Joseph Gifford, Mary Anthony, Pearl Primus, Talley Beatty, Valerie Bettis, Barton Mumaw, and Virginia Tanner. Her pupils also included John Garfield and Franchot Tone at the Group Theater, where she taught classes in movement for actors. In sum, Helen Tamiris rose above the crowd in the 1930s and 1940s as a vivid artist who cared deeply about the issues of her day, and at the same time, enlivened the dance world with her productions.

Lester Horton

Now we leave New York for a visit to California. We speak of American modern dance, but this really is a very big country. Even today, there are significant regional differences as you travel from one coast to the other. In the early 1900s, the Pacific coast was far away from New York, which was the center of the new dance. However, things were also happening out west, mainly around the magnetic figure of Lester Horton (1906 to 1953). His life and work are discussed in *Dance Perspectives,* Number 31.

When he was five years old, Horton, an Indiana boy, fell in love with Native American culture at a Wild West show, where he saw tribal dances. This brought him to dance. The fact that for two years he studied ballet, which had no connection at all to tribal dance, is characteristic of Horton's entire career. In 1928, on tour with *Hiawatha,* a dance drama based on Longfellow's poem for which Horton designed the costumes and lighting and also played the title role, he landed in California—and there he stayed. Horton's personal movement range was very limited. His imaginative movement and choreographic styles were not. You cannot describe Horton's output unless you use words like *changeable, restless,* and *variable.* We have met artists before who never settled into one style, but he took this quality to the nth degree.

Consider these pieces, set in the 1951 season: *Tropic Trio* included a Brazilian after-work dance of field hands; and *Cumbia* was a long, erotic Panamanian number in which the woman was sensually provocative but aloof, and the man challenged her with equal sensuality while manipulating burning candles. *On the Upbeat* had four lively sections: "Kathak," which was a vigorous, turning, (East) Indian dance with jangling ankle bells; "The Brushoff Blues," which was a campy treatment of a languid blues number; "Chasidic," which expressed an Eastern European, Jewish, joyful celebration of God, climaxing in fifteen successive leaps (almost undanceable) by the men; and *Pwe Bop*, which featured colorful costumes and a technical display. In *Another Touch of Klee*, Horton gave his visual sense free rein and came up with an imaginative movement fantasy in the spirit of Paul Klee's whimsical paintings. There was a lavish use of masks, ropes, and even soap bubbles. The score was by Stan Kenton. In previous seasons, he did a *Salome*, a *Lysistrata*, Mexican themes, an Aztec work, *Voodoo Ceremonial*, a Chinese fantasy, *An American in Paris*, and so on. For our purposes, we always like to hear about a new version of *Le Sacre du Printemps*, (The Rite of Spring). Horton's was done in 1937 in the Hollywood Bowl, with Bella Lewitzky as the Chosen One. In this production, the Stravinsky score and the angular, sensual movements of the dancers, along with their barefoot appearance, were labelled by some as "obscene," and raised a storm of protest almost as big as the original one in 1913.

Added to this wide-ranging approach to style was the fact that Horton could never be counted on to do the same number consistently. He changed titles, music, and phrases, to the point where his company members were confused about which version they were doing at a given performance. So there was no Horton repertory, nothing that could be passed on or preserved, because each season offered a totally new program. Incidentally, Horton was just as likely to produce works for the movies (he did the choreography for *The Phantom of the Opera*, and sixteen other films), or for nightclubs and shows, as he was for the dance theater. Well then, what did he contribute to the dance world? What made Joyce Trisler speak of the magic of his theater, which was not just an abstract artistic theater. It was also, after 1947, a building in Los Angeles. The realization of a Horton dream, it had actual, physical spaces for dance classes, for performances, and best of all, for constructing sets, props, and costumes. What made his followers like Frank Eng think of this building as *the* theater? as almost a religion? What made Alvin Ailey, years later, remember Horton as a wonderful model, one whom he always tried to imitate?

Horton was a talented, versatile, magnetic figure, who cast a spell on those around him. He was excited and stimulated by *things*—design materials like fabric, feathers, beads, colored paint, dyes, yarns, and also instruments like drums and other percussion devices—and his excitement was contagious. He was a prolific creator in movement and in design, and a born teacher. Horton's vision of art was grandiose and inspiring. He had great rapport with people of other ethnic groups. Native Americans, Mexicans, and blacks often visited and taught in his theater. His company was interracial well before the idea was fashionable. The downside of his insatiable appetite for creation was a lack of discipline and instability. Throughout his life, his prodigious activities fed an unfocussed personality, dropping him into depression, and turning him to alcohol. He abused his body and his store of energy, even after he had been warned by a heart attack and these abuses led to his death at forty-seven.

Horton's way of producing art meant that movements and other details were not refined; rhythmic counts weren't set. He was also open to accusations of flagrant imitation, because of the following. He used abstract platforms and columns to form sets (like Humphrey and Weidman). He combined mime with group and solo movements as well as words (including some of Lorca's poetry) in the service of dramatic and psychological subjects (like Humphrey). Horton even choreographed an *American Document* (but this was before Graham did). Later, he tapped into the social and political fomentation of the 1930s with *The Dictator, Strike*, and others (like Helen Tamiris). On the other hand, while Horton admired what he saw of these artists' works, keep in mind that first of all, he remained isolated in Los Angeles while they all clustered in New York City. Secondly, his similar works sometimes preceded theirs. It is a case of different sensitive minds picking up the same vibrations that are given off as a new cultural age begins, the spirit of an age, remember? In a way, it is fortunate that his interests were so varied, because through him the West Coast was introduced to the main currents of American modern dance.

The people in Horton's classes and his company, which was large and amorphous, were in a continuous state of flux. Among his better-known, highly talented dancers were: Carmen de Lavallade, Joyce Trisler, James Truitte, James Mitchell, Eleanor Brooks, Rudi Gernreich (later famous as the fashion designer), of course, Alvin Ailey, and from 1934 to 1950, a most important asset, Bella Lewitzky. We will hear a lot about Alvin Ailey when we come to the chapter on jazz and black dance. At that time, we will also meet Katherine Dunham, an early pioneer of black theater dance. Now we will get acquainted with Lester Horton's partner, Bella Lewitzky.

Bella Lewitzky

Lewitzky was born, in 1915, in a desert community of idealists. The idealism was not artistic, but political. Llano del Rio was a utopian socialist colony, engaged in an experiment of cooperative living. She was only three years old when the colony moved to North Carolina. However, her family stayed behind in Los Angeles and Bella was really raised on Llano del Rio's principles and its memories. When she became interested in dance, this strong sense of idealistic principle never left her.

In 1934, Bella Lewitzky joined Horton, first as a student, and then as a partner. She brought a first-rate performing ability and a flare for organizing class work to his unbounded conception of theater dance. She was blessed with the ability to understand what he wanted, to execute it beautifully, and to explain it clearly to others. Lewitzky became the instrument through which Horton realized his choreographic vision, and the disciplined mind and body through which he established his technique. Together, they dreamed about setting up a theater school, but this project remained on hold. Lewitzky assisted Horton in developing a basic technique of movement, with the goal of preparing dancers to perform any movement sequences they might wish to use in any style.

According to Joyce Trisler's evaluation in *Dance Perspectives*, Number 31, the Horton technique *was* successful in producing strong, versatile dancers *without* mannerisms. At the same time, dramatic projection was not neglected. Exacting balance studies made "legs and backs of steel." Horton-trained people were known for their high extensions and fluid back motion. The thirty-minute workout in elevation that was part of every class enabled them to do aerial movements with ease. They were good with turns, falls, and sequences that rose from the floor into the air and returned. They gained a broad vocabulary of ethnic gestures; and at the same time, they learned facility in moving different parts of the body in different modes and rhythms from challenging exercises in coordination. The one drawback Trisler noted was the frequency of back and knee injuries, which she attributed to carelessness in "over-stretching," and to improper exercises for the knees. No doubt Horton was the main offender. According to Lewitzky, his classes were so strenuous that they were "heroic," and he didn't bother with careful warm-ups.

At the school, Bella Lewitzky not only taught the technique, she was the ultimate demonstration model. The word was out: "If Bella can't do it, it can't be done." She was also Horton's outstanding performer. Her 1937 role in *Salome* was described by a reviewer in this way: "She danced with the grace and seduction of the panther, the sinuousness of the snake, the fleetness of the deer, the delicacy of the bird, and the strength and pride of the lion. The audience was held at a tension seldom experienced in the theater." The Horton-Lewitzky association must have been rewarding for both. It also, like many other dance alliances we have already observed, had more than its share of rough spots. The two artists had opposite personalities. She was a disciplined, well-organized perfectionist. He was a wildly creative, cavalier inventor. She wanted a small, well-trained company. He loved to fill the studio—and the stage—with large groups of excited people.

Then, in 1939, Newell Taylor Reynolds appeared at the theater, first as a student at the school, and then as a company member. In 1940, Newell and Bella married, and danced together in *Romeo and Juliet*, a duet which Horton choreographed for them. In 1941, World War II arrived. Company men were drafted. Newell went to work at Lockheed. Horton began to accept engagements at nightclubs, taking the company to the Follies Bergères in New York. The more serious-minded Bella regarded nightclub engagements as a commercial sellout of her art. In 1944, she injured her foot and ended up in Chicago to be near her husband Newell, who was stationed there in the navy. This was the first time Lewitzky and Horton went their separate ways.

In 1946, they got together with Newell, back in Los Angeles, with the intention of making the old dream come true: a permanent home for a dance theater school and company. This time, after two years of working long hours each day, and with the help of dedicated friends and dancers, they achieved their goal. In May 1948, the Dance Theater was initiated with a fourth version of *Salome*, complete with Greek chorus; *Total Incantation*, a simple view of Native American coming-of-age and marriage rituals spruced up with lavish costumes and props; and *The Beloved*, a dance drama inspired by a newspaper story about a man who beat his adulterous wife to death with a Bible.

Frank Eng, who managed the Dance Theater after Bella and Newell left, and indeed for ten years after Lester Horton's death, saw this performance before he knew any of the people involved, as a critic for the *Los Angeles Daily News*. He wrote (in *Dance Perspectives*, Number 31) that *The Beloved* was a miracle in its combination of Lewitzky's "fantastic technique" and Horton's "flawless choreographic craftsmanship." The dance "raped" his senses to such a degree that he was in a state of shock for the rest of the program. But by the theater's second season, the strain between the principals was not only beginning to tell on Lewitzky and Horton; it had affected the entire company, causing people to take sides and expend endless energy defending one or the other. In 1950, the partnership was dissolved. The money involved was negligible. It was purely a question of personality.

On her own, Bella Lewitzky taught children and adults, choreographed, and danced. Then, in 1955, when her daughter Nora Elizabeth Reynolds was born, she shifted her interests from performing to teaching, with an emphasis on teaching children, so that she could become a "proper" mother. As the years passed, she came up with inventive approaches to early childhood training that integrated dance with all the theater arts. Once her daughter Nora became an independent dance student, circumstances drew Bella back again into a full-time career as a dance artist, at the head of her own company. In 1971, Bella Lewitzky brought the company east for its concert debut in New York. It was not the group, whose choreography by Lewitzky was criticized as derivative, that won praise. Rather it was Bella herself, then fifty-six, who received rave reviews. Clive Barnes wrote in *The New York Times*: "Bella Lewitzky is a remarkable woman, one of America's great modern dancers. *On the Brink* struck me as one of the great individual performances of a contemporary modern dancer. Her technique is remarkable, and she has a most exquisite, natural sense of movement." During the same period, Bella was chosen to form the dance department at a newly formed California Institute of the Arts in Valencia, thirty-five miles north of Los Angeles. In 1978, Lewitzky won a *Dance Magazine* award both for her own dancing and for her nationwide influence on dance education.

Questions for Review

1.   Why wasn't Tamiris in the mainstream of modern dance?

2.   Discuss the problems in organizing the dance community.

3.   How would you characterize Lester Horton's style?

4.   What were Bella Lewitzky's contributions to dance education?

27 MID-CENTURY MODERN DANCE

ANNA SOKOLOW AND JOSÉ LIMÓN

The Influence of Modern Dance

By the 1940s, modern dance was a fact of life in America, even if the ordinary citizen never heard of it. Like a stone dropped into the cultural pool, the ripples created by modern dance touched distant shores of everyday life in education, entertainment, fashion, and therapy. Young people in public schools and colleges were learning creative rhythms that were adapted from modern dance systems. Broadway musical shows, movies, nightclub revues, and later, TV, all showed the strong imprint of modern dance in both choreography and general staging. Women were wearing fitted leotard tops together with bias-cut flared skirts copied from a dance teacher's outfit. In psychiatric hospitals, expressive movement was tried as a means of releasing patients' pent-up emotions. Even at religious conferences, there was talk of including dance in ritual worship.

The moving forces behind these activities were the dozens, and then the hundreds, of followers of each of the people discussed so far, and the hundreds more who in turn learned from them or were inspired from afar. This also happened in ballet of course, except for one big difference. From its early beginnings, and through all its changes down to the present, modern dance has embodied the idea that one becomes a modern dancer (rather than a ballet dancer) to create compositions, rather than to interpret the choreography of others. This means that each company assembled by a modern dancer becomes a breeding ground for new choreographers who break away to form their own individual styles, companies, and schools. Conversely, when you come across a modern dancer, it is of great interest to trace from where he or she came. Just as we say in psychological jargon, "I know where you're coming from," to show we understand that person, so it is in art, the more we know about a person's background, the closer we feel to him or her.

To mention just a few examples in theater dance, we find that Valerie Bettis and Mary Anthony started out as performers and teachers with Hanya Holm. Pearl Lang, Jane Dudley, and Jean Erdman began as soloists in the Martha Graham Company. Katherine Litz, Sybil Shearer, Joseph Gifford, and others began their careers in the Humphrey-Wiedman Company. Then all these artists went on to create works for themselves and their own companies. Similarly, in education, we find that Martha Hill, a member of the Martha Graham Company from 1929 to 1931, did an outstanding job at Bennington and Julliard, just as Pauline Koner, a beautiful performer of the works of Doris Humphrey and José Limón, went on to direct modern dance studies at the North Carolina School of the Arts.

You can see the very real problem that now confronts the historian. With so many distinguished artists, who is to be presented here? My solution is to pick two individuals, Anna Sokolow and José Limón both of whom have had a tremendous impact on audiences, students, and other modern dancers. My hope is that these discussions will give you starting points and approaches for further research on any other dancers who pique your interest.

Anna Sokolow

Anna Sokolow (born in 1912) found her inspiration and direction in life through Martha Graham, in whose company she danced from 1930 to 1938. When Sokolow first created her own dances (which she did as early as 1934), she immediately expressed her anger at social injustice, something that never disappeared from her work. Unlike Tamiris, however, who treated these themes with an upbeat directness, Sokolow developed a style that was ironic, subtle, and finally, grim. A typical Sokolow concert including three of her best-known pieces—*Dreams, Lyric Suite,* and *Time Plus Seven*—leaves an impression of bitter suffering.

Dreams (1961) is Sokolow's indictment of Nazi Germany, a series of nightmarish scenes presented with forceful, dramatic impact, to the accompaniment of Bach, Webern, Teo Macero, and utterances of human horror. A girl in white climbs convulsively over an unending line of bodies. Men and women run desperately at hopeless attempts at escape, but to no avail. A woman seeks sanctuary at doors behind which religious hymns can be heard. People gasp, fall, scream silently, and clutch at each other. Perhaps the most shocking episode features an actual child, a spindle-legged pathetic creature who walks in bewilderment toward a woman bent in abject despair.

Lyric Suite (1953), performed to a harsh score by Alban Berg, is made up of four solos expressing introspective sorrow, fear, twitching anxiety, and lonesome defiance; a duet of unsure love; and finally, a quartet of lyrical serenity. *Time Plus Seven* (1968, score by Teo Macero) opens with a pop poster of weird exhibitionists crying out, "Pow!" "Bam!" and "Maharishi!" The second part shows couples going through *Vogue*-type poses of fashionable dance and disinterested chatter. The third section is a sharply mechanized ballet of kooky automatism. The closing movement presents a bloody quartet of wounded soldiers, piling on each other in grotesque, passive slow motion. While there are occasional moments of humor in this portrayal of today's world, the whole piece is driven home with its acid disgust.

Another probing Sokolow work is *Rooms* (1955, music by Kenyon Hopkins). There is a group of eight young men and women. But it is not actually a group, because the piece reveals that each is imprisoned in the self, grappling alone with his or her psychological demons. The stage is set with eight chairs. Each dancer moves in isolation on a chair, the chair symbolizing a private prison. The solitude is present even in the duet, where a male and female pulse and crack their hands against each other, trying in vain to "break through." It is present when three "couples" dance together, their legs and arms reaching past one another in desire that returns to each self, unfulfilled. Sokolow was quoted by Joseph Gale in *Dance Magazine*:

> Perhaps for what I am, there will always be an underlying note in my work of how I feel about life. I just don't think it's a bowl of cherries. This is not a utopia after all, so why delude ourselves? If somebody feels and wants to speak the truth about it, why not?

She probably said this with a trace of an ironic smile that was in keeping with the quiet self-assurance of her personal manner. Sokolow believed that audiences who see only gloom in her choreography have not uncovered the basic harmony and structure that are also present.

> If Louis Horst were alive, he'd say to me, "That's perfect construction," which it is. Every single work I do has that. There is nothing haphazard. Every casual-looking, spontaneous movement is thought out and worked out and the performer then is trained to understand.

This reflects her long stay with Graham, at which time she studied composition with Louis Horst, and then went on to become his teaching assistant.

In that capacity, and on her own, she has always been generous with teaching and advice for scores of American dancers and students.

In 1970, she worked with Ray Cook at Dartmouth College. Cook, who had spent four years in Sokolow's dance company, was now resident teacher and choreographer at Dartmouth. She was setting scenes from Samuel Beckett's *Act Without Words* for a student demonstration. Beckett's script is a chillingly simple description of a man flung into the desert. Water is dangled in front of him, and ropes and cubes appear on the stage. But no matter what he tries, he cannot reach the water and collapses. While he lies inert, the water comes within reach, but he makes no attempt to get it, and the piece ends as he stares at his own hands.

Ray Cook stood quietly waiting for Miss Sokolow's instructions: "Go offstage. Don't think of dancing. Feel rather like a man wandering around for hours in a desolate place—covered with dust—hot—no food. Fling yourself on the stage, any way you want to."

The dancer walked into the wings. Suddenly he catapulted himself onstage, held himself in suspension, turned slowly, and sank to the floor.

"Try it again. Do all the preparation offstage. Run in and throw yourself on the ground."

He did.

"Do it again. That's good. Feel as though you fell over a rock."

Miss Sokolow explained that her art must have structure, technique, and content. By structure, she meant that the piece must grow as an organic whole, with the parts carefully shaped in relation to one another and according to the classical principles of thematic statement, development, and resolution. When she taught the demonstration class, Sokolow's attitude toward technique combined an understanding of the physical side with words like these:

> The back holds the body straight . . . Work with the neck. Without the neck there is no head . . . What's missing in your movement is muscle...All motion should light up . . . Your head must always indicate focus . . .I don't believe in positions—I must see how the movement got there.

The content is her reason for doing a piece. An idea may come from music, poetry, the Bible, or a play. One student observer asked, "Do you always work with man's loneliness?"

"No," she answered, "but I have a lot. It seems to come out that way." The final product is shaped with the dancer, as we saw.

> I start with a conception, not a blueprint. The dancer or actor gets specific directions. If it doesn't come out, I do what I can with verbal imagery to make it come out.

Thus do many choreographers use their "live" material. They don't invent and control every last gesture. They conceive the look and feel of the dance landscape, but then allow the qualities of individual dancers to help color in the details.

Like Tamiris, Sokolow has never limited social responsibility to her own creations. In 1939, when she resided in Mexico City as a teacher and choreographer, she formed a modern dance group there, the first one that country had ever had. While in Mexico, she did her own version of Lorca's *Lament for Ignacio Sanchez Mejias*, (music by S. Revueltas). Then, in 1953, she made her first visit to Israel, and helped the young Yemenite company, Inbal, to take on a more professional attitude. She has returned to Israel as an advisor to the dance artists of the country, as well as a choreographer, at least thirty times in the years since.

José Limón

As Anna Sokolow had absorbed the importance of structure from Louis Horst, José Limón (1908 to 1972) inherited his deep respect for structure from Doris Humphrey. Although their styles and views of the world were very different, both Sokolow and Limón shared the philosophy that marked the modern dance choreographers of their generation: that choreography demanded formally disciplined treatment of movement themes. When José Limón appeared in *Lament for Ignacio Sanchez Mejias* (choreographed by Doris Humphrey), he was hailed by critics and the public alike as the leading male dancer of American modern dance. But that wasn't all. From then until the middle 1950s, he also came through as one of the most important choreographers in the field. For example, his masterpiece entitled *The Moor's Pavane* (1949, music by Purcell) entered the repertoire of the American Ballet Theater, the Royal Danish Ballet, the Royal Swedish Ballet, the Joffrey Company, the National Ballet of Canada, and others, something few other modern choreographers can claim.

Although Limón, born in Mexico in 1908, came with his family to the U.S. when he was a little boy, he never lost his attachment to Spanish-Mexican styles of art. His movement technique, known by the proud, high carriage of his torso, arms, and head, clearly reflects that heritage. However, while he was born surrounded by dance and music (and played Bach on the organ), he started out to be a painter. After a short stay at UCLA where he found academic art education dull and irrelevant, he went to New York to study painting. But there he was only frustrated in his love for El Greco, because everyone in New York was busily imitating the French Impressionists.

Then, in 1928, he chanced to attend a dance concert held by Harold Kreutzberg. We noted in an earlier chapter how Ted Shawn was inspired by seeing Ruth St. Denis dance. Well, when Limón saw Kreutzberg on tour from Germany, he was overwhelmed in the same way. Years later, he wrote his reaction. His words are included in Selma Jeanne Cohen's *The Modern Dance, Seven Statements of Belief*:

> I saw that a man could, with dignity and a towering majesty, dance. Not mince, prance, cavort, do "fancy dancing" or "show-off" steps. No. Dance as Michelangelo's visions dance and as the music of Bach dances.

Thus was Limón's direction in life determined and he set about finding a modern dance school. By the time he got to the Humphrey-Weidman Company in 1930, he had reached the advanced age of twenty-two and had to work very hard to achieve balance and coordination. Work hard he could, and he did, and succeeded magnificently—and not only in controlling his body. By 1931, he was already choreographing:

> In Doris Humphrey I found a master who knew that every dancer, being an individual, was an instrument unique and distinct from any other, and that in consequence that this dancer must ultimately find his own dance as she had found hers.

In 1937, he won a scholarship to the Bennington College dance school where he produced a group work entitled *Danza de la Muerte* (Dance of Death) with music by Henry Clark and Norman Lloyd. This subject, which we discussed in the chapter on the Middle Ages, fascinates many a choreographer. In addition to his personal background in the Spanish dance style, Limón was drawn like so many modern dancers to the fate of the Spanish people during and after their repressive civil war.

In World War II, José Limón was drafted into the army where he was placed in special services as an entertainer. But although he did it as conscientiously as he did everything, Limón did not like entertaining.

> I discovered that the commercial form and the serious form of the modern dance were incompatible . . . the serious dance demands incorruptibility that makes no concessions to so-called popular taste.

Limón struggled to keep his muscles in shape and when the army released him, he went to ballet classes and back to the Humphrey-Weidman Company where he resumed performing. Then he went out on his own (along with costume designer Pauline Lawrence, whom he married in 1942) to form a fine company with Pauline Koner, Lucas Hoving, Ruth Currier, and Betty Jones.

The Moor's Pavane. Just as you can study Doris Humphrey's *Lament* as a splendid example of the use of poetry with movement, so you can also

José Limón's work, "The Moor's Pavane," is a modern dance classic.

study *The Moor's Pavane* as choreography that brilliantly combines expressive dramatic conflict with musical form. (Here too, Walter Strate made a film using the original cast.) *The Moor's Pavane* can be used as an example of the theme of this history: namely, that traditions in Western theater dance recur constantly, varied as they may be in different times and places.

A pavane is a dance form of pompous, proud steps that can be traced to the strictly formal court life in Spain during the Inquisition. Choreographer José Limón was imbued with the spirit and culture of that country. The *content* of the work, based on Shakespeare's play *Othello*, concerns jealous plotting at court, passionate love, and murder to avenge dishonor. The *setting* is Renaissance Italy, where court dancing appears at the beginning of this history as a forerunner of ballet.

Purcell's music reminds us again of the close ties between dance and music. Purcell lived and wrote in England in the seventeenth century, after Shakespeare's death. He wrote numerous suites that were simple arrangements of fast and slow dances. However, as a reflection of the Baroque spirit (which is grand, elaborate, and theatrical), Purcell's music contains elements of heroic emotion that were most suitable for the high-flown visions of Limón and Shakespeare.

The *structure* of *The Moor's Pavane* is the musical A-B-A-B-A. The A sections are visually shaped and formed like actual court dances. We see the four dramatic characters—the Moor (Othello), his wife (Desdemona), a friend (Iago, the villainous courtier), and his wife (Emilia)—move together in stately, gracious patterns. This is also a rondo form, with the constant return to a choral theme. The plot builds in the B sections, where the characters express their relationships in telling gestures, the action moves forward, and the piece builds to its tragic climax.

There Is A Time is another Limón piece with an especially satisfying structure. Its content is based on a passage from Ecclesiastes. "To everything there is a season: a time to be born, to die, to plant, to kill, to mourn, to dance, to love, to hate…a time for war, a time for peace." Again we have a rondo, with each emotional phrase expressed in a dramatic section that is linked to the next one by a chorus. In the choral sections, the whole group moves in a circle to show us both the closeness of the community and the continuity of its existence. Norman dello Joio wrote the music to suit this biblical theme.

The Exiles (1950, with music by Arnold Schönberg) also has a biblical base. It is a duet portraying Adam and Eve and it falls into two parts. "The Flight" shows the shame and despair of expulsion, and "The Remembrance" recalls the joyful innocence of Paradise. There is a short conclusion, returning to the theme of exile but on a more resigned note. The choreography is clear both dramatically and formally. At times, it is even literal in its indication of body self-consciousness. However, it also develops gestures into passages of movement which are beautiful and deeply stirring emotionally.

The Winged (1966) is not one of Limón's famous works. It is mentioned here not only because it emerged at its Connecticut College premiere as a masterpiece, but because its content has relevance to the entire field of dance. *The Winged* is developed like a theme with variations that explore all aspects of flight: psychological, mythological, and literal. The unifying theme of flight is always present in the use of off-balance bodies and outstretched arms. In the twenty or so sections that make up the presentation, there are an antagonistic duo, love, whimsy, greed in a delightfully humorous section entitled "East of Harpies," soaring patterns of design, the eagle, the phoenix, the Furies, and so on. With great creative inventiveness, an endless series of moods and ideas is spun forth.

Nonstop Flight. In the chapter on Martha Graham, I spoke of a lecture to her students about flight: "The meaning of flight—anything cleaving through space…the spectator does not have to analyze what flight means, but he should have the feeling or sensation of flight." Now please consider this idea: the art of dance is really all about flight, no matter what the style. This point was made one hundred and fifty years earlier in the

Romantic ballet. The great ballets produced then in France, and later in Russia, all featured winged creatures. They were symbolic of flight, of the spiritual half of man's nature, of the poetic fantasy that lifts people on wings of ecstasy and vision, away from everyday physical reality. Modern dancers appeared at first to reverse this principle. Mary Wigman and Martha Graham certainly related downward to the stage floor as much as, or more than, they did to the upper reaches of space. But even when a dance piece is rooted deep in the earth (or in daily experience), if it is successfully composed and well performed, the audience feels stimulated, excited, energized, in short, uplifted. And while it is fair to say that a good work of art in any medium communicates the artist's flight of fancy, in dance, where the instrument is the physical body of the dancer, there is a unique type of flight. The spectator "cleaves through space" vicariously (kinesthetically), and is uplifted beyond the realm of ordinary movement sensations.

Questions for Review

1. In what ways has Anna Sokolow made her presence felt in the world of modern dance?

2. Have you ever seen a Sokolow piece? What was your impression?

3. Describe José Limón's choreography in *The Moor's Pavane* or *There is a Time*.

4. What is the origin of the stylistic components of the Limón technique?

28 AFRO-AMERICAN DANCERS

JAZZ BEAT

To introduce the topic of black dancers in America, we pose two hard questions: (1) Who gets the credit for bringing black artists into the mainstream of contemporary dance? 2) Is the dance world fully integrated even today? The question of credit is one that we face in every phase of history. There are no exact beginnings, moments when we can say with confidence that this was the first modern dancer, this was the first classical ballet, and so on. There are always forerunners, artists and events containing hints of things to come. This part of the story is no exception. John Martin in his *Book of the Dance* mentions Hemsley Winfield, Edna Guy, and Wilson Williams, early black modern dancers who gave recitals in the 1930s and formed organizations like the Negro Dance Theater. In 1931, we hear about Gluck-Sandor and Felicia Sorel inviting Randolph Sawyer to join them in an "integrated" company. In 1933, Ruth Page, who we will meet in Chapter 29, choreographed *La Guiablesse* (to music by William Grant Still) in Chicago, for herself and fifty black dancers. The star of this piece was Katherine Dunham, and it is Dunham who now deserves our attention.

Katherine Dunham

Katherine Dunham was born in Chicago, in 1914. She first made a name for herself in that city, in 1933, as a star and a performer in Ruth Page's *La Guiablesse*. In recognition of Page's help, when Dunham became director of the Chicago branch of the Federal Theater, she made Ruth Page's famous

Frankie and Johnny one of its first productions. Like most dancers of her day, Dunham went on to New York where, in 1938, she formed her own company. For this company, and also for Broadway musicals, she choreographed a Brazilian number entitled *Bahiana*; a hot, fast Cuban piece entitled *Shore Excursion*; and *Barrelhouse*, a piece about Chicago urban life. Dunham appeared in Broadway shows like *Cabin in the Sky* and Hollywood movies like *Star Spangled Rhythm*. But her outstanding successes were the smashing *Tropical Revues* in the 1940s that she staged and performed with her company.

In 1945, Katherine Dunham opened her own school with these goals: "To establish a technique that would be as important to the white man as to the Negro...To take our dance out of the burlesque—to make it a more dignified art." Ironically, at the time Dunham was doing her best work (during the 1930s and 1940s), modern dancers and political liberals were stubbornly colorblind. They refused to speak about someone as Jewish, Italian, Irish, or black. They were all people—human beings. Any other label was racist. Hitler had just shown the world what can happen when you concentrate on people's origins. Therefore, the liberal dance-establishment people were not impressed with Dunham's goal of concentrating on "Negro" culture. (At that time *Negro* was a respectable term. *Black* and *Afro-American* did not take hold until the 1960s.) These same people had a hard time accepting jazz as an art form. In the intellectual climate of the 1930s, *Art* was always said with a capital *A*. Art included only high-minded, noble, dramatic expressions of humanity. It automatically excluded anything that might be commercially successful. "Entertainment" was not a worthy goal, and jazz was a very popular form of entertainment.

Furthermore, there was a problem with the sexual aspect of jazz. We have seen that modern dancers, from the very beginning, had no hesitation in portraying sexual love or even nudity. But they saw this as high morality, not carnal titillation. Sex was not equated with a "good time," but regarded as a noble fulfillment of man's deepest nature. This attitude was reflected in the physical movements that choreographers used to show a man and woman in love. In Graham's *Appalachian Spring*, when the husband caresses his bride's hip, the gesture is tender, lyrical, practically spiritual. Man and Woman in Humphrey's *Day on Earth* move toward one another with devotion, not lust.

As you know, jazz takes a different view of the body, which comes from its African origin. But regardless of negative moralistic and artistic attitudes, that no professional dancer or audience member today is unaware of the jazz style is certainly in large part due to Dunham and the success of her aims. Throughout this history we have seen how Western choreographers and directors have injected folk or ethnic dance forms into their creations.

You may remember many examples from the chapters on ballet. As far back as the eighteenth century, French folk figures were introduced into

La Fille Mal Gardée. Through the nineteenth century, all the great classics contained folk-dance passages, like the Hungarian *czardas* in *Coppélia*, and the Spanish and Russian dances in *The Nutcracker*. In the early twentieth century, Nijinsky turned to primitive ritual dance in *The Rite of Spring*, while dozens of modern dancers incorporated ancient, primitive, or folk dancing in their choreography. Think of Isadora Duncan in her Greek tunic; of the Oriental influence on Ruth St. Denis; of the biblical themes in the work of Martha Graham; and of the religious ritual of the Shakers as used by Doris Humphrey.

It is not surprising to find that jazz also swept through Western theater dance, where choreographers and directors have always been on the lookout for fresh material to rejuvenate tired blood. It is difficult to think of two movement styles that have less in common than jazz and classical ballet. However, in fact, these two styles are combined in the eclectic dance that we see on today's stages. Almost without exception, ballet and modern-dance choreographers eventually incorporated syncopated rhythms as well as physical gestures of jazz, in a variety of their compositions.

Aside from the influence of her own wildly successful productions, Katherine Dunham's contributions to the art were made through members of her company (like Talley Beatty), teachers at her school (like Geoffrey Holder), and black dancers who were inspired by her choreography (like Clive Thompson). Keep in mind also that Katherine Dunham was never a mere "entertainer." She was also an anthropologistwho studied cult and possession-trance dancing in the Caribbean. In retrospect, with the acceptance of jazz as one of the significant ingredients in American dance, we can appreciate Katherine Dunham in the role of a modern dance pioneer.

Jazz

Now we arrive at another one of those topics that does not lend itself to convenient tailoring in an academic work: jazz. You may not be able to define jazz, but chances are that you are familiar with it. Even outside of dance and music, we say something is "jazzy" when we mean it's lively, snappy, and out of the ordinary—it swings.

Marshall and Jean Stearns, in their book *Jazz Dance*, tell us that the origin of jazz is ethnic: first of all in the music and movement of primitive tribal Africa, and then in the developments among African slaves who were brought to the West Indies and the American South. As we have seen, there is a great range of movement styles in African tribal dance. If we want to single out the characteristics that jazz inherited from Africa, we can best do so, as we did with Oriental dance, by looking at African dance motion in contrast to European. This helps us pick out a number of things:

1.   The crouch, that is, legs bent at knee and ankle, with the spine flexible and loose.

2.   A strong attack that propels movement sharply back and forth.

3.   Movement that starts from the pelvic region and continues outward; at the same time, movement that may appear in an isolated limb, such as a hand, head, or one shoulder.

4.   Movement that shimmies, shakes, and trembles.

5.   A tendency to improvise, often satirically, which allows for freedom of individual expression.

Since their arrival in the West, slaves used their ancient songs and dances as a way of staying alive. At the same time, in the islands of the Caribbean, they came into contact with Spanish folk dance, and then after 1800, with upper-class dances from Europe. They were quick to imitate these, and combine them with their native forms. In their imitations of the white folks' dances, the slaves slyly mocked the pretensions of their "upper-class" masters. This is the element in jazz that has remained: the mocking irony; the subtle protest that is embodied in the casual flick of one shoulder, or one hip, or any limb of the body. Soon there were dozens of variations on European quadrilles. The body was held elegantly, and the feet did steps and floor patterns of dances from the Renaissance courts— with the addition of hip and shoulder motions. The rhythm and the basic movement propulsion were taken directly from Africa. You can recognize popular American "ballroom" dances—like the Charleston, the jitterbug, the rumba, the samba, the conga—in these hybrid forms.

The slaves took another element of African dance—a step-dance somewhat like a flat-footed jig, with the addition of hip movements—and developed it with endless variations into a form known as the *juba*. The juba, as we saw in the discussion on minstrel dance in Chapter 20, became an eccentric, shuffling circle dance. Two men in the center performed different figures, which were called out rhythmically. These figures were taken up by the men circling the two in the center. The men watching the duo alternately watched their movements and responded by clapping. The central figures might improvise animal motions and other gestures, such as the Pigeon Wing, the Yaller Cat, and so on. They gave a similar treatment to another African circle dance which became the very popular Ring Shout. Here the main elements were clapping, stamping, and shuffling with rhythmic heel tapping. And then there was the church, where slaves escaped from the horror of daily life by singing, stamping their feet, and clapping their hands in religious ecstasy.

The outstanding characteristic of these activities was the swinging, stamping, tapping, syncopated rhythms, all of which led to the *tap dance*. As we noted earlier, it was out of the question for blacks to be allowed

inside a respectable theater (except to clean it). The only performing out-
lets left to blacks were lower-class dives and bawdy houses, where they
performed with men of another despised minority, the Irish. Fortunately,
their lowly status did not stop these performers from creating countless
variations on their original material, like the *soft shoe*, which evolved
around 1900. Tap dancing, like Spanish dancing, goes in and out of fashion. It has been very hot since the release of the movie *Tap*, starring
Gregory Hines. In *Dance Magazine* (December 1988), Hines praises the old
tap dance greats, who taught him the trade. The film *Tap* presents master
hoofers Jimmy Slyde, Harold Nicholas, Bunny Briggs, Sandman Sims,
Steve Condos, Pat Rico, and Arthur Duncan. There were others: Charles
"Honi" Coles, Chuck Green, Buster Brown, Foster Johnson, Eddie Brown,
Leon Collins, and Charles "Cookie" Cook. Hines's co-star, Sammy Davis,
Jr., began his career as a child tap dancer.

Like every good artist, Gregory Hines wants to push his material
beyond the expected, to break out of the conventional, to play dangerously.
All good tappers, he believes, revere improvisation within the frame of a
dance. They play their instruments which, as for all dancers, are their bodies, with the help or hindrance of the floor. Hines carries with him a
portable stage, his own "percussive instrument," made of quarter-inch,
tongue-and-groove oak, miked with an audio pickup, so the audience can
hear the foot landing even when it is placed softly.

Through the twentieth century, the story of jazz and tap dance cuts
back and forth between white and black show business communities,
nightclubs, movies, and concert stages. Jazz is a particularly fascinating
subject because of its attraction as a form of vernacular dance, in addition
to its great appeal as entertainment. From African Americans, jazz spread
to the whole white American population, and from there to Europe and the
rest of the world. You might want to consider what basic qualities of jazz
caused it to become the most popular social dance expression of the twentieth century, particularly for young adults. More importantly, for our purposes, jazz, as a style, has inspired innumerable ballet and modern dance
choreographers. The swinging rhythms and pelvic thrusts of jazz movement express a sexual abandon that the guardians of social morality have
always found offensive. And while early modern dance devotees considered themselves anything but guardians of social morality, they too saw
jazz as a vulgar, commercialized entertainment, not to be admitted to the
halls of art. Dutiful mothers who, in the name of edification, took their
children to modern dance concerts, would do anything to steer them away
from jazz musicians and dancers.

Further, with its isolated, throw-away gestures of hand, shoulder,
head, and hip, jazz also expresses an attitude of mockery. This was uncomfortable for many among the doers and fans of early modern dance who
took themselves and life very seriously. Therefore when Dunham devel-

oped a repertory of dances that put the culture of her people on the stage, and at the same time, made a tremendous hit as a theatrically exciting choreographer, it took a while before serious dancers and the serious dance public could bring themselves to treat her compositions with great artistic respect.

Pearl Primus. During this same period, Pearl Primus (born in 1919), another black American dancer, started out like Dunham as a trained anthropologist, and went on to a career as an enormously successful, serious concert dancer. Primus studied with Martha Graham and Charles Weidman. Inspired by her research of African culture, she composed pieces about the black experience in Africa, and then the black experience in America. In 1943, she created *African Ceremonial* (a fertility rite in the Belgian Congo), *Strange Fruit* (a reaction to a lynching), *Rock Daniel* (a lesson in jazz), and *Hard Time Blues*, a protest against sharecropping. All these dances were cheered by audiences and critics alike.

Remember what Doris Humphry said about the content of a dance work? That it is important only to the choreographer? This was born out by Margaret Lloyd who, as the dance critic for the *Christian Science Monitor* from 1936 to 1960, saw all the major works of that period. This is what she said in *The Borzoi Book of Modern Dance* about *Hard Time Blues*, which was Pearl Primus's angry outcry against the lot of the sharecropper:

> *Hard Time Blues* is phenomenal for its excursions into space and stopovers on top of it. Pearl takes a running jump, lands in an upper corner and sits there, unconcernedly paddling the air with her legs. She does it repeatedly, from one side of the stage, then the other, apparently unaware of the involuntary gasps from the audience . . . For me it was exultant with mastery over the law of gravitation, and the poor sharecroppers were forgotten.

Primus, like Dunham, had a strong influence on her contemporaries. Other black dance artists made effective use of their inspiration and of the jazz style.

Alvin Ailey and Black Dance

When we discuss black dance artists like Alvin Ailey (1931 to 1989), we deal with the second question raised at the beginning of this chapter: Is the dance world fully integrated today? Although our subject is dance, we are unable to ignore the issues of racial prejudice that are raised by the term *black dance*. So, after we deal with the bare facts of Ailey's biography and his two masterpieces, *Blues Suite* and *Revelations*, we'll make a stab at the whole question of black ethnic culture and its connection with our story of Western theater dance.

Alvin Ailey was born in Texas. Like José Limón, he stumbled into dance while headed for a different course of study. In Ailey's case, it was foreign languages at UCLA. After a chance visit to Lester Horton's Dance Theater, he stayed on and became completely involved. He tells us in *Dance Magazine*: "Lester did it all. He designed the costumes, taught us about lighting, fabrics, make-up; he taught us how to sew. You can teach people a lot, if you teach with love, by showing them what you want with patience." Perhaps most important for Ailey's work was the Horton technique, which used ethnic as well as modern material, for example, jazz steps and isolated movements of the hip and torso in a "sort of Afro-Asian way."

After Horton's death in 1953, Ailey choreographed for the company. Then he went east to New York to study with all the well-known modern dance artists, as well as to take acting classes and to perform in Broadway musical shows. In 1958, he formed the Alvin Ailey American Dance Theater, which immediately attracted wide audiences with its theatrical repertory and electrifying performances. The Alvin Ailey Company has never suffered from a shortage of excellent, exciting dancers, many of whom appeared first in other companies, and some of whom went on to star elsewhere, or to found their own groups. Particularly outstanding among the men are Miguel Godreau, Dudley Williams, and Clive Thompson. Noteworthy among the women are Carmen de Lavallade, Sara Yarborough, and Consuelo Atlas. There is one star dancer, however, with whom the company was identified for many years: Judith Jamison.

Judith Jamison. This is the way Olga Maynard describes the dancing of the almost six-foot-tall Jamison in *Dance Magazine* (November, 1972): "We look upon her as we might a temple dancer—with a sense of religiosity, of awe. Judith Jamison is the prototype of countless carved and sculptured goddesses, ancient priestesses of the dance."

Jamison, born in Philadelphia, in 1944, started dance lessons when she was six, with Marian Cuyjet. Although the curriculum was the usual mishmash of ballet, tap, acrobatic, and primitive, Cuyjet gave her students something more. She encouraged the talented Judith to study with any well-known teacher who gave classes in town. So she took classical ballet lessons from Antony Tudor, Swoboda, and Celli. Agnes de Mille saw Judith in class, when she was a magnificent dancer of seventeen, and grabbed her for a part in an American Ballet Theater production. The production was dropped, but its star, Carmen de Lavallade, took the shy Jamison under her care, and led her to Alvin Ailey. Judith Jamison entered the company in 1965. In 1972, Ailey choreographed *Cry* for Jamison. Judith Jamison said:

> I think Alvin tried to get rid of all the hurt, all the ugly degradation and humiliation of black women in *Cry*.

> This is Alvin's work but, when I dance it, it is mine too. I create something then. Dance is a very perfect thing. You give yourself to it, yet you have to prove your power over it.

Time and again, the extraordinarily gifted Judith Jamison proved her power over dance, and over its audiences.

Ailey was a prolific creator, and not only for his own company. He had the honor in 1966 of choreographing Samuel Barber's *Antony and Cleopatra*, the opening production at the new Metropolitan Opera House; and in 1972, he did the choreography for Leonard Bernstein's *Mass*, which was performed at the Kennedy Center in Washington, D.C. His interests always spanned the whole field of dance. Ailey made a number of ballets for the American Ballet Theater, and set himself the task of providing a repertory company for modern dance classics. To this end, for the Alvin Ailey Company, he revived works by Ted Shawn, May O'Donnell, Katherine Dunham, and Pearl Primus. In addition, he included in the repertory of his own company works by white modern dance artists like José Limón, John Butler, Lucas Hoving, Paul Sanasardo, and Joyce Trisler; as well as blacks like Donald McKayle, Talley Beatty, and Geoffrey Holder.

Two of Ailey's early compositions remain great hits. *Blues Suite* and *Revelations*. *Blues Suite* (1958), performed to traditional blues songs, is just that: a series of separate dances—solos and small-numbers, groups—each one expressing the mood of a blues song. There is lost innocence, despair, social protest, anger, lost love, and high-stepping, honky-tonk revelry. For example, in *The House of the Rising Sun*, three young women lament their grim fate as prostitutes. The whole ensemble opens and closes the piece with *Good Morning Blues*. The groupings, and even some of the songs, have changed through the years, something right in keeping with a blues piece, which is always an expression of the singer's (or dancer's) feeling at the moment.

Revelations (1960) is also arranged to traditional songs, in this case, spirituals and gospel songs. (Again, scenes have been changed at various performances.) Men and women huddle close for physical comfort while their arms reach outward and upward for spiritual salvation. There is a proud procession of figures, dressed up in shining white clothes and with the women carrying parasols, going to church. "Wading in the Water" is a baptism ritual where bodies undulate from head to toe in waves while long yards of chiffon are waved to reinforce the physical motion. The smashing finale, "Rocka My Soul In the Bosom of Abraham" takes place inside the church. Women are sitting on stools. Their men arrive. They rock, circle one another, clap in mounting excitement, and reach a frenzy of religious joy while experiencing revelation. These two numbers have stirred audiences deeply all over America and on tour throughout the world.

Ailey's masterpieces touch feelings that all people share, but they are distinctly rooted in the culture of black Americans. Even more specifically,

Judith Jamison moves with elegance in Alvin Ailey's all-time favorite, "Revelations."

Revelations is set in the South, during an earlier period of this century, and is composed of scenes showing a particular community of people in their church and in a dance hall. It also shows the feelings and attitudes they have about themselves and about what is happening. In other words, the content—the subject, the theme, the specific action on stage—has an ethnic root. To make the point, let us compare the similarities and contrast the differences of *Revelations* and *The Moor's Pavane*. Limón's piece, you will remember, is set in Renaissance Italy. Its content concerns the feelings and actions of a man (who happens to be black) when he is goaded by a lying "friend" into murdering his innocent wife.

Both works express emotions through dance movements. They were composed according to traditional principles of Western theater dance, that is, structured by unified but contrasting scenes that build to a climax. The two owe a great deal to the musical selections chosen for accompaniment. Each was created to involve its audience in its forceful artistry. And both were, and are, highly successful. The differences lie in specifics of content, setting, costumes, gesture and action, and rhythm, in short, in specifics of style. The styles that Limón drew upon were Spanish, noble,

Shakespearean, and of the Italian Renaissance. Whereas Ailey's specific styles derived from black southern America, ordinary folks, and jazz.

To sum up, we are talking about cultural heritage and ethnic roots, as well as our central subject of traditions in Western theater dance. We have seen through this history how a choreographer may fit into a trend like Romantic ballet or modern dance. Yet at the same time, his works bear a personal stamp. And while we know that each person is unique, we also recognize that personality (and therefore artistic style) is shaped by one's heredity as well as by one's cultural upbringing. In the case of Limón, we can find traces of Spanish-Mexican and of Renaissance culture, without stirring up any big problems. But when we go on to consider the blackness of Ailey's heritage, we confront a big problem indeed.

Controversial Rhythms

Suddenly, like Alvin Ailey, Donald McKayle, Talley Beatty, Eleo Pomare, Gus Solomons, Jr., and Katherine Dunham and Pearl Primus before them, we are enmeshed in one of the major problems of American life: its multiracial composition and the black struggle for recognition and equality of status. The difficult question of race is raised because while it is primarily political and sociological, it has many ramifications for the dance-art world. If our goal is greater appreciation, then at least a beginning must be made toward understanding these thorny issues. A brief discussion of the conflicting approaches of four major black modern dance artists—Donald McKayle, Talley Beatty, Eleo Pomare, and Gus Solomons, Jr.—is in order. To illustrate the differing sensibilities of these artists, we hark back to 1959, just after Alvin Ailey did *Blues Suite*, and just before he did *Revelations*. Two other dances were produced that gained immediate recognition for their choreographers: Donald McKayle's *Rainbow 'Round My Shoulder* and Talley Beatty's *Road of the Phoebe Snow*.

McKayle: *Rainbow 'Round My Shoulder* (1959). *Rainbow 'Round My Shoulder* is in a rondo form. It presents a line of men in a prison chain gang. They are linked together by a dreary work refrain, punctuated by memories, dreams, and letters from the outside. The accompaniment is prison songs. Again, as in *Blues Suite*, each song expresses a different mood for each guy. One dreams of a graceful sweetheart; one is high on thoughts of staying with Nancy and keeping her drunk and juicy on brandy all the time; one can't read a letter without crying, because the time of his jail term is so long.

As in *The Moor's Pavane*, the scenes are linked together by a refrain in which all the chained men take part, "I've got a rainbow tied all around my shoulder—my Lord, I'm goin' home." The tempo quickens as the refrain is heard in counterpoint to *Take This Hammer*, and a man wildly breaks free. Bang! Everything freezes. A man has been shot while trying to escape. The last mournful song shows the prisoners carrying off the dead man, their spirits beaten down in despair. The men's movement themes include percussive contractions of the torso, and kneeling lunges. They stick pretty much to a line formation. Their imagined women move according to their individual characters: lyrically; in ballet poses; and in twists with a syncopated beat.

Talley Beatty: *Road of The Phoebe Snow* (1959). Talley Beatty's *Road of the Phoebe Snow* is set in Chicago's black ghetto near the railroad tracks where the express train, called *Phoebe Snow*, thunders in from Hoboken. The action, set to selected jazz pieces by Duke Ellington, is violent. Young people hang around together. A boy and a girl casually make out. Another boy and girl are seriously, tenderly in love. The girl's wholehearted love, reserved for only one boy, offends the onlookers. They separate the couple, beat up the boy and make moves on the girl. She runs from them, falls onto the tracks, and the gang watches in horror as the flashing lights of the *Phoebe Snow* announce the train's arrival and her end. Just as Donald McKayle did, Talley Beatty chose movement expressive of the characters and their emotions: youths hold their bodies with an aggressive shoulder pushed forward; there are slow, supportive lyrical motions for the couple in love; and bodies contract in horror at the finale. In other words, the approach taken by both McKayle and Beatty is the one with whom we are now familiar in modern dance.

Beatty identified the sources of his art first of all as the Katherine Dunham technique with its Afro-Cuban rhythms that made him aware of the pulse in the center of the body; and secondly, his studies with Martha Graham. But central to his creations are the black experience. He tells us:

> All my works reflect the crippling process that the Negro in this society has to go through. Physically I've left the little ghetto area in Chicago, but in a sense I've never moved away from this involvement. Every deep thought must come from this experience.

Before our next two black artists—Gus Solomons, Jr., and Eleo Pomare—gained recognition in dance, the 1960s were upon us with two developments noteworthy for this history: (1) the Civil Rights movement; and (2) the dance avant-garde, led by Merce Cunningham and Alwin Nikolais, whom we will meet in Chapter 31. The Civil Rights movement put a spotlight on black culture. It also led to the expression of anger by artists like Eleo Pomare.

Eleo Pomare: *Blues for the Jungle* (1966). Pomare's *Blues for the Jungle* is a collage of scenes and musical episodes that depict the horrors of black life, from slaves on auction blocks to prostitutes and junkies twitching on contemporary urban streets. Pomare (interviewed in *Dance Magazine*) expressed contempt for other black choreographers:

> They continue to paint our people the way whites want to see them. I set out to give a sharp, truthful picture of the black situation. Entertainment is the last thing on my list!

With *Blues for the Jungle*, Pomare claimed he had changed the direction of black dance. "Its characters cause an actual confrontation with the audience," he said. To critics who charged that his choreography was rough and undisciplined, he had this reply:

> Standards and values of whites no longer concern me. If whites don't understand me, well I'm not talking to them anyway. My dances are not directed to the white "sophisticates," but to the whole community.

Gus Solomons, Jr.: *City/Motion/Space/Game* **(1968).** In contrast to all this heat and anger came the cool formalism of Gus Solomons, Jr. His work *City/Motion/Space/Game* has neither emotional nor dramatic content, and in fact, its verbal message contains the philosophy that "art is play," which he accepted from Merce Cunningham, of whose group he was a member for a time. What the audience sees in this "video dance," simultaneously broadcast on two different television channels, is Gus Solomons, Jr. himself impassively performing a series of random dance movements in a junkyard, a studio, and on the Boston Common. Sometimes he uses props such as a jacket balanced on a lifted leg, or a sweatshirt that is taken on and off while he is running in a circle. Some scenes are speeded up or run backward, and presented in deliberately artificial greens and pinks. When you tire of watching Solomons, a magnificent, long-limbed dancer, you can focus on the verbal accompaniment, which explains the philosophy behind the dance: "An IBM machine doesn't have a beginning, a middle and an end. Why should my dance? The form is really just the amount of time it takes. The art-game is the game of life."

Gus Solomons, Jr. began dancing after being diverted from his studies in architecture, which may in part explain why he identifies his choreographic interests as concerning space, weights, and balances. When he extends this approach to the dancer's instrument, the body, he is led to making observations (quoted in *Dance Scope*, Spring 1967) about the Negro physique and culture, in contrast to the white:

> The jazz dance came out of Negro culture as jazz did. Certain structural things make it very difficult for me to do ballet movement. The physical bone

structure: forelimbs are longer in proportion to upper limbs than in white stock; calves tend to be less full, while thighs and buttocks are fuller. The lower spine tends to have a curvature. It presents a problem when one tries to fit into an established pattern of dance like ballet, which was invented on white European bodies.

Donald McKayle, as quoted in Selma Jeanne Cohen's *The Modern Dance, Seven Statements of Belief*, stands in direct opposition to Solomons. In matters of choreography, he sought meaningful experience. In matters of race, he was firm: "Classification according to arbitrary ethnic groups is ridiculous and misleading." He dismissed as nonsense talk of "the Negro physique or that fallacious old bromide about Negro rhythm."

We are in no position to resolve these differences. But we should be aware of them. The last word on problems of integration and separate identity are Alvin Ailey's, because through his company that has travelled abroad so widely (sometimes on tours sponsored by the State Department), he has presented and popularized his people as images of black America. Most of his dancers have always been black, but this was despite his efforts to make the company integrated, which was his ideal. He simply could not find the dancers he wanted outside of the black community:

> I've always felt that my company should be integrated. Lester Horton's company was integrated, there were blacks, Asians, Mexicans, Indians and whites and it all worked. He was doing what I'm still doing now. He was trying to erase the idea of color.

At the same time, Ailey told *Dance Magazine* in 1978:

> The black dancers are rather close anyway, like a family. I'm pleased that my company has become the kind of place where choreographers—many of them black—can come and make their statements.

For most people at a dance concert, of course, none of this controversy about race means anything. All they really care about is what they see before them. And as far as audiences were concerned, each one of the above black choreographers, including Gus Solomons, Jr., who allied himself with the abstract avant-garde, made the stage come alive with exciting dance movements, inside and outside of the jazz idiom. Up to now, we have surveyed the scene through the 1960s. Moving ahead through the 1970s and 1980s, we find that the work of black artists is constantly expanding. Pause for a moment in 1979, and see what you had. In the spring of that year, in New York City alone, there were three complete *series* of black theater dance, which included performances by seventeen companies. Alvin Ailey's Company, in its twenty-first year, was still packing them in, and the Dance Theater of Harlem was stronger than ever. Listen to this review of Pearl Primus, in *Dance Magazine*, June, 1979:

> I don't know how many times she has performed the famous African dance *Fanga*, but on this occasion she gave the impression of complete spontaneity, an instinctive delight in motion. Her robust frame was alive with a sensuous fluidity and rhythmic vitality that were positively contagious. I have seldom seen a dancer with such a distinctive sense of her own weight, and such an essential connection to the ground.
>
> This, I thought, is what dancing is all about.

For many other dance fans, however, dancing is still all about ballet. Next, we will look at the modern American ballet scene.

Questions for Review

1. How did Katherine Dunham contribute to the advancement of black dancers?

2. Describe Pearl Primus's choreographic output.

3. What made the Alvin Ailey Company such a hit?

29 REVIVAL OF AMERICAN BALLET

NEW YORK CITY BALLET FROM THE 1930s TO THE PRESENT

The American Golden Age: 1940 to 1970

In its long life, the art of ballet has gone through many cycles of prosperity and recession. During the 1800s, we watched the rise and fall of the great romantic eras in France and Denmark, and the classical era in Petipa's Russia. So far, in the 1900s, we have followed the magnificent achievements of Diaghilev's Ballets Russes and the British Royal Ballet. We come now to another golden age, modern ballet in America from 1940 to 1970. Those years saw an upsurge in creativity and the appearance of styles that were uniquely American. The dates, of course, are arbitrary. Great productions have continued to be performed up to the present day. Nevertheless, these tend to be enlargements and combinations of original works done during that period.

Achievements in modern American ballet, beginning in the 1930s, centered around the names of a few dancer-choreographers: George Balanchine, Jerome Robbins, Agnes de Mille, Antony Tudor, Eugene Loring, William Dollar, The Christensen brothers, and Ruth Page. After them, performers entered the scene both to inspire choreographers and to create fans among the public. Then there were the multitudes of people who made their contributions in teaching, in writing scenarios, in composing music, and in organizing companies. These included artists who, like Antony Tudor, had already made their mark in England: Alicia Markova,

Anton Dolin, and Hugh Laing. There were artists who had been connected with Sergei Diaghilev, or one of the many Ballets Russes companies that followed his: George Balanchine, Michel Fokine, Leonide Massine, Bronislava Nijinska, Mikhail Mordkin, and Adolph Bolm. There were others who started out in America, such as Robbins, de Mille, Loring, Dollar, the Christensen brothers, and Page. We will now look at how all this energy was focused and gave shape to a national American ballet.

Lincoln Kirstein. Lincoln Kirstein (born in 1907) came from a wealthy Boston family. Like Diaghilev, young Kirstein had dabbled in several arts before he devoted himself entirely to dance—his first love. Here his vision exceeded even Diaghilev's. No less than Ninette de Valois, he wanted to found a school and a company, a repertory and an audience for home-grown ballet—in his case on American soil. Except that he was to choose a Russian to realize his plans.

George Balanchine. George Balanchine (1904 to 1983) started life in St. Petersburg where he studied first ballet and then music. Then he did some experimental choreography which created a sensation. It was well received by younger people and severely criticized by ballet traditionalists, who were very much in control, despite the political revolution of 1917. In 1924, Balanchine managed to leave the Soviet Union with a small touring company, never to return, except while on tour with the New York City Ballet much later. On his exodus with him, in addition to Alexandra Danilova—who later became a great ballerina—was Balanchine's first wife, Tamara Geva. (He later married the dancers Vera Zorina, Maria Tallchief, and Tanaquil LeClerc.)

In Europe, the small Russian band came to the attention of Diaghilev, who immediately auditioned and hired the dancers, and appointed Balanchine chief choreographer of the Ballets Russes. During the 1920s, the young artist created about a dozen works for the Ballets Russes, two of which, *Apollo* and *Progidal Son*, have become classics of the international repertory. After Diaghilev's death, Balanchine drifted around, although he was by no means idle. He supervised Serge Lifar's first production for the Paris Opera and made a number of ballets for Vera Nemtchinova's small company, for the Cochran Revue of 1930 on a tiny English stage, and finally for his own company, Les Ballets 1933.

Lincoln Kirstein had been impressed by Balanchine's *Apollo* in 1927. In 1933, he sailed for Europe to seek out Balanchine and persuade him to come to America because "no one else could do dances like these." Since all Balanchine's European ventures seemed to be leading nowhere, he readily accepted Kirstein's invitation to transplant his art to the New World. Balanchine was not the first ballet missionary of his day to reach America's shores. Several Russians and even some Americans had already attracted followers. I am not only speaking of inspiring figures like Fanny Elssler and Anna Pavlova, whose tours across America left ecstatic visions behind them. There were also a dedicated few who settled among the people and succeeded in converting a number of young Americans into acceptable ballet dancers, and a larger number into ticket buyers for ballet performances. The most notable among the dancers were Adolph Bolm, Mikhail Mordkin, Ruth Page, and the Christensen brothers. A brief word about each is in order here.

Adolph Bolm. After Adolph Bolm (1884 to 1951), a Diaghilev dancer, was injured during the 1917 American tour of the Ballets Russes, he remained behind in this country for medical care; and then he stayed to perform, to choreograph, and to teach. In the opinion of Willam Christensen, Bolm was the greatest mime and character dancer of his time. He created new audiences for ballet when he toured the "women's club" circuit with his own Ballet Intime, giving talks along with performances.

Bolm's partner in the Ballet Intime was Ruth Page, for whom he created *Birthday of the Infanta*, in 1919, to music by John Alden Carpenter. Bolm did choreography for the Metropolitan Opera and the Chicago Opera. When he was ballet master at the San Francisco Opera, he presented its first all-ballet evening in 1933, an event which launched the San Francisco Ballet Company. His most successful, lasting composition was *Peter and the Wolf* (to Prokofiev's music, in 1940) for the American Ballet Theater. Along the way, Bolm helped to set a high standard for classical training in the U.S.

Mikhail Mordkin. Mikhail Mordkin (1880 to 1944) had been a soloist and ballet master at Moscow's Bolshoi Ballet, and he also partnered Anna Pavlova on tours in Europe and America. In 1923, he settled in the United States where he taught, choreographed, and organized the Mordkin Ballet, a company whose chief importance was its use as a starting point for the American Ballet Theater.

The Christensen brothers. William (born in 1902, and who later changed his name to Willam), Howard (1904 to 1989), and Lew (1909 to 1984) Christensen were third-generation Americans in a talented, ambitious, musical family that migrated in 1854 from Denmark to Utah so that they could join the Mormon community. All three were active in creating a strong ballet tradition in the American West. They laid the groundwork for the San Francisco Ballet which became the oldest, continuously running ballet company in America. They also established Ballet West in Utah.

In their companies and associated schools, the Christensens were responsible for training skillful dancers who have added a lot to the dance scene across the entire country. Of course, their primary aim was to feed their own productions, *not* to enrich other companies. However, New York always was—and has remained—the capital of the American dance world. Everyone "out of town" knows they risk losing their people to this magnetic city. Here are only some of the Christensen-trained dancers who left to make their reputations in the East: Cynthia Gregory, Harold Lang, Janet Reed, James Starbuck, Scott Douglas, Conrad Ludlow, Suki Schorer, and Michael Smuin.

Willam Christensen mounted the first full-length *Swan Lake* in the United States. Lew Christensen was the first native-born *danseur noble*. As a member of Balanchine's first company, he danced the lead in *Apollo*. For Lincoln Kirstein, he choreographed and starred in *Filling Station* (1938), which was about a gangland shooting at a gas station, one of the first "all-American ballets," with music by Virgil Thompson, decor by Paul Cadmus, and libretto by Lincoln Kirstein. The dancers at the premiere included Erick Hawkins, who was later to make a name for himself as Martha Graham's partner and then on his own as a modern dancer; Michael Kidd, who later choreographed *On Stage* for ballet theater, in 1945, to music by Norman Dello Joio; and Todd Bolender, who created in 1951 *The Miraculous Mandarin*, to Bela Bartok's music, for the New York City Ballet.

Ruth Page. Little Ruth (1905 to 1991), daughter of a professional pianist in Indianapolis, entertained her parents' artistic guests by dancing around with a scarf. When Page was a teenager, Anna Pavlova invited the graceful girl to study ballet in Chicago, and then to join her company on a tour of South America. That was *not* a bad beginning for a dance career, one that more than fulfilled the promise of those early years. After the Pavlova tour, Ruth Page went to New York, where she studied with Adolph Bolm; and as we saw, she soon became his partner. When she married Tom Fisher, a Chicago attorney, and they went to Monte Carlo for their honeymoon, she took classes with dancers from the Ballets Russes, and joined that company for a season. In 1928, Page assembled her own small company, and toured the Orient.

Back home, in 1933, Ruth Page was asked to arrange productions for the Chicago World's Fair. She staged *La Guiablesse*, with a large cast of black dancers, herself, and Katherine Dunham in the leading roles. This was an important event for black dance in America. On another trip to Europe in 1934, she met Harold Kreutzberg, a German modern dancer, and for the next three years they toured together. In 1938, Page formed a company with Bentley Stone, who had danced for a year with the Ballet Rambert. Together, with the support of the Federal Theater Project, they created *Frankie and Johnny*, a theatrically effective ballad (to a jazzy score by J. Moross) about a prostitute who shoots her unfaithful lover. For ten years, the popular Page-Stone Ballet toured the U.S. In other words, Ruth Page was always quick to try new styles and ideas.

Finally, Ruth Page made her mark as an opera choreographer. All through this history, we have met choreographers who have worked at the opera, most recently Bolm and the Christensens. Their work has consisted of arranging dance numbers within opera productions. Page had a fresh angle. For her own ballet company, she created a repertory *based* on the stories and music of operas, but transformed into complete dance works that were performed separately. For example, in 1938, she did *Guns and Castanets* (*Carmen*), in 1955, *Susannah and the Barber* (*The Barber of Seville*), and in 1957, *Revenge* (*Il Trovatore*).

Afro-American Ballet Dancers. We have just seen how Ruth Page staged *La Guiablesse* for black dancers, led by Katherine Dunham. It is no surprise to find talented Afro-Americans trained in modern dance and jazz styles. It is not widely known, however, that during this period a number of Afro-Americans were studying, and some were even performing in, classical ballet. Zita D. Allen, in her article "Blacks and Ballet," (*Dance Magazine*, July 1976) tells us that in the 1920s and 1930s, native-born black youngsters, like native-born whites, began to dream of careers in ballet. For the blacks, however, it wasn't easy even to enroll in classes. But they persevered, and gradually, white teachers like Fred Christensen (a member of the famous Utah family) and Karel Shook took them in.

Their initial opportunities to perform professionally arose when white choreographers created a ballet with an Afro-American theme. In 1940, Agnes de Mille's *Black Ritual* for the American Ballet Theater had an all-black cast. In 1946, Talley Beatty danced the lead in the Ballet Society production of Lew Christensen's *Blackface*. In 1952, Louis Johnson starred in Jerome Robbins's *Ballade* for the New York City Ballet. A few black dancers were accepted into major ballet companies: Janet Collins was the prima ballerina at the Metropolitan Opera Ballet from 1951 to 1954; Raven Wilkinson became a member of the Ballet Russe de Monte Carlo in 1954; Arthur Mitchell was an outstanding solo dancer in the New York City Ballet, which he joined in 1956.

Three all-black companies were started: the American Negro Ballet, by the German Baron Eugene Von Grona in 1935; The First Negro Classic Ballet by Richard Rickhard, a German-English emigré in 1949; and the All Male Negro Dance Theater by the English dancer Aubrey Hitchens in 1954. These companies all had high ideals, ambitious aims, and got good notices. But they did not last more than a few years, mostly defeated by the lack of financial support. At last, the Dance Theater of Harlem came into being. We shall follow this company's great success in the next chapter.

Balanchine

In 1934, George Balanchine and Lincoln Kirstein founded The School of American Ballet; and a year later a performing group from its students. During the next decade, the school continued to thrive, and a host of well-trained dancers began to emerge, but as yet no stable company was formed from these ranks. Instead, a large number of productions were mounted for short-lived groups that had names like the American Ballet (for a while, the resident company of the Metropolitan Opera), Ballet Caravan, the Dance Players, and Ballet Society. Balanchine was responsible for much of the choreography presented by these groups and in a minute we will survey his works. This most prolific ballet master occasionally moved outside of the classical ballet to the glamorous fields of show business and the movies.

Balanchine's smash hit *Slaughter on Tenth Avenue* provided the danced climax of *On Your Toes*, a 1936 show about a ballet troupe that featured music by Richard Rodgers, lyrics by Lorenz Hart, and scenery by Jo Mielzner. Like other popular American works—*Frankie and Johnnie*, *Filling Station*, *Billy the Kid*, *Fall River Legend*, *Undertow*, and *West Side Story*—*Slaughter on Tenth Avenue* also had a theme of violence. One of Balanchine's wives, Tamara Geva, starred in the ballet on Broadway. Another, younger wife, Vera Zorina, appeared in the film made in 1939. Audiences and critics liked both women in the role. Zorina became identified with it, however, because a film plays to many more people than a Broadway show. The plot concerns a jealous ballet star who hires gangsters to shoot a tap dancer, whose popular style threatens to steal the limelight away from the old-fashioned ballet performer. This time, the shooting is prevented because the tap dancer (brilliantly danced by Ray Bolger, both at the stage premiere and later in the movie version) keeps dancing furiously until the police come to arrest the gangster. (Remember, in *Giselle*, how Albrecht danced to keep alive until the arrival of the dawn?)

Balanchine continued to choreograph successfully for a number of Broadway and Hollywood musicals. He even arranged a circus polka for fifty elephants in the Ringling Brothers Circus, and got Stravinsky to compose the musical score! For these diversions, Balanchine was rewarded with a luxurious lifestyle. The ballet world benefited from a new respect for ballet and trained dancers, both in the musical theater and among the public at large.

In 1948, Balanchine produced *Orpheus* for the Ballet Society, to a commissioned score by Stravinsky, with sculpted scenery by Isamu Noguchi. Once again, Stravinsky and Balanchine labored together and brought forth a masterpiece. In the serene, spare, neoclassic manner of their earlier *Apollo*, this *Orpheus* spins the Greek tale of Orpheus, a musician who descends into Hades to reclaim his dead wife, Euridice. Maria Tallchief was married to Balanchine from 1946 to 1952. Once again, in *Orpheus*, a Balanchine wife danced the lead role in one of the master's works. Undoubtedly, Tallchief was also one source of inspiration for the choreography, as she had been when she created the role of Coquette in his *Night Shadow* (1946). This ballet was made for the Ballet Russe de Monte Carlo, discussed in Chapter 17. After the illustrious premiere of *Orpheus* at the New York City Center, which already housed a drama and an opera company, the management invited Kirstein to bring in this current group, which naturally featured Balanchine's choreography, as the official ballet company of the Center. So the New York City Ballet was finally born, as a public institution with a permanent home, although support came from the city and not from the American nation as a whole.

Balanchine-ballet. The style of the New York City Ballet has been known by the one word: *Balanchine-ballet*. First of all, the company has a certain "look," a certain style of moving. You see, the master personally shaped his "dance instruments" (the members of the company), starting with the daily technique class, where the underlying principle was *speed*. In fact, even before that, there was preselection of dancers based on body build: streamlined girls with long legs and necks, who were exceedingly thin. The males were less characteristic, and in fact, less important. Maybe this is because, as Balanchine often said, "Ballet is woman," or else because he, like every other ballet master, always had available far more talented, willing, female material than male with which to work.

We have to pause here for just a minute, to ponder Balanchine's ideal raw material, and the effect his image of "woman" was to have. If you look at photographs of prima ballerinas here and overseas, before the 1950s, and compare them with photographs of today's female stars, you will see what I mean. Balanchine's model woman was a leggy stick figure, capable of speeding like a rocket or twisting like a pretzel. That became the fashion, the appearance for which all female dancers still strive. Gone are any signs of a bosom or rounded hips. Dancers today are as preoccupied with losing weight as they are with mastering turns and leaps.

After the "look" and the dance style, Balanchine-ballet also refers to the repertory. For example the 1966 season of the company presented thirty-six Balanchine works, four by Jerome Robbins, and seven by all others combined. The listing included a few names of classical works, like *Don Quixote* (1965), *Firebird* (1949), and *Nutcracker* (1954). But these were all new Balanchine versions which condensed the dramatic action, included group passages with intricate combinations, streamlined the spatial design, and speeded up the rhythmic development.

For the most part, Balanchine's works are without any plot. There is a visual orchestration of a musical score, but no dramatic characters or strong emotions. His spatial groupings are simple. Dancers are often

George Balanchine directs Merrill Ashley, a ballerina with the Balanchine "look."

linked to one another, holding hands, forming chains, weaving in and out and under one another's arms. A male may partner two or three females simultaneously. Flashing, brilliant leg work justifies the classroom emphasis on *fast*! At all times the movements complement the musical moods and structures. Occasionally there are implied hints of a plot. In 1934, *Serenade* was composed in this manner to a Tchaikovsky composition, with a suggestion of a hidden romance. *Scotch Symphony* (1952, to a Mendelssohn score) contains references to *La Sylphide* in the costuming and occasional gestures. *Stars and Stripes* (1958) is set to Sousa parade marches and shows American drum majorettes and snappy cadets. *Concerto Barocco* (1940) presents motions as crisp as the notes on the pages of the Bach musical score. *Allegro Brillante* (1956) to a Tchaikovsky piano concerto is full of twinkling, cascading patterns.

In *Agon* (1957), Balanchine was motivated by the same idea as Stravinsky: to make a modern interpretation of seventeenth-century dance patterns. *Agon* emerges as an insolent, syncopated parody of a preclassical dance suite, a kind of "in" joke with upturned feet and saucy hip lines. It contains a wealth of witty, exciting passages. *Episodes* (1959) explores unexpected juxtapositions of movement, to a dissonant score by Webern.

Bugaku (1963) combines the artificiality of Japanese mannerisms with that of balletic mannerisms, to a score by Toshiro Mayuzumi, in the style of ancient Japanese court music. Ravel's *La Valse* (1951) conveys the romantic emotionalism of flirtations in a nineteenth-century ballroom, which builds to a frenzied gaiety as Death lures the Maiden away from her lover. *Raymonda Variations* (1946) embodies the purest classical formalism in patterns and structure, to a score by Glazunov. *Tarantella* (1964, to music by Gottschalk) is a lusty good-humored, pas de deux, with the female turning and prancing on her magic toes, and the male bounding about the stage like a rubber ball.

The above list does not include half the works of this prolific artist. The dance technique is always classical ballet, with the woman working *en point*. However, according to the theme, movements of other styles are worked in, such as military salutes, a square-dance slide, a Hungarian czardas, or a Highland fling. The *neo* in the term *neoclassic* refers to a modern styling. The legs are perhaps parallel instead of turned out, the foot is flexed instead of pointed, or the hand may be bent sharply at the wrist. The neoclassic style is also seen in the streamlining. Large groups are cut down to a small number, and one is always conscious of the modern emphasis on speed. To watch one of these plotless compositions in a crisp, faultless performance by the New York City Ballet, which functions precisely like a magnificent, impersonal, well-oiled machine, is to experience Balanchine-ballet. Even before the master's death, Jerome Robbins shared some of his directoral responsibilities and functions. But neither under Robbins's direction, nor in 1991, with Peter Martins at the helm, has the style noticeably changed.

Questions for Review

1.   Discuss the contributions of Ruth Page and the Christensen brothers to the development of American ballet.

2.   What was interesting about the Stravinsky-Balanchine artistic relationship?

30 THE MANY STYLES OF AMERICAN BALLET

AMERICAN BALLET FROM THE 1930s TO THE PRESENT

American Ballet Theater

There is a second American company of international stature, the American Ballet Theater, and this one has a much broader stylistic base than the New York City Ballet. In fact, from the very beginning, the ideal of the American Ballet Theater was to present great ballets in all styles, from a number of historical periods. The American Ballet Theater was born at the end of 1939, almost a decade before the New York City Ballet, when Richard Pleasant became manager of the two-year-old Mordkin Ballet. Pleasant's approach was the opposite of Kirstein's. Instead of a one-man company, he wanted to form a versatile ensemble, capable of reviving great classics from the past as well as doing justice to new works by a variety of choreographers. The company was to function like a fine symphony orchestra, which performs recognized musical masterworks as well as new, specially commissioned compositions. In the years from 1940 to the present, this company has had some brilliant successes in striving toward these ambitious goals. However, it has never enjoyed the economic security of the New York City Ballet.

Despite the fact that Lucia Chase, a wealthy woman who was also an accomplished dancer (in the Mordkin Company), backed the far-reaching program from its start, the American Ballet Theater still does not have a permanent home or a public charter. As a result, performance quality sometimes suffers. From an historian's viewpoint, however, this company has

Mikhail Baryshnikov follows a pose of master choreographer Jerome Robbins.

been the major American showcase for the great classics, and has also contributed enormously to the ballet repertory of our time. The American Ballet Theater has commissioned over one hundred ballets from a host of choreographers. These include already established figures like Antony Tudor, Leonide Massine, Michel Fokine, and even George Balanchine; as well as others who first became famous through this company like Agnes de Mille, Jerome Robbins, and Herbert Ross. However, in typical ballet fashion, none of these choreographers stayed firmly tied to this one company.

Agnes de Mille. Agnes de Mille (born in 1909) is a rare example of a successful dancer-choreographer who has also written most informatively about the field in books like *Dance To The Piper* (1952). Her first efforts were devoted to concert tours in Europe with programs of mimed sketches that were mostly solo. In England, she studied at Ballet Rambert and appeared with Antony Tudor for a while. Then, back in the United States, she helped launch the American Ballet Theater, both as a dancer and as a major choreographer.

Agnes de Mille created a number of outstanding pieces in an open, energetic style. The best known is *Rodeo*. It was actually created in 1942 for the Ballet Russe de Monte Carlo, which commissioned Aaron Copland to do the music and Oliver Smith the sets. However, it soon became an important fixture of the new American Ballet Theater. *Rodeo* is an exuberant picture of life on a ranch, where cowboys spend their time trying to master frisky horses and attractive women. The leading female role is that of a cowgirl who wears pants and boots and who tries to match the men in ranching skills. Eventually, she blossoms out in a dress and happily settles for being the center of male attention at a dance. De Mille achieved a spirited climax in the ballet with a lively American square dance, and thus a new folk idiom was added to the "character" vocabulary of the ballet.

Another ballet of de Mille's was also based on a bit of American lore, a real historical event that soon took on the dimension of legend. In 1948, to music by Eliot Gould, she created *Fall River Legend*, a psychological portrait of Lizzie Borden who had been accused of killing both her parents with an axe in a New England town in 1892. Then, the American Ballet Theater premiered her *Three Virgins and a Devil*, with music by Respighi, in 1941. This was a sharp, amusing medieval morality play about the Devil, who sets out to corrupt three women on their way to church. The ballet had a star-studded cast that included de Mille herself, Lucia Chase, Eugene Loring, and a newcomer—Jerome Robbins.

Jerome Robbins. Jerome Robbins (born in 1918) is surely the most important native American ballet choreographer to appear so far. He has been intimately connected with both major American companies, producing *Fancy Free* (1944, music by Leonard Bernstein), *Interplay* (1945, music by Eliot Gould), and *Les Noces* (1965, music by Stravinsky) for the American Ballet Theater. He then joined the New York City Ballet to do *The Cage* (1951, music by Stravinsky), *Afternoon of a Faun* (1953, music by Debussy), *Fanfare* (1953, music by Benjamin Britten), *Concert* (1956, music by Chopin), and *Dances At A Gathering* (1969, music also by Chopin). At first glance, Robbins appears to work in a variety of styles: jazzy American in *Fancy Free* and *Interplay*; ballet satire in *Concert*; musical compositions which go as far as *Fanfare* in visualizing the characteristics of specific instruments of an orchestra; pure plotless dance in *Dances At A Gathering*; modern dramatic metaphor in *The Cage*; and new versions of notorious works like *Les Noces* and *Afternoon of a Faun*.

However, a closer look reveals a strong personal style that is uniquely Robbins's. Each Robbins ballet, no matter what its content or message, is carefully structured, and above all, each one treats its dance figures not as sleek machine parts in the Balanchine manner, but as warm, live people who really see one another. At times, they even look directly and personally at the audience. They make significant human gestures that convey

Dancers of American Ballet Theater in a scene from Tudor's "Leaves are Fading."

clear emotions. These often express tender friendship, although the dark side is also present in a work like *The Cage*, where grasping, insectlike females use males for their own satisfaction and then cruelly destroy them.

When Robbins remade two Diaghilev ballets, he treated the themes more sympathetically than they had been in the originals. His *Les Noces* was not less vigorous than Nijinska's original, but his version has a more gentle, communal-folk quality than the earlier, roughly primitive ballet. Similarly, in his *Afternoon of a Faun*, the two figures are actually genuine dancers at rest, rather than an unreal male animal who is discovered by a row of stiff maidens. Robbins arranged this for the New York City Ballet in 1953. This was performed to the same Debussy score that Nijinsky used, but it is simplified to a pas de deux set in a dance studio. The "faun" is a self-involved male dancer, whose kiss with his female partner is only another expression of his narcissistic self-love.

Even Robbins's plotless works involve genuine, moody young people. In *Moves* (1959), deliberately created to be danced in silence, he presents male teenagers showing off in friendly competition, and girls making lazy or sharp motions, at times linking arms in mutual support. One girl broods apart from the others, and is gently comforted by a young man. *Dances At A Gathering*, performed to melodious Chopin selections, unfolds scene after scene of vivacious young people thoughtfully sensing each other and the world around them in lovely arrangements of gestures, steps, and groupings.

Robbins produced the masterpiece, *Dances At A Gathering*, twenty-five years after his first ballet, *Fancy Free*, burst upon the New York scene and announced the presence of a fresh choreographic genius. *Fancy Free*, performed to a brash jazz score by Leonard Bernstein, is a solidly American piece about three sailors on leave, lightheartedly competing for the attention of available girls. It made a sensation at the premiere in 1944 while World War II was still very much in progress, and sailors were a common sight. But popularity did not come because of patriotism in wartime. The ballet drew excellent notices for its "real" people and inventive humor as recently as in a 1970s revival.

It is no wonder that like Agnes de Mille, Jerome Robbins choreographed for Broadway musicals with enormous success. De Mille's contribution to *Oklahoma* in 1943, and Robbins's to *West Side Story* in 1957, made theater history.

Comparing the two masters—Balanchine and Robbins—we can think of Balanchine as a contemporary Petipa, a neoclassicist. We can then place Robbins as a contemporary Fokine, a neoromanticist, to use a fancy term. Fokine's vision of dance was as a vehicle for expressing different moods, and for suiting the gesture to the theme. His great works are simple in pattern, designed less to dazzle the viewer than to move him with a human portrait or an emotional fantasy. The same can be said for Robbins's ballets, such as the three sailors on leave in *Fancy Free*, the frolic in *Interplay*, the earthy Russian folk wedding in *Les Noces*, and his later Chopin works. They all breathe with a live directness. Even the "avant-garde" *Watermill* that he created in 1972 for the New York City Ballet, in the words of *Dance Magazine* critic Doris Hering, "presents a man and his cycle of life...tenderly, majestically...The ballet takes an hour but seems like a minute." Hering's companion thought it lovely, but said *Watermill* was "not dance." (This comment is often made about the avant-garde, as you will see later, when we take up that provocative topic.

A Wide Spectrum of Styles

Now we take note of other important works that are identified with the American scene and particularly with the American Ballet Theater, although several had their first performances elsewhere and were taken into the company later. These few examples will give you some idea of the range of styles that the company explored, according to their wide-ranging policy. Eugene Loring's *Billy the Kid* (1938), like Agnes de Mille's *Rodeo*, is a ballet about American frontier life, and it too employs a fine score by Aaron Copland. However, in mood and content they are quite different. The theme for *Billy the Kid* had been suggested by Lincoln Kirstein, in order to supply the Ballet Caravan with a representative "American" work for its repertory. Therefore *Billy the Kid* presents the legend of a dashing young outlaw who killed a large number of people, and was finally brought down by a sheriff with whom he had once been friends. *Billy the Kid* had its premiere with the Ballet Caravan in Chicago. Then, in 1940, the American Ballet Theater presented it, and did so repeatedly thereafter. In fact, this was to become one of the most popular works in the American Ballet Theater repertory, with its strong, dramatic scenes, and its free, open movements of American pioneers.

In a completely different mode, the American Ballet Theater presented a *Pas de Quatre* that Anton Dolin reconstructed in 1941 from lithographs and reviews of the famous original performance, given in 1845. (To refresh your memory, reread the appropriate passages in Chapter 14.) Dolin's version has moments that gently poke fun at the competitive spirit of the ballet stars Taglioni, Grisi, Cerrito, and Grahn, who are the "characters" in his ballet. Another interesting work frequently danced by the American Ballet Theater is *Caprichos*, choreographed in 1950 by Herbert Ross, to music by Bartók. *Caprichos* contains an unsympathetic, ironic view of useless, bored people in a cruel society. The ballet's four scenes bring to life four etchings by Goya, in compositions of exaggerated gestures, built on a footing of ballet technique.

In 1967, Eliot Feld's *Harbinger*, to music by Prokofiev, was premiered by the American Ballet Theater, and critics immediately hailed the young choreographer as an important new talent. *Harbinger* has no plot, but like Jerome Robbins's ballets, it deals with personal relationships. Eliot Feld (born in 1943) has proved the critics' favorable predictions to be right, producing other successful works for the American Ballet Theater and then for his own company. These include *At Midnight* (1967, music by Mahler), which concerns the struggles of love, and *Intermezzo* (1969), which presents three couples who are ballroom dancing to Brahms's music.

In 1980, Lucia Chase and Oliver Smith, the original directors of the American Ballet Theater, stepped down and appointed Mikhail Baryshnikov in their stead. Baryshnikov, the Russian superstar who made audiences scream with approval at his fantastic performances, continued the company's broad repertory policy, until he left his post in 1990. As of 1992, the repertory continues to range over the whole stylistic mixture of contemporary dance. Its recent programs include a new version of *Coppélia*; an evening-length *Don Quixote* by Soviet dancer Vladimir Vasiliev; and works by avant-garde and Postmodern choreographers like Merce Cunningham, Twyla Tharp, and David Gordon.

Money and Ballet. So, from almost a complete void in the first decades of this century, by 1960, a splendid active ballet scene of international importance had developed in the United States. This did not happen through the efforts of artists alone. The New York City Ballet flourished through George Balanchine's talent, combined with Lincoln Kirstein's vision and money. The American Ballet Theater developed from Mikhail Mordkin's modest group into a company of international stature through Lucia Chase's untiring efforts—and money.

Ballet is an unbelievably expensive activity. Time and place for music rehearsals, splendor of scenery and costumes, publicity, and so on, all cost a lot of money. Take the single item of toe shoes. At over ten dollars a pair, a corps dancer can go through nine pairs a week! It is no wonder that the annual budget for a regularly performing company runs into millions of dollars. Therefore the story of the two companies that put the United States on the map of the ballet world features wealthy dedicated patrons, as well as brilliant dance artists. Because of the existence of these two world-class companies, dance was "in," and everybody wanted to get into the act. There was a huge growth in the number of dancers around, and they all wanted to take part in the national ballet scene. Who was going to pay?

Keep in mind that when we speak of a "national" ballet in America, the word *national* refers to the scope and character of the country's ballet life and not to any government charter or large-scale subsidy. To this day, dance in the United States is supported by ticket buyers and private patrons, with only occasional grants from a public source. This provides an enviable amount of artistic freedom, but at the same time it imposes constricting practical limitations. Ours is the only industrialized nation without a tradition of public support for its artists. This changed a tiny bit in the 1960s, when we got a National Council for the Arts and Humanities, and a number of state arts committees. In addition, private philanthropy— corporate foundations—did respond generously to the growing public interest in dance. During the 1960s, *three thousand* arts centers were built! And dance concerts and companies were funded to fill them. It was at this time that a number of new ballet companies sprang into existence. Here we will discuss only two: the Joffrey Ballet and the Dance Theater of Harlem.

Joffrey Ballet

In Seattle, a doctor sent the sickly child Robert Joffrey (1930 to 1988) to dance for his health. He took to it immediately, and went on to New York to study, perform, and choreograph. Together with Gerald Arpino (born in 1928), he fulfilled his dream of starting a company. They sought a style for the Joffrey Ballet that would give them a niche not occupied by the New York City Ballet or the American Ballet Theater. They found a successful approach in the combination of youthful energy and sensation, and a policy of updating productions or dropping those that didn't fit. The Joffrey Ballet began with a single concert in 1954, and grew to take up residence as the official company of the New York City Center in 1966. (By then, Balanchine's company had left the City Center and moved to a new home at the glamorous Lincoln Center State Theater.) Robert Joffrey spent his time and energy organizing performances, teaching, and setting up first a school, and then Joffrey II, a young apprentice group to feed the parent company. Therefore, by default, the Joffrey Ballet at first resembled the New York City Ballet in that its repertory was largely the work of one choreographer. Gerald Arpino has given the company at least forty works, beginning with ballets like *Viva Vivaldi* (1965) and *Olympics* (1966, to a score by T. Mayuzumi).

For years, *Viva Vivaldi* was the signature work of the Joffrey Ballet. Set with a Spanish flavor to a Vivaldi concerto arranged for guitar and orchestra, the dance contrasts a wispy, delicate women's section with a flamboyant male competition. *Olympics* presents an all-male cast in a zestful impression of the international athletic games. Gradually, however, the Joffrey company began to resemble the American Ballet Theater. It featured new productions of unusual, but well-known works of the international ballet repertory, such as Massine's *Three-Cornered Hat*, Fokine's *Petrouchka*, Cranko's *Romeo and Juliet*, Kurt Joos's *The Green Table*, Ashton's *Illuminations*, and Anna Sokolow's *Opus 65*. It also took works by Postmodernist Laura Dean, and commissioned new pieces by Alvin Ailey and Twyla Tharp. Finally, Robert Joffrey contributed only a few, but some of the company's most interesting works. *Astarte* (1967) was a fascinating pas de deux that included an insistently loud, electronic score; piercing lights that played on the faces of the audience as well as the stage; and a backdrop of huge filmed images of the performers—all elements of the contemporary avant-garde style.

Then, shortly before his death, Joffrey staged *Rite of Spring* (*Sacre du Printemps*). This production is of special interest to us, not just because I have used it as a recurrent theme, but because it was an attempt to reconstruct the original Nijinsky version. Yes, it was possible, because Millicent Hodson, a dance historian, had dug out the pertinent material. Alongside of performances at the New York City Center, there was a three-day public seminar about the work at the Lincoln Center Library. The conclusion of critic Mindy Aloff, in the April 1988 issue of *Dance Magazine*, was that Joffrey's *Sacre du Printemps* was fairly authentic. As to its effectiveness, however, she voiced reservations. It lacked Nijinsky's effort "to reconsider the dynamic qualities of classic dancing from a new perspective." But at some moments the ballet had "an infectious appeal." Certainly, we can applaud the choreographer's commitment to this ambitious project. Furthermore, productions such as this require considerable financial backing. At various times, Joffrey succeeded in getting support from Rebekah Harkness, the Ford Foundation, and the New York City Center, where it has been a resident company. However, money problems have been a constant source of anxiety.

Dance Theater of Harlem

In 1969, Arthur Mitchell (born in 1934), a brilliant and charismatic soloist of the New York City Ballet, who also happened to be black, had a strong reaction to the assassination of the Reverend Martin Luther King, Jr. He left the company where he had worked so hard and given so much pleasure to found a classical ballet company in Harlem. It was his way of giving something back. As we saw in Chapter 28, while there were plenty of black performers starring in successful modern-dance and jazz companies, there were few opportunities for them in classical ballet. And yes, there were a number of talented blacks, with excellent training in ballet. So with the encouragement of both Balanchine and Kirstein, the collaboration of Karel Shook (born in 1920, in Washington), and with the help of a Ford Foundation grant, Mitchell started a school (in 1969) and a company (in 1972).

The Dance Theater of Harlem became a top-notch ensemble. The dancers are known for fine technique; and beyond that, for giving full-blown, theatrical performances that delight their audiences. Its prima ballerina (unofficially, because few contemporary companies still use that title) is Virginia Johnson. Virginia Johnson was born in 1950, and brought up in Washington, D.C. Johnson told Marilyn Hunt (*Dance Magazine* October 1990):

> When I graduated from Mary Day's Washington School of Ballet, and they said, "Maybe you should look for a jazz company or a modern dance company," I felt like I was being banished from the world I knew. But there was really no place for me to go.

Then she found herself with the Dance Theater of Harlem and "the thing that I wanted most but didn't dare ask for had happened." Twenty years later, as Hunt tells us:

> Virginia Johnson is a favorite from New York City to the USSR . . . Her dancing goes straight to the heart . . .
> She believes in what she is doing, and she moves you by means of classical ballet itself, without heavy emoting. Her musicality, lyricism and dramatic

One of Dance Theater of Harlem's star couples, Virginia Johnson and Donald Williams, in Balanchine's "Allegro Brillante."

intensity make a rare and ever-fresh combination. Her seeming physical fragility paradoxically affirms the resilience of the human spirit.

At the same time she is a willowy, elegant five feet eight inches tall, possessed of perfect line, perfect proportion. As Balanchine said of her, "there's more to see."

The repertory of the Dance Theater of Harlem includes plotless Balanchine pieces, dramatic ballets by Agnes de Mille and Antony Tudor, classics like Fokine's *The Firebird*, and a *Giselle* set by Frederic Franklin that remains true to the traditional choreography, even though it takes place on a plantation in pre-Civil-War Louisiana. In 1989, the Dance Theater of Harlem celebrated its twentieth birthday, and got great reviews. Then suddenly there was trouble. The Dance Theater of Harlem closed down in May 1990. Was it because there were no dancers? no audience? no choreographers? Not at all—there was no money.

Here, however, we had a double whammy: lack of money combined with racial prejudice. The question was, where would the dancers go? Oh, with their fantastic talents and skills, they could always find work in modern dance or show business. But they were trained, talented classical ballet dancers and that's where their interests lay. Take Ronald Perry, who was going to be the first black American *danseur noble*, according to critics like Clive Barnes. He didn't want to settle for less. So while he was hired as a soloist by the American Ballet Theater, he did not receive the major roles in *Swan Lake* and *The Sleeping Beauty* to which he felt entitled. As Lowell Smith, another member of the Dance Theater of Harlem, told Martha Ullman West of *Dance Magazine* (October 1990): "A black dancer can do five pirouettes, double tours, sixes up the ying yang, but he still won't get the roles." Fortunately, sponsors rushed to the bankrupt company's aid, and it is back in business, in better shape than ever. But the crisis points up the tenacious grip of racial prejudice.

Regional Companies. The dance explosion in the 1960s was not confined to New York. This period also saw the development of regional ballet, with new companies springing up or old ones maturing, all over the country. The San Francisco Ballet, and Ballet West in Utah, both connected with the work of the Christensen brothers, expanded rapidly. So did the Pennsylvania Ballet, the Boston Ballet, the Atlanta Ballet, the Los Angeles Ballet, and others. In the 1990s, there are three things to keep in mind about the ballet art in the United States:

1.   There are dozens of first-rate American companies, with a repertory of "American" ballets, which are well received on tours abroad as well as at home. Ballet is part of the scene in every region of this large country.

2.   The stylistic lines between companies are blurring and dissolving as choreographers, artistic directors, and starring dancers move around from one ensemble to another. In choreography, stylistic lines between modern dance, ballet, and jazz are also blurring.

3.   Money has always been a problem for the American dance art, and the picture in the 1990s is not any better. In fact, given the general financial situation in the United States, support of dance may well weaken.

Dancers in the Golden Age of American Ballet

Up to this point, I have paid little attention to individual dancers in the chapters on American ballet. It's a real shame, because when you come right down to it, it's the dancers you see at the ballet, not an abstract choreographic vision. Unfortunately, however, performers come and go. A dancer's performing career is painfully short. What remains is repertory, style, and historical tradition. These facets change much more slowly than the lists of company membership. Nevertheless, there are performers who not only were outstanding in their day, but some who were so impressive that they stimulated the public and choreographers to a high degree, both individually and as teams (partners). The first group of great classical dancers in American ballet all came from abroad.

Alexandra Danilova and Frederic Franklin. Like Balanchine, Danilova was Russian born (1904) and trained. She danced leading roles in Diaghilev's company, then as prima ballerina in the Ballet Russe de Monte Carlo, and finally in the American Ballet Theater. When she was partnered by the British-born (1914) Frederic Franklin, Walter Terry (in *The Ballet Companion*) tells us the electrifying team was adored by the public: "Both were ebullient by nature, both had a feel for the bravura and both projected (when suitable) bubbling humor."

Alicia Markova and Anton Dolin. Also highly popular, but in a more restrained style, was the British-born duo, Markova (born in 1910) and Dolin (born in 1904). Walter Terry rated their *Giselle* (staged by Dolin) as the finest of their era. During their years with the American Ballet Theater, they appeared in many classical roles.

Alicia Alonso and Igor Youskevitch. Terry reports that the Cuban "fiery Alonso" (born in 1921) and the Russian-born (1912) "dapper premier *danseur* Youskevitch," both in their own company and at the American Ballet Theater, also had their triumphs in *Giselle* and other classics. Terry noted: "For a time, New York balletomanes formed separate camps (as did the highly partisan followers of Taglioni and Elssler), one hailing the younger team of Alonso-Youskevitch, and the other singing the praises of their incomparable Markova-Dolin."

Nora Kaye. Balletomanes did not confine their admiration to the classical styles. Nora Kaye (born in 1920) attracted a tremendous following as the greatest dramatic ballerina of the mid-twentieth century (in my opinion and that of Walter Terry). Kaye threw herself into her roles like a "method" actress. In *Giselle*, her mad scene projected a passionate, neurotic woman, rather than a fragile, romantic girl. Terry relates that at one performance Kaye danced Blanche in *A Streetcar Named Desire* (choreographed by modern dancer Valerie Bettis). She was about to be ravished by Stanley (danced by Igor Youskevitch):

> Kaye, her fists clenched and held high, was doing violent turns. Youskevitch stepped in a fraction too soon to grab her. He was hit on the temple by a Kaye fist and knocked cold.
> Improvising, the ballerina did an erotic and intensely dynamic dance over the inert body. "What else could I do?" she asked after the performance.

"Short of lying down and pulling Igor on top of me, I couldn't think of any other way to end the scene."

Maria Tallchief. Our first, great, home-grown classical ballerina, Tallchief was born in 1925 on an Indian reservation in Oklahoma. (Her father was a full-blooded Osage, while her mother was of Scottish-Irish descent.) As a child, she performed Native American dances. Her family moved to Los Angeles in 1933 so that she and her sister Marjorie Tallchief (also a dancer) could get professional training. When she was twelve years old, she studied with Bronislava Nijinska, and later with David Lichine. In 1940, she made her first professional appearance in Nijinska's *Chopin Concerto*. In 1942, she joined the Ballet Russe de Monte Carlo and within a few years she was a soloist—and Balanchine's third wife. Tallchief was a major dancer in the New York City Ballet from its beginnings until the 1960s. She created a large number of roles in Balanchine ballets. After she left his company, she appeared with many companies on her own and with the brilliant Danish dancer, Erik Bruhn.

In 1962, I had the pleasure of interviewing the ballerina. She said she had never had any interest in choreography, but enjoyed almost all the roles she had danced, especially those in *Swan Lake*, *Firebird*, and *Miss Julie*. A real trouper, Tallchief performed all over America, where audiences were always receptive, although working conditions were sometimes tough. She lamented:

Sometimes the stage was so cramped, I felt I should dance with my elbows squeezed tight against my body . . .
There was that dreadful moment when I was dancing with a regional ballet company, in one of their costumes, and I felt the zipper pop. Suddenly there was Erik Bruhn, partnering my costume instead of me!

Tallchief has been called "cold." This label came, it seemed to me, from her awesome mastery of technique. For example, in her performance of the *grand pas* from *Raymonda* (with the American Ballet Theater), I found her manner imperial, pure, almost sculptured. Her approach was to produce a series of exquisite pictures, moving from one perfect pose to another, rather than to give a fluid sense of movement through space and time.

Carla Fracci. Fracci was born in Italy, in 1936. Although she was the prima ballerina of the La Scala company in the late 1950s, she is in this section because she joined the American Ballet Theater in 1967, where she became America's most notable interpreter of Romantic roles. Partnered by Erik Bruhn, hers was considered *the* Giselle of the 1960s. For her beautiful performances in the American Ballet Theater's *La Sylphide*, she has been called the Taglioni of the mid-twentieth century. In *Dance Magazine*,

January 1974, Tobi Tobias wrote: "Fracci conveys the whole emotional tenor of the Romantic era...She doesn't perform just to perform. She has something to say, a spiritual communication...Her dancing isn't technical. It's grace and beauty. It's poetry." Unlike the Taglioni-like Fracci, the dancers we are about to discuss all enjoyed outstanding careers in the New York City Ballet, where the Romantic style is not prominent.

Melissa Hayden. Born in Canada (in 1923), Hayden received her serious training in the U.S. She appeared with the American Ballet Theater and elsewhere, but from 1950 until 1973, she gained an international reputation as a principal dancer in the New York City Ballet, and as the creator of roles for a number of choreographers. Hayden is not known for the great classical roles, but for the modern pieces in which her unique dramatic ability comes through. I'll never forget her performance in Todd Bolender's unfortunately short-lived version of *The Miraculous Mandarin* (1951). She made the role of the prostitute a driven, predatory figure who focused the whole action. In a 1966 Boston concert, Melissa Hayden flew through space in Balanchine's *Thais*, executing this romantic dance with a surging exhilaration and an intensity that kept me at the edge of my seat. In a 1967 interview, she told me: "I love to move in space—like ice skating—across the floor. . . . Abstract ballets are more difficult. It is the most natural thing to react to people onstage. The relationship must be physical, not mental. Its quality depends on the choreographer."

Jacques d'Amboise. Born in Massachusetts (1934), d'Amboise developed into one of the finest interpreters of Balanchine's neoclassicism. D'Amboise frequently partnered Melissa Hayden. Both were completely at home in the classics. In 1970, I saw them do an elegant *Swan Lake* in the finest tradition, as guests of the Boston Ballet Company. At that same performance, the unabashed exhibitionism of Balanchine's pas de deux from *Sylvia* (music by Tchaikovsky), allowed them to pull out all the stops. Hayden's easy command of tricky footwork, quick balances, and fast turns, and d'Amboise's exciting *jetés* and *cabrioles* (a leap in which one leg is thrown upward and then both legs are beaten together) provided all the virtuosity an audience could want.

Edward Villella. Born in New York (1937), Villella was for many years a rarity in Balanchine's New York City Ballet in that he was an outstanding male dancer. Villella's dynamism and irresistible, virile energy made him a public favorite. In the early 1960s, when American companies had few men of the stature of Russian and Danish stars, I remember well how Villella's loyal fans were torn by the arrival in the West of Rudolf Nureyev. Edward Villella was superb in Balanchine's *Prodigal Son*. In a 1966 performance, he seemed to me to dance like one possessed. Leaping into the air with pent-up vitality, he combined unbelievable elevation with fantastic expressiveness. Then, his slide down from this peak allowed him to show brutish drunkenness, dehumanized sexuality, and a final crawl home for forgiveness—all magnificently danced and acted.

Edward Villella and Patricia McBride were a gratifying New York City Ballet team. McBride, born in New Jersey (1942), grew constantly in stature, beginning in the late 1950s, not only in technical virtuosity but also in generosity of spirit. When McBride appeared with Villella in a pas de deux like the "Rubies" section in Balanchine's *Jewels* or the master's Tchaikovsky pas de deux, it suddenly became obvious what ballet was all about. Darting around the stage together, she plunging daringly into space and he catching her at the last moment, they made gems of these little pieces because they always manifested that slight restraint that kept exhibitionism in the realm of art—distinct from circus acrobatics.

Appearing on the same stage (at a benefit for the Boston Ballet) with Villella and McBride, two other memorable dancers deserve special mention here as stars of the golden age of American dance: Carmen de Lavallade and Geoffrey Holder. These two are more a team in personal life (husband and wife) than in dance.

Carmen de Lavallade. Born in Los Angeles (1931), de Lavallade is a special kind of dancer, equally at home in ballet, modern dance, Broadway shows, movies, and television. In dancers who have tremendous technical facility but no commitment to communication, this kind of versatile ease often makes for slickness. However, Carmen de Lavallade yields to no one in giving the fullest value to the motivations behind every movement. As a result, she involves audiences so deeply in the emotions of her role that they may well miss the difficulty of her technical feats.

In a 1968 interview, when I tried to pinpoint the secrets of her artistry, she gave the credit to the Lester Horton Theater: "They taught everything with a dramatic image. Movements—no matter how abstract—were always given to you to do 'as if' you were a certain person, in a certain situation. This is a great help in enlivening a part." That certainly isn't a sufficient explanation, but of course it is really not possible to define the secret of artistry. In any case, de Lavallade has been enormously successful in everything she has done, which includes the film *Carmen Jones*, the Broadway musical *House of Flowers* (where she met and married Geoffrey Holder), Metropolitan Opera productions, the TV production of John Butler's *Amahl and the Night Visitors*, touring with Alvin Ailey's company, and as a guest artist with the American Ballet Theater, dancing *The Four Marys*, created specially for her by Agnes de Mille.

When de Lavallade received a *Dance Magazine* award in 1967, television producer Pamela Ilott put into words what many viewers have felt: "There is in Carmen de Lavallade what can only be described as the really pure flame of someone who really cares intensely about things that are beautiful and meaningful. And that shines through her dance."

Geoffrey Holder. Born in 1930 in Haiti, Holder is, like his wife, a most impressive dancer; and like her, he has appeared in a variety of productions at the Metropolitan Opera, with John Butler's company, and with his own group. In a 1966 Boston performance of *Dougla*, he seemed to embody the most beautiful features of an ancient tribal culture. I still remember his six-foot, six-inch presence clothed in fluid draperies, making simple, noble gestures or arresting staccato movements, his head tilted on his magnificent trunk, bent forward or majestically erect. Unlike his wife, Holder is also known as a fine choreographer. He choreographed *Three Songs in One* for Carmen de Lavallade at the 1966 Dance Festival in Central Park. It was unanimously proclaimed the most memorable performance at the festival. He also choreographed for Ailey's company, for the Dance Theater of Harlem, and for the film *Live and Let Die*.

Suzanne Farrell. Born in 1945 in Ohio, Farrell became the New York City Ballet's leading ballerina during the late 1960s. George Balanchine called her his muse. For her he created many roles, notably the part of Dulcinea in *Don Quixote* (1965). Farrell's style was very personal, called in turn "cool" and "sultry" by Marcia Siegel, in *At the Vanishing Point*. In *Dancers, Buildings and People in the Streets*, critic Edwin Denby wrote: "As Dulcinea, pensive young Suzanne Farrell is ravishing in the lucid grace of her mime and of her miraculous dancing...Lovely Farrell is at her loveliest in *Meditation* (Balanchine 1963). You see her yield completely, fainting with a soft abandon in a supported deep backbend, and before you see the recovery, she is already standing apart, mild and free."

Peter Martins. Martins frequently partnered Farrell. Born in Denmark in 1946, he was a solo dancer at the Royal Danish Ballet before he joined the New York City Ballet in 1969. Within a short time, he was delighting New York audiences with his elegant, exciting partnering and Robbins's inspired choreography. Robbins created roles for him in *The Goldberg Variations* (1971) and *Piano Concerto in G* (1975). In 1972, Balanchine choreographed parts for him in two Stravinsky ballets: *Duo Concertant* and *Violin Concerto*.

There were many other fine dancers during the American golden age who have not been mentioned above; and in the years since that time, there have been dozens more—maybe hundreds! There is simply not enough space to describe the qualities of these worthy artists. Keep in mind, however, that they are often the main attraction in a ballet performance. Audiences tend to identify dancers with the art of ballet, rather than choreographers and composers. You undoubtedly have your own lists of favorite performers. Now, in a single bound, we leave the dramatic heat of these passionate ballet dancers to plunge into the frigid abstractions of the new avant-garde.

Questions for Review

1. Why do we call Jerome Robbins "the Fokine of American ballet"?

2. Contrast the two major American ballet companies as to their approaches to repertory.

3. Who supports American ballet financially?

4. How would you describe the style of American dancers in comparison to that of English dancers?

31 BODIES
IN MOTION

MERCE CUNNINGHAM AND ALWIN NIKOLAIS

A New Avant-garde

We have already noticed in our history that as the pendulum of fashion in the dance art swings back and forth, it knocks down many of the accepted beliefs of each generation. At the same time, it brings into prominence theories that stand in direct opposition to those produced in the previous generation. The style known as modern dance had come into being in a spirit of freedom and rebellion against the entire field of ballet, which the new breed condemned for its sterility and lack of significance. By the middle of the twentieth century, a new revolt was necessary in modern dance itself, because the territory was overpopulated by tiresome imitators of the great pioneers. Thus there were too many "introspective" dances, and too many copies of familiar gestures. Further, once the "conventional" modern dancers had won the field and had been accepted, they proceeded to defeat their own aims by becoming too competent in technique.

Remember that modern dance was originally allied closely with primitive movement, and even with that of children, exploring what Martha Graham called "divine awkwardness." But gradually, the younger modern dancers mastered many schools of modern as well as classical ballet. They became so highly proficient that they found it easier to execute slick, mechanically brilliant movements than to explore the emotional source of gesture—the original impetus for modern dance. In an interview, Pauline Koner, a first-rate artist who came to prominence in Doris Humphrey's company, lectured against these tendencies: "Of course you have to have that much technique—but you don't have to show it off for its own sake! You must be motivated even to make an entrance on the stage—else why perform at all?" Koner, like Humphrey, believed that the choreographer's craft was to organize all the elements of a composition so that they expressed and communicated the artist's inner life of feeling.

Aside from developments *within* the dance world, in the 1950s and 1960s, the cultural climate of all the Western arts was changing sharply as painters, sculptors, musicians, and writers questioned the practices of their forerunners. The members of this avant-garde turned against the content of social realism and Freudian psychology of the 1930s and 1940s. They rebelled against the conventional structures that provided theme and development, climax and resolution, or contrast and unity. Instead, they focused on the *materials* of their art.

For their outlook on life and the world, the new creators turned to Eastern philosophies and theories of chance and indeterminacy. From their viewpoint, artists should erase the boundaries between one art and another, and break down the barriers between art and life. The creed, the mission of these artists, was to open themselves—and their audiences—to an awareness of the whole world, and everything in it. In fact, they asked: Why should there be a distinction at all between artists and viewers? Because artists are also people, it stands to reason that all people have a desire to create. At the very least, these artists invited their audiences to participate with them in art events.

This avant-garde reached back to pre-World War I experiments, when surrealism, dada, and atonal music were used in Diaghilev's Ballets Russes. This time around, there were added features. In the new 1960s music, there were sounds generated by electronic audio tape and by computers. Developments in painting and sculpture were labelled "pop," "minimal," "collage," "found art," or "nonobjective." Artworks might include the meticulous representation of familiar objects like soup cans, or improvised "action" paintings, where a model covered with paint might roll on a canvas. A poem might consist of one word, repeated forward and backward. And for every work, and every artist, there was a complete aesthetic philosophy. In fact, you might keep in mind that *the concept was as important, if not more important, than the artwork itself.*

Happenings. The outstanding expression of the mid-century avant-garde was the *happening*. It embodied two ideas: (1) art is play, with the added element that the player "observes" or is aware of the game; and (2) a real, fully realized artwork may well be consumed, used up, in the process of creation. Since the heyday of happenings occurred during the 1960s, you may never have attended one. You would have enjoyed some tremendously, as you would a party, when everything works just right. If you have any kind of critical sense, you would also have found some of them boring, or irritating beyond endurance. You must keep in mind, however, that according to the avant-garde philosophy, if you were bored, it was because you didn't participate in the proper spirit and the fault was yours.

Don't let the word *happening* confuse you. This is a planned activity, by one artist or several, although the preparation leaves room both for improvisations and unplanned occurrences. Here are examples of happenings and other avant-garde works, none of which lend themselves to exact classification. The first example, along with essays on the avant-garde, is described in Michael Kirby's book *The Art of Time*. Examples 2 and 4 are discussed in *The New American Arts* by Richard Kostelanetz.

1. Claes Oldenburg did a piece called *Washes*, set at a swimming pool. A girl lay floating on her back, covered with balloons. A man exploded the balloons by biting them. The "lifeguard" walked around helping with props, such as turning a record player on and off. Four men held a red clothesline in the water, and pushed sections of silver flue pipe back and forth along the rope.

2. In Robert Rauschenberg's *Pelican*, set on a skating rink, the performers wore roller skates and had parachutes attached to their backs.

3. Rauschenberg arranged a complex production at New York's Twenty-fifth Street Armory. He told Richard Kostelanetz for a *New York Times* article which described the event:

> My theater piece begins with an authentic tennis game with rackets wired for transmission of sound. The sounds of balls hitting rackets will control the lights. During the game, the sounds will turn out the lights one by one . . . A modestly choreographed cast of from 300 to 500 persons will enter to be observed and projected by infrared television onto the screens.

4. John Cage's musical composition 4'33 (four minutes and thirty-three seconds of silence) allowed any incidental sounds in the concert hall to be part of the piece.

5. One summer day in San Francisco, Ann Halprin took dancers and architects to the seashore and gave them the task of building driftwood structures. The result was a village, with housing that reflected the personal needs of the builders. As Jack Anderson describes the project in *Dance Magazine* (November 1966):

> A glamorous, athletic girl built a kind of sun-deck on which she could bask beneath the open sky like a goddess in a house of light. A more retiring boy dug into the sand to build a cave-like place for contemplation. A team of workers built a structure resembling a temple. Other people built a playhouse, a public forum, a house with water flowing through it, a gate, a lean-to, and a snug husband-and-wife house just big enough for two.

The artists ate, talked, and slept in their village, and didn't want to leave it the next day.

6. This is what I found at Brandeis University, in January 1967, when I struggled up an icy hill with a friend to attend a performance of the Once Group from Ann Arbor, Michigan. On the stage, a silent procession of black-clad bodies with flashing red lights sat down at a table. A voice came over the sound system:

> Do you want to see a dirty film? Anyone who wants to see a dirty film, take off your shoes and stand on your seat. Come on now, I see two people standing. Aren't there any more who want to see a dirty film? Don't be shy. Just stand on your seats.

Soon there were over one hundred young people standing on their seats, and yet the monologue continued for at least ten minutes, pleading that more than two people should respond. Even the stalwart seat standers tried to move the action along by hissing and clapping. Then finally, a fuzzy, dim film of a gyrating nude female was projected on a brick wall.

"Now," said the taped Big Brother, "everybody undress and change clothes with the person sitting next to you." This time, there was less audience participation than before, although we did notice on the side balcony a tall boy exchanging sweaters and boots with a tall girl. Someone handed out Italian bread and chocolate. Then a balloon descended from the ceiling, swelled, and burst. All of this took well over an hour, punctuated by girls flashing spotlights in our eyes, and loud noises like bomb explosions and jet planes erupting from the mike. I had sunglasses but no earplugs to defend myself. And so it went. There were several "centers" of avant-garde experimentation. One was at Black Mountain College, where John Cage (1912-1992) was recognized as a pacesetter, if not *the* most important leader of the new wave, through his own work and that of students like David Tudor. Another center was in New York City, where all kinds of artists have always rubbed elbows with one another. There was also a center in San Francisco, under Ann Halprin's innovative direction.

Ann Halprin. Halprin (born in 1920, and later changed her name to Anna) started out as a dancer, studying at the University of Wisconsin with Margaret H'Doubler and appearing with Humphrey and Weidman in the show *Sing Out Sweet Land*. She taught in her own studio in San Francisco from 1948 to 1955. Then she broke away from conventional dance, and founded the Dancers Workshop. The idea was to explore the possibilities of body movement in collaboration with avant-garde painters, architects, musicians, and dancers.

Halprin's central interest was in freeing, not just the dancer, but the person. She sought the artist in everybody as a means of (Gestalt) therapy.

Many of her exercises used "free association." Through her work, dancers developed deep concentration, that is, the ability to enter a special "dance state." Her methods emphasized improvisation, the use of language, and tasks, like building the driftwood village described above.

Because Halprin is a dancer, and because John Cage has been associated since the 1940s with Merce Cunningham, the effect of these developments on the dance art was tremendous. A new style was born, one in which the avant-garde dancers bent over backward to avoid any hint of significance, emotion, plot, or traditional form in their works. Not surprisingly, these new revolutionaries appealed to a small, devoted following, quite unlike the wide, general audience that flocked to the stirring programs of the passionate or jazzy modern dancers. The outstanding dance artist of the avant-garde was, and is, Merce Cunningham.

Merce Cunningham

Before Cunningham, dance expressed emotions: ecstasy, fear, anger, and frustration. It made statements about human dignity, freedom, anxiety, and brotherhood. It was performed by dancers who were trained to project feelings dramatically. After Cunningham's appearance, dance was for and about movement. It presented trained bodies with expressionless faces, moving about in space. Or, it discarded all the trappings of art and showed ordinary people randomly doing things. Before Cunningham, dance was composed according to formal principles. It was accompanied by music that reinforced the moods of the dance. After Cunningham, dance dispensed with recognizable themes and structures. The artist worked by trial and error, or by chance methods. An artwork might have been produced according to a mathematical formula, or to test the limits of time, space, or an idea. The accompaniment he chose might have been silence, broken by the rustling of the audience, music having no connection with the action, or words uttered by the performers themselves.

In other words, the avant-garde turned its back on the discoveries of modern dance, and set out to invent a new art form. In its heyday during the 1960s, the avant-garde and its followers were a thriving cult with full-fledged prophets like Merce Cunningham's musical director, John Cage, Marshall McLuhan, a Canadian humanities professor, and beyond them, the Hindu and Buddhist sages of the Orient. Years later, we can look back and see the avant-garde as one more new wave, becoming absorbed in the vast sea of dance history. Like the early modern dancers, as well as the innovators of the Ballets Russes, this avant-garde also made—and continues to make—its contributions through the vision and talent of each individual artist. Of the hundreds who have worked in this form, you will now meet a select few, beginning with Merce Cunningham.

Born in Centralia, Washington (1919), Merce asked to take dancing lessons in his home town, when he was twelve. The available teacher, a Mrs. Barrett, was experienced in vaudeville as well as in the circus where she had been a bareback rider. Seeing a "natural dancer" in the boy, she provided his first performing experience by taking him on tour with her daughter. In 1937, after high school graduation, Cunningham went away to study acting at the Cornish School in Seattle. But once more, he was drawn toward dance. He studied with Bonnie Bird, a Graham dancer, and made the acquaintance of John Cage, who played the piano accompaniment in class.

By 1940, Merce Cunningham was in New York, a soloist in Martha Graham's company, where until 1945 he created a series of brilliant, soaring roles in Graham masterworks like *Letter To The World* and *Every Soul Is A Circus*. Always an independent thinker, even before he left Graham, Cunningham was already studying ballet technique, something that few modern dancers were doing then. He spent two years at the American School of Ballet, gaining the dexterity and speed that are necessary to ballet technique. He was also experimenting with new artistic approaches and his own movement techniques. In 1942, he did original pieces with Jean Erdman (another Graham soloist) to music by Norman Lloyd and John Cage. In 1943, Agnes de Mille invited Merce Cunningham to be in a musical play on Broadway, where many dance artists were appearing. He rehearsed for a solo role in *One Touch of Venus*, but withdrew before the opening because he felt so ridiculous. In the same way, at the Graham Company he found it nonsense that each particular movement you were given meant something specific.

Then, in 1944, he gave a joint recital with John Cage at the Humphrey-Weidman studio. The critic Edwin Denby wrote: "I have never seen a first recital that combined such impeccable taste, such originality of dance material, so sure a manner of presentation." From then on, Cunningham and Cage gave annual recitals in New York, and at various colleges, where they aroused strong feelings, many of them negative. Painters and musicians were warmer fans of theirs than other modern dancers. Robert Rauschenberg, making a splash in th e visual arts,worked with Cunninhgham on many of his pieces. Jasper Johns and Andy Warhol were also collaborators. In 1947, the first commission for the Cunningham-Cage team came from the Ballet Society, for whom they created *The Seasons*, with decor by Isamu Noguchi.

That same year, they began to spend their summers at Black Mountain College in North Carolina, teaching and performing experimental pieces. In 1952, Cage put on *Theater Piece #1*, which, with its mixture of dancing, slides, poetry, films, and unplanned activities, was a forerunner of the mixed-media pieces and happenings of the 1960s. Cunningham supported himself and his performances by teaching. In 1949, he formed a

New York City Ballet dancers perform in Merce Cunningham's "Summerspace."

company from his pupils, among them Judith Dunn, Viola Farber, Paul Taylor, Remy Charlip, and Carolyn Brown. In the summer of 1953, the company was invited to reside as a unit at Black Mountain College. Cunningham made new pieces like *Collage* and *Suite by Chance*, which featured Christian Wolff's electronic score, the first to be written for a dance.

From then on, he continued to turn out works that drew devoted fans who were delighted by the originality of Cunningham's approach and the wonderfully concentrated performances of the choreographer and his company. Although the concert programs never differentiated among the dancers, Carolyn Brown was an unforgettable soloist, bringing an extra quality of magnetism to her every appearance. On the other hand, many in the audiences were alienated by the absence of clear content, and by the lack of connection with the frequently disturbing sound-score accompaniment, which featured nerve-shattering volume, inanity, or discordant shrieks.

Major works in the Cunningham repertory include: *Antic Meet*, music by Cage, 1958; *Summerspace*, music by M. Feldman, 1958; *Crises*, music by Nancarrow, 1960; *Field Dances*, music by Cage, 1963; *Winterbranch*, music by LaMonte Young, 1964; *How To Pass, Kick, Fall and Run*, to accompaniment of stories by John Cage, 1965; *Scramble*, music by Ichiyanagi, 1967; and *Rainforest*, music by Tudor, 1968. Cunningham started a series of *Events* in 1964. Consecutively numbered, they reached 143 in 1976. A highly successful four-week New York season in 1988 demonstrated Cunningham's continuing inventiveness with works like *Fabrications* and *Eleven*.

The outstanding feature of Merce Cunningham's dance compositions is their attention to the details of movement and its variations. Through his long career, he has never departed from the conviction that the wonderful thing about dance is motion. In 1951, he wrote: "Technique is the disciplining of one's energies through physical action in order to free that energy in its highest possible physical and spiritual form." By 1968, he had replaced the word *spiritual* with the word *interest*. He said, "Dancing provides something—an amplification of energy—that is not provided any other way, and that's what interests me." Spiritual or not, Cunningham's choreography is about movement. "I begin with moving around," he told me in 1970. "It doesn't come from an idea about something." Sometimes it was a sequence that he developed in the studio, at other times it was a movement idea. He described *Winterbranch* as "various kinds of falls," and *Summerspace* as "steps that carry one through a space and not only into it, like the passage of birds or automobiles relentlessly throbbing along turnpikes." About *Crises* he commented: "I was interested in the possibilities of people being together, and then it occurred to me that there were several ways that people could be together—by supporting each other, or hanging on to each other, or one could be attached without holding. Then it occurred to me to try elastics."

At this point, having a movement theme, Cunningham often used chance means to develop his material. The method goes something like this. Let's say he decided on a walking step for two dancers. On a series of cards he would note arm movements: swinging, lifting, holding still. On another series of cards he would note body directions: forward, backward, sideways, or diagonal. On another series he would note levels: high, medium, low, on the floor, or off the floor. On other cards he would note speeds: fast, slow, or moderate. On others, he would note dynamics: sharp, smooth, or uneven. Then he would note stage space: center, from the wings, or in front. He would flip his cards and get the first phrase of the dance: from opposite sides of the stage two figures enter, one backward in a low crouch, with arms swinging wildly; the other moves sideways in an uneven, limping gait, holding the arms quietly overhead.

Why go through all this rigamarole? Wouldn't it be easier to plan something mentally? Cunningham said:

> The feeling I have when I compose in this way is that I am in touch with a natural resource far greater than my own personal inventiveness could ever be . . .it is a mode of freeing my imagination from its own clichés.

Did he eliminate parts that he didn't like?

> I don't discard, but I simply look at what comes up and attempt to deal with it, and not to make the decision by saying well this isn't good, or I don't like that.

Some things don't work for practical reasons—the dancer might have to be up in the air in one movement and in the next one on his head. But even that would be possible if you could assume that something could go on in between. That's the kind of thing I would allow for naturally, since I always think we are human beings.

But Cunningham never allowed himself to be bound by rules—even his own. There were times when he *did* choose consciously. When he choreographed *Scramble*, for instance, we learn from Calvin Tompkins's piece in *The New Yorker* (May 1968):

He would change the movement if it did not seem to work well, or if the dancer felt uncomfortable doing it. Sometimes he would see something unexpected that he liked and would incorporate it. . . . Until the last minute he experimented with the order of the sequences, and added whole new passages.

In an interview, I asked him about music. Did he ever feel that the inane repetitions or intolerable, high-decibel sounds produced by John Cage or LaMonte Young might negate interest in the onstage movement? Cunningham answered:

Perhaps the sound and movement work to support each other. Perhaps if the music had not been "negating the movement," then it would have been less interesting!

The sounds, movement and decor are made separately—they are made without one dictating to the other. It's not a case of "you have to follow me, or support me"—they are simply three separate acts which are allowed to coexist. It seems to me we can't have colonialism anymore!

To the question of meaning in a dance, he replied:

A dance produces a kind of effect, but I don't plan it specifically. One brings one's own experience to anything. That's perfectly legitimate. That's what it's all about. One doesn't have to be told how to react. One reacts. And I don't have to force people to feel something.

Take *Winterbranch*. Cunningham said it was about various kinds of falls. He was interested "in the possibility of having a person dragged out of the area while lying or sitting down." Cunningham has never denied that his dances present human beings in motion, and that these human activities bear connotations. This artist was aware, you see, that when human beings fall, or when they are dragged, it is because they are sick, old, hurt, or dying. In connection with *Winterbranch*, for which Robert Rauschenberg arranged the décor and lighting, Cunningham said:

There is a streak of violence in me....I asked him to think of the light as though it were night instead of day. I don't mean night as referred to in romantic pieces, but night as it is in our time with automobiles on highways, and flashlights in faces, and the eyes being deceived about shapes by the way light hits them.

The sound element is an electronic extension of two different sounds, one low and one high, which go on continuously for most of the piece: fifteen minutes.

Winterbranch assaults the audience. Brilliant lights flash on and off at irregular intervals, sometimes turned right into the eyes of the spectators. The sounds rumble and screech unbearably. It is not surprising that the piece caused a furor everywhere. In Europe, people thought it was about the Holocaust. In Japan, they said it was about the atomic bomb. In New York, some saw it as terror on a subway train. So you see, it really is very simple. Go and look and listen, and make of the activities whatever you will. A dance work is an object for you to perceive, no more and no less. Will you like it? You will if you let yourself. Says Merce:

What gets in the way is a mind saying "Oh no, that's wrong," or "that shouldn't be done." Well, what if you got rid of all those and just said, "This is what it is. Maybe if I look at it for a while, it might grow interesting!"

This philosophy is expressed in one of the little stories that John Cage tells in *How To Pass, Kick, Fall and Run*, a work that is opposite in tone to *Winterbranch*. Its playful sequences are bouncy and light. The accompaniment consists of Cage's wry anecdotes, each one read in exactly one minute, regardless of the story's length:

At the New School, once, I was substituting for Henry Cowell, teaching a class in Oriental music. I had told him I didn't know anything about the subject. He said, "That's all right. Just go where the records are. Take one out. Play it and then discuss it with the class."

Well, I took out the first record. It was an LP of a Buddhist service. It began with a short microtonal chant with sliding tones, then settled into a single loud reiterated percussive beat. The noise continued relentlessly for about fifteen minutes with no perceptible variations.

A lady got up and screamed, and then yelled, "Take it off. I can't bear it any longer." I took it off. A man in the class then said angrily, "Why'd you take it off? I was just getting interested."

Alwin Nikolais

The work of Alwin Nikolais (born in 1912) resembles Merce Cunningham's in that its content lies in the art form itself, rather than in dramatic, psychological, or emotional statements. Nikolais once said he was fed up with seeing modern dancers writhing on the floor to express their sexual frustrations, something that a good many young women were doing in the 1940s and 1950s, in ludicrous imitations of Martha Graham. In fact, Nikolais carried his preference for abstract designs over emotional communication into a plea for male liberation:

> I have particular points of view about the difference between the male and female mind in respect to abstraction . . .What I'd like to point out is that the male is far more inclined to the abstract, and the field of dance is overpoweringly female and matriarchal. I hope fervently for the time when the sociodynamic climate will re-establish the male in a more just position in the modern dance world.

The above comment was written before 1965 (it appears in Cohen's *The Modern Dance, Seven Statements of Belief*) at a time when the great women— Duncan, St. Denis, Wigman, Graham, Humphrey, Holm—who had indeed dominated the field, were giving way to the men: Cunningham, Paul Taylor, José Limón, Alvin Ailey, Erick Hawkins, John Butler, Murray Louis, and Nikolais himself. We will drop this controversial subject by noting that fine female artists like Twyla Tharp continued to be outstanding in the use of the "abstract" as well!

Born in Connecticut, Nikolais leaned toward theater arts since his youth. He hung around the local "little theater," where he learned stagecraft by trying things out, a method which was to become a lifelong approach to his creations. He enjoyed piano lessons and painting, and by the time he was sixteen, he was a piano accompanist for the silent movies. This required continuous improvisation to suit the action and mood of a film. From this, he went on to become an accompanist for dance classes.

In 1933, he attended a concert by Mary Wigman, the German modern dancer. The percussion instruments that accompanied the dancers made a deeper impression on him than their movements. This led him to Hartford, where Truda Kaschman ran a Wigman school. He wanted percussion lessons, but Kaschman persuaded him to take dance classes as well. At the same time, he directed the Hartford Marionette Theater. The next step was being a choreographer for the Federal Theater productions in Hartford. Deep in the Depression, many American artists were given a boost by the U.S. government, which supported all kinds of theater projects. I've already mentioned that Katherine Dunham worked for the Federal Theater in Chicago, and Helen Tamiris was active in the Federal Theater in New York.

By the late 1930s, Nikolais was already part of the modern dance world, studying in the summer sessions of Bennington College with the great choreographers of that time. He was particularly attracted to Hanya

Holm, whose dance technique was less personal and "psychological" than Martha Graham's. And he continued percussion studies with Francesca Boaz. Still in Hartford, he produced his first full evening of pure dance in 1939: *Eight Column Line*, with soloists and chorus to music by Ernst Krenek. Army service in World War II interrupted his career as it did millions of other people's, but it served to deepen his conviction that there was more to the world than personal drama. In 1947, he became an assistant to Hanya Holm, and then head of the Dance Department at the Henry Street Playhouse. Here he made dance plays for children, gave dance classes, and put together his own company. In 1953, Alwin Nikolais produced *Masks, Props and Mobiles*, and also wrote his first electronic score.

Electronic Scores. An electronic score is music that uses magnetic tape, like the kind in your cassette-tape recorder. But it uses the tape not only to record and play back music, but also as a special kind of musical instrument in itself. With the aid of equipment like tape recorders, computers, and synthesizers, any kind of sound can be used as a base, and then scrambled around any way one likes: speeded up, slowed down, made louder or softer, emphasizing a higher or lower pitch, played backward or forward, with some sounds left out and others put in. In other words, a musician composes and edits an electronic score directly through electronic gadgets, which then play it back without the need for human performers.

At this point, Nikolais set out on the artistic route which he was to follow from then on. His most important productions include: *Kaleidoscope* (1956), *Totem* (1959), *Imago* (1963), *Sanctum* (1964), *Somniloquy* and *Triptych* (1967), *Tent* and *Limbo* (1968), *Echo* (1969), *Structures* (1970), *Scenario* (1971), *Grotto* (1973), and *Temple* and *The Tribe* (1975).

Unlike Cunningham, Nikolais plans, controls, and creates all the elements of his pieces. In fact, he does this more than any other choreographer of ballet or modern dance, past or present. Martha Graham once wrote:

> When you work in the theater, you collaborate at almost every step. The task is to fuse many individual artistic acts into one single act: dance, music, setting, lighting, costumes....It is not really natural for artists to work together—we are at the mercy of time and of each other, and this makes it all very risky.

The only major dance figure to whom the above does not apply is Alwin Nikolais. When his company appears in concert, everything you see will have been created by Nikolais: the theme, the movement, the electronic scores (which he prepares with a Moog synthesizer), the lighting, and the designs for props and costumes. And while, again, unlike Cunningham, he does not perform himself, like Cunningham he has personally trained all his dancers. Led by the excellent performers Murray Louis, Carolyn Carlson, and Phyllis Lamhut, Nikolais dancers are unisex instruments.

Alwin Nikolais's company in a light moment from "Tower."

They move freely, energetically, and with fine control, but their identities as males or females playing certain characters are lost behind the masks, helmets, tubes, and yards of fluid material that cover them.

Nikolais compares his approach to creating a piece to that of a writer of science fiction. That is, he sets certain conditions for the environment. Let's say he ties a metallic disk to each dancer's ankle, or crisscrosses the stage space with elastic bands, or seats the dancers on benches and covers them and their benches with lengths of jersey. Then he experiments. What possibilities are opened up for movement? How will this change the shape of the bodies in space? What effect will these limitations have?

His early work presented the construction of elements without specific content. Then, in the late 1960s, he began to design his theater pieces with a central idea. In *Sanctum*, for example, he played with motifs "suggesting place, thing, state of mind, in which sanctuary is possible." In *Imago*, each section was organized around a theme. *Dignitaries* had off-balance side leans, contrasted with abrupt changes of position. In *Mantis*, the arms were extended with bonelike appendages and explored slow, sinuous patterns. *Fence* broke the stage space with parallel elastic lines along which the figures draped themselves. *Boulevard* made a series of dance jokes, with its crowd of figures careening about in ballooning fabrics.

Nikolais has been highly praised for his originality. His approach has influenced many artists in the theater, TV, and advertising. Others have criticized him for being "dehumanized." To Nikolais, the great thing about modern art is that it frees the artist from the literal. He tells us in *The Modern Dance, Seven Statements of Belief*, edited by Selma Jeanne Cohen:

> To me, abstraction does not eliminate emotion. . . . I look upon statements that describe my work as cold and calculating and out-of-this-world dehumanization with considerable scepticism. . . . The greatest gift given to man is his ability to think in terms of abstraction, and his ability of transcendence. Although we need our moments of hearts and flowers, we need also to see the other side of the universal fence.

Nikolais advises audiences to watch his dances in much the same way they might listen to music, to enjoy the sight of motion and let it create within them their own references and understandings. This goes along with his belief that we experience our world through the shapes of things, and the way they move and sound.

Ten years after Merce Cunningham and Alwin Nikolais began exploring fresh approaches to art, a number of young dancers who had been drawn to their classes, performances, and companies banded together loosely for further experimentation. Their meeting place was the Judson Church in Manhattan, which became known as the Judson Dance Theater. In the next chapter, we will meet a number of artists who followed Cunningham and Nikolais, as well as a number who went off on their own, in the tradition of the avant-garde.

Questions for Review

1.   What were *happenings* in the 1960s?

2.   Discuss the changes that took place in modern dance, under the leadership of Merce Cunningham and John Cage.

3.   What is unique in the work of Alwin Nikolais?

32 MOVEMENT ABSTRACTIONS AND BEYOND

MAJOR FIGURES OF THE AVANT-GARDE

You may have noticed the oddness of the phrase that closed the preceding chapter: *the tradition of the avant-garde.* After all, the very idea of an avant-garde is to overturn traditions. Nevertheless, if the ideas expressed by Cunningham, Nikolais, Cage, Rauschenberg, and Halprin influenced the thoughts and work of other dance artists—and indeed they did—then it makes sense to speak of the tradition of the avant-garde. In fact, we shall soon see how the mid-century avant-garde became such a part of mainstream dance that a new "rebellion" took place within its ranks. First, let's consider five avant-gardists chosen arbitrarily from a larger number who have achieved fame here and abroad: Paul Taylor, Murray Louis, Erick Hawkins, Pilobolus (which is actually a group), and Twyla Tharp.

Paul Taylor

Paul Taylor (born in1930) has refused to stay with any one style. His works range from lyrical pieces that reflect music to collections of bizarre and gruesome images of behavior. Like José Limón, he originally wanted to be a painter and didn't study dance until he was over twenty. Born in Pittsburgh, Pennsylvania, he was studying art in college when he changed his interest. In 1979, he told *Dance Scope*: "On a flat canvas, painting is an illusion created through the use of color, depth, space, and so on, but I found that more and more I was opting for real space, real bodies, real movement. I saw more dance and that seemed much closer to meeting my needs."

Paul Taylor composed his first dance piece in 1953: *Hobo Ballet*, to music by Ponchielli. Almost as soon as he began learning dance technique he was performing, first with Pearl Lang and Merce Cunningham, and then as a soloist from 1955 to 1961 with Martha Graham. In other words, Taylor quickly emerged a natural dance artist. His stage appearances drew enthusiastic reviews for the big-bodied, elegantly fluid, yet forceful dancer. In 1959, *Episodes* was a rare collaborative effort by George Balanchine and Martha Graham to music by Webern. In the end, each famous artist independently created a section of the work. The only thing the two parts had in common was Taylor, who was featured as a soloist in both sections. Looking back on this, he said, "I was scared to death working with *The* Balanchine. I had an instinctive liking for Graham technique, felt close to it and though I was mostly untrained at the time, I learned it very quickly. Ballet was harder only because it was foreign to my nature, to my body." In the end, he absorbed the different approaches and drew on what he needed for the more than fifty varied compositions he turned out through the years.

Like Balanchine and Graham, Taylor pays close attention to the human material in his company. In fact, although he believes that the craft of choreography can be taught, he wrote an essay in *The Modern Dance, Seven Statements of Belief* (edited by Selma Jeanne Cohen), called Down With Choreography.

Here he claims that not enough attention is paid to the personal qualities of dancers who are, after all, what the audience sees. One dancer weights movements as though he were pressing against the heaviness of water. He makes you aware of energy, gravity. Another is slender and tall, with a reedy, organic continuity. These qualities inspire and influence Taylor's choreographic approach. Taylor's attitude toward music is also very much his own. He has been known to change scores in the middle of doing a piece. Clive Barnes tells about watching Taylor's company rehearse a new work for which the music had not yet been written. Instead of counting out the rhythms with appropriate periods of silence, they were practicing to *Rite of Spring* because Taylor happened to have that record and he liked working to music even when it was not the final accompaniment.

Here are a few examples from his very large repertory. *Aureole* (1962) is a lovely lyrical piece, costumed in simple white, which expresses the music of Handel that accompanies it. It is almost like a Balanchine ballet, except for the most unconventional use of curved body shapes, group formations, and transitions. The ballet star Rudolf Nureyev has appeared in it. But then, that doesn't tell us much, because the flamboyant Nureyev has also danced in Martha Graham's works, for example, the role that Erick Hawkins created in *Night Journey*. In 1963, Taylor created *Scudorama* to music by Charles Jackson. Program notes include quotations from Dante that hint at Purgatory. Dramatic moments include humans slithering across the ground, dragging themselves and others, and the lead male handling the lead female as a butcher might a carcass of meat. These movement images do indeed create a despairing portrait of unrealized life.

Agathe's Tale (1967), to music by Carlos Surinach, is a sly, irreverent medieval piece. Agathe, a maiden who perhaps had saved her virgin love too long, is seduced by Satan, a foul fiend and icy lover in the guise of a monk. She then goes off with Pan. Insinuating movements and clever use of props, like a prayer bench that becomes a bed, lend an outrageously ribald air. That same year saw *Lento,* a fluid musical composition to music by Haydn that contains simple, clean, and formal patterns. At the same time, one section melts into another: a dancer holds another aloft at a climactic moment, and then is swept away by a group surging across the stage. Thus the featured couple disappears into the crowd as a camera dissolves one shot into another. A movement piece of another kind is *Esplanade* (1975), to music by Bach. Taylor was inspired by the image of a girl running for a bus: "That started me on that piece which really doesn't have a single dance step in it. It's walking, running, rolling, sliding, hopping, jumping."

Taylor spoke to *Dance Scope* about his work *Polaris,* specifically about its stage set: a square cage made of metal piping, designed, as are many of Taylor's sets and costumes, by artist Alex Katz:

> It's an enclosure that defines space, a cube within the cube of the stage space. I couldn't ignore the dramatic possibilities of the inside and the outside. The movement is abstract but lively. To build up the dramatic moment of the dancers emerging and, believe me, they don't creep out they *blast* out . . . That enclosure is like the life of a family.

To make the dance stay in the audience's minds longer, Taylor had the whole dance repeated to another score at a different pace. Thus we are let in on the secrets of the choreographer's craft. We are conscious of the effect of tempo changes on space and dynamics, of different lighting, of each dancer in a part. Because of works like *Polaris,* Taylor has gained worldwide attention for his continuing inventiveness, the source of which varies from one piece to another. His more than fifty works have won many prizes and are represented in the repertory of the Royal Danish Ballet and the Dutch National Ballet. Outstanding later works include *Lost, Found and Lost* (1982) and *Last Look* (1985).

Murray Louis. Louis was born (in 1926) in New York. He studied dance with Ann Halprin and with Nikolais, whom he assisted at the Henry Street Playhouse from 1949 on, as a teacher and the leading member of his company. At the same time that he danced with Nikolais, from 1953 on, Louis also danced and performed, often on tour, with his own company, which included Phyllis Lamhut and Bill Frank.

Unlike Alwin Nikolais, a magician who worked his wonders from the wings, Murray Louis himself was the lead instrument of his own choreography. Inventively designed costumes and sets were contributed by other artists, as was the musical accompaniment, which was most often an electronic score by Nikolais. Because Louis was an intensely brilliant dancer and loved to experiment with movement—especially isolated gestures of arms and legs—even though his range of emotional concerns was narrow, he created a series of stunning dance pieces that contain overtones of foolish, weird, and devotional human behavior.

For example, *Junk Dances*, performed to a collage of pop music (1964), which became the Louis trademark, is a satire of modern living that presents a blank-faced couple moving among plastic objects that they obsessively pick up and discard. *Chimera*, performed to a Nikolais score (1966), is a solo that revealed Louis's stamina, since it lasted for thirty minutes. More important, it was engaging for the entire time. The dance opened with Louis in an enveloping stretch fabric beneath which he shaped grotesque and comical forms. Then he shed this cocoon and moved in a fluid style that reminded one of Oriental dance (reinforced by wailing tones in the accompaniment). In the final part, he freed himself so that he could perform ordinary movements, which alternated with satirical asides of deep contemplation. The dance, through its progression from constriction to freedom, evoked thoughts of creation and self-realization.

Other major works in the Louis repertory include: *Bach Suite* (1956), *Calligraph for Martyrs* (1961) and *Facets* (1962), both with scores by Nikolais, *Interims* to music by Lukas Foss (1963), and a full-length work, *Sheherazade* (1975), which demonstrates the way tradition in dance history is updated. Louis choreographed the title role of Sheherazade for a male dancer, Michael Ballard, who rippled and undulated in sensual romanticism. Louis chose a man for the part because he wanted it to be "sensual, not sexy."

In sum, one can find three major areas in Murray Louis's art. First of all, he creates from a sense of comedy, that most rare and welcome theatrical gift. Secondly, he designs beautiful patterns of abstract motion that evoke ideas about experience. Thirdly, he goes the route of so many dance artists, from Balanchine and Fokine to Isadora Duncan and Doris Humphrey, in doing pieces that present reactions to great musical scores. Louis's responses to Bach, Tchaikovsky, Ravel, Satie, and others tend to be clean, light, and angular in style.

Erick Hawkins. Erick Hawkins, born in Trinidad (in 1909), first made his name in modern dance, as did Merce Cunningham, as a leading soloist with Martha Graham. He danced with her from 1938 to 1951, when her company was at the height of its popularity. It was therefore a surprise to many when Hawkins turned up on his own in the late 1940s as a choreographer of fluid, low-energy, abstract works. He has continued to work in that vein. Along with his lyrical, sometimes bizarre, movements, Hawkins's choreography features liquid percussion accompaniment by Lucia Dlugoszewski. He uses masks, plumage, and brief body coverings, designed mostly by Ralph Dorazio, to evoke primitive Native Americans.

Because he uses his dancers as moving objects rather than as individual human beings, and because of the low-key dynamics and the emphasis on visual design, watching the works of Erick Hawkins is like viewing pictures and sculpture in an art gallery. The dances, although they are only slightly differentiated from one another in line and dynamics, are gratifying to watch. The artist has an obvious regard for the creation of harmonious and aesthetically pleasing movement patterns that are clean and open. Hawkins claims to strive for "the most beautiful dance" which he describes as "effortless . . .that lets itself happen . . . that loves gravity rather than fights gravity . . . that hangs and falls . . . that can stand still . . ." And he developed his own physical technique "so that movement flows, the technique allowing the body to move without tension."

His philosophical ideas come from the Orient: "Enlightenment is recognizing that constant element in human suffering and saying, 'okay it's fine. There's no point to kick against bricks'...And that makes for serenity and that serenity is the height of human culture." The above quotations are found in an elaborate program booklet issued in 1964 by the Guinn Company, and in an article by Beverly Brown for *Dance Scope.* Although Hawkins has his share of ardent followers, he also has many critics who complain about the soporific absence of energy in his creations, which include *Here and Now With Watchers* (1957), *8 Clear Places* (1960), *Cantilever* (1963), *Geography of Noon* (1964), and *Greek Dreams with Flute* (1973).

Pilobolus. Not an individual but a group, Pilobolus is included here because of its fresh approach to movement, and even more because of its unique character as a cooperative enterprise. As we've often noted, modern dance is an art form dominated by eccentric individuals, each of whom has created compositions and companies according to a personal inner vision. In contrast, Pilobolus is a small unit of about six dancers who create works collectively. It has functioned that way since its beginning, despite the fact that it loses and gains members every now and then. Pilobolus started out with four young men who had no dance technique aside from that offered by Alison Chase at Dartmouth College from 1970 to 1971.

Critic Iris Fanger observed them in the studio and the theater, and wrote about their choreography in *Dance Magazine* (July 1974):

When the dancers came together there was little planning ahead; more trying out of forms and action with analysis afterward of how to improve what they had created. One of the men came up with the idea of using the girls as hats...

Their first work, *Pilobolus,* contains the large multiple body structures, combined in gravity-defying balances which flow from one shape into another like the continuous splitting of an amoeba.

Since then, such works as *Ocellus* and *Spyrogyra* have further explored the kinaesthetic elements of space with spectacular leaps and spins. The coiling and release of tension creates an energy level of whirlwind force, and seems to produce exhilaration, rather than exhaustion, in the performers. . . .

The key term for Pilobolus technique is "linkage," a new way of linking bodies, and strength of arms and torso.

Pilobolus works have been well received in hundreds of performances in American colleges and theaters, as well as abroad in Israel, Scotland, Germany, Italy, and elsewhere.

Twyla Tharp

We now come to Twyla Tharp (born in 1942), a woman who ranks in talent with any of the above-mentioned people in the new wave of modern dance that arose in the 1950s. She surpasses all of them in the general public's recognition of her work in ballet, Broadway musical shows, and TV. In fact, in 1976, after she did *Push Comes to Shove* for Mikhail Baryshnikov and the American Ballet Theater, which was featured in stories by *Time, Newsweek,* and other national publications, she became such a cult figure that the blunt Twyla-Tharp haircut was copied by women all over the country.

Tharp arrived on the scene in the 1960s, after the face of the dance world had been radically altered by Cunningham, Nikolais, and their followers. What Tharp did was to build magnificently on Cunningham's approach to dance, presenting energetic bodies moving in infinite variations through time and space. She also absorbed the experiments that dancers were making at Black Mountain College, the Judson Theater, and elsewhere, and like them, found original ways to use all the elements of dance. As in Cunningham's work, Tharp's criteria for choreography has not been emotional expression or subject matter, but interest.

Tharp designs each composition to work out a problem, to test the limits of a structural concept. In the late 1960s, she told me: "The structure is of interest to me—it's what keeps on challenging me, keeps me going." Take *The One Hundreds,* for example, a piece composed in 1970. Its material is one hundred dance phrases, each exactly eleven seconds long. In unison, two dancers perform all the phrases, separating them with four-second pauses. A quick calculation will show you that twenty-five minutes have passed. Now, five dancers perform the one hundred phrases, except that this time, each performer does only twenty of them, and there are no pauses. Another three and a half minutes have passed. In the third and final section, which lasts exactly eleven seconds, one hundred dancers are supposed to appear simultaneously, each one dancing a different, single phrase.

Tharp admits freely that the piece is done not with one hundred dancers, but with only about twenty-seven. It was made during a two-day residency at the University of Massachusetts, so that as many students as possible could dance together with the company. As she put it: "The big catch is that nobody watching can count to one hundred in eleven seconds so we can get away with twenty-seven people. It looks like a mob." Just as the choreographic structure of *The One Hundreds* interests Tharp, so do the practical problems of organizing such a piece. The first two sections were prepared with her company, taking hundreds of hours to rehearse the complete opening duet, and then about another one hundred hours to rehearse the twenty dancers. During their stay at the university, five minutes of rehearsal allowed more than twenty trained dancers to teach one eleven-second phrase to twenty-seven students. Tharp says, "It's an interesting study in deterioration."

Another example of her structural approach is *Disperse*, made in 1967. There is an opening movement section, which is then repeated four times. But in each repetition, the movement takes up two-thirds of the space and two-thirds of the time used in the preceding section. The total time of the piece is twenty-one minutes, and you can imagine that figuring out the time and volume of each part requires a complicated calculation, not to mention planning and executing the actual movements.

Beyond structure, Tharp's other interests are also conceptual. She is concerned with what happens to dance in various performing areas, and has done pieces for museums, outdoor fields, and gymnasiums. She draws on a wide range of accompaniment, from the sounds of the dancers' feet hitting the floor, to scores by Haydn and Jelly Roll Morton. We have seen that innumerable mixed-media artists were playing around with all these elements in the 1960s. Where Twyla Tharp surpassed her colleagues was in the central role she gave to dancing, which she invested with an original, high-voltage style, endlessly fascinating and exciting to audiences.

Tharp is a child of the affluent, irreverent generation that grew up after World War II. From childhood music and dance lessons in Indiana and California, and then in New York, from studies in fine arts at Barnard College, and studio classes in all the major dance techniques she gained a practical and theoretical knowledge of music, an understanding of artistic structure in space and time, and a fine command of dance. For dance technique, she sought out the top people in each field: modern with Martha Graham, Merce Cunningham, and Alwin Nikolais; ballet with Igor

Schwezoff who was trained in Leningrad; and jazz with the leading teachers Matt Mattox and Luigi. On technique, Tharp has said: "Ballet technique is the technique most worth investing your time in. It is the most thorough, the most versatile, the most logical, rigorous and elegant. I think jazz technique is very important, too."

She joined the Paul Taylor Dance Company for a year and then struck out on her own in 1965. In her early efforts, Tharp, like Isadora Duncan, Paul Taylor, and the Judson dancers before her, threw out everything that was conventionally accepted as dance. Her first piece was *Tank Dive*. It took four minutes and had three scenes, which were separated by blackouts. The three scenes consisted of: (1) Tharp onstage striking a couple of poses; (2) Two men and two women (nondancers) exchanging flags; (3) Tharp swinging around a pole.

She continued in this minimal style for several years, then gradually she set about reinventing dance. By 1970, Tharp was creating dances that demanded great virtuosity, and she began to attract favorable reviews and a following. Because she favored ballet and jazz techniques, Tharp developed a personal style that seemed to combine their strengths. Balletic control enables her dancers to make changes of direction and height at breathtaking speed, while jazz gives them loose, casual-looking limbs and upper bodies that express Tharp's "so what?" attitude. In *Shapes of Change*, Marcia Siegel describes Twyla Tharp's style this way:

> Tharp's dancers look as if they could move any way at all. They sometimes jerk, twitch, go off balance, shake their heads unaccountably. They twist, glide, slump into momentary repose. Most of all they flow.
> Tharp's flow is one of the most remarkable things about her choreography and one of the most consistent. She sees both the dancer's steps and the sequence of the whole dance as one continuous filament of movement. Her dance always has a surging propulsiveness.

You may remember that Doris Humphrey said that the audience is comparatively indifferent to the subject matter of the choreography. What the audience does respond to is the artist's enthusiasm and talent, which make a work exciting. This has been born out repeatedly in Twyla Tharp's choreography in works like *The Catherine Wheel* (1981) and *In the Upper Room* (1987). Tharp's company's performances have always been first-rate, for which credit must go to dancers like Sara Rudner, Rose Marie Wright, Shelley Washington, and Tom Rawe. They have kept and held the interested attention of diverse audiences, and led producers of "establishment" entertainment to seek out Tharp.

Thus, in addition to the fifty or so "modern dance" works that she made, the Joffrey Ballet commissioned from her both *Deuce Coupe* (1973) and *As Time Goes By*. Tharp's other achievements include: a one-woman show during a Broadway season; choreographing movies like *Hair*, *Ragtime*, and *Amadeus,* and *Singing in the Rain* for Broadway; making *Push Comes to Shove* with and for ballet superstar Baryshnikov; and joining the American Ballet Theater (in 1988) as artistic associate and resident choreographer.

Finally, she is interested in video. Tharp has made a few works for TV like the TV special *Making Television Dance* (1977). While dance is the dominant component of these pieces, she uses the camera to reverse the image, or to show one part of the dancer's body in the foreground, and her face in the background. She has been quoted in *Dance Magazine:* "It is clear to me that the future of dance is in cassettes, not in live performance. It may not be in the next five years, or the next ten, but ultimately that's what it's all about."

Which brings us back to Merce Cunningham, who is also interested in making the camera dance. He has made many video pieces, using all kinds of camera experiments. For example, in *Blue Studio* he imposes five segments of himself dancing on the blue (or outside) area of the videotape, which creates the effect of seeing Cunningham dancing with a second Cunningham and then a third, a fourth, and a fifth. There are now courses in video dance, which has become a new field for the experimental dancers. It is ironic that the very artists who proclaimed that they were not interested in repertory—in preserving their works for repeat performances—are the ones who are working with video cassettes, which of course will be available for endless viewings in the future.

In addition to all the above-mentioned productions, think back to *Watermill,* the piece that Jerome Robbins did for the New York City Ballet, and *Astarte* that Robert Joffrey did for his own company. You see, the avant-garde has made its mark everywhere in dance. Even the "postmodern" choreographer David Gordon did a work in the 1980s for the American Ballet Theater. This brings us to the latest new wave in dance. During the 1970s, a group that consciously remained out in left field was labelled "postmodern" and the label stuck. Sally Banes, in her book *Terpsichore in Sneakers, Post-modern Dance,* describes the origin of this ardent band as the Judson Dance Theater.

Judson Dance Theater. A dance composition class was offered at Merce Cunningham's New York studio in 1960, taught by company member Robert Dunn. Dunn had studied music composition with John Cage. In 1962, Dunn organized the first of many concerts for his students at the Judson Church, which later became known as the Judson Dance Theater. Postmodern dance consists primarily of the dancers and choreographers (joined at times by musicians, poets, and painters) who took part in these events, or were in their audiences. They include (among others): Trisha Brown, Lucinda Childs, Judith Dunn, Ruth Emerson, David Gordon, Alex and Deborah Hay, Meredith Monk, Robert Morris, Steve Paxton, Yvonne Rainer, Robert Rauschenberg, and Robert Wilson. To illustrate postmodern dance, here is a brief write-up of one artist, Meredith Monk, again, an arbitrary choice.

Edward Villella in a serene moment from Jerome Robbins's "Watermill."

Meredith Monk. Monk was born (in 1943) in Lima, Peru, while her mother, a singer, was on tour. She studied every kind of movement, beginning with Dalcroze eurhythmics and mime; ballet with Mia Slavenska; modern dance with Martha Graham and members of Merce Cunningham's and Alwin Nikolais's companies; and improvisation at a summer workshop with Ann Halprin. As a teenager, she composed music, and also tried her hand at writing. She began producing her carefully arranged, poetic, and sometimes expressive dance-theater pieces in 1964. (Expressive! you see again, in every style there are good artists who will *not* stay within the tight confines of criteria and labels that critics devise for them.) We will look at *Paris/Venice/Milan/Chacon.*

Paris/Venice/Milan/Chacon is a trilogy, composed in collaboration with a participant, Ping Chong. Just because there are four parts in the title, you cannot assume in a postmodern work that there are four parts in the dance. There are in fact three sections, and they were composed at different times. *Paris* (1973) is a duet for Monk, who is costumed with a mustache and a long skirt, and Chong, a man who wears a feminine-looking hood. To the accompaniment of a repetitive piano score by Monk, the two walk, sit stiffly, hold hands, bow, hum a folk song, weep, and wave their arms about. In *Venice/Milan* (first shown in 1976), after an introductory entrance of a group of gondoliers, the *Paris* couple reappears, dressed up in evening clothes. A masked man in black lace joins the scene; a noblewoman welcomes guests and turns cartwheels; a visitor in a turban, dancing on a diagonal path, brings gifts; and mysterious things happen to people. The couple is out of place, constantly blundering in this atmosphere of decadent refinement. *Chacon* (presented in 1974) is set in a small town in New Mexico. We are told it is about immigrants and forefathers, with a number of different ethnic strains: Oriental, black, Jewish, and Scandinavian. The action is danced, mimed, and sung to live, improvised sound produced by sand-filled beer cans being shaken. In the background, a performer creates the scenery before your eyes by painting a landscape mural on brown wrapping paper.

Obviously, you have to see these works to receive their impact. To get an idea of why Monk has gained a devoted following, listen to these comments. Doris Hering, in her review of this piece in *Dance Magazine* (July 1977), praised the marvelous idea behind this surrealistic travelogue. She found *Paris* a study in "emotionless emotion"; she saw "sharp and funny images" in *Chacon*; and in *Venice/Milan*, she perceived "keen observations mixed with the deliberately homemade look associated with the aleatory theater of the fifties." (You should know that *aleatory* means random, dependent on chance.) "I have always believed," Hering wrote, "that Meredith Monk was among the chosen few who received the 'sensation fresh' and transmitted it to us that way." Robb Baker, in his article on Meredith Monk (*Dance Magazine*, April 1976), wrote that for him, she was an impressive, interesting and exciting artist—a conceptual genius.

Mark Morris. We conclude this chapter with an artist who, in the "tradition" of the avant-garde and the postmodern, doesn't fit easily into a category. Perhaps we shall have to call Mark Morris a post-post-modern dancer. Morris was born in 1956, in Seattle. In a 1986 piece about Morris in *The New Yorker*, Arlene Croce supported my thesis: "Morris is the clearest illustration we have, at the moment, of the principle of succession and how it works in dance: each new master assimilates the past in all its variety and becomes our guide to the future."

In *Dance Magazine* (September 1986), John Gruen tells us that when Mark was six, he enjoyed dancing to music. Spanish dance became his first passion. Talented and open, he went on from there to ballet classes, to modern dance, and then to performances with New York companies like Eliot Feld's, Twyla Tharp's, and Laura Dean's. In 1980, he formed his own group and immediately attracted critical interest. Morris told Gruen: "When I finally saw the New York City Ballet performing I just about passed out. What I learned from Balanchine is that you can do whatever you want."There is nothing Morris doesn't use. You can find in his work a random assortment of dance styles including modern, ballet, Spanish flamenco, jazz, and classical Hindu. His pieces include *Mort subite*, a piece commissioned in 1986 by the Boston Ballet, where he was artistic director for a time. Also in 1986, the Dance Umbrella commissioned two works, *Soap Powders* and *Detergents and Striptease*.

Mark Morris is restless, in career moves as well as choreography. In 1989, he turned up in Belgium as director of the Ballet of the Twentieth Century, after Béjart had a fight with the management. Journalists in Brussels, who wanted Béjart back, hissed Morris for scandalous nudity. Then, in 1990, Morris collaborated with Baryshnikov and a group of first-rate dancers on the White Oak Project in Florida. At the same time, his contract in Belgium having run out, Morris toured the United States with his own company called Monnaie Dance Group. Reviews of Morris's work are sometimes ecstatic. Nancy Dalva, in *Dance Magazine* (January 1991), used phrases like these:

> *Dido* is a tragic work but its existence makes people glad . . . *L'Allegro* is so beautiful it made me cry . . . He has found a new way to make dances that embodies the old ways . . .
> The poet Richard Howard suggested after seeing *L'Allegro* that the second half was an extended image of heaven . . .
> Morris is both sublimely allusive . . . and gloriously accessible . . . the choreography fuses with the music in extraordinarily memorable images . . . It is impossible to single out the most beautiful image, for one ravishing scene follows another . . .

Surveying the latest avant-garde movement which began in the 1950s, from the perspective of the 1990s, we find once again that this group of highly individualistic dancers, who set out to break with tradition, functions very much like generations of artists always have in the past. They make use of what interests them in and out of the dance world and discard or revitalize what has grown stale. Acceptance by the public (or publics, because it is obvious that as artists differ in their approach to the world, so do audiences) is not determined by novelty alone. Rather dance artists gain their reputations andr followings in proportion to the richness and complexity of their creations.

Questions for Review

1. Have you seen any works by Paul Taylor, Murray Louis, Erick Hawkins, or Twyla Tharp? How would you describe them? Did you find them enjoyable, or at least interesting?

2. In what ways, if any, is postmodern dance "farther out" than the avant-garde?

33 EPILOGUE

THE JUDGMENT OF HISTORY

Coda: Carnival of Styles

What styles characterize our dance world in the 1990s? The Western dance art is as diverse as the restless human society that surrounds it. This is a catchall age, perhaps a transitional period. Nothing from the human past or present is considered alien. Dance artists draw freely on all the traditions that have developed through the centuries. Perhaps if there is one overriding characteristic of the Western dance art today, it is its ever-changing personality. It's a chameleon that refuses to be fixed in place. There is a constant foraging for new experiences and perceptions, for originality, and for novelty.

Separating dance styles with labels like "ballet," "modern dance," "modern ballet," and "avant-garde" was useful in dealing with the past. This is no longer necessary. In the present, all styles are intermingled, not only in one company's repertory, but within a single choreographic work. If you look at the diversity of programs presented in any one month, it is immediately apparent that a great many styles exist side by side. There are preservations, revivals, and fresh versions of traditional works. There are stagings of authentic dance forms that are really outside of Western culture. In new creations, there is much that is original, alongside of borrowings and influences from other times and places.

Mikhail Baryshnikov

The superb artist with whom I will close the curtain is also outstanding as a representative of the dance world. In his career up to the present and in the constellation of brilliant artists and great companies that have been involved with this superstar, we see the major facets of the dance art today. Baryshnikov was born in Latvia, in 1948. At eighteen, he joined the Kirov Ballet, and went directly into the company's group of soloists. When he toured with the company in London and the Netherlands in 1970, he was hailed as phenomenal, of a quality unknown in the West. On tour in 1974, he asked for and was granted asylum in Canada. Like Nureyev, Makarova, and the Panovs, Baryshnikov left the USSR not because of political tyranny, but because he wanted a wider artistic experience. From 1974 to 1978, Mikhail Baryshnikov (known as Misha by his colleagues) was a guest artist with a number of companies until he settled in with the American Ballet Theater. He was immediately partnered with the magnificent ballerina Gelsey Kirkland.

Gelsey Kirkland. Kirkland (born in Pennsylvania, in 1953), had just shocked balletomanes by leaving the New York City Ballet where she had risen rapidly to major roles and stardom. At the American Ballet Theater, in 1978, Baryshnikov built a full-length version of the Petipa-Minkus *Don Quixote* around Kirkland's fabulous technique. She was pictured in the role of Kitri on the cover of *Time* magazine, in her breathtaking *jeté* kick, where one foot nearly touches the back of her head.

The Baryshnikov-Kirkland team won great renown from 1974 until 1983, particularly for their *Giselle*. Like the ballet, this partnership had a tragic ending. Kirkland left the American Ballet Theater and wrote (with her husband Greg Lawrence) *Dancing on My Grave*. In the book, the ballerina confesses that one of the reasons she was able to perform night after night with such wild abandon and such feats of speed and brilliance was cocaine. The accusation is made that the American Ballet Theater management, including Baryshnikov, was aware of the habit which was killing her. But they ignored it because of the tremendous box office. You will be glad to hear that Kirkland kicked her habit with Greg Lawrence's help, and went on to make a successful comeback with the British Royal Ballet.

While Baryshnikov was at the American Ballet Theater, in addition to performing in the classical repertory, he created roles in works by Eliot Feld, Paul Taylor, and Twyla Tharp. In 1978, at the age of thirty, Baryshnikov left the American Ballet Theater to join the New York City Ballet. He did this, according to Gennady Smakov in his book about Baryshnikov, *From Russia to the West*, because he felt he had reached his peak and wanted fresh challenges. Baryshnikov regarded Balanchine as the

Versatile superstar Baryshnikov in Balanchine's "Prodigal Son."

"crystallization of Russian classicism." Eighteen months later, he left the New York City Ballet with new insight into choreography, but also with the realization that Balanchine's approach was in fact a culmination of the romantic era, not the classical. Because Balanchine idolized women, his choreography was not beneficial for male dancers. Specifically, Balanchine's movement style was bad for Baryshnikov's body.

In 1980, Baryshnikov was back at the American Ballet Theater - as artistic director. He not only staged elaborate new productions of classics like *Swan Lake* and *Giselle*, but also secured for the company eight Balanchine ballets and a number of works by avant-gardists like Merce Cunningham, Paul Taylor, Mark Morris, and David Gordon. In addition to commissioning her works, Baryshnikov made Twyla Tharp an artistic associate at the American Ballet Theater. He also raised the training of his dancers to a very high level, and inspired them with his own continuing performances. Along the way, Baryshnikov has appeared in films: *Turning Point, Giselle,* and in 1985, *White Nights,* in which his co-star was the fabulous tap dancer Gregory Hines. Both Hines and Baryshnikov shared in the choreography of the opening sequence, which included a staged performance of Roland Petit's *Le Jeune Homme et La Mort.* Baryshnikov also acted on Broadway in *Metamorphosis.* In 1987, Baryshnikov (together with Rudolf Nureyev) danced at the opening of the Martha Graham season in *Appalachian Spring.* (World-renowned Russian ballerina Maya Plisetskaya appeared in a solo on that same program.) Later in the season, Baryshnikov danced in *El Penitente,* one of Graham's greatest early pieces.

In 1990, Baryshnikov left the American Ballet Theater, just as its fiftieth anniversary gala was about to take place. That year, he produced and starred in Mark Morris's White Oak Project. In 1992, Mikhail Baryshnikov appeared at Saks Fifth Avenue. Was he dancing at a department store? No, he was launching a line of perfume and beauty products. Thus one of the greatest dancers of the twentieth century, at forty-four, plunged into the world of commerce. However, Misha is still very prominent in dance. Baryshnikov aside, judging by the quantity and quality of dance events that take place on our stages today, we would have to conclude that the art form is robust and dynamic.

Judgment of the Past. This work is finished, but it's not complete. That's obvious in regard to the future. The story of dance will move on as long as there are people to carry it forward. But what of the past? Have we formed a picture of the important figures, the ones who, in the judgment of history, are the most creative, interesting, and influential in dance? The phrase that should give you pause, as it does me, is *the judgment of history.* Can't you just see it? A huge stage, floating in the rarified atmosphere we call the past, is crowded with dancers who are jostling one another, trying to be noticed. Where is the godlike judge called history, surveying this dance world with all-seeing, impartial wisdom?

One thing is sure, it's not I! My prejudices and preferences, consciously and subconsciously, affected the choice of topics in every chapter. This was true both for the hundreds of events and people I was familiar with personally, as well as the thousands with which I wasn't. In both cases, I checked the writings of other authors. As often as not, no two agreed with one another on how to evaluate a given person, or whether to include an individual at all! Let's face it, everybody looks at the world through a screen of temperament, age, gender, and opinions. An artist who is most worthy in the eyes of one beholder, may not impress another at all. Remember too that artists themselves are not innocent regarding their reputations. There are those who have the connections and a knack for getting known that matches their artistic ability, indeed, sometimes exceeds it. And there are those who are too immersed in their work, or lack the traits necessary to court the public's fancy. Many in the second group, regardless of talent, sink out of sight.

Finally, all writers, even compilers of encyclopedias and dictionaries, must ignore worthy figures because of space and deadline limitations. In my original outline for this book, companies like the Washington National Ballet were listed, as well as details about dancers like Esther Junger, Katherine Litz, Sybil Shearer, and James Waring. Sadly, they remained in the wings, because the manuscript was too long. So where does all this leave us? We can follow the current scene in dance through newspapers, magazines, books, and, of course, at concerts. We can also dig further into dance history.

Historians of the Future. Autobiographies, playbills, letters, and other documents that relate to dance are available. One can read about individuals, art styles, and social conditions of a period and compare the opinions of different writers on a dancer's style and output. This is how history gets revised. It is also how dance scholars find insight and much of interest along the way. There is a need for further historical exploration. Anyone interested in dance history can play a part. Names from the past can be hunted down. The Dance Library at Lincoln Center in New York and CORD (the Committee On Research in Dance) are both excellent sources of material and ideas. On with the Dance!

BIBLIOGRAPHY

Factual References

CHUJOY, ANATOLE, and MANCHESTER, P.W. *Dance Encyclopedia*. New York: Simon & Schuster, 1967.

CLARKE, MARY, and VAUGHAN, DAVID. *The Encyclopedia of Dance and Ballet*. London: Pitman Publishing, 1977.

KOEGLER, HORST. *The Concise Oxford Dictionary of Ballet*. London: Oxford University Press, 1977.

KRAUS, RICHARD; HILSENDAGER, SARAH CHAPMAN and DIXON, BRENDA. *History of the Dance in Art and Education*. Englewood Cliffs, New Jersey: Prentice Hall, 1991.

McDONAGH, DON. *Complete Guide to Modern Dance*. New York: Praeger, Popular Library, 1977.

General Works for all Periods and Styles

COHEN, SELMA JEANNE. *Dance as a Theater Art*. New York: Dodd, Mead, 1975.

LABAN, RUDOLF. *The Mastery of Movement*. London: MacDonald & Evans, 1960.

DE MILLE, AGNES. *The Book of the Dance*. New York: Golden Press, 1963.

———. *Dance to the Piper*. Boston: Little, Brown, 1951.

MAGRIEL, PAUL, ED. *Chronicles of the American Dance*. New York: Da Capo, 1970.

SORELL, WALTER. *The Dance Has Many Faces*. New York: Columbia University Press, 1966.

———. *The Dance Through the Ages*. New York: Grosset & Dunlap, 1967.

Criticism and Aesthetics

DENBY, EDWIN. *Dancers, Buildings, and People in the Streets*. New York: Horizon Press, 1965.
———. *Looking at the Dance*. New York: Horizon Press, 1968.
SIEGEL, MARCIA B. *The Shapes of Change*. Boston: Houghton Mifflin, 1979.
———. *At the Vanishing Point*. New York: Saturday Review Press, 1972.

Periodicals for all Periods and Styles

Note: The specific issue referred to on a given topic is cited in the text.
Ballet Annual. A. & C. Black, 4 Soho Square, London.
Ballet Review. Dance Research Foundation, 46 Morton St., New York, NY 10014.
Dance and Dancers. Hansom Books, P.O. Box 294, 2 & 4 Old Pye St., London SW1P 2LR, United Kingdom.
Dance Chronicle. Marcel Dekker, 270 Madison Ave., New York, NY 10016.
Dance Index. Out of print.
Dance Magazine. 33 West 60th St., New York, NY 10023.
Dance Perspectives. Out of print.
Dance Scope. American Dance Guild, 1133 Broadway, New York, NY 10010.

Primitive, Ancient, Ethnic, and Folk Dance

BOURGUIGNON, ERIKA. *Trance Dance*. New York: Dance Perspectives #35, Autumn, 1968.
BLUM, ODETTE. *Dance in Ghana*, New York: Dance Perspectives # 56, Winter 1973.
COTLOW, LEWIS. *In Search of the Primitive*. Boston: Little, Brown, 1966.
DUNHAM, KATHERINE. *Journey to Accompong, New York*: Henry Holt, 1946.
ELLFELDT, LOIS. *Dance From Magic to Art*. Dubuque: Wm. C. Brown, 1976.
ELLIS, HAVELOCK. "The Art of Dancing" in *The Dance of Life*. Boston: Houghton Mifflin, 1923.
FRAZER, SIR JAMES. *The Golden Bough*. New York: Macmillan, 1947.
Hoffman, Malvina. *Heads and Tales*. New York: Bonanza, 1936.
LA MERI. *Spanish Dancing*. New York: A.S. Barnes, 1948.
LANGE, RODERYK. *The Nature of Dance, An Anthropological Perspective*. London: MacDonald & Evans, 1975.
LAWLER, LILLIAN B. *The Dance in Ancient Greece*. Middletown, Connecticut: Wesleyan University Press, 1964.
LOMAX, ALAN, "CHOREOMETRICS AND ETHNOGRAPHIC FILMMAKING" IN *FILMMAKERS NEWSLETTER*, VOLUME 4, NUMBER 4, FEBRUARY 1971.
MEGGERS, BETTY J. *Amazonia*. Chicago: Aldine, 1971.
NAGLER, A.M. *A Source Book in Theatrical History*. New York: Dover, 1952.
POWER, EILEEN. *Medieval People*. New York: Doubleday, 1954.
SACHS, CURT. *World History of the Dance*. New York: W.W. Norton, 1937.
SARABHAI, MRINALINI. *The Eight Nayikas*, New York: Dance Perspectives # 24 1965.

European Ballet

ARBEAU, THOINOT. *Orchesography*. Translated by Mary Stewart Evans. New York: Dover, 1967.

BALANCHINE, GEORGE. *New Complete Stories of the Great Ballets*. New York: Doubleday, 1968.

BEAUMONT, CYRIL W. *The Ballet Called Giselle*. New York: Dance Horizons, 1969.

————. *The Ballet Called Swan Lake*. London: C.W. Beaumont, 1952.

————. *Complete Book of Ballets*. New York: Grosset & Dunlap, 1938.

BLASIS, CARLO. *An Elementary Treatise Upon the Theory and Practice of the Art of Dancing*. Translated by Mary Stewart Evans. New York: Kamin, 1944.

BRUHN, ERIK, and MOORE, LILLIAN. *Bournonville and Ballet Technique*. London: Adam & Charles Black, 1961.

BUCKLE, RICHARD. *Diaghilev*. New York: Atheneum, 1979.

FISKE, ROGER. *Ballet Music*. London: George G. Harrap, 1958.

FOKINE, MICHEL. *Memoirs of a Ballet Master*. Translated by Vitale Fokine. London: Constable, 1961.

FRASER, ANTONIA. *Mary Queen of Scots*. New York: Dell, 1969.

GUEST, IVOR. *Fanny Elssler*. Middletown, Connecticut: Wesleyan University Press, 1970.

————. *The Romantic Ballet in Paris*. Middletown, Connecticut: Wesleyan University Press, 1966.

HORST, LOUIS. *Pre-Classic Dance Forms*. New York: The Dance Observer, 1940.

KARSAVINA, TAMARA. *Theater Street*. New York: E.P. Dutton, 1931.

KIRSTEIN, LINCOLN. *Movement and Metaphor*. New York: Praeger, 1970.

MAGRIEL, PAUL, ED. *Nijinsky, Pavlova, Duncan*. New York: Da Capo, 1977.

NOVERRE, JEAN GEORGES. *Letters on Dancing and Ballets*. Translated by Cyril W. Beaumont. New York: Dance Horizons, 1966.

PERCIVAL, JOHN. *The World of Diaghilev*. New York: Harmony Books, 1971.

RAMBERT, MARIE. *Quicksilver*. London: Macmillan, 1972.

ROSLAVLEVA, NATALIA. *Era of the Russian Ballet*. New York: E.P. Dutton, 1966.

DE VALOIS, NINETTE. *Invitation to the Ballet*. London: John Lane/Bodley Head 1937.

————. *Come Dance With Me*. London: Hamish Hamilton 1957.

VAUGHAN, DAVID. *Frederick Ashton and His Ballets*. New York: Alfred A. Knopf, 1977.

Dance in America

BANES, SALLY. *Terpsichore in Sneakers, Post-modern Dance*. Boston: Houghton Mifflin, 1980.

BOND, CHRYSTELLE T. *A Chronicle of Dance in Baltimore 1780-1814*. New York: Dance Perspectives #66, Summer 1976.

COHEN, SELMA JEANNE. *Doris Humphrey: An Artist First*. Middletown, Connecticut: Wesleyan University Press, 1972.

————. *The Modern Dance, Seven Statements of Belief*. Middletown, Connecticut: Wesleyan University Press, 1966.

DUNCAN, IRMA. *Duncan Dancer*. Middletown, Connecticut: Wesleyan University Press, 1966.

DUNCAN, ISADORA. *My Life*. Garden City, New York: Garden City Publishing, 1927.

GRAHAM, MARTHA. *The Notebooks of Martha Graham*. Introduced by Nancy Wilson Ross. New York: Harcourt Brace Jovanovich, 1973.

HUMPHREY, DORIS. *The Art of Making Dances*. New York: Grove, 1959.

KIRBY, MICHAEL. *The Art of Time*. New York: E.P. Dutton, 1969.

KIRKLAND, GELSEY, and LAWRENCE, GREG. *Dancing on My Grave*. New York, Doubleday, 1986.

LLOYD, MARGARET. *The Borzoi Book of Modern Dance*. New York: Alfred A. Knopf, 1949.

MARTIN, JOHN. *Book of the Dance*. New York: Tudor, 1963.

MAYNARD, OLGA. *The American Ballet*. Philadelphia: Macrae Smith, 1959.

MAZO, JOSEPH H. *Prime Movers: The Makers of Modern Dance in America*. New York: William Morrow, 1977.

McDONAGH, DON. *Martha Graham*. New York: Praeger, Popular Library, 1973.

ROGERS, FREDERICK RAND. *Dance: A Basic Educational Technique*. New York: Macmillan, 1941.

SCHNEIDER, GRETCHEN ADEL. *Pigeon Wings and Polkas: The Dance of California Miners*. New York: Dance Perspectives #39, Winter 1969.

SCHNEIDER, ILYA ILYICH. *Isadora Duncan, The Russian Years*. New York: Harcourt, Brace & World, 1968.

SHAWN, TED. *Dance We Must*. Lee, Massachusetts: Jacob's Pillow, 1950.

SMAKOV, GENNADY. *From Russia to the West*. New York: Farrar, Straus, and Giroux, 1981.

STEARNS, MARSHALL, and STEARNS, JEAN. *Jazz Dance*. New York: Macmillan, 1968.

TAPER, BERNARD. *Balanchine*. London: Collins, 1964.

TERRY, WALTER. *The Ballet Companion*. New York: Dodd, Mead, 1968.

———. *Miss Ruth*. New York: Dodd, Mead, 1969.

VAN CLEEF, JOY. *Rural Felicity: Social Dance in 18th-Century Connecticut*. New York: Dance Perspectives #65, Spring 1976.

WIGMAN, MARY. *The Language of Dance*. Translated by Walter Sorell. Middletown, Connecticut: Wesleyan University Press 1966.

INDEX